Seeking the first farmers in western Sjælland, Denmark

Dedication

In memory of Mads Esbjerg and Egon Iversen
With deep thanks to all the members of the field crews over the years
With great appreciation to Jens Nielsen, Nanna Noe-Nygaard, and Lisbeth Pedersen and the support
of the Kalundborg Museum
With deep gratitude to the Kalundborg Archaeological Association
With sincere thanks to those institutions that provided funding – Wisconsin Alumni Research
Foundation, Fullbright Foundation, the U.S. National Science Foundation, National Geographic Society,
the Danish Research Council, and the Carlsberg Foundation
With great love for Anne Birgitte Gebauer

Seeking the first farmers in western Sjælland, Denmark

The archaeology of the transition to agriculture in Northern Europe

T. Douglas Price

 OXBOW | books
Oxford & Philadelphia

Published in the United Kingdom in 2022 by
OXBOW BOOKS
The Old Music Hall, 106-108 Cowley Road, Oxford, OX4 1JE

and in the United States by
OXBOW BOOKS
1950 Lawrence Road, Havertown, PA 19083

Hardback edition: ISBN 978-1-78925-765-6
Digital Edition: ISBN 978-1-78925-766-3

A CIP record for this book is available from the British Library

Library of Congress Control Number: 2022935176

Printed in the United Kingdom by Short Run Press

For a complete list of Oxbow titles, please contact:

UNITED KINGDOM
Oxbow Books
Telephone (01865) 241249
Email: oxbow@oxbowbooks.com
www.oxbowbooks.com

UNITED STATES OF AMERICA
Oxbow Books
Telephone (610) 853-9131, Fax (610) 853-9146
Email: queries@casemateacademic.com
www.casemateacademic.com/oxbow

Oxbow Books is part of the Casemate Group

Contents

List of figures

List of tables

Foreword

At the end of the road

It can become a condition of life to research the transition from hunter and gatherer communities to early farming cultures. In *Seeking the First Farmers in Western Sjælland, Denmark*, Professor T. Douglas Price gathers the results from *c.* 35 years of archaeological and scientific studies of Stone Age settlements in West Zealand to provide new knowledge for this important cultural change.

The studies were anchored in a collaboration between the University of Wisconsin, USA, and Kalundborg Museum, Denmark, within the framework of The Saltbæk Vig Archaeological Project. In this book, Doug not only considers the archaeological and scientific results of fieldwork but, equally important, he links sociological and cross-cultural observations to the international collaboration that unfolded over a number of years between the University and the Museum (now West Zealand Provincial Museum). It is rare, if ever, that results from an international and long-standing archaeological collaboration are brought to an end that way. As former head of Kalundborg Museum, I am happy to provide some introductory words along the way.

Initially, I would like to thank Doug for both a long-term collaboration and friendship. For many years as museum director in Kalundborg, in the spring I often faced the questions of when our American migratory birds would land, and what new the field season was expected to bring. I therefore write the foreword in gratitude to all who followed the project with interest, who supported it financially, who gave permissions, and laid the groundwork. Similarly, it is on my mind to thank everyone who participated and supported the project, whether it was practical and formal tasks to be solved or when it became difficult and major bumps had to be resolved. The Saltbæk Vig Archaeological Project fortunately had many opportunities to celebrate milestones (Figs F.1 and F.7) and give thanks along the way.

The present publication collects the main archaeological and scientific results of the project. Equally important, however, are the numerous cross-cultural and inter-ethnic connections that the project originated over the years. It created numerous friendships across the Atlantic, some even with marriages and children as a result. Several students in the USA and Denmark have completed their studies by writing dissertations based on materials from the Saltbæk Vig project. Others inspired by it wrote a PhD dissertation on the basis of materials from other West Zealand sites and carried out archaeological excavations in the Kalundborg area with resulting publications

Fig. F.1. Top: presentation of the publication Smakkerup Huse in 2005 in Kalundborg Museum's lecture hall. In addition to the book, the highlight of the reception was a traditional Danish layer cake decorated like the Stars and Stripes (bottom). It was eaten to the last crumb (photos: (top) Gunnar Jørgensen and (bottom) Mads Findal Andreasen).

(Stafford 1999; Fischer *et al.* 2021). And then Kalundborg Museum got quite unexpected materials to examine the early Danish emigration to the United States (Pedersen 1999; Pedersen and Findal Andreasen 2000; 2002; Pedersen and Lund 2010). The final results from this study are about to be published.

Over the years, American institutions financed significant parts of the Saltbæk Vig Archaeological Project and consequently provided the basic substance for numerous scientific publications of archaeological material from the Kalundborg area. That was definitely beyond our imagination when Doug, my future husband, Anders Fischer and I met in the mid-1970s at the Department of Prehistoric Archaeology in Copenhagen, and Doug from time to time visited our home. The idea began to develop after 1984, when Doug visited Anders' and my home in Kalundborg. I, as the newly appointed director of Kalundborg Museum. faced explicit expectations of running a popular and research-oriented cultural history museum (Bagger 1984). Kalundborg Museum was then and is still known for extensive and well-lit ethnological collections. But the Kalundborg area is archaeologically very rich. The area is not only favored with significant Stone Age settlements both inland around the Åmose basins (Fig. F.3) and along the coasts in, for example, the Saltbæk Vig region. Numerous sites, now protected, especially dolmens and burial chambers, adorn the landscape which some of the country's early farming families built as burial monuments in the centuries after 4000 BC.

Fig. F.2. Search for submerged islets in Saltbæk Vig in 1994. Douglas Price was himself in the water while inspector Ole Petersen, Saltbæk Protected Area, sat at the helm (photo: Anders Fischer).

Fig. F.3. 'Karoline's dysse' at Gravhøjsmarken on the east bank of Lille Åmose, 2021. Here, amateur archaeologist Max Raffn collected Early Neolithic settlement material for exploratory studies, cf. Chapter 5 (photo: Lisbeth Pedersen).

Remains from the Bronze Age and not least from the Iron Age and Viking Age also attract much attention. In the same way, the history of the town of Kalundborg itself stimulates archaeological engagement. For here sit the ruins of a medieval castle, the country's largest collection of medieval stone houses, and a unique five-tower church that tempt one to pursue medieval archeological issues (Pedersen 2013, 245–72). So, there was plenty to tackle for a newly appointed museum director, inspired not least by amateur archaeologist Egon Iversen's information about many new exciting finds and archeological sites in the area. Numerous emergency excavations quickly overrode any desire for real research studies. Gitte Gebauer came to the museum and excavated, among other things, an Early Neolithic long mound, which the sea was slowly but surely destroying (Gebauer 1988). Doug also saw the Kalundborg region's archaeological research potential when we went on a trip with Egon. The ideas for an American–Danish archaeological project began to simmer. They were later inspired by the experiences from the marine and land excavations related to The Great Belt Fixed Link, which Anders and I directed on behalf of our respective institutions (Fischer 1997).

Colleagues from other Danish archaeological institutions joined in, and The Saltbæk Vig Archaeological Project became a reality in 1988 (Fig. F.4). The museum's newly established amateur archeology association was quickly included. For several winters in a row, the members reconnoitered available fields according to principles, methods, and classifications that Anders Fischer had developed. Anders was also responsible for significant parts of the teaching and training of the amateurs who, with widely differing backgrounds and approaches to archeology, met around a common interest. Ander's vision and passion for exploring the Stone Age inspired the group.

Many of the association's members participated in the surveys and, if possible, in the excavations (Figs F.5 and F.6). Most everyone followed the progress of the project on visits to the excavations. The Kalundborg Archaeological Association has thus over the years practiced what we now call citizen science, where citizens contribute to scientific data collection and research. Basically, the archeology association continued the tradition behind the establishment of Kalundborg Museum in 1908 (Pedersen 1992; 2018). The members thus formed an important archaeological group that allowed me to fulfill the stated expectations of developing Kalundborg Museum into an open, popular, and research-based cultural history museum. Kalundborg Archaeological Association deserves my unreserved tribute and thanks.

Many friends and colleagues welcomed the Saltbæk Vig Project. Several commented positively on the special research environment which, for a number of years, revolved around the museum. Others were more skeptical. Doubt lost momentum when Doug Price, in 2006, received one of Danish archeology's greatest honorary awards, the Erik Westerby Prize, for his pioneering efforts in exploring the older Stone Age remains in Denmark.

Now the materials from The Saltbæk Vig Archaeological Project have been arranged, processed, published, and put on shelves so that others can use the results in future research. At the end of the road, I extend my heartfelt thanks to the professionals, board members, landowners, local people, amateur archaeologists, and friends who have helped carry the project through. Employees at Kalundborg Museum deserve their share of tribute for providing a solid operational base for the project.

I allow myself to highlight Gitte Gebauer, who has been an essential partner, professionally and cross-culturally, in the project. Gitte worked as the leader of a rescue excavation project at the Kalundborg Museum in 1985 and continued as an important cross-cultural partner in the Saltbæk Vig Project. Thank you for your professionalism, your perseverance, and your friendship. Discussions between Anders, Doug, Gitte, and I in the 1980s led to the formulation of *The Saltbæk Vig Project*. As a result of the present publication, Stone Age settlements in the Kalundborg area have now been placed in a local and, not the least, global perspective. In addition, I would like to express my heartfelt gratitude to Douglas for his trust in the ability of the Kalundborg Museum to create a platform for archaeological collaboration, as well as an introduction to American culture and ways of thinking, in short: The American Ways. Douglas Price now gets the floor.

Lisbeth Pedersen
Kalundborg Museum director, retired

Fig. F.4. Initial working group at the memorial stone for the embankment of Saltbæk in 1989 (photo: Anders Fischer).

Fig. F.5. One day's harvest (1990). From left to right are forester Erik Nielsen, grocer Margit Jørgensen, fish buyer Egon Iversen, and farm owner Aage Petersen (photo: Anders Fischer).

References

Bagger, T. H. 1984. *Tiltrædelsestale for Lisbeth Pedersen, Kalundborg og Omegns Museum*. 1. marts 1984. Kalundborg: Kalundborg Museums Administrative Arkiv.

Fischer, A. 1997. People and the sea – settlement and fishing along the Mesolithic coast. In L. Pedersen, A. Fischer and B. Aaby (eds), *The Danish Storebælt Since the Ice Age – Man Sea and Forest*, 63–77. Copenhagen: Storebælt Fixed Link.

Fischer, A., Gotfredsen, A.B., Meadows, J., Pedersen, L. and Stafford, M. 2021. The Rødhals kitchen midden – marine adaptations at the end of the Mesolithic world. *Journal of Archaeological Sciences Reports*. [10.1016/j.jasrep.2021.103102]

Fig. F.6. Trench at Smakkerup Huse, 1989. American field archaeologists and Danish natural science archaeologists are studying Stone Age layers in the cove (photo: Anders Fischer).

Fig. F.7. Project party in the Knights' Hall at Kalundborg Museum, 1995. The hall in Lindegården was a nice setting when landowners, museum staff, board members, friends, and Danish and American participants met for a 5-year project celebration with grilled wild pig, wine, coffee, and cake (photo: Anders Fischer).

Gebauer, A. B. 1988. The long dolmen at Asnæs Forskov, West Zealand. *Journal of Danish Archaeology* 7, 40–52.

Pedersen, L. 1992. Kalundborg og Omegns Museum gennem 80 år. *Kalundborgs Historie* 4, 223–227.

Pedersen, L. (ed.) 2013. *Menneskers veje - kulturhistoriske essays i 100-året for Kalundborg Museum.* Kalundborg: Kalundborg Museum.

Pedersen, L. 2018. Tekstiler som museumsgenstande og folkeminder – stof til eftertanker. *Dragtjournalen Årgang* 12(16), 31–48.

Pedersen, L. and Findal Andreasen, M. 2000. 'Kurs imod det Punkt af Horisonten, hvor Solen hver Aften gaar ned'. En udvandrerhistorie fra Sæby sogn i Vestsjælland. *Fra Holbæk Amt. Årbogen for kulturhistorien i Holbæk Amt* 2000, 9–26.

Pedersen, L. and Findal Andreasen, M. 2002. Vestsjællændere i Den Amerikanske Borgerkrig – fra asken i ilden. *Fra Holbæk Amt. Årbogen for kulturhistorien i Holbæk Amt.* 2002, 9–26.

Pedersen, L. and Lund, G. 2010. Ulkestrup Mark – Nordvestsjællands Tahrirplads – et fortællested om demokratiets udvikling i Danmark. *Fra Nordvestsjælland. Årbogen for kulturhistorien i Nordvestsjælland* 2010, 128–145.

Stafford, M. 1999. *From Forager to Farmer in Flint. A Lithic Analysis of the Prehistoric Transition to Agriculture in Southern Scandinavia.* Aarhus: Aarhus University Press.

Preface

Friends and colleagues often asked what I was working on. I told them that I was trying to write a book about our archaeological investigations in Denmark over the last 30 years, that I wanted it to be both academic and personal, to describe the actual *process of research*, because most projects involve elements of both. Friends and colleagues nodded knowingly, and the conversation quickly shifted to other subjects.

Facts and feelings. Writing such a book is not a straightforward or easy task. If I make it too personal, it will lose academic credibility and if I write it too formally or technically, it will be boring and ignore many important aspects of the decisions that were made and directions that were taken. An academic slant to a narrative tends to ignore the individuals that were involved and the interpersonal interactions that are such a critical component of most research. I have been thinking about this volume for a number of years and have probably delayed starting it for several more because I was not quite sure how to manage this personal/academic schizophrenia that is generally dismissed in writing about the study of the past – or most academic subjects for that matter.

My solution to this dilemma is to provide an introduction to each chapter that discusses some of the more personal aspects of the research. In this way I can introduce each phase of our study within the context in which decisions were made. Each chapter will deal with one of the components of the project – survey, testing, and excavations. The bulk of each chapter will be a more technical scientific report on our investigations. Some parts of this work have already been published and are presented here in condensed form. This includes the excavations at Smakkerup Huse (Price and Gebauer 2005), Dragsholm (Price *et al.* 2007), and Asnæs Havnemark (Price *et al.* 2018). You can judge for yourself if my personal/academic approach has worked and helped you understand how archaeological (and many kinds of) research happens, at least from my perspective.

Since 1989 I have been doing archaeology in northwestern Sjælland, Denmark, at a series of different places. I was in Denmark summer and sometimes fall almost every year since 1989. We surveyed 25 km² of a coastal area and excavated a number of Late Mesolithic localities – coastal sites, inland sites, burial sites, fishing sites, shell middens. I have counted hundreds of thousands of flint and other stone artifacts, hundreds of pieces of pottery, excavated kilos and kilos of animal bones, submitted tens of radiocarbon dates, and recorded lots of stratigraphic sections, feature drawings, and floor plans. I have also visited numerous other excavations in the region, attended a number of meetings, and spoken at length with other archaeologists. I have had a pretty good look at the Stone Age in this area.

I want to tell you about the archaeological research that we did in western Sjælland, Denmark, largely between 1985 and 2010. That 25 years is a large chunk of any life and a big part of mine. Many things happened in my life in that period in addition to archaeology, and those events no doubt affected the research that we did and how I thought about it. This book is really about what I have learned.

I was a professor of European archaeology at the University of Wisconsin-Madison for many years, from 1974 until 2010 when I retired. A big part of my research interest involved the Mesolithic and Neolithic in northern Europe – the last hunters and the first farmers. My PhD thesis dealt with sites from the Mesolithic in the Netherlands but, shortly after I finished my PhD in 1975, my interests turned to Denmark and the Mesolithic there. Mesolithic sites in the Netherlands, for the most part, were small, thin scatters of little stone tools and pieces of charcoal. Mesolithic sites in Denmark were often large and well preserved, with bone and even wood among the finds. Much more could be learned about the past with such material.

I was very fortunate to attend the first Mesolithic Congress in Warsaw in 1973 (Fig. 0.1). I had no idea at the time that the meeting would have such an impact on my research and my life. There were only 50 some people attending – mostly traditional typologists from Eastern Europe. There were lots of maps with arrows and what seemed like hundreds of slides of artifact drawings. Much of Mesolithic research at that time was about classification and culture history. There were also a few young folks asking questions about people, landscapes, culture, and behavior. The younger group hit it off. A number of friendships were formed that continue to this day, more than 45 years later. I met Søren Andersen, Lars Larsson, Stig Welinder, Erik Brinch Petersen, and Peter Woodman, among others. It was an exciting time – a small group of young rebels versus the established hierarchy. That wonderful experience in Warsaw drew me deeper into the Mesolithic. Of course, these friends are now the old and, in some cases, dead guys that may or may not make it to the next Mesolithic Congress.

Fig. 0.1. Warsaw. First Mesolithic Congress, 1973.

I traveled to Denmark in the summer of 1978 and joined Erik Brinch Petersen (Fig. 0.2), participating in the Mesolithic excavations at Vedbæk, north of Copenhagen. We agreed on further collaboration and I got some funding and took students there to dig in 1980, 1982, and 1983. That was my first experience in Danish archaeology (Price and Brinch Petersen 1987). It made quite an impression in terms of the richness of the sites, the care in excavation, and the quality of the archaeological materials (Petersen 2015). It also inspired an interest in what I termed complex hunter-gatherers and an edited book (1985) called *Prehistoric Hunter-Gatherers: The Emergence of Cultural Complexity* (Price and Brown 1985a). I wrote then that the Mesolithic hunter-gatherers of southern Scandinavia were structured in complex societies with hierarchical organization and status differentiation. But I no longer believe that. After many years digging in the Mesolithic, it is my sense that these were just regular hunters and gatherers. More on this in the concluding chapter as part of what I have learned.

The most important thing that happened to me in this period was meeting my future wife, Anne Birgitte Gebauer, in Denmark in the mid 1980s (Fig. 0.3). Gitte is also an archaeologist, interested in the Early Neolithic and especially pottery and megalithic tombs from that period. At that time, Gitte was excavating an important Neolithic tomb near a town called Kalundborg in western Sjælland (Gebauer 1988). Gitte moved to Madison in 1987. We got married in April 1989 and our daughter Annalise was born in 1990. In that same year we bought a new house together in Madison and collected a new Volvo station wagon in Gothenburg, Sweden. We were established. I was 45 years old.

A friend from previous years in Copenhagen, Lisbeth Pedersen (Fig. 0.4), was then the director of the local museum in Kalundborg and we began discussing the possibility of a large project in the Kalundborg area. I clearly remember going with Lisbeth, Anders Fischer, and 'Columbus' out to the Saltbæk Vig (a *vig* is a bay in Danish) in 1985 to discuss the possibilities and potential for such a project. Columbus took us to some of the sites in the area. There seemed to be a lot of Mesolithic.

Egon Iversen was a special person (Fig. 0.4). Columbus was his nickname, known and used by everyone. He was a fish monger, buying and selling fish around the island of Sjælland. He spoke loudly and came to the fore in any conversation, or any group. He reminded me of Popeye, with huge forearms on his large frame, and a jolly, flushed red face. He was also a self-taught amateur archaeologist who had found or

Fig. 0.2. Erik Brinch Petersen.

Fig. 0.3. Jens Nielsen and Anne Birgitte Gebauer.

Fig. 0.4. *Lisbeth Pedersen and Columbus (photo: Anders Fischer 2017).*

visited most of the archaeological sites in the area and knew as much as anyone about the Stone Age archaeology of the Kalundborg region. He was intense about the archaeology of his homeland, a force of nature, cheerful, full of humor, and outgoing. One of my favorite stories about Columbus concerned the family of hedgehogs that lived in his backyard and how he would often get day-old pastries from the local baker to feed them. Columbus also successfully taught the American students to say *øl* (beer) and *ål* (eel) in Danish, an important distinction. Columbus passed away in 2018.

The Saltbæk Vig lies within the Kalundborg Kommune (municipality) and was under the administrative responsibility of the Kalundborg og Omegns Museum, the collaborating institution for the Saltbæk Vig project. Lisbeth Pedersen was a major driving force behind this project. Anders Fischer, also an archaeologist and husband to Lisbeth, was an important partner in this endeavor, providing advice and some information on the Stone Age.

I made an agreement with Lisbeth to try and get a project running focused on the Stone Age around the Saltbæk Vig. I also clearly remember going with Lisbeth in 1988 to the National Museum in Copenhagen to talk with the state archaeologist, Olaf Olsen, about why an American should be allowed to work in Denmark. I wouldn't say he was particularly friendly or welcoming, but we did get his approval.

I was fortunate to obtain funding from the National Science Foundation (NSF) in the United States. In 1989 Gitte and I began this investigation of the Late Mesolithic and Early Neolithic around the Saltbæk Vig. Our project was planned at the outset to be a long-term look at the Mesolithic and Neolithic in western Sjælland. We intended to survey the fields around the Saltbæk Vig, mapping artifact concentrations, and identifying potential places for more intensive investigation. The next stage would require a couple of years for testing some of the interesting places we had identified to see if they were of sufficient content for full-scale excavation, planned for the last several years of the project. I had promised Gitte that we would spend part of each year in Denmark and this project combined archaeology and marriage quite nicely. Anne Birgitte Gebauer was the co-director of the Saltbæk Vig project and this work could not have been done without her energy, knowledge, and abilities. Gitte chose not to be a co-author on this manuscript, but her role in the success of the Saltbæk Vig project is paramount.

The harvest was late in the fall of 1989. It wasn't possible to do fieldwalking in search of artifacts and sites until the crops had been taken off the fields. So we started with some test excavations at Lindebjerg and Smakkerup Huse, described in Chapter 3. We made a major commitment to the area in 1994 and purchased a cabin, known as a summerhouse, on the peninsula of Røsnæs just east of the Saltbæk Vig area, overlooking the Kalundborg fjord and the Storebælt. This has been our home away from home for the last 25 years. We feel a strong attachment to the area and are very much at home there.

This book chronicles my growth and development as an archaeologist and the experiences I had in Denmark in the pursuit of answers to questions about the transition to agriculture in prehistory. The first part of the story involves the Saltbæk Vig project in western Sjælland. Chapter One provides some background to Danish prehistory and the area. Chapter 2 concerns our fieldwalking in the Saltbæk Vig study area, locating archaeological sites. Chapter 3 deals with the testing phase of our project where we more closely examined some of the sites we had found. Chapter 4 is brief report on the full-scale excavations at Smakkerup Huse that concluded the Saltbæk Vig component of this research. The locations of our excavations in Western Sjælland are shown in Figure 1.20. At the end of the Saltbæk Vig project there were still many unanswered questions and the project expanded beyond the Saltbæk Vig to include excavations at an inland site called Trustrup, to coastal sites at Dragsholm and Bøgebjerg, and to a Mesolithic shell midden at Fårevejle. Our last excavations took place in 2007 near the end of the peninsula of Asnæs, not far from the town of Kalundborg. These were all Late Mesolithic sites occupied close to the time of the transition to agriculture. The first and last chapters provide a broader view of the issues and questions that drove this study. The intervening chapters provide some of the details and experiences that conditioned my ideas and conclusions.

Acknowledgements

There are so many people and institutions that should be acknowledged and thanked for their support in such a long-term undertaking. It is not possible to remember them all and I will certainly fail to list some, but the students, colleagues, and the local people where we were excavating made my life good and meant that doing archaeology in western Sjælland was very rewarding, both personally and academically. Major thanks must go to Anne Birgitte for all her work, care, and support through these years. This would not have happened without her. She was involved in many of the strategic decisions made regarding the project. She also provided most of the pottery descriptions and classifications found in this volume. She should really be co-author of this volume.

First and foremost we acknowledge and thank Lisbeth Pedersen for her vision, support, and hospitality. Lisbeth has always been most helpful, hospitable, and supportive — a true friend. Lisbeth and the Kalundborg Museum were our liaison and home base for many years of this project. The staff of the museum (Jimmy, Irene, and Kurt) were most helpful and thoughtful as a rowdy group of Americans descended on them every year.

Jens Nielsen of the museum was an important member of the project and responsible for a substantial part of the work we have been able to do. Jens and I worked together for more than 15 years. Jens did most of the work and research with wood that is described in this volume. Jens is a terrific archaeologist, colleague, and friend and kept things going on many occasions.

The people of Saltbæk Vig area were, in almost every case, welcoming and kind. We would especially acknowledge the assistance of Ole Petersen, the Overseer of the Saltbæk Vig Company property and a genuine help in our work, Åge and Vagn Jacobsen, Viggo Illerman Hansen, Steen Christensen, Slagter Erik, Eirik Vinsand, and many others. The Kähler Foundation and the Saltbæk Vig A/S gave permission for us to survey much of the coastal area of the project. The Kalundborg Arkæologiske Forening, a vibrant society of amateur archaeologists, has been an important partner in the survey project, using their winter weekends to survey fields in the project area. The time, the energy, and the help of these kind and active people cannot be repaid.

There are others I must mention. Anders Fischer, also a specialist in the Mesolithic, provided help in a variety of ways and was available to answer our many questions. Nanna Noe-Nygaard, a Danish geologist and archaeozoologist at the University of Copenhagen, joined the project during the excavations at Smakkerup Huse and worked with us from that time (Fig. 0.5). Nanna helped with the funding for the project among many other things. A number of Nanna's students participated in the project and made substantial contributions. Nanna was involved in training some of the American students as well. Nanna's knowledge of the geology of our research area and her enthusiasm were an important part of what we accomplished. Many of the geological observations reported in this volume were hers. Nanna has become a dear friend.

There are many others involved who contributed in various ways and to whom I owe many thanks, including Charlie Christensen, Helle Juel Jensen, Else Kolstrup, Kristian Kristiansen, Lars Larsson, Torsten Madsen, Per Person, Peter Rasmussen, and Karl-Göran Sjøgren. Max Raffn was heavily involved in our adventures at Trustrup. Niels Hartman assisted us though the period of the field survey. Søren Andersen spent a lot of time with us at Dragsholm. Per Paulsen (see Fig. 7.8) and Peter Vang Petersen excavated with us at Fårevejle for some days. Both are dear friends. Peter Woodman from Cork, Ireland, another dear friend, helped us get started at Fårevejle. Peter is now departed and deeply missed. Harry Madsen and his wife Else for 45 years had farmed one of the areas we surveyed and were most gracious and hospitable. We remember them fondly, although I suppose they are both gone now as well.

The project would not have been possible nor as much fun without the American, Danish, and British students that joined us: Lone Andersen, Christian Hans Abildtrup, Joel Boaz, Jennifer Doerfler, Mads Esbjerg, Paul Flanagan, Carolyn Freiwald, Mikael P. Jensen, Kasper Johansen, Mike Kimball, Ingrid Kostin, Lene Laursen, Mollie Lyons, Louise Martens, Tia Nielsen, Bettina Olsen, Kristian Petersen, Annalise Price, Erika Price, Anne Raun, Ken Ritchie, Anthony Ruter, Rob Schmidt, Elizabeth Severson, Terry Slocum, Michael Stafford, Todd Surovel, Ed Swanson, Tina Thurston, Signe Uhfeldt Hede, and Beth Workmaster. Some of these individuals appear in Figure 0.6. Mike Stafford did his PhD on stone tools from the Mesolithic and Neolithic in western Sjælland. Ken Ritchie did most of the identification and discussion of the fish bone

Fig. 0.5. Nanna Noe-Nygaard.

Fig. 0.6. Jens Nielsen, Tony Ruter, Ken Ritchie, Terry Slocum, and Doug Price leaving the museum for a day of fieldwork.

from our excavations as part of his PhD thesis at the University of Wisconsin-Madison. Kurt Gron did the same, including the PhD, with the animal remains. Ken and Lone together helped enormously with the chapter on Fårevejle.

Kasper Johansen and Mikael Jensen were high school students in Kalundborg who joined us for several seasons. Kasper went on to study archaeology in Aarhus. Mads Esbjerg was a geology student we lost to leukemia much too early. Ken and Lone got married, have two kids, and live in Denmark. Lone works for the Herning Museum. Ruter got his PhD in geology in Copenhagen and is still in Denmark. Two of my daughters joined us in the excavations for days or weeks. My youngest daughter Annalise is a Danish citizen and lives on the island of Sjælland. Freiwald, Kimball, Surovel, and Thurston are professors in Departments of Anthropology in the US. Stafford is the director of the Cranbrook Institute of Science in Detroit. Gron has a post-doc at the University of Durham.

The last several seasons of fieldwork were pure joy. The average age of the crew was somewhere over 40. Most of us had been together over several seasons and everyone knew what to do. The students had a house and a car and we had our summerhouse. I had learned enough about directing excavations by that time that I was more relaxed and easier to deal with. I really miss those days in the field, working together toward a common goal – it was a special time. We also took a road trip each year to see archaeological places in northern Europe. Visits to the Danish island of Bornholm, to the Bronze Age rock carvings in Bohuslan, Sweden, and to the island of Rügen and to Peenemünde, near the town of Greifswald in northeast Germany, were good examples and good times. It was quite an adventure.

I must also say what a pleasure it has been to work with the staff of Oxbow Books. I wish Julie Gardiner could always be my editor. Jess Hawxwell made an outstanding contribution as well. I very much appreciate the job that Oxbow does, not just for me, but for the entire field. Thank you!

Doug Price
Kalundborg, Denmark

Chapter 1

Setting the table – an introduction

This chapter is intended to provide some background and context for the archaeological fieldwork that we did in northwestern Sjælland between 1989 and 2010. Initially there is a summary of Danish prehistory to place the Mesolithic and Neolithic in a larger context and also to emphasize the importance of myriad changes that came with the arrival of the Neolithic. Hopefully, this volume also conveys some sense of the exceptional archaeology that exists in the small country of Denmark. Denmark is about one-half the size of the U.S. state of South Carolina. If you want more information on the archaeology of the larger region of northern Europe, I wrote a detailed, illustrated volume called *Ancient Scandinavia* a few years ago (2015).

In this chapter, I also discuss the history of archaeological research in northwestern Sjælland to provide some background to our project. Monumental tombs get their own introduction as the most visible and powerful reminders of the past on the Danish landscape today. Many of these are Neolithic in age. A description of the landscape is essential to understanding that past as well, and a short geographic tour is offered. Finally, there is a brief introduction to the organization of this volume.

A final note. Dates are given in both BP (before present) and BC (before Christ) formats, always cal (calibrated). I try to provide BC dates in most instances. It is also the case that present convention in radiocarbon dating involves presentation of a range of dates and probabilities that are complicated to explain, and I avoid those where possible by giving an approximate date within the range. For those who prefer the probability distributions and range reports of radiocarbon dates, most of the determinations we obtained are published in this volume or in the original reports and can be evaluated there.

The Danish past

The prehistoric archaeology of Denmark extends from the Late Paleolithic period through the Viking Age. These periods are shown in a chronological chart in Figure 1.1. In the following pages, I describe the Paleolithic, the Mesolithic, and the Neolithic, the periods of interest in this volume. Readers interested in later periods of Danish prehistory are referred to my 2015 volume, *Ancient Scandinavia*.

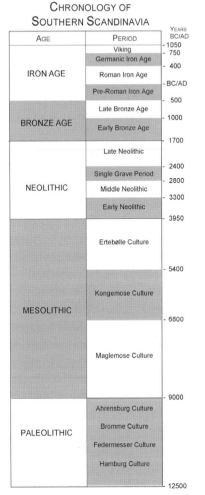

Fig. 1.1. A chronological chart of the Danish past.

Late Paleolithic

We begin at the bottom of the chart with the Late Paleolithic. The first inhabitants of Denmark entered northernmost Germany and southern Scandinavia from the south around 12,500 BC, shortly after sheets of glacial ice disappeared from the continent and the Danish Isles. There is no definitive evidence for any earlier human presence in Scandinavia. These early groups were primarily reindeer hunters and left small scatters of flint tools, rock, and charcoal at the places where they stopped. Only rarely are the remains of the animals they killed or the outlines of the tents they erected found. A series of named archaeological cultures filled this time period until around the end of the Pleistocene at 9700 BC. The Hamburgian, the Bromme, and the Ahrensburgian cultures are known for their shouldered and tanged spear and arrow points used to hunt reindeer (Fig. 1.2). A fourth culture, the Federmesser, appeared during a slightly warmer episode; these people hunted large game such as elk, red deer, and aurochs (wild cattle); reindeer were largely absent at the time. Human settlement very gradually moved further and further north during the Late Paleolithic as climate improved and the landscape became more hospitable. The Ahrensburgian people appear to have had a marine component to their diet and eventually expanded along the coast of Scandinavia to the Arctic Circle.

There were also connections to the east as genes and a distinct lithic technology appear to have come into this northern corner of Scandinavia. Geneticists have examined aDNA in human remains from that region and concluded that Scandinavia was originally colonized from two different directions, one from the south and the other from the northeast (Günther *et al.* 2018). Studies of lithic artifacts suggest that

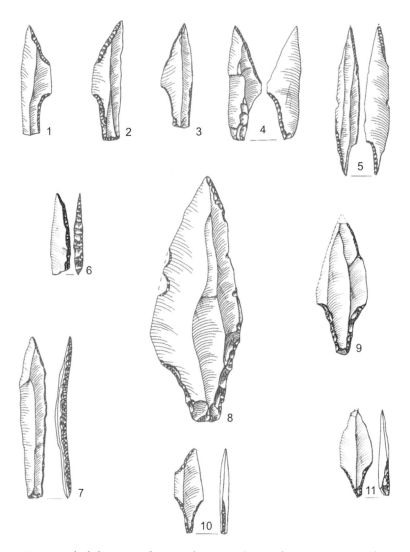

Fig. 1.2. Paleolithic points from southern Scandinavia (Vang Petersen 2008).

an eastern influence was responsible for the stone tools seen in the Mesolithic of northeastern Scandinavia (Sørensen *et al.* 2013).

Early Mesolithic: Maglemose

As the last Paleolithic hunters were entering the far north of Scandinavia at the beginning of the Holocene Epoch, 9700 BC, the Mesolithic period was getting underway in southern Scandinavia. The same basic chronology of Mesolithic cultures is seen across the entire southern region – Maglemose, Kongemose, and Ertebølle are the names given to Early, Middle, and Late Mesolithic. During the Holocene, the fresh, barren landscape exposed at the end of the Pleistocene grew heavily forested and was inhabited by a litany of wild game and vegetation. Red deer, roe deer, and wild boar were the primary prey of hunters in the later Mesolithic. Hazelnuts and acorns were available in mast in the forests. Fish, shellfish, and marine mammals filled the seas. Freshwater fish were an important resource beginning in the Early Mesolithic (Boethius 2018).

The first period of the Mesolithic, the Maglemosian, was primarily a coastal adaptation along the North Sea and western Baltic shores. Most of the known sites, however, were inland summer occupations, as the coastal areas from the early Holocene are now submerged. Maglemosian assemblages date from the early part of the Holocene in northern Europe, approximately 8900–6400 BC. This Early Mesolithic culture is known primarily from finds of distinctive small blades and microliths, used for arrowheads and cutting edges. Subtle changes in axes, microliths, and blade production techniques mark different phases of Maglemose culture. Both core and flake axes are known from the period. Flake axes appear early and core axes were added slightly later. Early flake axes have symmetrical surface retouch and are flaked on the sides as well; later flake axes show no surface retouch and have asymmetrical edge retouch. Lancette microliths and rather irregular blades mark the older half of the period; triangular microliths and thinner, more regular blades made with a soft hammer technique are found in the second half.

Maglemosian materials in the Saltbæk Vig are known only from stray finds of projectile points that have been collected, primarily in the higher, sandy spots in the research area. These places may have held more open forest, and hence more game, in the early Holocene. The coastline in Denmark until the end of the Maglemosian period was tens of kilometers to the north and is now beneath the waters of the North Sea (Astrup 2019).

Middle Mesolithic: Kongemose

Kongemose lithic assemblages are recognized primarily by distinctive projectile points and cores. A few microliths continue to appear in the earliest part (Blak phase) of the Kongemose (Sørensen 1996), but most projectile points are trapezoidal or rhombic forms made from segments of broad blades, sometimes using the microburin technique. The younger Kongemose has some very large points with an oblique edge, a form seen also in the Early Neolithic. Burins and blade knives with curved backing retouch are common in Kongemose assemblages; scrapers and borers are rare. Microblades were made from distinctive handle cores which are shaped from a heavy core early and from a heavy flake later in the Kongemose.

Both core and flake axes are known from the Kongemose but are difficult to distinguish. A flake axe retains its original bulbar surface as one side and the leading edge includes this original flake surface. Kongemose flake axes show no surface retouch and have asymmetric edge retouch. Core axes often are narrow and have a rhombic or irregular cross-section; one-third are pointed and chisel forms are also known. There is also an unusual long, pointed tool known as a *spidsvåpen* ('pointed weapon') from this period.

Given current knowledge of sea level changes in the Saltbæk Vig area during the early Holocene, it is clear that some coastal Kongemose settlements today lie underwater not far from the modern coastline (Astrup 2019). Only a few sites from the younger part of this period have been found at elevations between 0 and –1.2 m below sea level on reclaimed land in the study area of the Saltbæk Vig. The flint artifacts at these younger Kongemose sites are heavily marine and bog patinated and the sites have usually been extensively eroded by the rising seas.

Late Mesolithic: Ertebølle

The biggest challenge in the lives of these hunter-gatherers in southern Scandinavia came from rising sea levels. Early Holocene human groups in this area were primarily focused on terrestrial resources, as the sea was lower and quite distant from much of southern Scandinavia. Continued melting of glacial ice refilled the seas and flooded large areas of dry land on the floor of what became the North Sea. By around 4000 BC the present shorelines of the region had been reached by the sea. Late Mesolithic hunter-gatherers focused on marine resources. Residence was concentrated on the coasts and more than half of the diet came from fish, shellfish, and marine mammals. Huge piles of oyster shells – the famous *køkkenmøddinger* (kitchen middens) – document the presence of Mesolithic groups in certain coastal regions of southern Scandinavia (Andersen 2004).

The Ertebølle period (EBK), the last part of the Mesolithic, extends from 5400 BC to approximately 4000 BC. Several distinct phases are recognized within the Ertebølle period (Hartz and Lübke 2006). Settlements often appear to have been permanently occupied, predominantly in coastal locations, often for hundreds of years; so that several phases may be represented at the same location. A variety of more specialized camps and activity areas are also known in southern Scandinavia. These successful groups of fisher-hunter-gatherers constructed an effective technology of wood, stone, and eventually ceramics (Fig. 1.3) to best utilize their environment both on land and sea; boats and paddles, bows and arrows, and a variety of other fishing and hunting equipment were in use.

Projectile points were transverse in form and became smaller and more symmetrical through time (Fischer 1989). Early points are oblique, made on soft hammer blades. Soft hammer technique was not used as frequently in the Middle Ertebølle but re-emerges in the last phase. Cores in Middle Ertebølle were globular with large round platforms; blades were rather straight and flat with rounded distal ends. Conical cores with prepared edges were more common in Late Ertebølle.

Both core and flake axes were present; flake axes increased from approximately 10% initially to being numerically dominant in the Middle and Late Ertebølle. Early Ertebølle flake axes were side retouched from the bulbar face; later examples were symmetrically surface retouched. Flake axes in the latest Ertebølle were side trimmed, usually in two directions, and smaller, with a wide bit. Core axes in the early part of the Ertebølle were diamond shaped in cross-section, becoming rectangular or trapezoidal through time. 'Specialized' core axes (exhibiting a bit fashioned with perpendicular laminar flake scars) were present only in the Late Ertebølle. A few examples in Sjælland also showed some edge polishing (Stafford 1999).

Blade knives with transverse retouch are common as settlement and grave finds. Blade knives with a concave retouch on the distal end are typical of the later stages of the Ertebølle. Blade knives with curved backing along one edge and partial retouch at one end of the cutting edge are present in the Late Ertebølle and Early Neolithic. Scrapers and borers vary in number in different phases but are more common later. Early Ertebølle borers were large and made on flakes or cores; late examples were smaller, made on blades. Drills made on blades in the Ertebølle were characterized by parallel-sided, narrow bits. Fine denticulated pieces are known from western Denmark in the Late Mesolithic and Early Neolithic but were absent on Sjælland until the beginning of the Neolithic (Juel Jensen 1994). These denticulated tools were made on blades in the Mesolithic and on the edges, often concave, of small flakes in the Early Neolithic.

There are also several types of groundstone artifacts from the Mesolithic period. The trindøkse typically is a cylinder of hard, heavy diabase or greenstone that is shaped by pecking (Fig. 6.12). The butt end is tapered and nicely rounded; the bit end is typically rounded on one side and polished to a flat or concave edge on the other. These axes are found throughout the Mesolithic period beginning in the younger Maglemosian. Limhamn axes are made from a large flake of greenstone and have a polished cutting edge. These axes are known exclusively from Sweden in earlier periods and also on Sjælland during the Ertebølle, more commonly in the later part of the period. The distinctive and formidable amphibolite shoe-last adze, perhaps a kind of battle axe, was imported from Central or Eastern Europe during the later part of the Ertebølle period (Fischer 1982). This adze is also considered to be a wood-working tool.

Pottery appears in Middle EBK in the form of pointed base cooking pots; slightly later in time shallow, oval lamp bowls are also found. This pottery is usually thick-walled, coarsely tempered, and poorly fired (Koch 1998). It seems certain today that the Ertebølle pottery had its origins to the east, rather than the south (Hallgren 2004; Hartz *et al.* 2011, 465–484; 2012).

Ertebølle people carved animal effigies and pendants in amber (Fig. 1.4). Exchange operated on a small scale and certain products of the Neolithic farmers to the south found their way to Mesolithic groups in southern Scandinavia. There was also some exchange among groups of Mesolithic hunter-gatherers. But, for whatever reason, these people resisted the introduction of agriculture for more than 1000 years. Farmers appeared to the south in northern Germany by 5500 BC, only 100 km or so distant, but farming did not arrive in Scandinavia until around 4000 BC.

Fig. 1.3. An Ertebølle pot (National Museum, Copenhagen).

Early Neolithic: Older Funnel Beaker (TRB): ENI and ENII

The introduction of agriculture was remarkably rapid when it finally took place. There appears to be a chronological and stratigraphic break between the Late Mesolithic and Early Neolithic (Hartz and Lübke 2006). Within a few hundred years, farming practices and evidence of domesticates had spread from northern Germany to the limits of cultivation in Middle Sweden and the Oslo Fjord in Norway. The Michelsberg Culture, a Neolithic group in France and Germany, may have been the source of many of the immigrant farm-

Fig. 1.4. Amber figurines (National Museum, Copenhagen).

ers who found their way to southern Scandinavia (Fig. 1.5). At the same time stable isotope analysis of human bone collagen indicates that a full farming economy was not established before the 3rd millennium BC on a general scale (Terberger *et al.* 2018).

Domesticated plants and especially animals defined these early agricultural groups, along with their distinctive Funnel Beaker pottery and the new polished stone axes. People typically lived on individual farms and may have moved when their land had been cultivated for some years. However substantial cultural layers suggest that some settlements were inhabited more permanently from around 3800 BC, e.g., Lisbjerg Skole in Jutland (Skousen 2008, 126–51) and Smedegade on Bornholm (Nielsen and Nielsen 2020, 79–92). During the late part of the Early Neolithic, small hamlets with several contemporary houses appear (e.g., Ullerødgård on Zealand; Rosenberg 2006). In contrast to the earlier hunters-fishers and gatherers, the early farmers invested large amounts of time and resources in constructing tombs for their ancestors as well as enclosures that may have served as meeting places for large gatherings. More

Fig 1.5. Major Early Neolithic cultures in Central and Northern Europe (courtesy of RGZM, Gronenborn 2010).

long-distance exchange is evidenced, particularly in axes, but in other objects as well. The first clear evidence for metal – copper – began to appear by the Early Neolithic, probably coming from central Europe (Klassen 2004; Budd *et al.* 2020; Gebauer *et al.* 2020).

The beginning of the Neolithic in southern Scandinavia, around 4000 BC, is associated with Funnel Beaker pottery, monumental earthen graves, flint mines, and bog sacrifices (Price 1995; Koch 1998; Sørensen 2015). The Early Neolithic can be separated into two main phases, based on changes in Funnel Beaker pottery. The earliest Funnel Beaker ceramics seem to be a combination of Late Ertebølle and TRB forms found in a transitional phase that lasts perhaps 100 years (Koch 1998; Müller 2011b). Body sherds of utilitarian wares in the early Funnel Beaker period are not noticeably different from Late Ertebølle pottery (Koch 1998). However, rim sherds and decorated pieces provide distinct chronological markers. Pottery is occasionally found on the surface at Early Neolithic sites, but it is rare because of its friable nature.

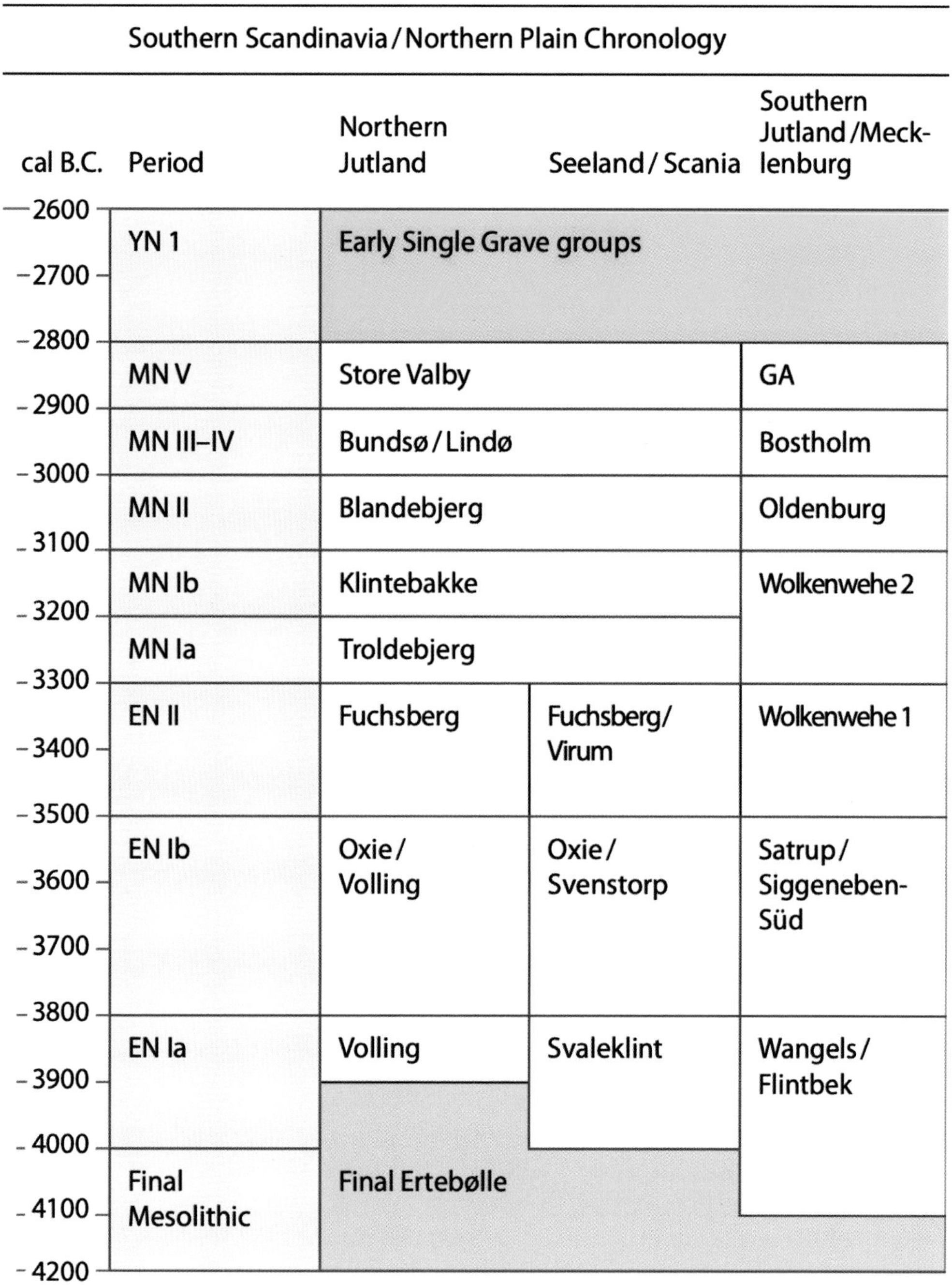

Southern Scandinavia / Northern Plain Chronology

cal B.C.	Period	Northern Jutland	Seeland / Scania	Southern Jutland / Mecklenburg
—2600 —2700	YN 1	Early Single Grave groups		
—2800 —2900	MN V	Store Valby		GA
—3000	MN III–IV	Bundsø / Lindø		Bostholm
—3100	MN II	Blandebjerg		Oldenburg
—3200	MN Ib	Klintebakke		Wolkenwehe 2
—3300	MN Ia	Troldebjerg		
—3400 —3500	EN II	Fuchsberg	Fuchsberg/ Virum	Wolkenwehe 1
—3600 —3700	EN Ib	Oxie / Volling	Oxie / Svenstorp	Satrup/ Siggeneben- Süd
—3800 —3900 —4000	EN Ia	Volling	Svaleklint	Wangels / Flintbek
—4100 —4200	Final Mesolithic	Final Ertebølle		

Fig. 1.6. A chronological chart for TRB pottery in southern Scandinavia (from Müller et al. 2010).

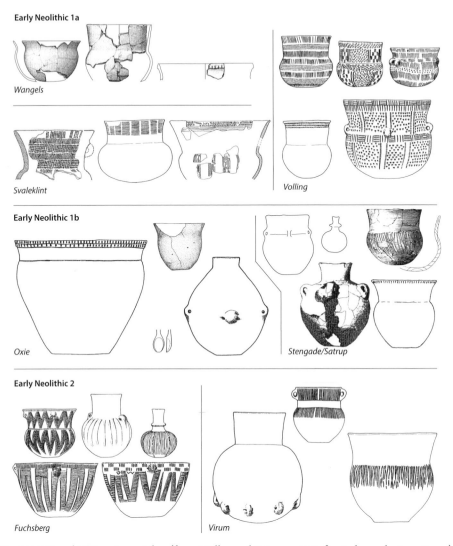

Fig. 1.7. ENI and ENII pottery styles. (from Müller and Petersen 2014, fig. 3, drawn by Ines Reese).

A chronological chart for TRB in southern Scandinavia is provided in Figure 1.6. The two major phases are Early Neolithic I and Early Neolithic II. ENI runs from approximately 4100 in northern Germany and perhaps 4000 BC in Scania and to 3500 BC in Denmark and ENII lasts from 3500 to 3300 BC. Some, primarily German, researchers (e.g., Müller *et al.* 2010) divide ENI into two phases: ENIa (4000–3800 BC) and ENIb (3800–3500 BC). Pottery from the Early Neolithic is one of the more diagnostic materials, in addition to the polished flint pointed-butt axes (Sørensen 2020). The first manifestation of this Early Neolithic is seen on coastal sites in northern

Germany, especially at the site of Wangels (Hartz *et al.* 2002) and has been termed the Wangels group (Klassen 2004). After 3900 BC, the Wangels group was replaced by Siggeneben-Süd–Stengade II group which was also found further east in Germany, almost to the Polish border, as well as in the southernmost of the Danish islands, specifically on Falster, Langeland, and parts of southern Funen.

The earliest style of TRB pottery in Denmark is known as Oxie, after the Swedish type site, and occurs from northern Germany through eastern Jutland, the Danish islands, and in southwestern Sweden (Fig. 1.7). Oxie materials date from 3950–3500 BC according to Klassen (2004) or 3958–3797 BC per Skousen (2008). Oxie pottery is usually undecorated with a flat bottom. Decoration is occasionally found (10%) around the rim, produced with fingernail or fingertip.

Svaleklint and Volling were the subsequent ENI pottery styles (Fig. 1.7). Svaleklint is found in eastern and southern Denmark, while Volling appears in the northern and central parts of Jutland. Contemporary groups in Sweden are termed Svenstrup, Mossby, and Siretorp. Svaleklint pottery is typical of the later part of period EN I between 3800 and 3500 BC (Ebbesen and Mahler 1980; Madsen and Petersen 1984; Koch 1998; Klassen 2004; Skousen 2008; Madsen 2019). Svaleklint pottery is characterized by Funnel Neck beakers with a vertical or slightly flared necks, a rounded belly and a flat or rounded base. The inventory also includes lugged beakers, flasks and jars, collared flasks, as well as clay discs. Decoration is infrequent and usually placed below the rim. Designs are made with stick impressions, stab-and-drag, and twisted, two-stranded cord. Rows of vertical strokes are a common design. Some beakers have a decoration of alternating horizontal and vertical designs that are repeated on the neck and belly. Svaleklint pottery is related to the contemporary Volling style in western Denmark.

Volling style as noted is characteristic of later ENI in northern and central Jutland and dates from approximately 3800 BC until 3500 BC, but the degree of contemporaneity with Oxie style is debated (Klassen 2004). Volling vessel shapes include Funnel Neck beakers, lugged beakers, flasks and jars, collared flasks, and clay discs. Volling style is primarily characterized by a rich decoration that may cover the entire surface of certain beakers and some other vessel types. The decoration typically combines horizontal and vertical designs that are repeated on the neck and belly. Decoration techniques include stab-and-drag, twisted two-stranded cord, and various imprints. In northern Jutland, Volling style is extended in ENII in the form of the Lokes Hede style.

ENII dates from 3500 to 3300 BC and involves Fuchsberg and Virum ceramic styles, which dominated in Jutland and the Danish islands respectively. The inventory of vessel types in both styles included Funnel Neck beakers, lugged beakers, flasks, and jars, collared flasks, and clay discs. A new phenomenon was vertical striations as belly design on Funnel Neck beakers. Impressions of whipped cord were frequently used for decoration in both styles. Fuchsberg is primarily characterized by richly decorated bowls and lugged beakers with large chevron designs filled with horizontal impressions of whipped cord, cardium, twisted cord, or chisel stamp (Andersen and Madsen 1978). Virum style includes rim designs of various imprints, rows of short strokes, and horizontal lines. While the neck is usually undecorated, some lugged beakers and jars may have complex neck designs such as hanging semicircles. The vertical lines on the belly may be combined with a ladder design (Ebbesen 2011).

Several important changes can be seen in ENII. Exchange of local and exotic materials appears to have intensified. Domesticates were more common in ENII and the first plow marks have been observed (Thrane 1991). However, cereal cultivation appears to be limited; specialized hunting and fishing sites are still in use. Settlement expands and there is an initial occupation of areas with heavier soils. Residential sites are found in both coastal and inland contexts and appear to be smaller and more ephemeral than Late Mesolithic occupations (Madsen and Jensen 1982).

Earthen long barrows were replaced by megalithic dolmens – large stone cists, covered with a round or rectangular mound, circumscribed by a line of huge stones. Such tomb construction, known from much of the Atlantic façade of Europe and the western Mediterranean, appears to have originated in Brittany after 5000 BC. Another type of site dating to ENII is the causewayed camp, a type of enclosed, regional ceremonial center (Andersen, N.H. 1990; 1993). These are large open areas encircled by natural or built defenses, such as palisades and ditches, on natural promontories or heights (Andersen, N.H. 1993).

The transition from Late Ertebølle to the Early Neolithic is not readily apparent in most lithic materials. One major change from the Mesolithic to the Neolithic is the shift from core axes to polished flint axes and chisels. Polished axes provide one of the hallmark chronological markers for the Neolithic (Fig. 1.8). Shape of the butt end of the axe and the extent of polishing define specific chronological intervals (Nielsen 1977; Stafford 1999; Sørensen 2014). Pointed-butted axes characterize ENI. Thin-butted polished flint axes appear toward the end of ENI, dating from 3800 to 3500 BC, and are more generally associated with Svaleklint and Volling pottery styles. Thin-butted axes with two- or four-sided polish continue until replaced by a variety of thick-butted axes in the Middle Neolithic (MNV), associated with Store Valby

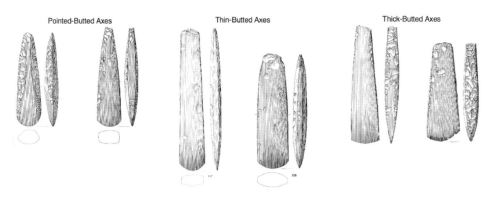

Fig. 1.8. Neolithic polished stone axes (National Museum, Copenhagen).

ceramics. Other kinds of thick-butted axes continue to be used during the Battle Axe and Late Neolithic dagger period.

These polished axes are made from large blocks of high-quality flint and finely flaked into a quadriform shape (Vemming and Madsen 1983; Stafford 1998). The flint for such axes often came from distant, flint-rich localities along certain coasts or from mines in the chalk belts of southern Scandinavia (Rudebeck 1987; Berggren *et al.* 2016). These early axes were highly polished on all four sides. The extent of the polish and the remarkable size of some of these axes, along with their discovery in hordes and offerings, suggests that at least some were important in terms of status and display (Stafford 1998; Klassen 2004; Bradley and Edmonds 2005).

Debitage from axe production is distinctive. The flakes from core axe manufacture are curved with an angular striking platform; quadriform production results in a flat, expanding flake terminating at the opposite end of the axe side or face (Vemming and Madsen 1983; Madsen 1984; Stafford 1998). These flakes have a striking platform perpendicular to the flake; that platform is often prepared and scarred.

Flake axes continued in use in the Early Neolithic and are difficult to distinguish from Late Ertebølle examples. Neolithic flake axes were usually made on more irregular pieces and had a side bulb and a pointed end. The flake axes often had symmetrical surface retouch and retouch on the sides as well, sometimes from the bulbar face. The distinctive Havnelev-type flake axe has a pronounced bulb near one of the corners of the cutting edge. In addition to flaked and polished flint axes, polygonal battle axes, pecked and ground from various types of stone, are occasionally found in the Early Neolithic.

Other artifacts in Early Neolithic flint assemblages include transverse points, scrapers, borers, and knives. Transverse points in the Early Neolithic typically have parallel sides and may be slightly smaller than Late Ertebølle examples. The edges of transverse points are sometimes retouched in two directions in the Neolithic and the butt end is occasionally retouched as well. Points are often made on flakes, occasionally removals from polished flint axes. Large rhombic points, perhaps spear tips, are also known from the Early Neolithic and are thicker and more irregular than earlier Kongemose forms. Scrapers are much more common at Neolithic sites and appear in a variety of sizes and shapes, generally larger than their Mesolithic predecessors. Heavy, rounded flake scrapers are typically Neolithic, with steeper and more shallow edge angles attributed to wood and skin working respectively (Juel Jensen 1994). Shouldered and beaked scrapers are known. Retouch on the bulbar surface of scrapers is a Neolithic trait. Drills in the Neolithic are commonly made on flakes and have converging, rather than parallel, edges on the bit. Burins are not frequently seen overall in the Neolithic but are common at some sites.

Recent genetic evidence is particularly informative. Several regional studies have documented varying degrees of interaction with local Mesolithic groups, ranging from gradual population admixture to almost complete replacement (e.g., Olalde *et al.* 2015; Hofmanová *et al.* 2016; Lazaridis 2018; Brace *et al.* 2019; Rivollat *et al.* 2020).

Early Middle Neolithic: Younger Funnel Beaker: MN A

From the beginning of the Middle Neolithic period around 3300 BC, substantial residential sites begin to re-appear on the coast as well as at inland locations and territorial boundaries among settlements appear to be in place, emphasized by the construction of one or more megalithic tombs in relation to settlements (Skaarup 1973; 1985; Madsen 1991). These tombs, known as *jættestue*, or passage graves, were erected in the younger Funnel Beaker period, from 3300 to 2800 BC. One of the major concentrations of megalithic, monumental tombs in Europe (see Fig. 1.18) is found in western Sjælland (Furholt 2011; Sørensen 2015).

The Middle Neolithic, which extends from 3300 BC until 2400 BC is a complex mixture of cultures and economies that vary over time and space in southern Scandinavia. The first half of this period, until 2800 BC, represents the later part of the Funnel Beaker period. The second half of the Middle Neolithic witnesses the arrival of two new and distinct groups, the Single Grave/Battle Axe Culture and the Pitted Ware Culture. Most of the chronological and cultural markers for this period are again based on ceramics.

There are significant differences seen in the lithic assemblages as well. Middle Neolithic sites are often large, with abundant flint artifacts, especially flake scrapers, borers, and polished axes (Vang Petersen 2008). Axes and blades are well made, somewhat smaller than previous forms, and often found in large depots/caches. Axes change dramatically during the period. Four-sided thin-butted axes and flake knives continue from the Early Neolithic into MN I. Some thin-butted axes are polished only on two sides during MN I–II. The amount of polishing on axes generally decreases through time. Thick-butted axes and chisels replace thin-butted forms after MN I and the *tværeoxe* (a pointed-butt adze) is known from this time. Simple, asymmetrical daggers begin to appear as well.

Later Middle Neolithic: Single Grave/Battle Axe Culture

The chronology of the Neolithic is shown Figure 1.9. The later Neolithic – the second half of the Middle Neolithic (MNB) and the Late Neolithic – was a time of dramatic change in southern Scandinavia as new groups entered the region from the south and east, probably in association with the expansion of the Yamnaya from Eastern Europe and western Asia (Allentoft *et al.* 2015). The second half of the Middle Neolithic (MNB) is known variously as Corded Ware/Battle Axe/Single Grave Culture and originated in east-central Europe. Pitted Ware Culture also appears in the MNB, between 3400 and 2400 BC, probably originating in eastern Middle Sweden.

Single Grave/Battle Axe culture is known primarily from graves and a number of excavated settlements. Graves are often found as sets of stone-lined cists. Battle axes, pecked and ground from a variety of types of hard stone, are found in grave deposits and rarely on the surface. Egfjord *et al.* (2021) have argued, on

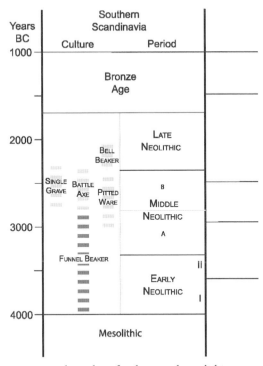

Fig. 1.9. Chronology for the Danish Neolithic.

the basis of the genomic analysis of three individuals from a Single Grave Culture cist at the site of Gjerrild in Djursland, Denmark, that the ancestors of these individuals were from the Yamnaya people. Settlement sites are large and rich. The only diagnostic flint types are axes and transverse arrowheads with polished side edges. Flint axes take a variety of forms including a two-sided thick-butted type, a two-sided thin-bladed thick-butted one, a large and highly polished four-sided thick-butted one, and the distinctive hollow-edged thick-butted form. The so-called B-type axe is characteristic for this period, with its angled, converging butt and straight sides, usually polished on two sides or not at all. The butt end of the axe shifts from a rectangular to square cross-section in the last part of the Middle Neolithic.

The Pitted Ware Culture, dating from approximately 3400–2400 BC appears to represent a return to a primarily hunting, gathering, and fishing adaptation. Some cultivation and herding continued in inland areas. A distinctive pottery is the hallmark of this period. Sites in southern Scandinavia are found primarily northeast of the distribution of Single Grave culture in Denmark and Scania, along the coast of the Limfjord and Kattegat. Lithic artifacts include cylindrical blade cores, long, tanged projectile points on blades, and burins.

Late Neolithic

The Late Neolithic began around 2350 BC and ended by 1700 BC with the start of the Early Bronze Age. The Late Neolithic includes two distinct groups. The Bell Beaker culture dates from approximately 2350–2000 BC. Arrowheads from this period are distinctively triangular in shape, surface retouched, and basally notched to create a small tang. While such points are found throughout Denmark, there are no examples from the Saltbæk Vig region. Only a handful of sites are known from this period, characterized by the bell-shaped ceramic forms. The Bell Beaker Culture in Denmark likely had a western origin and arrived in northern Jutland, perhaps to exploit the rich flint deposits located there. Bell Beaker users introduced more trade and more metal to a large region and may have been the catalyst for the onset of the Late Neolithic.

The Late Neolithic is also known as the Dagger Period because of the widespread distribution of these objects (Fig. 1.10). This period is characterized by the specialized production of flint daggers, surface retouched sickles, spoon-shaped scrapers, spear points, and arrowheads. Flake removals in dagger production show an angular platform and expanding flake. There are changes in dagger and arrowhead morphology though the period that provide chronological markers. Daggers shift from lanceolate form to fishtail hilts (Fig. 1.10), but complete daggers are rarely found in surface survey. Projectile points are surface retouched and evolve from broader triangular forms with tanged or flat bases to narrower triangular, barbed shapes. Blade production essentially stopped, but flint axes with flared edges were produced in large numbers. There was an increase in both copper and gold, occasionally found in graves. This period also witnessed a major intensification in exchange, leading to a series of innovations ranging from costume to burial ritual. Bronze began to appear after 2000 BC. Metal production was focused primarily on weapons – axes, spearheads, and swords.

In all likelihood the beginnings of inherited rank and the warrior ideology can be traced to this period (Vankilde 2019). The increase in conflict and wealth likely reflects pronounced social inequality which became manifest in the Bronze and Iron Ages. Population increase is indicated by the growing number of farmhouses, still isolated or grouped in small hamlets for the most part. House size increased during the Bronze Age reflecting a transformation in social and political relationships. Large halls and rich graves confirm the impression of status differentiation and hierarchically organized society. The larger houses or halls were the residences of the elite. A hierarchy with a large central farmstead or manor surrounded by smaller farms may be an emerging pattern of settlement in the later Bronze Age. Aristocrats and warriors traveled far and wide across much of Europe in search of wealth and knowledge (Kristiansen and Larsson 2006).

History of archaeological research

Northwest Zealand has a long history of archaeological research. The Danish National Museum has undertaken several major excavations in this area since the late

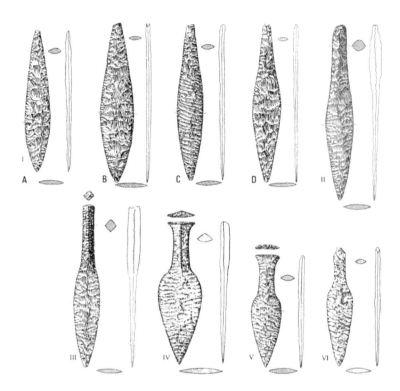

Fig. 1.10. Dagger types from the Late Neolithic of Denmark.

1800s. These projects have included both 'kitchen middens' (e.g., Kilsaas, Klintesø: Madsen *et al.* 1900) (Fig. 1.11) and inland settlements (Mullerup: Sarauw *et al.* 1903; Vinde-Helsinge Mose: Mathiassen 1948), from the Mesolithic; Neolithic excavations have focused largely on megalithic tombs (Olstrupgård: Müller 1918; Ebbesen 1975; Lindebjerg: Liversage 1981), but some coastal sites with a mixed hunting-farming economy have also been investigated (Ordrup Næs: Becker 1939; 1951; Ørnekul: Becker 1952).

The best way to understand this history of research is through the records of the *Sognebeskrivelse*, the national archaeological database. The *Kulturhistoriske Centralregister* (DKC) of the Danish Kulturarvsstyrelse maintains this archive of reported prehistoric sites in Denmark. This registry, also known as the Parish Register (*Sognebeskrivelse*), contains a sequentially numbered list of sites for each parish (*sogne*) in the country, along with the archives of the archaeological work that produced that information. This catalog is an essential database for any archaeological study.

The history of investigations in the Saltbæk Vig area is revealed in these records. A total of 501 reports of some 442 finds were made in the larger research area prior to the Saltbæk Vig Project. Four major activities produced 85% of these reports: the District Survey (*Herredsberejsning*) in 1881 and 1891, the Survey of Protected

Fig. 1.11. Photograph of shell midden excavation at Vejle Kro in 1896 (National Museum, Copenhagen).

Monuments (*Fredningsrejser*) in 1941, peat digging in the 1940s, and Therkel Mathiassen's survey of northwestern Sjælland between 1948 and 1956 (see below).

Recording of archaeological sites in the Saltbæk Vig area began in the 1860s when the steward of Lerchenborg manor, F. Beck, recorded the megalithic monuments belonging to the estate. The *Herredsberejsning*, made by H. Petersen in 1881 (Raklev and Tømmerup parishes) and by C. Neergaard in 1891 (Avnsø, Bjergsted, Bregninge, Viskinge, and Værslev parishes), was the first professional cataloging of archaeological sites and produced 20% of the present site records within the Saltbæk Vig area. This survey was concerned primarily with visible monuments in the landscape and most of the megalithic tombs (and only two settlements) were recorded.

Activities intensified in 1940s and 10% of the *Sognebeskrivelse* records were produced during this decade. P.V. Glob did a survey of protected monuments (the *Fredningsrejse*) in 1941 and peat digging during the later years of the Second World War uncovered a number of stray finds, one hoard, and one settlement.

A major survey of prehistoric remains in northwest Sjælland, from the end of the last glaciation until the end of the Iron Age about AD 1000, was made between 1948 and 1956 under the direction of Therkel Mathiassen (1959). A similar study had previously been done in Northwest Jutland (Mathiassen 1948), an area with different topography and patterns of prehistoric occupation. Mathiassen's goal was to compare the developmental trajectories of the settlement patterns in each area.

This survey involved the cataloging of museum collections and archives, followed by visits to landowners to record their private collections. Field reconnaissance of varying intensity was undertaken to locate sites and monuments not included in the files of the National Museum. The total area of the survey in northwest Zealand was approximately 1700 km^2. The results were published in tables and on maps showing the prehistoric habitation as a sequence of tombs and settlements through time. The parishes around the Saltbæk Vig were inspected between 1951 and 1953 in Mathiassen's project. This large-scale investigation produced 55% of the current *Sognebeskrivelse* records, including 83% of all known settlements, 43% of hoards, 76% of stray finds of axes, and 75% of other stray finds in the area.

Between Mathiassen's survey around the 1950s and 1990, archaeological work in the area involved the National Museum investigations of the long barrow at Lindebjerg (Liversage 1981) and various activities by amateur archaeologists. In

addition, Paludan-Müller wrote his Magister thesis on the distribution of Mesolithic sites in northwest Sjælland. Examination of the Mathiassen survey data
by Paludan-Müller (1978) took a strongly ecological perspective on changes in
settlement. On the basis of his observations, Paludan-Müller argued that the carrying capacity of the estuaries increased at the beginning of the High Atlantic
in the Early Ertebølle, making permanent residence possible for the first time.
Sedentism then resulted in increasing population and seasonal expansion to the
outer islands and inland regions during the later Ertebølle. Continued increases
in population would have demanded increased productivity. The only area where
that would have been feasible was in the climax forest in inland areas. Thus, at
the end of the Mesolithic, Paludan-Müller predicted a decrease in the number of
island sites and an increase in inland occupation reflecting greater manipulation
of the forest.

In the first part of the 21st century Almut Schülke studied the distribution of Neolithic tombs (see Fig. 1.16) and settlements across northwest Sjælland (2008; 2009a;
2009b; 2013; 2015). This work is discussed in more detail in the following section on
monumental tombs.

Several unusual places are noted in the *Sognebeskrivelse* listings. A thick midden
of oyster and mussel shells was reported in the last century along the banks of the
Bregninge Å (SB 22 – Viskinge parish). This midden could not be relocated by our
project survey. A number of finds in the bog area near Løgtvedgaard close to the
juncture of the Bregninge Å and the drainage of the Storemose likely document a
series of Neolithic votive offerings (Koch 1998). Finds from this locality included
pottery vessels, a human skull, antler, flint, and stone axes. These places were not
relocated. A Mesolithic site reported on an island in the middle of the Saltbæk Vig
(SB# 145 – Tømmerup parish) today lies at a depth of *c.* 50 cm beneath the surface
of the inlet. This site was reported at a time when lower water levels in the inlet
exposed the small island. We visited this site by boat and relocated its position in
the Saltbæk Vig.

Monumental tombs

Megalithic monuments in the Saltbæk
Vig region (Fig. 1.12) have attracted
most of the attention of archaeologists and account for 28% of the
Sognebeskrivelse records for the project area. The number of reported Neolithic tombs in the Saltbæk
Vig study area, more than 100, is
remarkable, although only about 30%
remain today. Sjælland has the highest

*Fig. 1.12. Long dolmen on the peninsula of Røsnæs
(drawing: Kurt Petersen).*

concentration of megalithic tombs in southern Scandinavia and one of the highest in all of Europe (Fig. 1.13).

Three major groups of Neolithic tombs can be distinguished: earthen long barrows, long dolmens, and other megaliths, and their distributions are of interest. The earthen barrows exhibit substantial variation in size. Normally, these barrows are low features (1–2 m in elevation) and vary in the length between ca. 10 m and 100 m. Radiocarbon dating indicates that the construction of earthen long barrows took place during ENI (*c.* 3950–3600 BC).

Long dolmens are a distinctive construction, often a combination of an earthen long barrow and one or more dolmens, with large stones placed along the edges of the barrow (Fig. 1.14). The long dolmens apparently represent a situation where a megalithic monument, a dolmen, was added to an earlier construction of the earthen long barrow (Madsen 1993; Müller 2011b). David Liversage (1981) of the National Museum conducted a series of investigations in 1966–1972 around the Early Neolithic

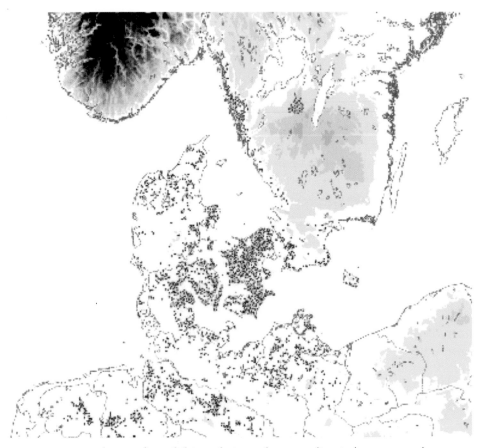

Fig. 1.13. Distribution of megalithic tombs in southern Scandinavia (Sørensen 2015).

long dolmen at Lindebjerg in the Saltbæk Vig area, purportedly one of the oldest in Denmark (*c.* 3800 BC).

The fill of the barrows often incorporates artifactual materials, suggesting that these monuments were built within or adjacent to Early Neolithic settlements. Thus, we have assumed that the distribution of long dolmens in the Saltbæk Vig area is a reflection of Early Neolithic occupation. There are approximately 20 long dolmens reported in the project area (see Fig.1.15). The majority of these, all but four, are located on the south side of the Saltbæk Vig itself. These long dolmens are rather evenly distributed from northeast to southwest and lie approximately halfway between the coastline of the Saltbæk Vig and the hills that mark the watershed to the next fjord at Kalundborg to the south. The exceptions are one mound at the north end of the Storemose and three at the eastern edge of the project in the area known as Vesterlyng (Becker 1947). The long dolmens occasionally occur in pairs; there are four such pairs along the south side of the Saltbæk Vig.

Fig. 1.14. Long dolmen.

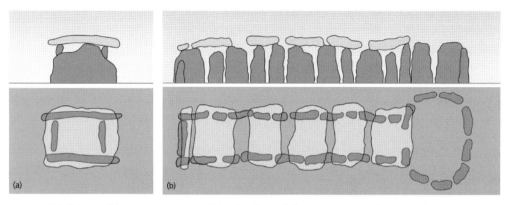

Fig. 1.15. (a) dolmen, (b) passage grave. Both kinds of megalithic tombs were often buried under a mound of earth.

The third group of Neolithic tombs includes megalithic dolmens and passage graves (Fig. 1.15) that date from ENII, *c.* 3500–3300 BC (Skaarup 1993). There are more than 90 megalithic tombs (dolmens and passage graves) in the Saltbæk Vig study area. These monuments show a more widespread distribution than the long dolmens (Fig. 1.16). Single or small groups of megaliths are found inland throughout the project area. There are clear clusters of these monuments on several hills in the area at Fibjerg, Lindebjerg, and Rungedyssebjerg. Although most megaliths occur on the south side of the inlet, there are several north of the Bregninge Å.

In sum, the date and location of barrows and megalithic tombs provides another source of information on the presence and distribution of Neolithic settlement and land use in the Saltbæk Vig region. The focus of these monuments is clearly on the south side of the inlet. Their distribution is widespread and fairly uniform across this area. Although the tombs concentrate in distinctive, higher locations, their broad distribution suggests that Neolithic settlement was common in the area. It is the case that the northeastern portion of the coast may have been less attractive for settlement as it is exposed to the predominant wind direction and subject to serious erosion.

Schülke (2015) suggests three functional kinds of monumental tombs among the dolmens and passage graves in the Saltbæk Vig area and environs: the closed single

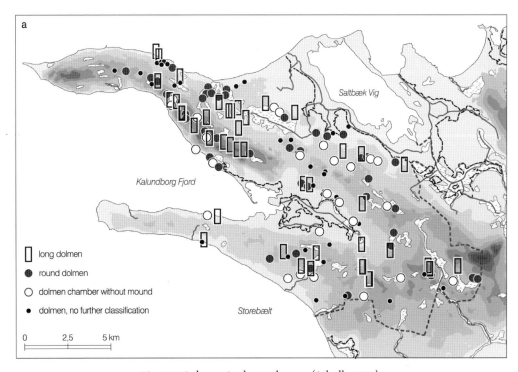

Fig. 1.16. Dolmens in the study area (Schulke 2015).

grave, the openable single grave, and the open collective grave. Generally, these monuments were variously placed close to the coast, on top of hills, on hillsides, in depressions, and conspicuously, e.g., on the east–west moraine-ridge of Røsnæs (Schülke 2009a). The problem is that we do not know if these different functional types are contemporaneous. If the argument for contemporaneity made in Sweden (Sjögren 2011; Blank *et al.* 2020) is valid here, then perhaps these different types are in use at the same time and reflect a society with a highly varied burial program. In phase EN I (as in the Ertebølle), settlements were placed in low-lying locations (0–20 m asl), either within 1.3 km of the former Early Neolithic coastline, or very close to the large inland freshwater basins like Lake Tissø and the Lille Åmose. In the next phase (EN II–MNA II) settlement density doubled and sites occurred further inland. This phase corresponds with the observed increase in cultivation and pasture land that marks agricultural intensification in southern Scandinavia.

An introduction to the region

Southern Scandinavia today is heavily agricultural with fields of wheat, barley, rape, potatoes, corn, soy, and sugar beets. The landscape is one of the more domesticated on earth – the opposite of wilderness – manifesting an ordered and serene surface, intensively farmed, pruned, and cultivated for 6000 years. The seas also provide important routes of transportation and communication throughout Scandinavia and must be considered in any overview. No spot in Denmark is more than 75 km from the sea and most are closer.

Geographically, southern Scandinavia includes Denmark, southern Sweden, the Oslo Fjord area, and the northernmost part of Germany, which was part of Denmark until the 19th century. Southern Scandinavia is different from the north, both today and in the past. This is the lowland zone. Rising from the sandy stretches of the North European Plain, the peninsula of Jutland extends as an entry point from the continent toward the rest of Scandinavia. Many islands dot the seascape. Denmark and southwestern Sweden were leveled by glacial ice, leaving a flat, hummocky topography with small rivers and numerous bogs and lakes inland, while several seas surround that surface. The highest elevation in Denmark is 171 m. The streams draining the area flow quietly into the Baltic, North Sea, Kattegat, and Skagerrak.

The island of Sjælland is roughly 100 km in diameter, the largest in Denmark and the most populous with 2.3 million people, about 40% of Denmark's total. Most of the population resides in the eastern third of the island in and around the city of Copenhagen, the cultural and political hub of the country. The island has a generally rolling landscape with major features today that are the remnants of sub-ice formations. The melting of the glacial ice that covered most of Denmark left a range of sub-ice features – terminal moraines, kames, eskers, outwash plains, and the like – that define the higher points on the landscape (Fig. 1.17).

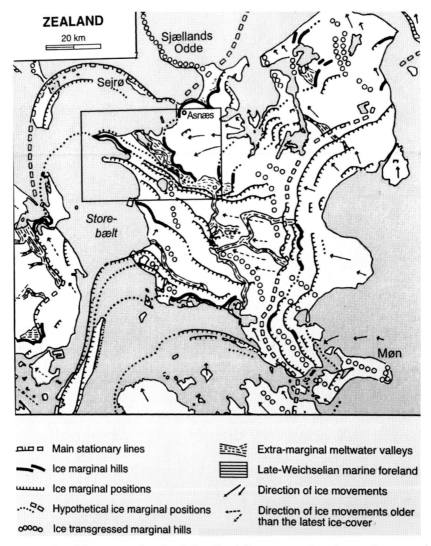

Fig. 1.17. Glacial features on the island of Sjælland (from Houmark-Nielsen and Kjær 2003).

The rise of sea level left a landscape of peninsulas and islands, of lakes and bogs. Western Sjælland, carved by the sea, has deep inlets and many peninsulas and smaller islands. The term 'fjord' is used for these inlets in Denmark, although they lack the high mountains and rocky cliffs that define such features in Norway. Someone, probably Anders Fischer, once told me that to really understand the Danish landscape you have to see it from the water and that is certainly true. It is also important to remember how much wetter this landscape would have been before field drainage and agriculture began to lower the water table. Fjords, lakes, and bogs would have dominated the landscape, putting higher, drier land at a premium.

The warming trend and melting ice at the end of the Pleistocene caused a dramatic rise in sea level during the first half of the Holocene (Astrup 2019). The seas flooded the North Sea basin. England was separated from the continent as the Channel filled with water and the dry land area known as Doggerland in the North Sea basin was transgressed and submerged *c.* 6500–6200 BC (Gaffney *et al.* 2007; 2009). The Dogger Bank, an upland area of Doggerland, remained an island until 5000 BC.

Much of the sea floor that today surrounds Denmark was dry land during the early Holocene, gradually inundated by rising seas and water tables. The present sea floor of southern Scandinavia contains abundant traces of submerged prehistoric landscapes. The sea reached modern levels around the end of the Atlantic climatic episode, *c.* 4000 BC, and even exceeded present levels a bit at that time. Geological investigations suggest that the coastline in the Early Neolithic was located at the present 2.5 m contour line in the Saltbæk Vig area (see Fig. 1.17; Hede 2003, 143–147) and that today's bogs were mostly open, shallow areas of salt or brackish water (Noe-Nygaard and Hede 2004). The coastal area would have been easily accessible by boat, while the inland, with its many wetlands, must have been difficult passage (Dalsgaard 1985). The western side of the island of Sjælland typifies this landscape (Hede 2003). Sea water gradually made its way into the Storebælt and completely changed the nature of this formerly inland area (Fig. 1.18). The rate of sea level rise varied but estimates suggest that the inhabitants would have been aware of changes (Astrup 2019).

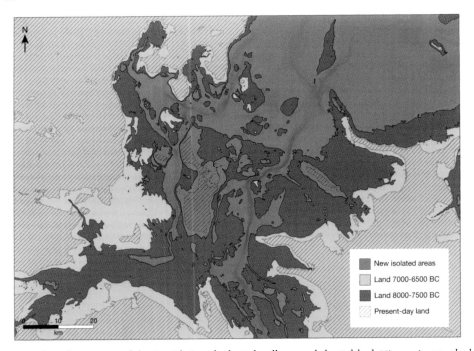

Fig. 1.18. The submergence of the Danish Storebælt. Kalundborg and the Saltbæk Vig are just to the left of the legend box (from Åstrup 2019).

A contour map (Fig. 1.19) of western Sjælland provides a good view of these features and offers a lesson in the geography of this region. This landscape was forged largely by periglacial events at the end of the Pleistocene. Melting of the ice sheet was uneven; northwest Sjælland initially became ice-free, followed by parts of central Sjælland (today's Åmose) where a meltwater lake formed amid the ice-covered remainder of the island. The major outlet for this meltwater was to the northwest, through the area of the Saltbæk Vig. Eventually the melting of the Storebælt glacier opened an outlet further to the south via the lake of Tissø and another river, the Halleby Å. A final re-advance of the glacier formed the steep hills at Bjergsted to the east and created the present watershed between the Saltbæk Vig and the Åmose basin in west-central Zealand. Terminal moraines from the huge ice sheets that covered much of Denmark provided the highlands (Verhøj and Bjergsted), peninsulas (Odsherred, Røsnæs and Asnæs), and islands (Nexselø and Serjerø), of the area. These terminal moraines have elevations up to 100 m and higher and divide the landscape into three drainages which follow the older meltwater courses: the Halleby Å drains the Store and Lille Åmose via Tissø, the Kjærby Å drains the Kalundborg region into the fjord, and the Saltbæk Vig area is itself drained by the Bregninge Å.

The many lakes and bogs of the region developed in the depressions left when remaining blocks of inactive ice finally melted (Hede 2003). The middle elevations of the area are composed of ground moraine and various outwash sediments of sand and gravel. The powerful meltwaters from Late Pleistocene ice sheets carried vast amounts of rock and sediment over the Bjergsted moraine and deposited them at the foot of the ridge. Much of the land to the west of Bjergsted Bakke has been exploited for many years for sand, gravel, and boulders. The larger materials, e.g., van-sized boulders, are found nearest the Bjergsted moraine. These boulders and gravel are an important natural resource and, for that reason, these deposits at the eastern end of the study area have largely been removed. Either there are active gravel pits or the land surface has been restored following quarrying activity in the area east of the village of Bregninge. These deposits grade to smaller sizes as one moves north and west from the moraine. Near the mouth of the Saltbæk Vig, approximately 16 km west from Bjergstad, the sediments are fine sands. These sands undoubtedly spilled out through the Saltbæk Vig and formed the very fine beach at Vesterlyng.

The vegetation and landscape development in Denmark over the last 15,000 years is documented in a number of pollen records from lakes, bogs, and kettle holes (e.g., Iversen 1973; Rasmussen 2005; Odgaard and Nielsen 2009; Mortensen *et al.* 2014). The succession of deciduous forest started in Denmark around 7000 BC. This forest contained a large variety of trees, dominated by lime (*Tilia*), elm (*Ulmus*), oak (*Quercus*), alder (*Alnus*), and ash (*Fraxinus*). These more shade-tolerant species gradually outcompeted the Boreal hazel (*Corylus*) and pine (*Pinus*) dominated forest. The primary forest was relatively dense (*c.* 90% of the area), with few and small open areas (Nielsen

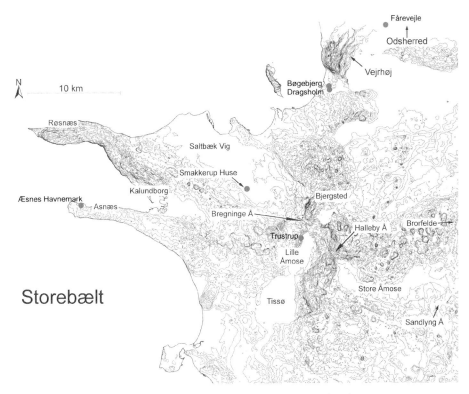

Fig. 1.19. Contour map of western Sjælland and location of sites excavated in this project. Contour interval is 5 m.

et al. 2012). The open areas have primarily been concentrated around wetlands and along the coasts. There is no indication of human impact on the vegetation before the Neolithic period.

With the arrival of the first farmers, major changes in the forest composition began. In eastern Denmark there is a marked decrease in lime, probably because the first farmers preferred the high-lying and drier soil often inhabited by lime. With the clearing of the lime forest, grasses (Poaceae), oak, elm, willow (*Salix*) and hazel temporally increased, as a secondary succession in the cleared areas. Despite these major changes in the composition of the forest, only an insignificant change in the ratio between forest and open land is observed. From around 3800 BP, a distinct increase in birch was caused by the repeated use of fire in clearing the forest. The extensive deforestation and burning resulted in a very open landscape in large parts of eastern Denmark (Andersen, S.H. 1993a). Birch disappears after 3400 BC and the continuing presence of grasses and ribwort plantain (*Plantago lanceolata*) indicate that cattle had become much more important. The presence of cereal pollen (Cerealia) indicates local cultivation.

Organization of this book

The general organization of this volume follows our program of fieldwork. Chapter 2 details our 1989–1992 survey of the Saltbæk Vig region north of Kalundborg, mapping the size, location, and contents of Mesolithic and Neolithic sites around the former coastline. The majority of Mesolithic settlements were from the later, Ertebølle period of the Mesolithic and were often defined by large, dense concentrations of lithic material. Chapter 3 describes the 2-year program of testing in 1993–1994 and excavation of some of the sites we had recorded. Chapter 4 is a report on several years (1989, 1995–1997) of a major excavation at a place called Smakkerup Huse at the head of the Saltbæk Vig inlet (Price and Gebauer 2005). The locations of our excavations in Western Sjælland are shown in Figure 1.20.

A note on field seasons

We conducted the field survey after harvest in the fall for 2 months in 1989 and 3 months in 1991. Gitte and I spent a couple of weeks in Kalundborg in the fall of 1990 doing some survey and artifact registration. Testing and excavation were done in the summer with seasons of 6 or 8 weeks.

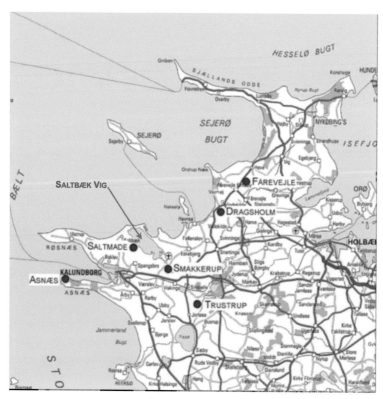

Fig. 1.20. Locations of excavations discussed in this volume.

Next, after the end of the Saltbæk Vig project, I wanted to look at inland settlement for comparison with all the coastal material we had collected and we began work at a place called Trustrup, in the Lille Åmose in west-central Sjælland (Chapter 5). Because of the importance of the burials at the site of Dragsholm and their role in discussions of the Mesolithic–Neolithic transition, I began excavations there in 2002 in the hopes of locating Early Neolithic levels with good preservation (Chapter 6). We spent three summer field seasons in very rich Mesolithic and Neolithic layers at Dragsholm. We also did some digging at the nearby Middle Mesolithic site of Bøgebjerg, 150 m north of our excavations at Dragsholm (Chapter 7).

From Dragsholm we headed north a half dozen kilometers to the Mesolithic shell midden at Fårevejle, described in Chapter 8. I wanted to see what shell middens were like compared to other Mesolithic sites and I hoped we might locate an Early Neolithic level in the midden. We spent two summers (2005–2006) at Fårevejle learning that these middens were quite variable in terms of artifact contents. Fårevejle did have massive accumulations of oyster shell, stone-lined hearths, and a good bit of Ertebølle pottery, including a fragment of a lovely little lamp. In 2007, our project moved again to a site called Asnæs Havnemark, along the coast at the end of the 10 km long, narrow peninsula of Asnæs just south of Kalundborg (Chapter 9). The location is very much focused on the sea as the peninsula is about 1 km wide at this point. Some of the major questions we pursued in all of this research – Mesolithic lifeways, the nature of the Mesolithic–Neolithic transition, the spread of agriculture, the emergence of inequality – are discussed in the final Chapter 10, Conclusions, along with some thoughts and feelings about the project as a whole and the questions we sought to answer.

Chapter 2

Archaeological survey

It is amazing to think how much has changed since we began our survey of the Saltbæk Vig area in 1989, both in terms of technology and the land itself. Of course, that was more than 30 years ago. In terms of technology and methodology, we were fieldwalking and mapping sites before the availability of the Global Positioning System (GPS) which meant a lot more time was spent in locating and measuring the places we found. No field computers, location satellites, georadar, laser measuring devices, or total stations were available. This was old-fashioned map, compass, and measuring tape archaeology.

On the other hand, much of the work we did simply could not be done today because of changes in land use, legislation, and farming practices. Legislation from the European Union now requires that plowed fields be planted in winter wheat or barley following harvest, so that vegetation covers the ground, hiding artifacts, during the prime fieldwalking seasons of late fall and spring. The goal is to reduce soil erosion, but it means that the bare ground surface is no longer visible. Moreover, since the time of the survey in the early 1990s, agricultural regulations have reduced the number of cultivated fields in the Saltbæk Vig area by as much as 25%. Large swathes have been planted in forest and pine plantation to reduce the amount of farmland on poor soils.

One of the things that we noticed years ago when talking to the farmers to obtain permission to survey their land was that very few were under 60 years of age. Most of those folks are gone now and, for the most part, no younger generation has taken their place. There are no more collections of ancient artifacts that the farmers discovered in their fields. The farmland has been purchased or leased by larger corporations using massive machinery to cultivate and harvest enormous fields in a more open landscape. The small farms have largely disappeared, and many young people have left the rural areas for larger towns and cities, a trend seen in many parts of the world.

Many of the small farms where we surveyed have now been merged into larger enterprises, sometimes making access more difficult. With the industrial revolution, new crops, all-field rotation, extensive drainage, and the addition of marl and fertilizers to the fields greatly raised productivity, supporting increased population and denser settlement in the cities. Today southern Scandinavia is industrially farmed by large agribusinesses that have created a species-poor landscape of enormous fields and little native vegetation in many areas (Christianson 1997). Heavy doses of fertilizer and pesticide are required to keep the fields fertile. The water drawn out by deeper plowing, irrigation, and animal use has lowered the water table considerably. The process is not necessarily good for the land or for archaeology.

Archaeological sites are damaged by heavy, deeper plowing and the absence of moisture means that organic materials like wood and even bone preserved in the ground for thousands of years are now disappearing (see also High *et al.* 2016). We saw this clearly during our excavations at Lindebjerg where a deep ditch had been cut through a Neolithic settlement, perhaps during the medieval period. The moisture remaining in the deeper ditch had preserved the bones that had fallen in from the Neolithic site while, less than a meter higher, the removal of moisture from a drop in the water table led to the disappearance or degradation of most of the faunal remains.

A note here. It seems important to point out several aspects of our project that are of relevance to archaeology today. First and foremost, a survey such as ours would be more difficult to conduct today. Agricultural activity continues to intensify in the fields that remain in the Saltbæk Vig region. Deep plowing carves further into sites already near the surface and will eventually eradicate them. Industrial consumption of water, field drainage, and well irrigation continue to lower the water table; conditions for the preservation of prehistoric materials deteriorate rapidly. Air pollution and its accompanying acidity also contribute to the destruction of archaeological materials. Over time, and not much time is left, the prehistory of this area will remain only as thin scatters of flint artifacts on the surface of the ground (e.g., High *et al.* 2016). Calls for more active programs of surface survey in Europe (e.g., Bintliff *et al.* 2000) need to be heeded quickly, if it is not already too late.

Survey of the Saltbæk Vig drainage, western Sjælland

The Saltbæk Vig Project was a regional archaeological investigation of the beginnings of agriculture in prehistoric southern Scandinavia, conducted largely from 1989 to 1997. Funding for this survey was provided by the National Geographic Society, the U.S. National Science Foundation, and the Fulbright Foundation, and these institutions are gratefully acknowledged. Survey was a way to take stock of the number and location of archaeological sites in an area that had not been systematically fieldwalked. At the time, and until today, most of Denmark has not been systematically surveyed.

The focus of the Saltbæk Vig project was on the Stone Age, especially the Mesolithic and Neolithic, and the transition between these two important periods. The archaeological survey was concentrated on those zones where Mesolithic and Early Neolithic settlements were most likely to be found, along the coast and the shores of low, wetland areas. The survey was intended to record all materials that were encountered, with the expectation that most of the finds would belong to the Stone Age. This indeed turned out to be the case.

The Saltbæk Vig itself was a small inlet on the west coast of Sjælland that became a lake when the attempted reclamation in the 1860s was unable to remove all the water (see Fig. 1.20). The research area covers almost 150 km² including the inlet. The actual area of field survey was concentrated along the coastlines of the lowered inlet and on elevations below 5 m asl. We chose the 5 m elevation rather arbitrarily as a way to keep the study area a feasible size for the time and personnel we had available. We also surveyed a few transects that crossed higher elevations as a check on our focus on the coastal areas. Approximately 22 km² were surveyed intensively by fieldwalking and more than 400 prehistoric localities were recorded, ranging from stray finds to large settlements.

Archaeological sites, of course, originally contained a wide range of artifacts and materials, both organic and inorganic, left behind by their inhabitants. The passage of time, however, has resulted in the degradation of many of these items. Organic objects, plant or animal remains, are usually missing from prehistoric sites, leaving only inorganic stone and pottery. Stone Age ceramics, however, rarely survive more than a few years on the surface of agricultural fields in northern Europe. Pottery is susceptible to the destructive forces of cultivation in summer and freeze/thaw cycles in winter.

Natural decay and more recent human activity mean that the most common arti-facts remaining on the surface of the ground in northern Europe are made of flint, commonly available in Denmark. Many studies have been made of what happens to stone artifacts in plowed fields (Mallouf 1981; Larsson and Olausson 1992; Dunnell and Simek 1995; Steinberg 1996; Boismier 1997; Noble *et al.* 2019). In general, such studies show that artifacts are not moved a significant distance from their original location. Under most circumstances, the distribution of materials reasonably reflects the location and size of the site underneath.

Our survey found and located prehistoric artifacts on the ground surface, either individually or in clusters, and recorded the distribution, content, and chronology of the material that was collected whenever possible. The types and styles of artifacts provided the diagnostic markers for various periods of the Stone Age (Fig. 2.1). This information can be used to make some estimates of the nature of human activity and settlement during different time periods in the past.

The chronological focus of the project was the later Mesolithic and the Early Neolithic, between approximately 5000 and 3300 BC. The introduction of farming in prehistoric Scandinavia is complex; the reasons for this transition are unclear and the subject of some debate. On the one hand, the Neolithic seems to come suddenly, shortly after 4000 BC, with the appearance of Funnel Necked Beaker (*Tragtbæger* or *Trichterbecker*, TRB) pottery, domesticated plants and animals, and earthen long barrows for burial across a broad area (Sørensen and Karg 2012). On the other hand, Mesolithic hunter-gatherers in Denmark had been in contact with farming popula-tions to the south in Poland and Germany for more than 1000 years before agriculture arrived. Farming did not become the primary means of subsistence for several hundred

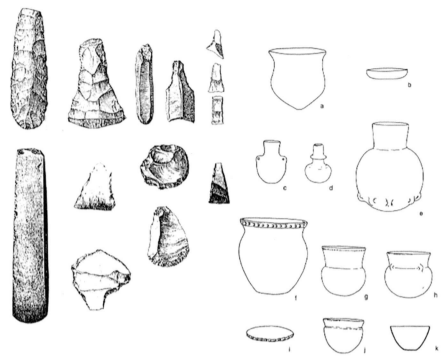

Fig. 2.1. Some diagnostic artifacts from Mesolithic and Neolithic. Top row is Mesolithic: core axe, flake axe, blade, blade knife, projectile points, Ertebølle pot (a) and clay lamp (b). Remaining are Neolithic: Polished flint axe, small flake axe, flake knife, 2 scrapers, 1 projectile point. Pottery includes a variety of funnel beakers as well more utilitarian ware such as the clay disk (i) and 2 bowls (j, k) (from Hartz and Lübke 2006).

years after the introduction of domesticated plants and animals. Thus, the transition in southern Scandinavia can be understood either as a rapid event or as a gradual process. Detailed evidence of the changes involved in the transition is still lacking in many areas. The Saltbæk Vig project was intended to obtain such information. The regional aspect of this study was considered important in order to assess changes through time within a specific geographic area.

This larger project involved several stages of fieldwork – survey, testing, excavation, and paleoenvironmental investigations – intended to learn more about the archaeological remains of the area and to obtain information on the nature of the transition to agriculture.

The archaeological survey of the Saltbæk Vig study area was initiated in 1989 (Gebauer and Price 1990) and largely completed by 1993. Some survey work continued for several years, however, in order to visit newly accessible areas and to return to some known localities to enlarge collections. The major goals during the survey stage were (a) to locate and identify prehistoric localities from the time covering the transition to agriculture, specifically from the Mesolithic and Neolithic, and (b) to record museum and amateur collections from the area. The recording of local collections was rather haphazard; many collections had been passed on to younger generations. Most of what we learned came from the field survey. The survey described here provided a foundation for the larger research project. Information from the survey and the analysis of surface collections was essential for the later testing and excavation components.

This report on the archaeological survey provides a description of the Saltbæk Vig area as well as the survey methods and results. Following this introduction, more detailed information on the landscape and geology, sediments and soils, sea level changes, and more recent changes in the landscape of the research area is provided. The archaeological survey is covered in the next section with a description of the survey zones, the methodology, and the information recorded for the site location, the artifacts collected, and chronological placement. A subsequent section of the report presents the results of the archaeological survey in a chronological framework with information on both time period and the location and distribution of sites. The following section contains an analysis of the survey information in terms of variables such as site size, settlement distribution, elevation, and soils. This section includes a comparison with both previous archaeological surveys and the information in the *Sognebeskrivelse*, or National Register of archaeological sites. The conclusion of this report provides a summary of the results of the archaeological survey and outlines some general trends in the evolution of prehistoric human settlement in the coastal region of the Saltbæk Vig drainage.

The research area

The Saltbæk Vig in northwestern Zealand, Denmark (Fig. 1.16), lies northeast of the town of Kalundborg. The Saltbæk Vig itself is a roughly rectangular former inlet of the Kattegat, approximately 9.61 × 3.75 km in size and 36 km^2 in surface area (Fig. 1.18). The research project area around this inlet is defined by the watershed and drainage of the Saltbæk Vig and the river which feeds into it, the Bregninge Å. This entire project area is approximately 16 km in length from northwest to southeast and 8.8 km in width, roughly 150 km^2 in area. Pronounced hills and ridges in the landscape define the borders of the project area around the Saltbæk Vig to the east, south, and west; the waters of the Storebælt and Kattegat lie to the west and north.

In the 1860s an attempt was made to drain the Saltbæk inlet and reclaim the sea floor for farmland. A series of dams were built, connecting the marine forelands at the mouth of the Vig and closing the inlet. Pumping systems were constructed to remove the seawater (Fig. 2.2). This reclamation project ultimately failed to completely drain the inlet, probably because of the deep sand deposits beneath the inlet. However, since that original attempt, water levels in the Saltbæk Vig have been artificially maintained below sea level by continued draining and pumping. The lake left behind in the

Fig. 2.2. Pumping station involved in drainage of Saltbæk Vig from 1895 (postcard).

former Saltbæk Vig is the third largest in Denmark. The water level in the inlet today is kept to 1.2–1.5 m below sea level. Because of this situation, a series of coastal Mesolithic localities, from the Late Kongemose and Early Ertebølle periods, are accessible on the former floor of the Saltbæk Vig and along its shores.

The Saltbæk Vig region is thinly populated, inhabited largely by farmers and laborers living in small villages or isolated farmsteads. Cultivation of most of the research area means that archaeological localities are usually exposed on the surface of the ground and amenable to surface reconnaissance and collection. Private ownership of much of the reclaimed land (essentially the area below the 0 m contour) by the Saltbæk Vig Company has limited the erection of summer cottages, common in many other coastal areas in Denmark. The area is peripheral to industrial development; construction has had only a minor impact. This coastline of northwest Sjælland was declared a protected wetland of international importance for sea birds in 1978.

Much of the area is accessible for archaeological fieldwork. Groundwater levels are close to the surface in the low meadows around the Saltbæk Vig, enhancing conditions for the preservation of organic materials. Archives at the National Museum record finds of artifacts and the bones of human and other animals from the first half of the 20th century. Several other localities with preserved organic material have been found since that time in bogs or during the investigation of megalithic tombs. These occurrences, even after a century of intensive drainage and cultivation, indicated that there were opportunities for finding localities with organic material, both in the waterlogged, lower areas and in the higher glacial and periglacial deposits. Such organic remains are essential to understanding the transition to agriculture.

Landscape and geology

This section provides some background on the research area around the Saltbæk Vig and includes a description of geology and the landscape, sediments, and soils in the region, the impact of Holocene sea level rise, and more recent changes in the landscape.

Perhaps the best way to visualize the project area starts from a small boat on the Saltbæk Vig itself. Although the water today is enriched with phosphates from agricultural fertilizers, there are flourishing populations of eel and zander, harvested commercially each year. Many species of birds are seen around the Saltbæk Vig; migratory waterfowl are especially abundant; the guns of duck hunters are frequently heard in season. Cormorants are common and easily spotted as they fly by or at their distinctive nesting areas, marked by the dead trees and vegetation killed off by their toxic feces.

The mouth of the Saltbæk Vig is crossed by a chain of small islands – Mulen, Lille Vrøj, Store Vrøj, and Krageø. Today these islands are connected by a series of constructed dikes that dam the Saltbæk Vig from the sea. These islands have some antiquity and are not completely a result of higher sea levels during the Holocene. The discovery of a Late Paleolithic projectile point on Vrøj documents its exist-ence as an elevated part of the landscape at the end of the Pleistocene. Our testing program also encountered glacial till in the subsoil of Store Vrøj, documenting its pre-Holocene existence. The peninsula of Alleshave, along the northeastern shore of the Saltbæk Vig, would have been a small island during the higher water levels of the middle Holocene.

The former shoreline of the Saltbæk Vig, prior to the damming and lowering of the water, is marked today by a drainage canal at the 0 m contour (Fig. 2.6). Above this canal, between +1.5 and +2.5 m above sea level, lies a pronounced beach ridge that more or less parallels the modern coast of the Saltbæk Vig throughout its cir-cumference. This beach ridge was formed at the end of the Atlantic climatic episode around 4000 BC, when sea level was higher than today, and marked the coastline of this area in the middle Holocene. The land between the 0 m canal and this beach ridge today is a combination of meadows, cultivated fields, and woodlands. Above the beach ridge are fields of wheat, clover, barley, beets, potatoes, and maize, which extend throughout the study area to the tops of the moraine ridges that mark its boundary (not shown).

The major stream in the area, the Bregninge Å, empties into the headwaters of the Saltbæk Vig and flows out through the drainage canals on either side of the inlet. The Bregninge Å was originally formed by one of the last powerful meltwater rivers running through the Saltbæk Vig area during the melting of the Storebælt glacier. From its mouth, the stream winds its way over 9 km to the southeast across bog and grassland. The Bregninge Å begins at the Avnsø, a small lake at the foot of the end moraine hills of Bjergsted Bakke on the southeastern edge of the research area. The stream today has been canalized along much of its course.

There are several smaller streams and creeks in the area. The Tranemose Canal drains the east and south, emptying into the Saltbæk Vig near Illerup Sand, likely following a former watercourse. Small streams, almost invisible today, run into the Saltbæk Vig on either side of Tømmerup Holme. A narrow stream near Asmindrup, locally known as *Asmindrupløbet*, runs through an area of several megalithic structures. On the northeastern edge of the Saltbæk Vig, a small, unnamed stream drains into wetlands in the area of the Arnakkebugt.

The project area encompasses a variety of topographical features that result from the glacial shaping of the landscape and the subsequent deposition of sedimentary materials. A broad diluvial plain characterizes the central part of the study area and underlies the Saltbæk Vig itself. Undulating end moraine hills rise to the east, west, and south of the inlet and define the larger borders of our study area.

A distinctive series of sandy, flat topped hills lie to the south and west of the Saltbæk inlet. Examples are seen at Lindebjerg, Rungedysse Bjerg, and Fibjerg. These elongated, plateau hills or kames were built up of horizontal layers of sand and gravel deposited during the Pleistocene in holes in the ice sheet (Strand Petersen 1985). Plateau hills are typically flat on top with relatively steep slopes. Based on the quantity and variety of finds from the survey, these hills were often the focus of hunting activities during the Mesolithic and of residence and tomb construction during the Neolithic. Better drainage, lighter tree cover, and more open forest in these lighter, sandy soils may have attracted prey, hunters, and early farming communities.

Dunes and beach ridges characterize the Kattegat coast of the Saltbæk Vig area. A rapid sea level rise (3–4 m per 100 years) took place between 8000 and 6000 BC and inundated the western part of the diluvial plain across the Sejerø Bay and brought sea water into the Saltbæk Vig area. Extensive beach ridges were piled up along the shore of the Saltbæk Vig and in the valley of the Bregninge Å. Offshore bars built up on higher points on the landscape at the northwest opening of Salbæk Vig, partly closing off the entrance.

Sediments and soils

Sediments and soils in the Saltbæk Vig area are typical for northwestern Zealand and are primarily the result of four major processes: the deposition of moraine by Late Pleistocene ice sheets, the subsequent outwash of layers of sand and gravel from the melting of the ice, the transgression of the sea, and the accumulation of organic deposits of peat and gyttja. The higher ridges surrounding the study area are composed of end and ground moraine with clayey soils. The south side and east end of the study area are covered with meltwater sands and gravel. The sandy kame hills along the south side of the Saltbæk Vig are included in these deposits. The middle elevations are primarily sand and peat.

Postglacial deposits atop the glacial surface include lacustrine and bog formations, along with eolian and marine sediments. The area below +5 m in elevation is dotted with fossil, buried, and extant bogs that developed in the hollows and depressions left when the remnants of the glacier finally melted. The Tranemose and the Storemose are two of the largest bogs in the Saltbæk Vig region; large bogs also cover parts of the diluvial plain along the Bregninge Å. The Tranemose lies southeast of the Saltbæk Vig in a broad depression among higher elevations. The Storemose lies to the northeast of the Saltbæk Vig and at one time drained into the Bregninge Å near the village of Bregninge. Both the Storemose and the Tranemose have been drained and exploited for peat in the last several centuries. In addition to these two large former wetland areas, there are many smaller bogs scattered throughout the project area.

The basin of the Saltbæk Vig itself is defined by Holocene marine deposits. The extent of these sediments essentially marks the maximum stand of the sea in the project area at the time of the transition to agriculture. Beach ridge deposits are found along most of the coast of the Saltbæk Vig and around the mouth, including the large islands. There are also two areas of surface eolian sand deposits along the coast of the Kattegat to the west (at Vollerup) and to the east (at Vesterlyng) of the Saltbæk Vig.

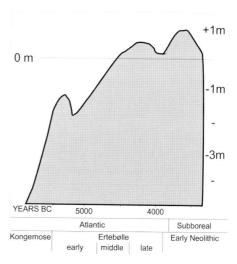

Fig. 2.3. Early Holocene sea level changes in western Sjælland.

Sea level changes

The rising waters of the sea during the Postglacial played a major role in the evolution of this area. The Saltbæk Vig lies in that part of Denmark where the land surface continues to rise due to isostatic rebound following the melting of continental ice. There are several reconstructed curves of sea level change from various parts of Zealand: at Vedbæk in the northeast corner of the island (Christensen 1982; 1993; 1995), at Trundholm Mose in the northwestern corner (Maagaard Jacobsen 1982; 1983), and at Halskov on the west coast (C. Christensen 1993; K. Christensen 1997). Halskov is the area closest to the Saltbæk Vig and likely the best model for the project area. The basic pattern revealed by this curve (Fig. 2.3) is one of a major rise in sea level during the Atlantic period, from –30 m to 0 m in less than a thousand years. At the end of the Atlantic and the beginning of the Subboreal period, there were two transgressions and regressions between +0.5 m and +2.0 m, termed the Littorina fluctuations (Christensen 1995). In some models these two are treated as one (Christensen 1995; Hede 2003).

Maximum sea level in the Saltbæk Vig area was reached during either the late Atlantic or early Subboreal transgression. Extrapolation from the maps of the isostatic rebound of the land surface in this area (Mertz 1924) provides an estimate of +1.5–2.5 m for the coastline at this time in the Saltbæk Vig area. This elevation correlates well with the beach ridge that rings the inlet and likely marks the maximum stand of the sea at the time of the Atlantic–Subboreal transition. It should be remembered that until it was dammed, the *vig* was open to the sea and tidal so that significant shellfish populations may have been supported in this area.

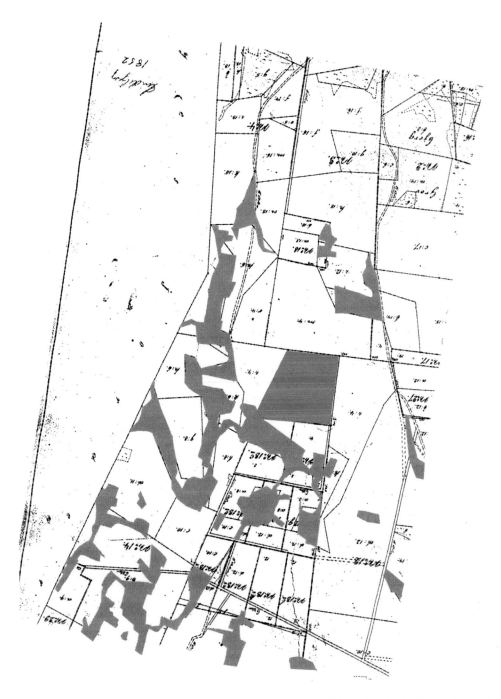

Fig. 2.4. 1852 Cadaster map of Lindebjerg area on the south side of the Saltbæk Vig. The pink area is the top of the Lindebjerg plateau. Blue marks areas of open water in 1852. Gone today.

Recent changes in the landscape

One of the more dramatic recent changes in the landscape in the Saltbæk Vig study area has been the lowering of the water table, particularly in the last 150 years. In addition to the pumping of the waters from the Saltbæk Vig itself, drainage pipes have been installed in many fields in this area to carry water away and into the canals around the Saltbæk Vig. Given the intentional lowering of the waters in the Saltbæk Vig and the continuous agricultural activities in this area over the last century, we would estimate that the water table has been lowered at least several meters since the Postglacial sea level maximum. Farmers have intentionally drained and filled small ponds and bogs to increase the amount of arable land and improve conditions for plowing. Repeated plowing, especially with heavy modern equipment, has leveled the landscape, in the process filling and burying former wetlands. The wetlands in this coastal area of northwestern Sjælland today occupy only a tiny fraction of their former extent at the beginning of the Subboreal period.

A series of maps of the area from 1852 provide a good indication of the amount of bog and surface water in the area of the Saltbæk Vig prior to its more recent reclamation and drainage for the development of agriculture. Figure 2.4 shows an area around the sandy hill of Lindebjerg on the 1852 map. In 1852, Lindebjerg, with a maximum elevation of 15 m, was almost completely surrounded by bog and wetlands at its base, *c.* 5 m above sea level.

Today there is very little evidence of these bogs at Lindebjerg. The surrounding fields have two or three small wet areas that are slowly disappearing. Clearly the lowering of the water table, along with the drainage and plowing of the fields, has dramatically changed the landscape. The reduction in wetlands around Lindebjerg is substantial and likely representative of the entire research area. We would estimate that perhaps 60–70% of the landscape of the Saltbæk Vig research area at one time was covered with wetlands. It is important to visualize the region around the Saltbæk Vig at the time of the transition to agriculture as largely wetlands, marsh and bog, with limited patches of higher, drier ground.

The archaeological survey

This area was selected for the research project for a number of reasons, including the intentional draining of the Saltbæk Vig, the limited modern development in the area, the extent of cultivation, the potential for preserved organic materials, and the presence of Early Neolithic remains.

Information for the archaeological survey comes from several sources.

Fig. 2.5. Field survey and artifact collection, Jordmor Site, Saltbæk Vig, Denmark.

Amateur archaeologists from the Kalundborg area – members of the local archaeolog-ical society – working in conjunction with the Kalundborg og Omegns Museum, have surveyed selected areas in the Saltbæk Vig. A second source of information came from the Tranemose region in the eastern part of the project area, intensively surveyed for some years by Jens Nielsen, an archaeologist at the Kalundborg og Omegns Museum and a member of the Saltbæk Vig project. Most of the survey data, however, comes from a full-coverage, systematic field survey by a trained crew including the author. This group examined all accessible plowed and open fields and surface exposures within the survey zone. Surveying was done in the fall of the year when agricultural fields had been harvested and replowed (Fig. 2.5). This systematic survey was carried out in September and October of 1989 by a crew of five, for 2 weeks in August of 1990 by two individuals, and in September, October, and November of 1991 by a crew of six or more.

Locality designation

All sites/localities were numbered consecutively within a parish using a six-letter code. The following parish abbreviations were used and are capitalized as the first three letters of the site designation: Avnsø = AVN, Bjersted = BJE, Bregninge = BRE, Kalundborg = KAL, Raklev = RAK, Tømmerup = TMM, Vorslev = VRS, and Viskinge = VIS. New find locations in each parish were designated consecutively with three letters starting with baa. Out of consideration for the varying alphabets in Denmark and the US, we decided to use all letters of the alphabet except i and u, because of potential confusion. In numbering the site/location within a parish, this 24-letter system was used in lower-case:

baa, bab, bac, bad ... bax, bay, baz,
bba, bbb, bbc, bbd . . . bbx, bby, bbz,

...

bza, bzb, bzc, bzd ... bzx, bzy, bzz.

For example, the first location/site in the Avnsø parish was designated as Avnsø no. baa – and the objects from it were marked AVNbaa.

The survey zone

The project area included the entire drainage of the Saltbæk Vig. However, the survey zone was limited to the coastal zone of the Saltbæk Vig supplemented by selected areas at higher elevation. The coastal zone in particular was chosen because Meso-lithic and Early Neolithic localities could be expected in this area. Since it was only feasible to survey a portion of the project area, just selected parts of the inland area were intensively surveyed. Figure 2.6 shows the location and distribution of the fields where intensive fieldwalking took place.

The survey zone included the following areas:

1. The prehistoric coastlines between approximately –1.2 m, the water level in the Saltbæk Vig, and +5 m around the entire inlet. This is the zone of Holocene

transgressions where many Late Mesolithic and Early Neolithic localities can be expected. Given that the maximum height of Holocene transgression in this area is approximately +2.5 m, the survey zone effectively includes the entire coastal area of the Saltbæk Vig from the later Mesolithic through the Neolithic. This area today is in part under cultivation in wheat, barley, and maize. There are also extensive meadows used for pasture at the lower elevations around the Saltbæk Vig. Intensive survey was not undertaken in areas of grass and pasture; these areas were walked and surface exposures examined, but a number of localities may have been missed because of the ground cover. Phosphate testing of subsurface samples was attempted in an effort to locate sites, but without success.

2. A series of four transects, radiating perpendicularly from the Saltbæk Vig to the edge of the research area (Fig. 2.6). The transects were 500 m wide and extended from the coastal survey zone around the inlet to the ridge tops marking the boundaries of the research area. These transects were designed to provide some information on the higher, inland areas of the Saltbæk Vig for comparison with the immediate coastal zone. The placement of the transects was largely arbitrary and intended to cover different parts of the project area. Transect A ran northeast–southwest roughly perpendicular to the southern shore of the Saltbæk Vig and parallel to the coast. This transect extended from the town of Illerup across the Tranemose to the 25 m contour, a distance of approximately 2 km. Transect B ran from the 5 m contour at the south shore of the Saltbæk Vig across Lindebjerg and to the town of Ubberup, a distance of approximately 1.5 km. We deliberately included the well-known area of Lindebjerg in the survey transect. Transect C was placed along the southern side of the Bregninge Å and extended for approximately 1 km to the southern edge of the project area. Transect D was located on the peninsula of Alleshave and extended across the top of the peninsula from one side to the other, a distance of roughly 1 km. All the accessible fields in these transects were surveyed.

3. Areas around long dolmens on the south side of the Saltbæk Vig. The monumental tombs of the first farmers provide evidence of habitation and land use. The earliest monuments, the earthen long barrows with wooden burial structures, appear around 3800 cal BC and are often located on top of earlier settlements. The only known earthen long barrow from the research area was incorporated in a long dolmen with stone chamber. In an attempt to locate other long barrows and Early Neolithic settlements, areas up to 300 m in diameter were surveyed around the long dolmens (Fig. 2.7).

The emphasis on the coastal zone is somewhat arbitrary but justified by what is known of the distribution of settlement in the later Mesolithic (Larson 1987; 1990; Price 1991; Brinch Petersen 1993). Although the coastal zone represents only a small fraction of the total landmass of southern Scandinavia, the majority of Mesolithic sites have been reported here (e.g., Andersen 1995; Larsson 1997). Coastal sites are

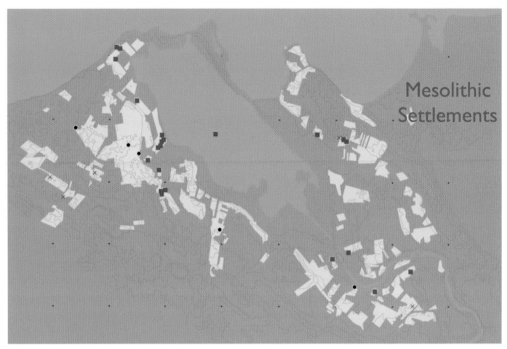

Fig. 2.6. Surveyed fields (lighter shading) and Mesolithic settlements in the Saltbæk Vig project area. Water levels are shown at present day heights. North is to the top. Grid points are spaced at 1 km intervals. Black dots are stray finds. The zero contour is the one closest to the water.

often larger, more substantial and more permanent (e.g., Madsen *et al.* 1900; Jonsson 1988; Andersen 1995). Inland settlements are generally smaller, seasonal, more limited in the material remains present, and probably represent seasonal extraction sites of coastal groups (e.g., Fischer 1993; 1997; Andersen 1995). Persson's (1999) compilation of radiocarbon dates from Mesolithic sites in these two zones in southern Scandinavia clearly demonstrates their relative utilization. The number of radiocarbon dates from the coastal region is several times greater than from inland localities.

There is some information from an archaeological survey conducted prior to the installation of a new gas pipeline across much of Denmark (Hertz *et al.* 1987). This survey, which took place from 1979 to 1986, covered a zone 300 km long and 10 m wide, a total of approximately 30 km². This survey was confined primarily to the interior of the country. A total of 644 settlements was recorded in the project, of which 132 belonged to the Stone Age. Of the Stone Age settlements, 29 were distinguishable as Mesolithic and 96 as Neolithic. Among the Mesolithic sites, approximately ten were Maglemose, three were Kongemose, and 11 from the Ertebølle period. Of these Mesolithic sites, 32% came from coastal zones that comprised less than 5% of the survey area. Clearly, the major proportion of Mesolithic settlement can be expected to occur in coastal contexts.

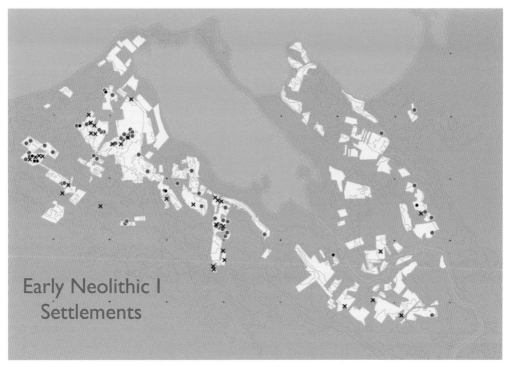

Fig. 2.7. Surveyed fields (lighter shading) and Early Neolithic settlements (blue circles) in the Saltbæk Vig project area. Water levels are shown at present day heights. North is to the top. Grid points are spaced at 1 km intervals. Black crosses are stray finds.

The earliest Neolithic settlements in Denmark and Scania are known from two contexts: either as continuations of Late Mesolithic occupations in coastal locations or as new inland sites – scatters of residential debris, usually discovered beneath long barrow excavations. Neolithic remains are found stratigraphically above Late Mesolithic along the coast at a number of sites (Andersen 1991; 1993a; 1993b). The earliest known grave from the Neolithic is the male burial from Dragsholm, northwest Zealand (Price *et al.* 2007). At Bjørnsholm, on the Limfjord in northern Jutland, both a long barrow and an Early Neolithic settlement are found above an earlier Mesolithic site (Andersen and Johansen 1992; Andersen 1993b). This pattern of coincidental barrow and settlement is repeated at a number of inland early TRB settlements in Denmark such as Lindebjerg (Liversage 1981), Stengade (Skaarup 1975), and Mosegården (Madsen and Petersen 1984). Early Neolithic residential sites in inland contexts appear smaller and more ephemeral than Late Mesolithic occupations (Madsen and Jensen 1982).

Survey methods

Survey of the Saltbæk Vig area involved intensive, full-coverage fieldwalking of all accessible fields in the survey zones defined for the project. Crews of 2–6 or more individuals conducted the primary survey of fields along parallel transects with a spacing of 5–15 m between surveyors, depending on conditions. Archaeological remains from all periods were recorded during the survey.

There were positive and negative aspects of the survey schedule and procedures with regard to the recovery of prehistoric materials. The survey was undertaken intensively by well-trained crew members. It is unlikely that many localities were missed in the fields that were walked. On the other hand, the majority of the survey took place during the autumn of the year. The optimum time for fieldwalking in Denmark is generally considered to be the early spring after the fields have been washed many times by the rain. In addition, in most cases the survey involved only one visit to a locality. We thoroughly collected each locality at the time of the visit, but it is well known that repeated visits to surface sites produce additional material (e.g., Johansson 1999).

It is also the case that the Holocene coastlines of Denmark have changed substantially over time through cycles of transgression and regression of the sea. Much of the coast from the Mesolithic and Early Neolithic has been heavily eroded. Many of the sites that we encountered during the survey had been redeposited to some extent. Johansson (1995) notes that virtually all Mesolithic sites in the Karrebæk-Dybsø fjord area (Fig. 2.8; Table 2.1) were heavily eroded by marine transgression. Such changes in the distribution of material makes assessment of site size more difficult.

A number of studies of stone artifacts on the surface of plowed fields have been undertaken (e.g., Mallouf 1981; Jacobsen 1984; Dunnell and Simek 1995; Steinberg 1996; Boismier 1997). In general, such studies show that artifacts are not moved a significant distance from their original location of deposition. As Jacobsen (1984) and others have pointed out for Scandinavia, the surface material reasonably reflects the location and size of the site underneath but is less useful for determination of the age and type of site. In our experience, artifact distribution is generally a good predictor of site size. This was less often the case, however, on the former sea floor of the project area where marine erosion had sometimes removed larger sites leaving only limited remains on the surface. In many instances, the more material found on the surface, the greater the likelihood that much of the actual site had been destroyed through plowing or other activities.

Worked flint is found in virtually every field along the coasts of northwestern Zealand. All flint artifacts observed during the survey were counted; the total count of artifacts in each field was tabulated. The strategy was to record the number of stray or background flints encountered in each field, to mark single finds of chronological significance, and to record the concentrations of artifacts that we encountered. When a large number of flints was found, a locality was declared. Generally this was a fairly straightforward decision. Most fields contained 1–20 stray pieces of worked flint (Fig. 2.9). More than 1–2 pieces per square meter usually indicated the location of a scatter or settlement.

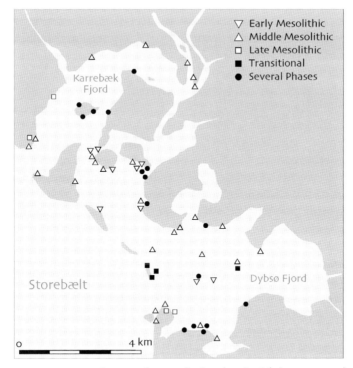

Fig. 2.8. Survey results in in the Karrebæk-Dybsø fjord (Johansson 1995).

Table 2.1. Number of sites and number of axes present by Mesolithic phase in the Karrebæk-Dybsø fjord system.

Phase	No. sites	No. axes				
		1–9	10–25	26–100	101–400	400–1000
Dragsbjerg	3	2	1	0	0	0
Møllekrog	6	1	0	3	2	0
Lundebakke	16	0	6	5	4	1
FIskerhus	12	3	1	1	3	3
Karrebæk	4	0	1	0	2	1
Humlebakke	4	1	0	2	1	0

When a concentration of artifacts was recognized, the interval between surveyors shifted to 1–3 m and the area was walked more intensively. Small flags were used to mark the position of artifacts; if the locality was large and artifacts abundant, flags were placed along the edges of the distribution. The use of the survey flags had two primary purposes: (1) to mark the topographic distribution of materials on the landscape, and (2) to allow us to measure the size of the locality. Length and width dimensions of the

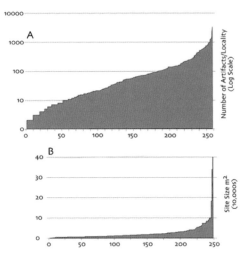

Fig. 2.9. A. Number of artifacts per locality, and B. Site size in m².

artifact scatters were recorded by pacing or meter tapes. In addition, the position of the locality in the field was recorded by pacing and/or measuring to adjacent roads or field margins.

Localities were collected as completely as possible and the artifacts taken to the museum to be washed, counted, and recorded. All diagnostic artifacts were noted, ceramics were described and analyzed, and this information added to the survey database. The survey collections and records are now archived with the museum and the site information has been put on file with the *Sognebeskrivelse*.

As with any project, methods changed some and improved as the survey continued. During the first season, flints were examined in the field, debitage was counted, and only diagnostic pieces were collected and returned to the museum. Background flint was not counted in the field during the first year of the survey. These procedures were revised for the subsequent seasons when the majority of the fields were walked.

Locality characterization

The word locality was used in the project for findspots to avoid the ambiguity inherent in the term 'site'. Single finds, lithic scatters, settlements, and graves are subsumed under the term locality. Each locality was marked on copies of the standard 4 cm topographic maps for Denmark and a survey form was completed to characterize the locality. Along with the site number, other recorded information included the UTM coordinates (Universal Transverse Mercator) and elevation of the place, the identity of the surveyors, a description of field conditions, an estimate of artifact visibility, the amount of time spent collecting the site, weather, soil type, the landowner and tenant if applicable, site size, site type, and an estimated age for the site. This information is part of the permanent archive of the survey.

Many of these categories are self-evident; others require some explanation. Several categories relate to collecting conditions. Field conditions, weather, soil type, and visibility are particularly relevant. *Field condition* refers to treatment of the ground surface and was noted as rough plowed, level plowed, second growth, or standing crop. *Visibility* was ranked in relative terms from very good to poor. *Soils* were generically described in the field in terms of sand, clay, and peat composition but the final designation for soil types on the survey forms was taken from the national soil map for the area. The designations that were used included diluvial gravel, diluvial sand, freshwater clay, freshwater peat, marine gravel, marine sand, moraine clay, and indeterminate.

Types of localities included stray find, lithic scatter, settlement, and grave. The terms lithic scatter and settlement were used in the field to distinguish small, low density scatters of artifacts from larger, higher density concentrations of material. In practice, however, the distinction is not meaningful. The distributions of both number of artifacts and size area by site show a continuous gradation. Test excavations at a number of these sites revealed some scatters to be more substantial and some designated settlements to be simple scatters. In sum, the distinction between lithic scatter and settlement is of little use in an area where there are hundreds of artifact concentrations of widely varying size and content.

In the final analysis, three terms were used to describe lithic finds: primary localities, stray finds, and secondary occurrences. *Primary localities* are concentrations of three or more artifacts with an identifiable chronological association. *Secondary occurrence* denotes the presence of artifacts from other time periods at a primary locality. *Stray finds* were unusual or diagnostic, single artifacts that were recorded because of their special character. For example, individual polished flint axes were recorded as stray finds, providing a means to examine the regional distribution of these distinctive artifacts. Stray finds were automatically assigned a locality size of 1 m².

Artifact characterization

The survey located prehistoric artifacts, either individually or in clusters. These artifacts were collected and taken to the museum. Pottery was described and assigned to a period based on known types, technique, shape, and decoration. Lithic materials were also classified and counted according to standard typological categories (Table 2.2). Several dimensions of the axes were measured and more specific subtypes of these artifacts were recorded.

Other information was recorded, including burned flint, patination, type of flint (Senonian vs Danien), and technique of blade production (hard vs soft hammer). Burned flint is common at Neolithic localities; its presence on the ground surface may mark the location of settlement or, in some cases, of megalithic tombs. Two primary types of flint are used for the manufacture of tools in the Stone Age of southern Scandinavia (Vang Petersen 2008). Senonian flint, darker, finer, and shinier, is more commonly used for artifacts than Danien flint which is lighter, coarser, and matte in appearance, and used primarily for axe production. Mesolithic materials from the Kongemose and Early Ertebølle often exhibit a heavy white patination caused by exposure to sea water. The oldest Mesolithic materials in the Saltbæk Vig region often have a reddish-brown, bog patination in addition to the white marine patina. Later Ertebølle artifacts usually exhibited some bog (iron) patination but were only occasionally marine patinated. Neolithic sites, generally found at or above 2.5 m, rarely exhibit marine patination.

Table 2.2. Lithic and ceramic categories.

Flake	Scraper
Blade	Scraper: large flake, skin
Microblade	Scraper: large flake, wood
Burnt piece	Scraper: side
	Scraper: end of blade
Microburin	Scraper: shouldered
Sickle blade	Scraper: round flake
	Scraper: double
Flake core	Scraper: beaked
Blade core	
Microblade core	Drill: small flake
Handle core	Drill: large flake
	Drill: blade
Retouched flake: lateral	Burin
Retouched flake: distal	
Retouched flake: bifacial	Axe: flake
	Axe: core
Skive kniv	Axe: specialized core
Flake knife	Axe: polished fragment
	Axe: pointed butt
Retouched blade: lateral	Axe: 2-sided thin butt
Retouched blade: distal	Axe: 4-sided thin butt
Blade knife	Axe: thin butt–thin blade
	Axe: thick butt
Denticulated flake	Chisel
Denticulated blade	Dagger
Denticulated piece: fine	Axe blank
Notched flake	
Notched blade	Pottery: Ertebølle
	Pottery: Neolithic
Point fragment	Pottery: Iron Age/later
Rhombic point	
Transverse point	
Transverse point: large	
Other point	

Soft and hard hammer blades were distinguished. The type of hammer used in blade production varies through the Stone Age (Vang Petersen 2008). The soft hammer technique, employing a mallet of bone, antler, or wood, can be recognized in both the general form of the blade and in the characteristics of the striking platform. This technique produces longer, more symmetrical, and more gracile blades than the use of a hard hammer. The striking platform on the blade is relatively small and has a distinct lip, compared to the larger platform and bulb seen in hard hammer technique. Hard blades were more common on Mesolithic sites. Hard hammers often produce impact fractures and crushing on the striking platform. Blades in general were more common on Mesolithic sites than on later ones (Table 2.3)

In the survey, flint axes were the main artifact type used to date Neolithic sites. Pointed-butted axes from EN I, thin-butted axes of different types from late EN I (c. 3800)–MN II, thick-butted axes and pointed but hollow edge axes from MN III/IV–V, thick-butted axes of type B from the Battle Axe Period and other types from the Late Neolithic. Ceramics were rare. In general, prehistoric pottery does not survive more than a few years on the surface of agricultural fields, subject to destruction by plowing and freeze-thaw activity. Ceramics from the Mesolithic and Bronze Age were not recovered during the survey. Occasional Neolithic and Iron Age pot sherds were collected.

Table 2.3 Percentages of blades to total flakes and blades at sites with more than ten blades and flakes.

Period	Ave.%	Sites	s.d.	Min	Max	n>10%
Mesolithic	21.9	25	10.7	7.1	42.8	23
Early Neolithic	8.6	13	6.6	1.0	25.0	4
Middle Neolithic	9.3	17	8.7	1.5	33.3	6
Late Neolithic	12.2	9	10.1	5.18	37.5	3

Extreme values (>50%) have been eliminated in these calculations.
n>10% shows the number of sites with more than 10% blades.

Neolithic ceramics were useful in determining the chronology of several sites where sufficient rim and decorated pieces could be collected.

Chronological characterization

An estimate of the approximate age of the survey localities was often possible based on the surface materials that were collected. The current chronology for the Stone Age in Denmark was used in this study. Table 2.4 provides the numbers used to construct Figure 2.12, below. A period and phase designation was employed when possible. Period refers to the more general age of the site, specifically Paleolithic, Mesolithic, Neolithic, Bronze Age, and Iron Age. Phase, or sub-period, designations were employed when warranted.

Within the survey area, the Paleolithic phases present included Bromme and Federmesser. Maglemose, Kongemose, and the early, middle and late phases of the Ertebølle (termed Trylleskove, Stationsvej, and Ålekistebro respectively) were distinguished in the Mesolithic (Vang Petersen 1984). Table 2.5 provides average flint artifact counts and site size by time period in the Saltbæk Vig survey. Neolithic sites are bigger than Mesolithic ones and Neolithic artifacts are more abundant.

The Neolithic was divided into five phases for purposes of the survey, based on changes in diagnostic materials, particularly polished flint axes as diagnostic ceramic materials were rarely recovered. The earliest Neolithic is a brief period of transition between the Late Mesolithic and the Early Neolithic; these localities contained artifacts from both phases (marked as M+N in Table 2.5). This phase is the equivalent of Koch's (1998) Phase 1, the period of the pointed butted flint axe. Early Neolithic includes late EN I, EN II, and MNA I–II (Koch's Ceramic Phase 2 and 3, the period of the thin-butted flint axe). Middle Neolithic incorporates MNA III–MNA V (Koch's Ceramic Phase 4, thick-butted flint axe type A). Single Grave Culture and Pitted Ware Culture are included with a third category, MNB. Late Neolithic is Dagger Period. Bronze and Iron Age materials were rare in the survey zone and no further subdivisions of these periods were made. Only general criteria for these divisions are described in the following paragraphs; details on the specific chronology and diagnostic materials are provided in the discussion of survey results below.

Table 2.4. Count of sites per period from various registration systems in western Sjælland.

Period	Saltbæk Vig Survey				Mathiassen Survey				Sognebeskrivelse			
	Primary	Stray	Total	%	Primary	Stray	Total	%	Primary	Stray	Total	%
Paleolithic	1	2	3	0.8	1	0	1	0.2	1	0	1	0.4
Maglemose	0	0	0	0.0	1	0	1	0.2	1	3	4	1.4
Kongemose	4	4	8	2.0	4	0	4	0.9	1	0	1	0.4
Ertebølle	28	7	35	8.8	5	0	5	1.1	6	4	10	3.5
M+N	6	0	6	1.5	0	0	0	0.0	2	1	3	1.1
Early Neolithic	58	32	90	22.6	8	112	120	27.1	17	64	81	28.4
Generic Mesolithic	16	10	26	6.5	2	20	22	5.0	3	5	8	2.8
Generic Neolithic	92	33	125	31.3	0	0	0	0.0	11	30	41	14.4
Generic Stone Age	27	15	42	10.5	0	0	0	0.0	60	35	95	33.3
MNA III–V	29	11	40	10.0	7	151	158	35.7	5	31	36	12.6
MNB SG/ PW	3	8	11	2.8	0	0	0	0.0	1	3	4	1.4
Late Neolithic	8	5	13	3.3	0	132	132	29.8	0	1	1	0.4
Bronze Age	8	2	10									
Iron Age	3	1	4									
Total Stone Age			399				443				285	

Table 2.5. Average flint artifact count and site size (m²) by time period in the Saltbæk Vig survey.

Period	Average flint	Average size
Kongemose	261	2693
Ertebølle	184	2236
Generic Mesolithic	53	1351
M+N	130	2230
Early Neolithic	424	4176
Middle Neolithic	233	3599
Late Neolithic	83	854
Generic Neolithic	68	1432
Generic Stone Age	54	782
Bronze Age	49	1400
Iron Age	95	646

Dating of the Mesolithic localities was based on elevation in the landscape (a few lower localities on older coastlines), blade and projectile point typology, and the presence or absence of core and flake axes. Mesolithic localities were recognized by the presence of large flint blades and core axes along with an absence of polished flint axes and pottery. Flint is of high quality and generally large size. Morphological types such as burins and borers are relatively common in surface collections. Scrapers are not often seen. Blade manufacturing techniques change during the Mesolithic, switching between hard and soft hammer techniques. Projectile points shift from geometric microliths in the Maglemose, to rhombic forms in the Kongemose, to transverse types in the Ertebølle. Transverse points become more symmetrical and narrower through the Ertebølle phase and into the Neolithic (Fischer *et al.* 1984).

There is a marked difference in the proportion of blades between Mesolithic and Neolithic sites. Comparison of the percentage of blades to total flakes and blades collected in the Saltbæk Vig survey is informative (Table 2.3). At Mesolithic sites, blades generally represent 10% or more of the total flakes and blades in the assemblage. Early Neolithic sites show the lowest proportion of blades with slight increases in the Middle and Late Neolithic. The minimum and maximum values provide an indication of the differences as well. While the ratio of blades to flakes is not an absolute criterion for distinguishing Mesolithic and Neolithic sites, it is clear that this difference is important.

In general terms, flint artifacts at Neolithic sites are more variable and less regular in shape and form than at Mesolithic settlements. The quality of work is not as careful. Smaller pieces of flint raw material were often used; cortex is more commonly seen on debitage and artifacts. As noted, blade production decreases dramatically in the Neolithic. The proportion of blades to flakes at Neolithic sites is normally less than half that in Mesolithic assemblages. Blades were made using a hard hammer from conical cores with prepared edges, but blade cores are rarely found at settlements (Vang Petersen 2008). Neolithic localities were generally distinguished by the presence of polished flint axes and a less regular flint artifact assemblage. Perhaps the most diagnostic objects on Neolithic sites are flakes from polished flint axes. Changes in the typology of polished flint axes and daggers, along with occasional ceramics, mark the various phases of the Neolithic.

Bronze and Iron Age materials were rare in the survey zone. These periods were identified by distinctive stone tools or ceramics. Bronze Age lithic assemblages are less distinctive than Mesolithic and Neolithic materials, larger and more coarsely made. Flint artifacts are generally less abundant at Bronze Age sites. There is virtually no flint at Iron Age sites, but the hard-fired pottery usually survives on the surface.

Generic localities

In an ideal world, distinctive types of flint tools and pottery would be found commonly during archaeological survey; sites could be readily identified and dated on the basis of the collected materials. In the real world, of course, archaeological sites on the surface are often represented only by a handful of flakes and a few retouched pieces. Frequently there are no diagnostic pieces; chronological placement is difficult. Projectile points are useful indicators of chronological period but are difficult to find on the surface. Scrapers appear on many Neolithic sites but are remarkably non-diagnostic. Axes are one of the better indicators of chronology and do turn up on surface sites. Core axes are Mesolithic; polished axes are Neolithic. Polished axes shift from pointed-butted to thin-butted in form in the Early Neolithic to thick-butted in the later Neolithic. While most Neolithic sites contain flakes from polished flint axes, larger diagnostic fragments or whole axes are not as common. The assessment of site chronology then becomes a more subjective endeavor.

Because of such difficulties in assessing chronology, we have used generic designations for some localities: Mesolithic, Neolithic, or Stone Age. These terms were employed when finer resolution of the age of the locality was not possible. Mesolithic and Neolithic localities could be separated, but no further distinction of phase could be made. Stone Age was used for Mesolithic or Neolithic localities that could not be distinguished.

The results of the survey

The survey revealed a variety of settlements (Table 2.6) primarily from the Mesolithic and Neolithic periods, including a number of important new localities. Settlement locations tend to be concentrated on higher points of land and peninsulas on or near the former coastline. The majority of localities are found on the south shore of the inlet, concentrated toward the mouth. Few localities were found in the valley of the Bregninge Å. The relative absence of localities in the four transects of the survey document the generally low density of inland settlement.

The systematic survey of the Saltbæk Vig covered approximately 22 km² of agricultural fields. This total area includes only actually surveyed fields. This fieldwork recorded 415 localities, including settlements, stray finds, and several graves. Fifty-five localities had previously been reported in the *Sognebeskrivelse* in the fields that we surveyed. The survey collected more than 50,000 artifacts, stored in the collections of the Kalundborg og Omegns Museum. These materials include some 40,000 flakes, more than 5000 blades, some 400 polished axes and fragments, more than 200 projectile points, more than 1000 pieces of pottery, and a variety of other flint and ground stone objects.

There are only three known Late Paleolithic find spots recorded in the survey. The vast majority of the localities belong to the Mesolithic and Neolithic periods. The most common category is generic Neolithic, but there are also a large number of Early Neolithic sites in the survey area. Ertebølle and Middle Neolithic sites make up the next most common categories. Bronze and Iron Age settlements were few in number and rarely observed during fieldwalking. Sites from these periods are generally located at higher elevations, above the boundaries of the survey zone.

The following paragraphs summarize the results of the survey. Major time periods of interest are discussed in chronological order. Important diagnostic indicators are described, primarily among the lithic artifacts. The occurrence and distribution of sites in each period is discussed. Maps of the distribution of localities from the Mesolithic and Early Neolithic periods are provided (see Figs 2.7 and 2.8). These maps of

Table 2.6. Average elevation of Saltbæk Vig survey settlements by time period.

Time period	Average elevation	No. sites
Mesolithic	+ 0.91 m	51
Neolithic	+5.73	183
Kongemose	−0.75	4
Early Ertebølle	−0.60	9
Late Ertebølle	+1.25	12
Transition	+5.08	6
Early Neolithic	+7.16	54
Middle Neolithic	+5.48	29
Late Neolithic	+3.12	8

the Saltbæk Vig region show the elevations for the area; the contour (green lines) interval is 5 m with the exception of the 2.5 m elevation, corresponding to the maximum sea level of the mid-Holocene (Table 2.6). The grid marks shown on this map correspond to the UTM coordinates at a 1 km interval. Surveyed fields are shown with a lighter shade on the maps.

Late Paleolithic

Late Paleolithic materials are found scattered across northern Europe from Britain to Poland and are characterized primarily by large, tanged points made of flint. These materials date from the end of the Pleistocene, between approximately 14,000 and 11,000 years ago. Most of the finds from this period are stray artifacts. Concentrations of artifacts from the Late Paleolithic in southern Scandinavia likely represent small, short-term camps, often located at strategic inland hunting spots.

Late Paleolithic remains in the Saltbæk Vig are known from only three localities, all in northwestern quadrant of the project area. Two are finds of isolated projectile points reported in the *Sognebeskrivelse*. One of these is an irregular Bromme point from the island of Vrøj at the mouth of the Saltbæk Vig (Fig. 2.10). The presence of this point suggests that the chain of islands across the mouth of the inlet existed before the end of the Pleistocene. A second point found in a collection donated to the museum many years ago was reported to have been found at Vollerup Overdrev (Raklev s.b. #252). This was described as a Lyngby point attached to a wooden shaft with skin strips; the artifact unfortunately no longer exists. The sandy area of Vollerup Overdrev has long been the focus of hunting activities, evidenced by the numerous finds of projectile points from all periods of the Stone Age. The third Late Paleolithic locality is a probable camp site from the Federmesser period, located along the northern shore of the east end of the Tranemose. This site was found by the amateur group in 1994 and is represented by a number of finds including 2 very fine blade cores, 1 frost-cracked flake, 2 burins, 1 scraper, 4 retouched blades, 11 flakes, 4 blades, and 6 burned pieces.

Early Mesolithic: Maglemose

The Maglemosian is an Early Mesolithic adaptation found from southern Scandinavia to Britain and along the Baltic coast to Poland. Maglemosian assemblages date from the early part of the Holocene in northern Europe, approximately 8900–6400 BC. Most of the known sites are inland summer occupations. The former coastal areas of the early Holocene are now submerged. Almost all reported Maglemose materials in

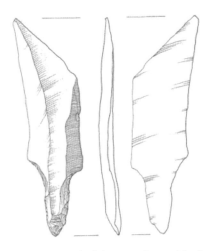

Fig. 2.10. Late Paleolithic point from Saltbæk Vig area (NM A46021), approximate length = 6.5 cm (drawing by Kurt Petersen).

Denmark are from inland locations. This Early Mesolithic culture is known primarily from stray finds of distinctive small microliths, used for arrowheads. Lancette microliths and rather irregular blades mark the older half of the period; triangular microliths and thinner, more regular blades made with soft hammer technique are found in the younger half.

Maglemosian materials in the Saltbæk Vig are known only from stray finds of projectile points on the south side of the Saltbæk Vig. Maglemosian microliths are found on a several of the higher, sandy areas of the survey region including Lindebjerg and Vollerup Overdrev. These better-drained areas may have supported less dense forest, and hence more game, in the early Holocene. A few microliths from the former island of Vrøj at the mouth of the Salt-bæk Vig indicate an Maglemose presence there as well. All of the region would have been inland during the first part of the Holocene. It is essential to remember that the coastline was tens of kilometers to the north and west.

Middle Mesolithic: Kongemose

Kongemose lithic assemblages are recognized primarily by their distinctive projectile points and cores. Eight younger Kongemose localities were found during the Salt-bæk Vig survey, including five concentrations of artifacts and three stray finds, in the northwest quadrant of Saltbæk Vig study area (Fig. 2.6, above). Settlements are found only in the lower areas of the reclaimed lands at elevations of –1 m or less. The flint artifacts at these younger Kongemose sites have been rolled and exhibit marine patination. The sites were eroded during periods of transgression and exposed to the open-air during times of regression. Stray finds come from inland areas usually in the form of distinctive Kongemose handle cores. Kongemose material also appears in very low frequency at other sites in the area, again in the form of handle cores or rhombic projectile points.

Late Mesolithic: Ertebølle

The Ertebølle, the late phase of the Mesolithic, extends from 5400 BC to *c.* 3950 BC. The majority of Mesolithic sites encountered during the Saltbæk Vig survey date from the Ertebølle period. Twenty-eight settlements were located around the coastline of the Saltbæk Vig compared to five in the Kongemose. Sites are more common south of the Saltbæk Vig but several were found to the north as well. There are inland settlements seen in the Tranemose and along the Bregninge Å, although the lower reaches of this stream would have been a marine environment during the later Mesolithic.

It is essential to remember that, during the later part of the Atlantic climatic epoch, sea level transgressed the modern coastline. Earlier sites lie on the former sea floor of the Saltbæk Vig, at elevations between –1 and + 1 m. Rising seas gradually forced settlement to higher ground. In most cases, Ertebølle sites were located at or below 3.0 m in elevation, emphasizing the coastal nature of occupation in this period. Later Ertebølle sites generally are found around +2 to +3 m directly at the coast during the Late Atlantic, at the height of the maximum Littorina coastline. The very latest Ertebølle sites may be slightly lower in elevation, dating from the time of a minor regression in sea level (Christensen 1995). Only a few stray finds and secondary occurrences of latest Ertebølle materials were found in the project area.

Late Mesolithic/earliest Neolithic transition sites

One major change from the Mesolithic to the Neolithic is the introduction of polished flint axes and chisels. The earliest type, the pointed-butt flint axe, is one of the best indicators of the presence of earliest Neolithic occupation, but only four of these axes have been identified in the survey. With one or two exceptions lithic artifacts are otherwise very similar across the transition (Stafford 1999). Ceramics from the Ertebølle and the earliest Funnel Beaker period were not recovered during the survey.

There are six settlements sites in the survey area that may date from the transition between the Late Mesolithic and the Early Neolithic. Five of these sites lie along the former south coast of the Saltbæk Vig, and one was found on the north slope of the hill of Lindebjerg. The predominance of material at these sites is Late Ertebølle including diagnostic pieces like specialized core axes with some identifiable artifacts from the Early Neolithic such as pointed-butt axes or polished axe fragments. The location of these sites corresponds well with what is known of the earliest Neolithic occupation. Such sites are usually situated on the coast, with Neolithic materials superseding Late Mesolithic deposits (Andersen 1993b).

Early Neolithic: older and middle Funnel Beaker

In the survey the 'Early Neolithic' was defined by the life span of the thin-butted flint axe, the most distinctive chronological marker in surface collections, in lieu of pottery. This long period of time includes late EN I, EN II, and MNA I–II (3950–2950 BC). This period includes both Phase 2 and 3 of Koch's 1998 ceramic chronology.

During the EN I period, residential sites in southern Scandinavia are found in both coastal and inland contexts. Settlements appear to be smaller and more ephemeral than Late Mesolithic occupations (Madsen and Jensen 1982). Sites from this period in Scania range from 400–800 m^2 (Larsson 1991). The second part of the Early Neolithic, EN II, is marked by major changes in settlement, subsistence, and tomb construction (Madsen and Jensen 1982). Causewayed enclosures are introduced. The number of known sites increases, and occupation evidence becomes more substantial. Settlements seem to expand, and there is an initial occupation of heavier, clay soils. Specialized hunting and fishing sites are still in use. Settlement size varies from small hunting sites of 100 m² to residential sites up to 8000 m². The first part of the Middle Neolithic, MNA I–II, is characterized by an intensification of many of the trends in the previous period. Settlements become larger and use more continuous.

The use of a long 'Early Neolithic' period in the survey was based on the absence of more diagnostic information in the surface collections. Only flakes or fragments of polished flint axes were found at most sites, making it impossible to rely on morphological changes in the axe types through time for dating. For the same reason polishing on all four sides versus two sides, could not be used as general criteria for separating EN and MNA axes.

On the other hand, a distinction between thin- and thick-butted axe fragments may be made based upon the cross-section. Thin-butted flint axes are rectangular in cross-section; their sides are convex and meet at slightly obtuse angles. In comparison, the later thick-butted flint axes have a rectangular or square cross-section with straight sides meeting at perpendicular angles. Other diagnostic types from this time period include thin-butted chisels, thin-butted, thin-bladed flint axes, an older type of flint dagger (*flintdolkstave*), polygonal battle axes, and thin-butted greenstone axes. However, these items were rarely encountered during fieldwalking in the Saltbæk Vig survey zone.

Other stone tools show some changes through this period. Flake axes continue in use through the Early Neolithic and are difficult to distinguish from Late Ertebølle examples. Neolithic axes are usually made on more irregular pieces and have a side bulb and a pointed end. The flake axes often have symmetrical surface thinning and side retouch as well, sometimes from the bulbar face. The distinctive Havnelev-type flake axe has a pronounced bulb near one of the corners of the cutting edge. In addition to flaked and polished axes, the polygonal battle axe is found in the Early Neolithic, pecked and ground from various types of stone.

Other artifacts in Early Neolithic assemblages include transverse points, scrapers, borers, and knives. Transverse points in the Early Neolithic typically have parallel sides and may be slightly smaller than Late Ertebølle examples. The edges of transverse points are sometimes retouched in two directions in the Neolithic and the butt end is occasionally retouched as well. Points are often made on flakes, occasionally removals from polished flint axes. Large rhombic points, perhaps spear tips, are also known from Early Neolithic and are thicker and more irregular than earlier Kongemose forms.

Scrapers are much more common at Neolithic sites and appear in a variety of sizes and shapes, generally larger than their Mesolithic predecessors. Heavy, rounded flake scrapers are typically Neolithic, with steeper and more shallow edge angles attributed to wood and skin working respectively (Juel Jensen 1994). Shouldered and beaked scrapers are known. Retouch on the bulbar surface of scrapers is a Neolithic trait.

Drills in the Neolithic are commonly made on flakes and have converging, rather than parallel, edges on the bit. Burins are not frequently seen overall in the Neolithic but are common at some sites.

A variety of flint knives are known from the Neolithic. Blade knives with curved backing on blade and partial retouch along the end of the cutting edge are common in the Early Neolithic, probably used as sickles. The ends of these knives may be retouched or snapped. Curved backing retouch on flakes marks TRB flake knives. Two notable forms are the *bue kniv* and *skive kniv*. The *bue kniv* was made on a flake with one straight edge and retouch or naturally backing on the curved, opposite edge. The *skive kniv* is a distinctive form with a short, extended wing, defined by concave retouch on both sides, leaving a straight, sharp, 1–2 cm long edge. Both the *bue kniv* and *skive kniv* are dated to the Funnel Beaker period. Fine denticulated pieces on the concave edge of flakes, absent in the Mesolithic of Zealand, are present in the Early Neolithic.

Early Neolithic sites are found in abundance throughout the project area (Fig. 2.7, above), concentrated in areas of sandy soils (see also Table 2.6). Settlements from this period number almost 60 and are concentrated on the south side of the Saltbæk Vig. There are very few sites in the region of the Bregninge Å and only a handful on the north side of the Saltbæk Vig. This pattern is generally confirmed by the distribution of stray finds, again largely thin-butted axes. There are a few coastal settlements from the Early Neolithic (e.g., at Illerup Sand) but the majority seem to be somewhat inland with clusters seen in the Tranemose and Storemose and around Lindebjerg, mimicking the distribution of long dolmens and other megalithic tombs (Fig. 1.13). Early Neolithic materials also show up secondarily at a number of sites in the area, but again largely along the south side of the Saltbæk Vig. At the same time, it is important to remember that the intensive survey discussed here was focused on the coastal zone and elevations below +5 m. Thus higher, more inland settlement would often not have appeared in the survey. There are a number of other EN sites in the Saltbæk Vig area seen in the distribution of the megalithic tombs and in the locations reported in the *Sognebeskrivelse*.

Middle Neolithic A III–V: late Funnel Beaker

Thick-butted flint axes with two-sided polish characterize the later Middle Neolithic period, MN A (3300–2800 BC). Type A of the thick-butted axes are straight and symmetrical along a longitudinal axis. The Bundsø and Lindø types have a rectangular cross-section, while the St Valby type has a square cross-section. These axes belong to the late Funnel Beaker period, MN A III–V (Nielsen 1979). Other diagnostic types include thick-butted chisels, thick- butted, thin-bladed flint axes, and pointed-butt, hollow edge flint axes.

The trend toward larger residential sites, often situated quite close together, continues during the final part of the Funnel Beaker period. On Langeland, for example, residential sites from MNA V vary in size between 70,000 m^2 and 2–300,000 m^2; some sites are located only 1 km apart (Skaarup 1985). Special sites for fishing and seal hunting occur but hunting and gathering activities are often incorporated at the coastal residential sites with red deer being the most commonly hunted game. Burials continue in the megalithic tombs but construction of new monuments has ceased. Flint axes and chisels are replacing the use of ceramics in ceremonial deposits.

Middle Neolithic materials in the Saltbæk Vig show a different distribution from the Early Neolithic. There are some 30 MN settlements in the survey, largely found on the south coast. These materials are concentrated in several areas on the coastal peninsulas of Kollen, Tømmerup Holme, and Løcns on the west side of the Saltbæk Vig. There also seems to be some substantial settlement beginning on the peninsula of Alleshave during this period. Again, the survey data emphasize coastal localities. Distinctive Middle Neolithic axes and chisels are the predominant type of stray finds and secondary artifacts at other sites.

Middle Neolithic A V–MN B: Pitted Ware culture

The Pitted Ware culture, dating from *c.* 3400–2500 BC, represents an economic adaptation focused on animal husbandry, hunting, fishing, and gathering concomitant with a deterioration in climate at this time (Rasmussen 1984; 1993; Iversen 2013). Pitted Ware sites are mainly found along the coast of Norway, Denmark, and Sweden. Cylindrical blade cores and tanged points belonging to the Pitted Ware culture are contemporaneous with the final Funnel Beaker period (MN A V) and continue into the early Battle Axe period.

In the Saltbæk Vig project area, Pitted Ware cylindrical blade cores and tanged points are seen only as occasional stray finds.

Middle Neolithic B: Battle Axe culture

The flint axes belonging to the Battle Axe culture, MN B (2800–2400 BC), are thick-butted axes of type B (Nielsen 1979). These axes are asymmetrical with a slightly curvilinear shape; one corner of the cutting edge is drooping. The butt end is set at an oblique angle to the body of the axe and may be crushed from being used as a hammer. In general type B axes are more coarsely manufactured than type A axes; cortex from the original flint nodule may be present on the butt end of the axe. A few type B axes are more luxurious, bigger, and with an all-over polish. Other types related to the Battle Axe period are thick-butted chisels, thick-butted, thin-bladed axes, thick-butted, hollow-edge axes/adzes, and transverse arrowheads with polished side edges. A series of ground stone battle axes together with the pottery can be divided into three stages MN B I–III. Unpolished flint tools cannot be distinguished from Funnel Beaker flint tools.

The Battle Axe period appears to be a continuation of the late Funnel Beaker in eastern Denmark. Settlements continue on the same sites or in the same local area; however, sites appear to be smaller and fewer. There might be an increased emphasis on cattle herding; barley is the dominant cereal. Hunting, fishing, and gathering supplement the economy. Megalithic tombs are re-used for burials. In the Saltbæk Vig project area, three Battle Axe sites were found on the southern coast of the Vig. Secondary finds occur throughout the area, including Alleshave.

Late Neolithic

Surface retouched flint tools, especially daggers, characterize the Late Neolithic (LN) period, (2400–1800 BC). A chronology of three sub-phases, LN I–III, is based on changes in the daggers from lanceolate to fishtail hilts and on the pottery (e.g., Lomborg 1975; Madsen 1978). Usually only fragments of these flint tools were found in the survey, but they were easily ascribed to the Late Neolithic period due to the surface retouch. Flake removals in dagger production are likewise distinctive and show an angular platform and expanding flake. Other surface retouched tools include spear points, arrowheads, sickles, and spoon-shaped scrapers (Fig. 2.11). Flint axes have flared edges in this period, and a new type of greenstone axes with shaft hole appear.

Generally the Late Neolithic appears to be a continuation of the Battle Axe subsistence and settlement pattern. Burials take place at the megalithic tombs or in newly constructed stone cists covered with a mound or placed in older mounds. In the Saltbæk Vig, however, the Late Neolithic localities from the survey show a new and distinctive distribution. Most of the eight settlements and a number of graves are located on the eastern and northern side of the Vig, particularly on the peninsula of Alleshave. Many of the stray and secondary finds likewise come from the northeast quarter of the survey area, indicating a significant shift in the location of occupation in the area.

Bronze Age

The Bronze Age is characterized by the introduction of bronze axes and daggers, but the basic traditions of Late Neolithic flint working continue. Many of the more utilitarian artifacts, such as scrapers, drills, and knives, cannot be readily distinguished from their Late Neolithic predecessors, but may be somewhat larger. Heavy, round, and spoon-shaped flake scrapers, borers and massive flint blade knives are common in the Bronze Age. Certain artifact types are very well made, including flint axes, daggers, projectile points, and sickles, but not often found during fieldwalking. Sickles show a shift from surface-retouched crescent-shaped

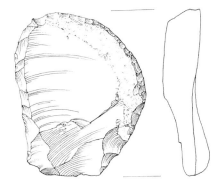

Fig. 2.11. Spoon-shaped scraper from the Neolithic. Approximately 4.2 cm in diameter (drawing: Kurt Petersen).

forms to retouched blades in the younger Bronze Age. Flint arrowheads have a distinctive shape in the Bronze Age – surface retouched with convex edges and a concave base, although a few transverse points continue in use. Blade production has largely ceased except for specialized knives and sickles.

Settlements from the Bronze Age are not common in the coastal areas of Denmark and only a few were recorded in the survey, all on the south side of the Saltbæk Vig, in the northwest quarter of the project area. Nevertheless, the pattern is quite distinct from what was observed in the Late Neolithic. The majority of Bronze Age sites reported here come from the Tranemose area as recorded by Jens Nielsen. Stray finds and secondary artifacts were also uncommon from this time period and emphasize the focus on the western portion of the research area.

Iron Age

Iron age sites are characterized primarily by distinctive, hard-fired pottery sherds. Iron Age settlements in the survey area number only three, but sherds of Iron Age pottery appear as secondary finds at a number of localities in the survey. The absence of flint material undoubtedly makes the recognition of Iron Age localities more difficult. In addition, it is clear that occupation from this period is more commonly found at higher elevations outside the survey area.

Generic sites

There were, of course, a number of localities encountered in the survey that could not be easily assigned to a specific chronological period. Often diagnostic artifacts were not recovered; some periods are simply not readily distinguished in small collections of lithic material. These sites have been grouped into three generic sets distinguished as Mesolithic, Neolithic, or Stone Age. Mesolithic assemblages have substantial numbers of blades and perhaps a core axe but cannot be easily assigned as to subperiod. Generic Neolithic collections usually contained fewer blades, smaller, more irregular flint pieces, and often small flakes or removals from polished flint axes. These materials, however, were not always sufficient to designate the appropriate phase of the Neolithic and thus the generic category was used. The group of Stone Age sites are those collections of lithic material generally lacking any diagnostic items. These localities might sometimes be distinguished by elevation but in general they could only be recognized as Stone Age.

The distribution of these generic sites is not particularly informative. Generic Mesolithic sites conform to the pattern noted earlier with a predominance of materials in coastal zones on the south side of the Saltbæk Vig. There are perhaps more indications of occupation on the peninsula of Alleshave than seen in the more specific data. This is also seen in the generic Neolithic distribution that draws attention to the point of Alleshave. Otherwise, this distribution generally emphasizes the concentration of activity on the south side of the Saltbæk Vig and particularly in the coastal peninsulas that contain such an abundance of material. The generic Stone age localities reflect the basic pattern of settlement seen in the data from more specific periods.

Analysis of data and maps

The location, size, and contents of the localities found during the Saltbæk Vig survey provide useful information on prehistoric settlement and land use in the project area. Other kinds of information are also available. The distribution of localities can be examined in relation to other features of the landscape such as elevation and soil. It is also useful to compare the information from the Saltbæk Vig survey with the existing record in the *Sognebeskrivelse*, with Mathiassen's original survey, and with other studies. These topics are discussed in the following paragraphs.

Site size

Some statistics about the size of sites and number of artifacts per site provide basic information on the dimensions of the collected materials. Table 2.5 provides these data for the survey area by time period. The largest single site contained almost 4000 pieces while the smallest localities were single finds. The average size of a surface collection from 46 Mesolithic settlements was 136 artifacts; the average size of a collection from the Neolithic localities was 186. The largest Mesolithic collection contained 494 pieces; the largest Neolithic site contained almost 4000 pieces.

The average collection size by period (Fig. 2.12) indicates some differences. Generic collections are almost by definition small in number because they did not contain diagnostic artifacts. Early Neolithic collections contained the most artifacts; Bronze and Iron Age collections were the smallest. Late Neolithic collections are generally smaller as well. Kongemose, Ertebølle and Middle Neolithic localities contained more than 150 artifacts each; transition sites were somewhat smaller.

A similar pattern can be seen in an examination of average site area by period (Fig. 2.12). Site area was measured in the field, defined by the boundaries of the distribution of artifacts. Site area is generally correlated with collection size. Kongemose sites are slightly larger than Ertebølle (2700 m² compared to 2235 m²), perhaps due in part to the more substantial erosion and dispersal of these materials and, in part, to the greater range of sites known from the Ertebølle. Transition sites are almost identical in size to the Ertebølle, likely because the earliest Neolithic settlements often lie directly on top of Late Ertebølle deposits.

Early Neolithic sites are the largest of any encountered in the survey, more than 4000 m² on average. This increase reflects several things. Early Neolithic sites are often found on higher, sandy soils where artifact visibility is greater and more material may be collected. As noted above, the Early Neolithic period as defined for the study includes EN I–II and MNA I–II. This is a long period of time, more than 800 years (*c.* 3800–3000 BC). Settlement relocation over short distances during this period would likely have created a number of very large localities in the survey area found as an accumulation of residences over time (Larsson 1988). The settlement concentrations described below provide likely examples of such large localities.

Middle Neolithic localities are slightly smaller than the Early Neolithic sites but still substantial, *c.* 3600 m². Late Neolithic localities are small, less than 1000 m², only about one-quarter the size of earlier Neolithic settlements. Once again, the changes that take place with the Late Neolithic are reflected in these differences. Bronze and Iron Age localities are also small in size, perhaps representing individual farmsteads.

Settlement concentrations

There are several places within the survey area with dense concentrations of artifacts over a large area. These zones were often collected in several different episodes and as several different sites. Sometimes these site groups were combined if chronology and adjacent location warranted such a decision. These concentrations are described here as a fairly typical pattern in the landscape, at places that were clearly favored for settlement. These zones of concentration are known from the Mesolithic (at Illerup) and Neolithic (at Illerup Sand, Tømmerup Holme, Kollen, Lindebjerg, and the Wild Boar sites).

The Mesolithic sites at Illerup likely lay along the sandy banks of an earlier stream through this area. Nevertheless, the general nature of the finds, the variety of axes and projectile points found, and the changes in the blade assemblages suggests a rather long-term utilization of this location and short distance shifting of settlement over time from the Late Kongemose through the early and middle phases of the Ertebølle. The shifts in settlement location may have been in response to the sequence of transgression and regression of the sea that characterized this period in the late Atlantic.

The Neolithic concentrations, with a few exceptions, are either on small peninsulas and bays along the former southern coast of the Saltbæk Vig, or on the distinctive sandy, plateau hills (e.g., Lindebjerg, Rungedysse Bjerg, and Fibjerg) away from the coast with both settlement and tomb remains. The pattern observed at Illerup Sand and elsewhere (Wild Boar, Lindebjerg, Tømmerup Holme, Kollen) of a number of concentrations from the roughly same time period in the same general area may reflect a picture of shifting settlement in the Neolithic as described by Larsson (1985; 1988) and others. Small settlements appear to have been moved every generation or so a few tens of meters from their original location. The general pattern observed from such concentrations of settlement and the likely repetition of settlement it suggests implies continued use of these 'fixed' locations.

Elevation

In general terms, Mesolithic sites are found in coastal locations and Neolithic sites tend to be placed higher and more inland. This pattern is confirmed in an examination of the localities from the Saltbæk Vig. Table 2.7 shows the average elevation by time period for all localities except stray finds. It should be remembered that these values are based on the surveyed sites, not on all of the Saltbæk Vig.

As can be seen in Table 2.7, there is a substantial difference in elevation between all Mesolithic sites and all Neolithic sites, +0.9 m vs +5.7 m. In terms of more specific chronological subdivisions, there is a clear trend toward higher elevation through the Mesolithic. Sites from the Mesolithic–Neolithic transition have a higher average elevation, but this is largely the contribution of one site on the hill of Lindebjerg. There is an interesting trend in the Neolithic as well, with a decrease in elevation through time. Late Neolithic sites tend to be found on Alleshave, which has a low elevation, and also tend to be more coastally oriented. The difference between Early and Middle Neolithic sites is more difficult to explain but may related to the preference of Early Neolithic sites for the sandy hills throughout the area.

The Late Mesolithic settlements were found exclusively at or below the 2.5 m contour, while Early Neolithic settlements were found at or above that elevation contour (Gebauer and Price 1990, fig. 2). The average elevation of the Late Mesolithic settlements is 1.74 m; the average elevation of the Early Neolithic settlements is 3.16 m (Hede 2003). The Late Mesolithic and Early Neolithic settlements occur along the irregular southwestern shore of the inlet, clustered toward the mouth of Saltbæk Vig (Figs 2.6 and 2.7). Mesolithic sites are generally closer to the water, while Neolithic sites concentrate on slightly more inland, sandy soils. The Mesolithic sites tend to be concentrated at sheltered locations on points of land and peninsulas at or close to the former coastline.

Soils

The distribution of localities by soil type is shown in Table 2.7. This information is provided only for settlements; stray finds do not reflect a choice of location for residence. Categories of soils have been described previously, taken from the national soil map of Denmark. Several patterns can be observed in the table.

As has been noted, Mesolithic settlements generally occur at low elevation along the coast of the Saltbæk Vig. Almost 80% of Mesolithic settlements are found in the marine sand or gravel deposits that cover this zone. Sites from the transition between the Mesolithic and Neolithic show a mixed distribution on different soils. Half of these six sites are on marine deposits and half are in diluvial sand or moraine clay. Sites from the Early Neolithic show a very different pattern in which ten of the eleven settlements are located on moraine clay. The distribution of megalithic structures in the project area (Fig. 1.16) generally conforms to the pattern seen for the Early Neolithic. There is a clear emphasis on the higher, more inland, moraine deposits. A few megaliths are located on the diluvial sand and gravel that forms many of the hills in the area; none are found on marine deposits.

Middle Neolithic settlements are also predominantly on the moraine clay but several sites are found in other contexts, perhaps emphasizing expansion over the area

Table 2.7. Distribution of sites by soil type in the Saltbæk Vig survey.

Soil	Meso	%	M+N	%	EN	%	MN	%	EGK	LN	Neo	%	Stone Age	%	Total
Diluvial gravel	1	2								2	7	8			10
Diluvial sand			2	33.3	1	9	4	13.8		1	11	12.5	2	5.9	21
Eolian sand											1	1.1			1
Freshwater peat	5	9.8					3	10.3			6	6.8	3	8.8	17
Freshwater clay							1	3.4			1	1.1	2	5.9	4
Marine gravel	7	13.7	1	16.7			1	3.4		4	11	12.5	4	11.8	28
Marine sand	33	64.7	2	33.3			2	6.9	1		6	6.8	5	14.7	49
Marine clay	3	5.9	1	16.7	10	91	17	58.6		1	41	46.6	17	50	91
Indeterminate	2	3.9			11		1	3.4			4	4.5	1	2.9	8
Total	51		6				29		1	8	88		34		229

and the utilization of more zones in the landscape. Late Neolithic settlements show another pattern, emphasizing the better drained gravel soils and residence closer to the coast. This shift strongly suggests a substantial change in subsistence activities during the Late Neolithic.

Comparison with other information

Although there is a sense that archaeological survey is common practice in Scandinavia (e.g., Larsson and Olausson 1992; Diinhoff 1998), research-oriented systematic fieldwalking is in fact rare. Most previous surveys have been opportunistic and focused on specific land forms, time periods, or artifact types. It is useful to compare the results of the Saltbæk Vig survey with other surveys of this area and elsewhere in Denmark in order to evaluate the utility of such information. In the following sections, comparison is made with the project of Mathiassen and with the records of the *Sognebeskrivelse*. Finally, comparison is made with the reported survey of the Karrebæk-Dybsø Fjord in southern Zealand (Fig. 2.12).

The Mathiassen survey

The results from the Saltbæk Vig survey can be compared with Mathiassen's survey of northwest Zealand. Mathiassen's regional study accounts for almost 50% of all archaeological activities in the area and has been a major source of information on the prehistory of Denmark for many years. Carried out between 1948 and 1956, this was a remarkably advanced project and provided a foundation for modern Danish archaeology. For these reasons it is useful to examine this study in some detail.

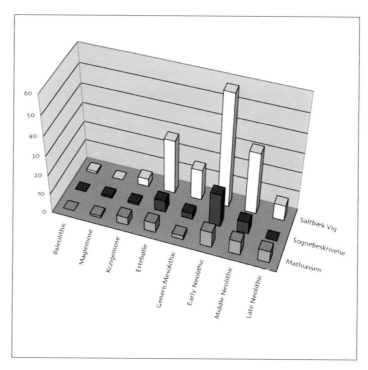

Fig. 2.12. Number of sites by time period from our survey, Mathiassen (1948), and the Sognebeskrivelse.

Northwest Zealand was chosen by Mathiassen for several reasons. The region was known to be very rich in prehistoric sites and included a variety of topographical features and different soil types. The National Museum had undertaken several large excavations in northwest Zealand and a large number of amateur archaeologists had worked in the region. The Åmose bog, where significant archaeological research had been done since 1938, was also part of this region. Finally, the area had been familiar to Mathiassen since his childhood. He grew up in Mullerup, on the west coast of northwest Zealand, where his father was a schoolteacher and his family had lived there for several generations.

Mathiassen's survey was the largest archaeological survey that has ever been undertaken in Denmark in terms of time depth and areal coverage. The survey covered a timespan from the Late Paleolithic to the end of the Viking period, *c*. AD 1000. The research area encompassed *c*. 1690 km² in 80 parishes. The field work was carried out by a group of young archaeologists and students. Each surveyor was assigned a district of one or more parishes. The survey of each parish was planned to take 14 days. Bicycles were used for transportation around the parish, each averaging a little more than 20 km² in size, meaning that each surveyor had to cover more than 1 km² per day.

The aim of that survey was to record all the prehistoric remains, both those already known and newly discovered materials. The instructions to surveyors describe three kinds of investigations to be carried out: fieldwalking, home visits, and the recording of specimens in known collections. The area was to be very thoroughly investigated by visiting all the landowners and by fieldwalking every square meter of accessible land. Fieldwalking was to be done in terrain suited for settlements, i.e., near coasts, streams, lakes, bogs, and on sandy soils, but other areas with plowed soil were to be included as well. Generous samples of flints and sherds were to be collected. Sites already known were to be revisited and more artifacts collected if possible. Plowed-over mounds and other unrecorded monuments were to be recorded.

One of the investigators, Holger Kapel, described his fieldwork in 1954 (*Holbæk Amtstidende* 25 November 1954):

> During the last 14 days or so I have worked for the National Museum recording prehistoric finds in Rørvig and Nykøbing parishes. This means that I have biked and walked through these parishes from one end to the other, from farm to farm, from field to field, in sunshine, in wind and in rain. I am based at the station in Rørvig (an excellent place), which allows me to divide my district in three areas of about even size. Every morning as soon as it is light, I leave this headquarter and usually do not return before it is time to put the light on my bicycle. After dinner I start again on the evening house visits. By a conservative estimate I have biked 250 km and walked 300 km during these 14 days.

The Mathiassen survey recorded about 2700 settlement sites, 3400 dolmens, mounds, and other burial sites, 240 secular or sacrificial deposits, roughly 50,000 artifacts, and numerous single finds. The results were published in 1959 as a series of 28 maps and a catalog recording the settlement patterns throughout the prehistory of the region. Several trends are observable in these data and have been discussed elsewhere (e.g., Thrane 1973; Paludan-Müller 1978).

The results indicated that northwest Zealand was only lightly occupied in the older Stone Age (Mesolithic) with concentrations of sites in certain areas, especially on islands, peninsulas, and in the areas of large, inland bogs. The Neolithic was divided into thin-butted axe (earlier), thick-butted axe (middle), and dagger (later) phases by Mathiassen. Stray finds of thin-butted axes and settlements from the earlier phase can be seen throughout northwest Zealand, along with long dolmens, round dolmens, and passage graves.

Mathiassen ended his published conclusions on a somewhat pessimistic note, leaving judgment to the future as to whether the results of the survey were worth the considerable effort that was invested. Very little actual analysis of the data was undertaken. Mathiassen's survey increased the number of known settlement sites and stray finds. The uneven coverage in fieldwalking, however, clearly created a bias in the distribution of stray finds of stone axes versus settlement sites. This bias may also produce a distribution pattern in favor of Neolithic land use in parishes with a high percentage of stray finds of stone axes since these are usually of Neolithic date. Mesolithic habitation on the other hand is more likely to be represented among the settlement sites. It is also clear that the concentrations of settlement seen on

Mathiassen's maps are largely a function of the intensity of the survey and the work of amateur collectors rather than the actual distribution of prehistoric activity.

Today most of the finds recorded during Mathiassen's survey in the Saltbæk Vig area exist only on paper; it is no longer possible to make a direct analysis of the material. Many of the artifacts he recorded in private collections had been lost by the time we visited the area, except for items donated to museums. Only retouched artifacts were brought back to the National Museum, while flakes and burned pieces were counted and left in the field. The generous samples of surface collected material called for in the instructions for survey were in fact fairly small. This is probably due to the limited time available for survey and to the fact that collections had to be brought back on foot or by bicycle. Inspection of the materials from Mathiassen's survey at the National Museum generally confirmed the content and dating assignments that were made.

Studies of the distribution of materials from Mathiassen's reconnaissance have generally supported his results. Thrane reported that subsequent survey in small areas in northwest Zealand simply added to the distribution of sites from Mathiassen's project. Thrane (1973) compared results from his survey with Mathiassen (1959) and found that (1) intensive survey added a large number of sites to the number of finds recorded by Mathiassen, and (2) the relative distribution of sites does not change with subsequent surveys.

Examination of the Mathiassen survey data by Paludan-Müller (1978) took a strongly ecological perspective on changes in settlement location. Paludan-Müller argued that the distributions reported by Mathiassen were not biased by variation in collecting strategies. He suggested that the survey data held a 'big information potential'. On the basis of his observations, Paludan-Müller argued that the carrying capacity of the estuaries increased at the beginning of the High Atlantic in the Early Ertebølle, making permanent residence possible for the first time. Sedentism then resulted in increasing population and seasonal expansion to the outer islands and inland regions during the later Ertebølle. Continued increases in population would have demanded increased productivity. The only area where that would have been feasible was in the climax forest in inland areas. Thus, at the end of the Mesolithic, Paludan-Müller would predict a decrease in the number of island sites and an increase in inland occupation reflecting greater manipulation of the forest.

The results of the Saltbæk Vig survey provide a somewhat different picture with regard to the representativeness of the Mathiassen survey. A summary of Mathiassen's findings for the Saltbæk Vig survey area is presented in Table 2.4. For the Mesolithic period, only four settlements and a few stray finds are recorded from the Saltbæk Vig area itself. The primary concentration of Early Neolithic finds is on the south side of the inlet and slightly away from the coast. There are eight settlements indicated for this phase. In the subsequent thick-butted axe phase of the Neolithic, finds and tombs continue to be found across northwest Zealand, with a slightly greater inland focus. In the Saltbæk Vig, concentration is again on the south side with more materials in the higher elevations of the research area. There are seven settlements reported for the Middle Neolithic. During the Late Neolithic dagger period, stray finds and settlements clearly decline in number across northwest Zealand. In the Saltbæk Vig area, stray finds are concentrated on the peninsula of Alleshave and only four settlements are recorded further south.

Overall the results of Mathiassen's investigations are mixed. The survey required a great deal of time and energy to conduct. It produced much new information about the prehistory of northwest Zealand. Many new settlements and stray finds were recorded and a number of important new finds were brought to the National Museum. Some general chronological trends in settlement density and location were noted and provide a sense of change in population and land use. On the other hand, the survey was rather cursory. The temporal and geographical placement of many of the collections is general and sometimes inaccurate. Certain periods, such as the Neolithic, are better represented in the survey and others, such as the older Stone Age, are under-represented. As can be seen from the results of the systematic survey reported here, the information from Mathiassen's survey is useful in terms of general trends, but less so in terms of the details and quantities of settlement remains. As to his own concerns about the value of the work, there is no doubt that this early survey raised questions about the prehistory of Denmark and inspired further research (e.g., Paludan-Müller 1978). It was in many ways a remarkable achievement, one unlikely to be repeated today.

Parish Register (Sognebeskrivelse)

The records of the Parish Register provide the most complete and comprehensive official catalog of archaeological information in Denmark, compiled for many years from a variety of sources. Comparison with the Saltbæk Vig survey data provides some indication of the coverage and accuracy of the *Sognebeskrivelse*.

Because the Saltbæk Vig survey focused on low elevations between 5 m asl and the present coastline, the vast majority of recorded materials were settlements and stray finds. There were no mounds and only a few tombs recorded in the survey. With regard to settlements, however, only a small proportion (less than 20%) of the localities found in intensive survey had been previously reported in the *Sognebeskrivelse*.

Table 2.4 also presents the numbers and kinds of finds by major periods as recorded in the *Sognebeskrivelse* for the *entire* project area. This information can be compared with the finds from the survey. (This comparison does not include the megalithic tombs.) The survey covered approximately 20 km² while the entire project area is roughly 115 km². There are approximately 284 sites in the project area listed in the *Sognebeskrivelse* compared to the 410 recorded in the survey. In other words, the density of sites found in the survey was approximately 20 per km², while the density of sites in the *Sognebeskrivelse* is approximately 2.5 per km².

The most obvious differences in the table can be seen in the percentages of sites by different periods. The general trends are similar but several contrasts can be noted.

There are three times as many Mesolithic sites recorded in the survey as were previously known from the entire project area in the *Sognebeskrivelse* (71 vs 23). There are
many more Neolithic sites found in the survey than reported in the *Sognebeskrivelse*
(305 vs 163). On the other hand, there are roughly the same number of Early Neolithic
sites (90 vs 81) because (1) polished flint axes are the most common item found in
private collections that were recorded by Mathiassen's survey and entered in the
Sognebeskrivelse, and (2) these records include all of the inland, higher elevations of
the research area. There are many more generic Stone Age sites in the *Sognebeskrivelse* because of the low number of diagnostic artifacts in many of the collections.
Stray finds of stone axes represent 31% of the localities in the *Sognebeskrivelse*. The
number of stray finds of axes without contextual information within the research
area is actually higher. Stray finds in the Kalundborg og Omegns Museum collections
for example, not recorded in the National Museum archives, have not been included
in these calculations.

The geographic distribution of sites varies between the survey and the *Sognebeskrivelse* as well. In the Ertebølle period, there are many more survey sites in a number
of different areas. The *Sognebeskrivelse* sites are concentrated along the coast in the
northeast quarter of the Saltbæk Vig. Sites from the time of the Mesolithic–Neolithic
transition are generally in the same locations in both records. Early Neolithic sites
in the *Sognebeskrivelse* are also concentrated on the south shore of the Saltbæk Vig;
the survey sites show more dispersal and the use of other areas. Middle Neolithic A
sites are poorly represented in the *Sognebeskrivelse*; the survey information indicates
many more sites in a variety of different areas. Late Neolithic materials are also only
lightly represented in the *Sognebeskrivelse* records.

Clearly only a small proportion of existing prehistoric localities have been recorded
in the *Sognebeskrivelse* for the Saltbæk Vig specifically and for northwestern Zealand
more generally. It was clear from the survey than many of the the listings for sites
were often inaccurate with regard to location and contents. During the course of the
survey, we sometimes were unable to locate reported sites in the *Sognebeskrivelse* in
the field. Chronological designation is difficult for these records since many of the
materials reported by the Mathiassen survey were non-diagnostic. Generic Stone Age
site is the most common category of settlements in the *Sognebeskrivelse*.

The Karrebæk-Dybsø fjord

The Karrebæk-Dybsø fjord in south Zealand, approximately 60 km south of the Saltbæk
Vig, provides another interesting comparison with more Stone Age data. The Karrebæk-Dybsø fjord system is larger than the Saltbæk Vig (c. 15 × 10 km) with a much more
extensive coastline due to its irregular shape and the presence of several large islands.
A long-term survey of Ertebølle sites around the coast of the fjord over a period of 40
years from 1958–1996 detected 97 localities (Johansson 1999), shown in Figure 2.9, above.

The results of the long-term survey of the Karrebæk-Dybsø fjord system can be
compared with those from the Saltbæk Vig. The chronological resolution of the

Karrebæk-Dybsø is greater because the repeated visits to sites over many years produced more diagnostic material. The number of sites per phase in the Ertebølle is shown in Table 2.1, above. Johansson (1999) recognized six phases of the Ertebølle in this area. The first two phases are Early Ertebølle; the third and fourth phase are Middle Ertebølle; the fifth phase, named Karrebæk, is late. The final Humlebakke phase is transitional between the Ertebølle and the Early Neolithic.

There are fewer sites from the Early Ertebølle, perhaps because more sites from this period are submerged in the Karrebæk-Dybsø area. The increase in larger sites in the later Ertebølle is typical as Middle and Late phase sites are often continuously occupied. The reduction in the number of sites in the transitional Humlebakke phase likely reflects the more terrestrial focus of the Early Neolithic and the shorter length of this 100 year-long period.

The distribution of the sites is also of interest. Sites from the early phases are known only from the outer part of the fjord system at lower elevations. Large sites from the Middle Ertebølle are found throughout the fjord system. The Late Ertebølle sites are found primarily in the outer fjord, again at slightly lower elevations, perhaps during the regression that marks the end of the Atlantic. Prime locations by deep stream channels in this shallow fjord were occupied through all phases of the Ertebølle.

The results of the Karrebæk-Dybsø fjord survey are similar to the Saltbæk Vig in general terms. In both areas the Mesolithic occupation is intensely coastal. In both areas there is an increase in both the number and size of sites during the Mesolithic. In both areas the number of transitional sites is small. More detailed comparison is difficult for two reasons: (1) different chronological schemes were used in the two areas, and (2) sea level changes have affected site visibility differentially. It appears that there are relatively fewer Late Ertebølle sites in the Karrebæk-Dybsø fjord region. In the Saltbæk Vig there was no obvious shift between the outer and inner fjord during the Mesolithic, as seen in the Karrebæk-Dybsø fjord region.

The Ystad Project

One of the more important archaeological investigations in Scandinavia in the last 50 years was the Ystad Project, a multidisciplinary study of settlement and land use by the University of Lund. The research area covered approximately 20 × 25 km around the city of Ystad in southernmost Skåne and was conducted in the 1980s (Berglund 1991; Larsson *et al.* 1992). The goal was to map the locations of archaeological sites and investigate changes in environmental conditions from the Late Mesolithic to the present day, using archaeological survey and excavation, historical documents, and environmental proxies such as pollen. This project provided a glimpse at the changes in human settlement in the countryside of Scandinavia for much of its prehistory.

It was possible to go into even more detail—to trace changes in human settlement and the environment over very long periods of time in specific places. The distribution of sites from the Neolithic, Bronze Age, Early Iron Age, and Viking periods is shown in Figure 2.13. The modern city of Ystad appears in the lower left of the map. The majority of human settlement is either in the glacial till soils to the west or along the two stream valleys in fine sand and gravel deposits to the east in the study area. Neolithic settlements in particular appear to be concentrated in the till, while Iron Age and Viking settlements, fewer in number, are found almost exclusively in the stream valleys. Settlement is rare outside the stream valleys in the eastern half of the study area.

A series of time slices can be used to describe some of the changes. The few Mesolithic sites in the area were focused on the coast. The first substantial inland settlements appeared during the Early Neolithic, occupied by farming populations cultivating the lighter coastal and upland soils to grow several species of wheat and barley and raise cattle and pigs. Only a few sites are known from this period and houses are rare.

Conclusions

The Saltbæk Vig archaeological survey recorded a number of new sites in a small area of northwest Zealand, Denmark. The purpose of this survey was to determine the size and distribution of sites from different time periods, but especially the Mesolithic and Neolithic. The survey was undertaken to provide a foundation for a longer-term project of research on the transition to agriculture and was a successful means of achieving this goal. More than 50 of the localities found during the survey have been tested for buried deposits and preserved materials. Excavations have been conducted at several of these sites, providing information the nature of settlement and subsistence in this area during the shift from foraging to farming.

For the moment, it is useful to consider what information is available from the survey itself. What can be said about human occupation in the Saltbæk Vig region during the earlier part of its prehistory on the basis of archaeological survey? The following paragraphs are intended to provide an overview of settlement patterns and site location.

Evidence for the initial human presence on the fresh landscape at the end of the Pleistocene is meager. At this time, the region was an interior area of a much larger and more continental Denmark; coastlines were several tens of kilometers distant. The Saltbæk Vig itself was a system of streams and lakes draining to the north. There are two tanged points from along the northwest edge of the project area that evidence some human presence in the region. The Federmesser occupation near the mouth of the Tranemose suggests somewhat more intensive use at that location.

The first Mesolithic materials from the Maglemosian appear only as stray finds of projectile points in the sandy hills and flats along the south side of the Saltbæk Vig. These materials may simply represent intermittent inland hunting in the more open parts of the forest. Several settlements are known from the later part of the Middle Mesolithic Kongemose. By this time sea levels had risen rapidly through stream valleys and low areas and begun to flood the Saltbæk Vig itself. Coastal locations in the upper

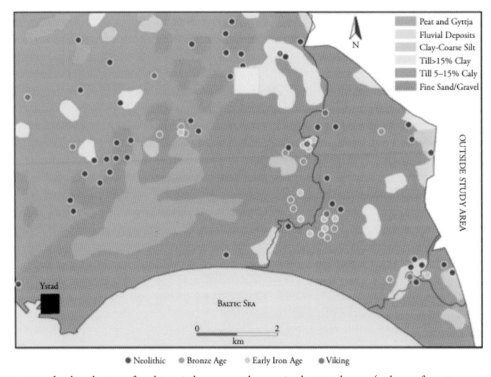

Fig. 2.13. *The distribution of prehistoric human settlement in the Ystad area. (redrawn from Larsson et al. 1993)*

elevations of the former sea floor along the south side of the Saltbæk Vig were favored, while stray finds of Kongemose artifacts indicate the use of the adjacent hinterlands.

A more visible human presence is seen in the Late Mesolithic. Ertebølle localities are more common along the coast of the Saltbæk Vig throughout this period (Fig. 2.7). Earlier settlements are found at slightly lower elevations and later Ertebølle sites are directly on the coastline of the higher sea levels at the end of the Atlantic climatic episode. Sites are substantial and rich in content. Most of the settlements from this period remain concentrated on the south side of the Saltbæk Vig, but new areas to the south and east are also occupied at this time. It seems clear that favored locations combined shelter and access to aquatic resources and that these places continued in use over long periods.

Fischer (1997) has promoted a model of Mesolithic settlement based on the assumption that sites were located at or near the best places for fishing with stationary structures such as weirs and traps. This 'fishing site model' focuses on river mouths and narrow places in the fjords and on headlands and islands where the sea floor has a gentle slope. In this context Fischer suggests a general pattern of settlement along the coasts in which a central site exploits an area of land and sea approximately 8 km in diameter. The central site is large and sedentary and often includes burials among the features. Smaller sites within the territory of this central place are thought to be the foci of various extraction activities.

This general pattern is seen in the Saltbæk Vig as well, although there appear to be several contemporary central sites in this area. The majority of Mesolithic localities are found in three clusters, on the islands at the mouth of the fjord, along stream channels on its south-central shore, or at the head of the fjord where it meets the Bregninge Å. Other localities are smaller and contain fewer artifacts. These three clusters are 2–4 km apart and likely represent contemporary settlements in the later Mesolithic of the Saltbæk Vig.

The first evidence of the Neolithic in this area is slight and appears in two contexts, coastal and inland. The general pattern seems to be one in which the earliest Neolithic is found on top of Late Ertebølle settlements or at new, inland localities (Andersen 1993a; 1995). There are several localities along the south shore of the Saltbæk Vig where both Late Mesolithic and Early Neolithic materials have been found together on the surface. These are the best candidates for sites that are transitional between foragers and farmers. Some of the earliest domestic cattle in Scandinavia are known from the coastal site of Smakkerup at the head of the Saltbæk Vig (Price and Gebauer 2005; Noe-Nygaard *et al.* 2005). The distribution of long dolmens, paralleling the coast of the Saltbæk Vig, may also reflect areas of human occupation in the earlier part of the Neolithic. A very early radiocarbon date for a Neolithic long barrow that was later incorporated in a long dolmen came from the flat sandy hill at Lindebjerg (Liversage 1981).

Early Neolithic remains are the most common, identifiable materials recovered in the survey. Settlement appeared more obviously in inland areas. Coastal zones were not abandoned, however, and there were several substantial settlements along the south shore of the Saltbæk Vig. The majority of sites, however, are now found away from the coast, utilizing higher, better drained areas, perhaps for pasture or agricultural fields. These areas are also occupied for long periods and there are indications of short-distance settlement relocation during this time. Outside the boundaries of the survey area, the distribution of megaliths (see Fig. 1.13) and Neolithic materials in the Sognebeskrivelse document the wider presence of the Early Neolithic.

Middle Neolithic materials also are concentrated on the south side of the Saltbæk Vig. There is some suggestion of more intensive use of the coast than in the preceding period. There is relatively little evidence of the Single Grave Culture and only a few settlements from that period are present. Pitted Ware Culture is represented by only a few stray finds.

A shift to new areas is clearly seen in the Late Neolithic, while at the same time the number of settlements decreased substantially from the Early and Middle Neolithic. This change suggests that substantial differences emerged in human settlement and activity at that time. Bronze and Iron Age materials are only lightly represented in the survey area and serve simply to document the continuing human use of the

Saltbæk Vig region. Better evidence for these later periods can be obtained from the records of the *Sognebeskrivelse*.

Some general trends can also be observed. The northwest quarter of the survey area witnesses most intensive occupation. This region offers an irregular coastline with freshwater streams, protected bays and peninsulas that may have provided more shelter and better fishing. Neolithic localities tend to be richer in terms of artifact density and more diverse in settlement size, yet some of the Mesolithic localities surpass Neolithic localities in size. This pattern does not suggest any dramatic changes in population density but may indicate a trend toward larger population and more varied economic organization in the Neolithic.

The survey has documented significant variation among the lithic assemblages collected at Neolithic localities in the project area. Production specialization appears to have been present at the settlement level in the Neolithic. Some localities contained extraordinary numbers of scrapers, axe production flakes, types of flint, or specialized tools. Sources for flint for the manufacture of small, expedient tools are apparently local; certain items such as axes, chisels, and some finished tools are made from high quality material. This quality material is likely exotic to the local area.

The survey itself was a productive endeavor, revealing a number of new sites for further investigation and increasing the collections of artifacts from the area. The chronology and distribution of materials in the Saltbæk Vig region provides an overview of Stone Age settlement through time. The survey results allow us to examine existing theories concerning pattern of settlement in different periods of the Stone Age. The survey also generated data for evaluating previous fieldwork and archives. In addition, the survey provided an in-depth familiarization with the area for the project participants and a marked appreciation for the hard work and hospitality of rural Danes. The survey established an essential foundation for the continuing project. As one of the first intensive, systematic fieldwalking surveys it also provides a baseline for the investigation of the focus and intensity of land use in the early Holocene.

Chapter 3

Site testing

An important part of the Saltbæk Vig project following the initial survey was testing those locations which might have significant buried materials. Over a 2-year period, during the summers of 1993 and 1994, we tested more than 50 localities, some by hand, others with machine, sometimes using phosphate testing, boring, and/or coring, or a combination. Phosphate testing involves mapping phosphate concentrations in the earth under the assumption that higher values are a result of human activity. Much of the testing was done using a small digging machine to open a trench or square for excavation. The decision about which sites to test was based on several factors including the expected richness of the location as originally determined in the field survey, the chronology, the setting in terms of the possibility of waterlogged deposits or good conditions for preservation, and accessibility. It was our goal in this testing phase to identify sites with substantial potential for large-scale excavation, from the Late Mesolithic and/or Early Neolithic, following our focus on the transition to agriculture.

We were looking for sites with good preservation and with primary *in situ* deposits, not redeposited materials which could be a mix of time periods and functions. While a large number of sites were tested, many failed to show promise for further excavation, and we did not continue at those locations. (Reports on each test were filed with the museum.) Rather than discuss each test site here, I have chosen to focus on 12 sites where we spent extra time with interesting results. A map of the location of these sites in the Saltbæk Vig area appears as Figure 3.1.

Our test excavations were essential both to locate sites for more intensive investigation and to obtain information on the age and contents of sites we could not excavate later. As it turned out, it was quite fortuitous that we tested a number or sites because in the end, due to constraints of time and money, we were able to conduct major excavations at just one site, Smakkerup Huse (VISbao).

A note about numbers: although we talk about the numbers of different objects at these sites, the usefulness of such counts depends on how much of the site was excavated, what part(s) of the site was excavated, the quality of the excavation, the use of water sieving, and other factors. So, these numbers are not really comparable among sites and do not mean a great deal other than in relative terms, a lot versus a little.

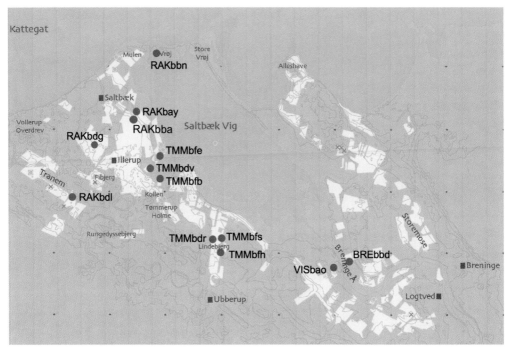

Fig. 3.1. A map of the location of the selected test sites in the Saltbæk Vig area. Labeled squares show modern towns. Grid points mark 1 km².

A note on gyttja: gyttja is a dark organic mud, normally a decomposed peat rich in nutrients, that has accumulated along the bottom of a marsh or lake. Gyttja is a common deposit with excellent preservation conditions often associated with outcast layers at Danish Mesolithic sites. An outcast layer contains materials lost or discarded into the water at coastal and lacustrine settlements.

A note on rolling and patination: the rolling of artifacts is caused by water movement and redeposition of materials; patination is a consequence of exposure on the surface near saltwater or to the iron-rich waters of the bogs. White patination is sometimes referred to as a marine patina resulting from exposure to seawater; a brown patina is often a result of burial in bog deposits.

1. TMMbdr (aka Lindebjerg)

The plateau hill at Lindebjerg is known from the excavation of one of the country's earliest long barrows dated to around 3800 cal BC (Tauber 1973; Liversage 1981; Schulz Paulsson (2010) argues that this early date may be from a settlement context beneath the long barrow). A total of six megaliths (sb. 38, 40–4), five settlements (sb. 50, 112, 129–31) and a cache (sb. 77) from the Funnel Beaker Culture (TRB) are registered on the hilltop and down its slopes. Furthermore, amateur archaeologists have zealously collected this area and documented the widespread occurrence of Neolithic material. Thus, it should be possible to find a TRB settlement similar in age to the long barrow.

Lindebjerg is one of a number of kames or plateau hills north of Kalundborg on the south side of the Saltbæk Vig. These hills were deposited in the ice sheets and appear very distinctive with steep sides and a flat top in the generally flat lands of the Saltbæk Vig. The hills are made up of gravel and/or sand (Nørrevang and Lundø 1979). The Lindebjerg hill is sand. Blowing sand with easterly winds from the hill of Lindebjerg has been a major problem for the farmers. The grounds of much of the hill were therefore planted with forest to keep the sand in place. The widespread sowing of winter wheats in recent years has made it possible to include more land in cultivation.

Systematic reconnaissance of the plateau in the winter of 1988–89 by the Kalundborg Museum showed that a relatively newly cultivated field on the west side of Lindebjerg was very rich in both flint and pottery from the Early Neolithic. The field had served as a sports ground until sometime in the 1930s, when it was planted with pine. The trees were felled in 1985 and the field has since been cultivated in winter rye. The field had thus been protected from cultivation and amateur collection.

Excavations were undertaken here in 1989 while we were waiting for the harvest and the clearance of cultivated fields for survey. A test excavation was done to investigate whether cultural layers and possible traces of houses were still preserved. We opened two perpendicular trenches to look for features and artifacts (Figs 3.2 and 3.3).

The surface of the trench was cleared by machine, followed by flat shoveling. The changes in fill color were highlighted and drawn in scale 1:20. Then the fill changes were dissected, unless they obviously originated from modern disturbances. These features were

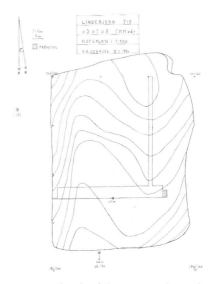

Fig. 3.2. Sketch of the excavated trenches at TMMbdr.

Fig. 3.3. Excavated trenches with features at TMMbdr.

drawn in section. At the eastern end of the wide trench, the remains of an old surface had been buried below later eolian sand deposits.

The clean, almost stone-free sandy soil was ideal for observing color changes (Fig. 3.4). The subsurface consisted of uniform yellow–brown sand, darker to the east, but the color gradually changed to lighter yellow/yellow–brown to the west. The soil was also reasonably moist but dried quickly. The previous forest had left some disturbances in the form of root runs, treefall pits, post holes, and there were tractor tire tracks in the subsoil. The loose soil had obviously also attracted underground residents with extensive animal passages, especially in the narrow trench.

Features

A number of color changes in the soil were interpreted as prehistoric features based on the clarity with which they appeared in the flat and in section. Many are, however, uncertain.

Post holes

There were nine scattered post holes, which did not form any recognizable system in terms of house yards or fences. The shape and size of the post holes were uneven, the depth varied from 11 cm to 23 cm but the fill was more or less uniform.

Pits

Fifteen prehistoric features were interpreted as pits of varying shape, size, depth, and volume. The fill usually consisted of gray–brown sand in lighter or darker tones, sometimes including extraneous mud or subsoil as a result of animal or root activity. None of these observations suggest a different age for these features, just as the finds indicated a dating to Early Neolithic TRB.

However, one of these features, A30, turned out to contain a complete vessel, probably from the pre-Roman Iron Age. The pot was sitting vertically at the bottom of the pit (Fig. 3.5). The pot was approximately 14 cm high and had a short neck with rounded, even rim and a heavily rounded belly and flat bottom. The vessel was asymmetrical with a ribbon shaped lower handle. There was no ornamentation or other surface treatment. Similar handled cups are known from pre-Roman Iron Age period I. Material from the Iron Age was also described in Liversage's (1981) report on the excavation of the long barrow. The pit fill was undisturbed and contained large amounts of Neolithic flint and ceramics which must be secondary to the pit's creation in the Iron Age. This late dating of pit A30 cast doubt as to whether all the features we uncovered are actually Neolithic.

As mentioned, an old surface, likely the Neolithic cultural layer, was preserved beneath eolian sand deposits in the first *c.* 15 m of the east end of the wide trench. The layer was only 3–4 cm thick and will disappear in a few years – streaks from plowing were already seen in several places. The layer contained some flint artifacts, flakes

Fig. 3.4. Excavation of the wide trench at Lindebjerg.

from four-sided polished axes, as well as a few sherds from TRB vessels and more recent pottery. Some irregular flat bottom depressions remained after the layer had been peeled away, where the remains of the culture layer were preserved. This Neolithic cultural layer probably extended across the entire field. However, cultivation has mixed it into the plow zone, where the protective eolian sand was thinner to the east. Most of the pottery originates from the west end of the broad trench.

Flint inventory

Waste flakes, cores, and burned pieces were counted separately, as were retouched pieces and tools (Table 3.1). Moreover, the flint is divided into loose finds in the cultural layer and finds from the features, finds from the older surface at the east end of the wide trench, as well as those from the plow layer. The three groups are about the

Fig. 3.5. Beth Workmaster excavating the Iron Age Vessel in Feature A30.

Table 3.1. Flint inventory from TMMbdr.

Type	Cultural layer and features	Older surface	Plow zone
Waste			
Flake	300	298	162
Burned	54	52	45
Core	14	1	7
Total waste	368	351	212
Tools			
Ret. flake	6	4	2
Pol. flake	17	7	6
Flake borer	3	0	2
Flake knife	2	0	2
Fine denticulate	3	0	0
Blades ± ret.	16	8	13
Blade knife	0	3	4
Scraper	1	0	4
Transverse point	2	1	3
Burin	2	0	1
Microblade	0	3	0
Total tools	21	15	25
Total flint	389	366	237

same size except that only half as much waste was found in the plow zone. The topsoil removed by the machine was not systematically sieved or examined. The distribution provides some clues about how many finds were removed by modern cultivation and ended up in the plow zone. The older surface at the east end of the wide trench contains a lot of flint, while the features in this part of the trench are not so common. The majority of the flint found in the features originates from the west end of the wide trench. This may reflect different areas of activity.

The retouched flint tools make up only a fraction of the total flint and show a clear dominance of tools made on flakes, including knives, e.g., a flake knife (Fig. 3.6), as well as large round scrapers with a flat edge intended for skins (one piece), a thick steep edge intended for wood (three pieces), and a snout-shaped edge (one piece). The source for the polished flakes was thin-butted flint axes – some with four-sided polishing. These axes were sometimes used as cores after discard (Fig. 3.7). Pieces with fine-denticulated retouch also point toward Early Neolithic TRB. Other types are hard to distinguish from Mesolithic objects, e.g., the flakes, blades, and transverse arrowheads. The vast majority of the flint assemblage can easily be placed in the older part of Funnel Beaker Culture.

Ceramic inventory

The pottery is also divided into three find categories, finds from features, finds from the older surface, as well as those from the plow layer and loose finds from the surface. Most of the pottery appears to be small and medium size funnel neck beakers and, due to heavy fragmentation, complete vessel profiles could not be reconstructed. The rims are vertical or slightly flared. The necks are concave and flared or more cylindrical, one example is very short. The transitions between neck and belly are smooth, occasionally marked by an incised line or a slight ledge. The bellies are evenly rounded and the bases flat. Two clay discs were part of the inventory as well as lugged vessels documented by a single perforated lug.

Only 8% of the sherds were decorated with an even number of rim sherds and side sherds. The designs include clay cordons with finger imprints, horizontal lines impressed with twisted, two stranded cord in addition to rows of pits and vertical strokes. Other decoration techniques include stab-and-drag, cardial shell and vertical or oblique stick impressions. The design of a clay cordon with finger impressions point is typical of the earliest pottery in period EN I, the Oxie Phase, and to a date between 4000 and 3800 BC or perhaps slightly younger (Nielsen 1985, 96; Koch 1998, 181; Klassen 2004; 2014; Skousen 2008, 125).

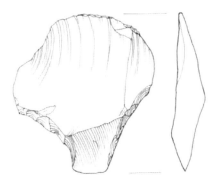

Fig. 3.6. Flake knife (Skive kniv) from BREbct, 4.5 cm in length (drawing: Kurt Petersen).

The remaining pottery belongs to the Svaleklint group, a local pottery style typical of the later part of period EN I, 3800–3500 BC (Ebbesen and Mahler 1980; Madsen and Petersen 1984; Koch 1998; Klassen 2004; Skousen 2008; Madsen 2019). Svaleklint pottery is characterized by funnel neck beakers with a relatively short, vertical or slightly flared neck, a rounded belly and a flat or rounded base. The inventory also includes lugged beakers and jars as well as clay discs. The decoration is primarily made with stick impressions, stab-and-drag and twisted, two stranded cord. Rows of vertical strokes are a common design. The decoration is typically composed of a combination of horizontal and vertical design, but due to fragmentation the design composition cannot be assessed in the pottery described here.

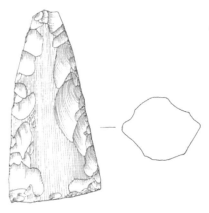

Fig. 3.7. Polished axe fragment used as a flake core, TMMbdr (drawing: Kurt Petersen).

Daub

Clay daub fragments should be a good indicator of nearby structures. Pieces of clay daub were found to the west in the wide trench. Two pieces clay daub emerged in feature A42 at the beginning of the narrow ditch. In addition, clay daub was found only to the south in the narrow trench. Several pieces show clear prints of timber. The spread of clay daub could indicate that there were two house areas within the excavated zone – at the west end of the wide trench and near pit A54. Since the dispersion coincides with the Neolithic materials and only four artifacts were found in the pit A30 with the Iron Age vessel, it is likely that the clay daub originated from the Neolithic settlement at the site.

Summary

The excavation thus resulted in the discovery of a settlement from the oldest part of the Neolithic culture, c. 4000–3500 B.C. The settlement may well have been contemporary with the early long barrow excavated by Liversage. The distribution of clay daub, in particular, could indicate that there have been at least two houses within or near the excavated area. The different distributions of artifacts might also reflect a difference in the activities between the west and east ends of the wide trench, respectively. Post holes and pits do not form a clear pattern to illuminate the activities. Furthermore, it is uncertain whether these features have the same age as the Neolithic settlement. A whole pre-Roman Iron Age clay vessel found on the bottom of one of the pits shows that at least one of the features must date to the Iron Age. This pit does not differ in any other way from the other pits in the square. Therefore, it cannot be excluded that these features have the same late date and that the Neolithic material is secondary. Nevertheless, the early pottery, axes, and likelihood of house construction mean that this site should be investigated more thoroughly.

2. TMMbfb (aka Kåstrup Holme)

The original 1989 field survey at the Kåstrup Holme site (TMMbfb) identified a promising concentration of flint artifacts along with a few pieces of bone. The site was registered as Tømmerup sogn, Ars herred (Holbæk), Vestsjællands amt, Stednummer 03.01.08, NM sb. Nr. 181. This was a large site, c. 5500 m², based on the distribution of lithic artifacts. The lithic material included core axes, flake axes (Fig. 3.8), and a few polished flint axes, suggesting both Mesolithic and Neolithic occupation. Modern truncation of the ridge top for house construction on which the site was located may have removed some of the settlement, but at the same time may have buried and protected lower areas. Elevation is approximately 2.5 m asl.

The site is on land belonging to several owners. We were not allowed to dig in the southern part of the field. At the test excavation in 1993, the site was investigated using an approximately 20 m long machine-dug trench (Trench 1) and seven test pits (T1–7). The find inventory comes partly from Ertebølle (e.g., a specialized core axe, Fig. 3.9) and partly from TRB (thin-butted polished flint axe, flake axe, transverse arrowheads). The purpose of the 1993 excavation was to locate waterlogged layers of preserved organic matter that could be related to on-site residential phases. There were no intact cultural layers or features.

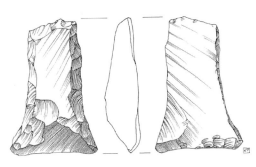

Fig. 3.8. A Mesolithic flake axe. Length approximately 10 cm (drawing: Kurt Petersen).

The material was probably washed into the layers in question during storms and transgressions/regressions. Despite the large artifact differences among the levels, there may not be much time difference between the different layers. The location of the actual place of residence is unknown.

The site is on a north–south ridge approximately 2.5 m above sea level; this rise extends from Illerup Sand to Kåstrup Holme but is interrupted by the Tranemose canal, draining the bog of Tranemose. The Subatlantic sea level rise was the highest transgression in Saltbæk Vig, where it reached 2.5 m above modern sea level. Massive shore formation is found along the entire south coast of the vig. The rise of the terrain here must at least be part of an old formation resulting from the Subatlantic transgression. The location is excellent for fishing and

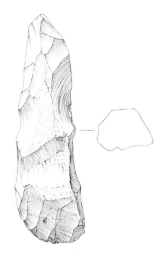

Fig. 3.9. Specialized core axe, with prepared bit (TMMbfd). Length is 11.3 cm (drawing: Kurt Petersen).

hunting at the mouth of the stream from Tranemose into the cove. In terms of site conservation, however, it has been an exposed location lacking shelter from wind and soil erosion.

The 20 m long machine-excavated trench (Trench 1) was laid out in the middle and perpendicular to the flint distribution. The machine began in the low area to the west and was to continue up the middle of the central finds area. However, the wet sand layers at the bottom were unstable and the trench collapsed repeatedly. We tried to dig a continuous trench over a 10–12 m stretch but failed. The trench was then continued by digging a series of 2 × 1 m squares. The profile was drawn in sequence as a continuous course was not possible.

In general, the top of the profile was plow zone above an eolian sand layer. Underneath there was a dark organic gyttja that could be followed everywhere except furthest west in the profile at 0.0 m. The middle part of the profile showed alternating layers of coarse and fine sand, with some layers laminated, probably the result of transgression. In some places there was a shoreline formation, most pronounced between 8.5 m and 12.0 m west. These must be near-beach deposits. At the bottom of the trench were alternating layers of dark organic gyttja and gray, usually finer, beach sand.

Cultural layers were nowhere to be found, although charcoal and artifacts were encountered in several places. Waste material and burnt flint were observed in connection with the upper organic horizon. Charcoal was found in the organic horizons in several places or scattered in gray layers of beach sand. The finds appear to have been transported from elsewhere. Charcoal lenses in Trench 1 decreased in some places from north to south which might indicate that the material was originally coming from the north. Lithic artifacts for various levels at the site are listed in Table 3.2.

The flat meadow area facing the cove east of the field road was the location of most of the test pits. The area was investigated by digging five tests (T1–5 of 1 m²). Pits T1–5 were at 20 m intervals in a north–south running row along the east side of the field road at a distance of 20 m from the road. Test pit T3 was placed a further 20 m east of T1. The deposition conditions proved to be complex. None of the test pits had exactly the same sequence of layers. Each contained over 50 artifacts: in T1 there was a flake axe; in T4 a TRB transverse arrowhead; in T5 two transverse arrowheads, probably from the Mesolithic and TRB respectively. These artifacts were found deep down and probably belonged to the deep shell layer, which also contained charcoal. T6 was excavated 20 m west of the field road and 20 m north of Trench 1. The stratigraphy corresponded to Trench 1. T7 was excavated 52 m east of the others, in the lowest meadow area to see if there was peat in the area and how deep it was; there were no artifacts.

The impression of the meadow area was that it has been filled and leveled by one or more transgressions; any elevations may have been completely removed by the Subatlantic transgression. The stratigraphy in the sample tests shows repeated deposits of beach sand and gravel. Artifacts were found in at least two levels and must have been water transported from elsewhere.

Table 3.2. Flint artifacts by layer at TMMbfb.

TMMbfb	Surface 1989	Surface 1993	T1	T1 under 75 cm	T2	T3	T4 Top 50 cm	T4 Top shell	T4 shell	T5	T6	T6	T6	Grøft 1	SUM
Flakes	171	4	36	58	33	22	18	1	16	36	14	51	26	3	489
Blades	16	0	6	6	3	3	5	0	5	9	5	3	4		65
Burned pieces	5	0	2	0	0	1	0	1	0	0	1	2	2	1	15
Flake core	3	1	1	1	0	0	1	0	1	1	0	1	0	0	10
Blade core	3	0	0	0	0	0	0	0	0	0	0	0	0	0	3
Flake, distal retouch	3	0	0	1	0	0	0	0	0	0	0	0	0	0	4
Blade knife	1	0	0	0	0	0	0	0	0	0	0	0	0	0	1
Arrowhead	0	1	0	0	0	0	0	0	0	2	0	0	0	0	4
Flake axe	1	0	0	0	0	0	0	0	0	0	0	0	0	0	1
Core axe	1	0	1	0	0	0	0	0	0	0	0	0	0	0	2
Polished axe	0	1	0	0	0	0	0	0	0	0	0	0	0	0	1
Flake scraper	1	0	0	0	0	0	0	0	0	0	0	0	0	0	1
Borer	1	1	0	0	0	0	0	0	0	0	0	0	0	0	2
Total flint	208	8	46	66	36	26	24	3	22	48	20	57	32	4	600

3. TMMbfe

Located inside the Saltbæk Vig drainage canal on rather flat ground, the dense distribution of flint artifacts at –1.0 m bsl appeared to date to the Ertebølle, Trylleskov phase. The site is approximately 8300 m² on the surface. Three trenches, 12 test pits, and borings were used in the evaluation. Surface collection from survey and artifacts from testing totaled 2050 pieces. An abundance of core axes and absence of flake axes, 15 blade knives, and dozens of cores were found. Moderate rolling and patination were observed. There was good preservation with antler, bone, and wood in the first test pit and also some oyster shell suggesting that there may have been a midden associated with this site. Some visible stratigraphy was present but was probably redeposited and thus of less interest. A radiocarbon date of 6110±70 BP (5045 BC median probability) may be from more recent wooden stakes. All this material appears to be in secondary position and thus of less interest for larger excavation in future.

4. TMMbdv (aka Saltmade, Viggo's site)

This was a promising locality with abundant lithics in a relatively dense concentration over an area of 6400 m² when recorded in the field survey. Preliminary testing at the site in 1993 revealed very good preservation of waterlogged materials at depth (Fig. 3.10). In 1994, bone, nutshell, and wood were collected in test pits at this sandy site, lying inside the beach ridge at an elevation of approximately 0.0 m asl. The predominance of core axes and the absence of pottery points to early Middle Ertebølle. The finds indicate secondarily deposited material but a very rich locality with very good preservation, including fish bone and wood. Secondary deposition and distance from settlement made this of less interest for more intensive excavation.

Stratigraphy at the site confirmed the underwater context of the deposits. The top of the profile was characterized by a 25 cm plow zone above an eolian sand. There were several layers beneath this sand that were waterlain and sometimes reworked. The gray sand layer was a mixture of gyttja and the eolian sand and continued to a depth of *c.* 120 cm. Some artifacts were found in this water redeposited layer. A shell layer with a sharp boundary was found at 120 cm beneath the gray sand and this appeared to have been the primary cultural layer at the site with the majority of artifacts and fauna. In all likelihood this was an outcast layer. A shell gyttja layer was found beneath the shell layer grading into a pure gyttja at the limits of excavations at 155 cm below the surface. The settlement itself must have been on higher ground nearby.

Fig. 3.10. Excavations at Viggo's site.

Flint material included a wide range of Mesolithic artifacts, dominated by core axes and projectile points. The flint finds are listed by layer in Table 3.3. Retouched tools by layer are provided in Table 3.4. Artifacts in the gray sand layer were less patinated and more rolled than those in the shell gyttja, while the artifacts in the shell layer were intermediate in condition.

The site is characterized by two superimposed deposits of outcast or redeposited materials with a general assemblage of artifacts and fauna that characterize Mesolithic settlements. Fauna identified from 64 fragments comprised red deer (43 fragments), roe deer (15). wild boar (5), and seal (1). Hazelnut shells were common in the cultural deposits at the site. Wood was also preserved and the remains of one or more fish

Table 3.3. Flint artifacts by layer at TMMbdv.

Saltmade flint	Gray sand	Shell layer	Shell gytja	Total	%
Unretouched flakes	465	2405	106	2976	79.80
Unretouched blades	72	440	14	526	14.1
Unretouched microblades	3	20	0	23	0.6
Cores	43	103	9	155	4.2
Retouched pieces	6	41	0	47	1.3
Worked flint	589	3009	129	3727	100
Burned flint	71	286	7	364	
Total flint	660	3295	136	4091	
Hammerstones	3	0	0	3	
Nodules	2	0	0	2	
Total flint	1914	9599	401	11914	
% by layer	16.10	8.06	3.40		

Table 3.4. Retouched tools by layer at TMMbdv.

Saltmade flint tools	Gray sand	Shell layer
Flake axes	0	0
Core axes	0	5
Axe sharpening flakes	2	3
Points	1	11
Blade knives	2	10
Flake knives	0	5
Retouched blades	1	1
Retouched flakes	0	5
Burins	0	1
Total	6	41

fences and parts of fish traps were uncovered. In one instance a partial section of a fish fence, knocked down and damaged by the sea, was uncovered in the excavations.

Jens Nielsen devoted his efforts at the site to the wooden stakes and provided substantial information. Jens recorded both vertical (16) and horizontal (12) wooden stakes, normally of hazel and often more than 25 cm in length. These stakes had been sharpened using a stone axe (Fig. 3.11) and were intended to be placed vertically in the sea floor, represented here by the shell gyttja. Two stakes were broken segments from bows

Two radiocarbon measurements from Copenhagen on wooden hazel stakes provided dates of 5140 cal BC (K-6381) and 5330 cal BC (K-6382) for the upper and lower levels with artifacts at the site. Several bone artifacts were recovered in the excavations, including a decorated bone awl (Fig. 3.12), although this cross-hatching may well be utilitarian. The site appears to be a Mesolithic settlement, but deposits are for the most part secondary and not as suitable for our research.

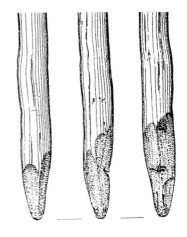

Fig. 3.11. Sharpened wooden stake, length = 12 cm (drawing: Kurt Petersen).

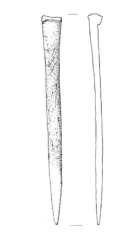

Fig. 3.12. Decorated bone awl, length = 7.2 cm (drawing: Kurt Petersen).

5. TMMbfh (aka Mollie's Site)

Located on the sandy plateau of Lindebjerg at an elevation of approximately 15 m asl, this Neolithic site is southeast of the long barrow excavated by the National Museum (Liversage 1981). The dense flint scatter covered roughly 2300 m² and surface finds included fine denticulated pieces, four-sided polished axe fragments, burned bone, daub, and lots of pottery.

The site was tested over two seasons in 1993 and 1994 with three test pits in the first year and three trenches in the second year (Fig. 3.13). Trench 1 was 46 m north–south in line with Test 3 from the previous year, with two 10 m trenches (2 and 3). Trench 2 ran east from Test 3 and Trench 3 was approximately 10 m south of Trench 2, also running north–south. Trench 4, connecting Trenches 2 and 3, was added during the course of the excavations. Our goal was to expose the black cultural layer seen in Test pit 3 across a broad area. There appeared to be two levels with cultural material. Level 1 was a mottled brown horizon directly below the plow zone with some artifacts. It was often separated from Level 2 by eolian sand. Level 2 was a black cultural

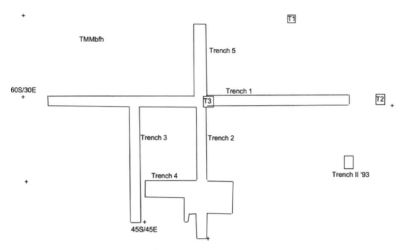

Fig. 3.13. Plan of excavations at TMMbfh.

Table 3.5. Number of identified bone fragments at TMMbfh.

Species	No. bone fragments (NF)
Cervus elaphus	4
Capreolus capreolus	2
Sus scrofa	5
Bos domesticus	4
Equus caballus	5
Capra ??	2
Total	22

horizon (probably a decomposed peat) with artifacts and features. This level is likely ENII based on the Virum style pottery recovered.

A stone-lined ditch was observed in Trench 3, probably medieval and perhaps for field drainage. Today this ditch lies beneath the plow zone, likely due to continuing movement and accumulation of sands on the glacial feature that is Lindebjerg. Bone materials from the earlier Neolithic horizon had fallen into the bottom of this stone-lined ditch when it was created and were much better preserved in the ditch than in the higher Neolithic horizon because there was more moisture at the bottom of the buried ditch.

A possible house floor was encountered in Trench 2 with a sandy layer, a greasy black level and a concentration of large sherds and flints. Trench 5 was added later in the excavation (6 × 1.5 m) from Trench 1 west from Trench 2. We also opened a few new test squares, 4 × 3 m north of Trench 2 and a 3 × 3 m area at the southeast corner of Trenches 2 and 4.

Artifacts from the site were numerous. Flint artifacts were common and typical of the Neolithic with a number of polished axe fragments, several fine denticulated pieces, and large transverse points or small flake axes. Pottery was common, belonging to the Late TRB. A number of pieces of burned daub, some with wattle impressions, were recovered. Bone was variably preserved but a number of pieces could be identified: cow bones and horn core were usually clear (Table 3.5). Horse and cow appeared to be the dominant fauna at the site although the horse is unexpected and may well be younger. A number of features were preserved including fireplaces and at least one possible house floor. There were also more recent features in the deposits including tree falls and the drainage ditch. This is clearly an interesting Neolithic site, but it is too late for information on the transition to agriculture and for that reason, no further work was planned at this site.

6. TMMbfs

This was an Early Neolithic site at the front of the Lindebjerg plateau with estimated size of 3300 m². It was an open level field and finds from the surface survey included a quantity of TRB pottery, a large number of polished axe fragments, including two thick-butted forms, daub, and large transverse points. A number of large stones were reported to have been removed from this area so that there may have been a megalithic monument here.

Three test pits and two trenches at this site revealed a cultural layer beneath the plow zone with some artifacts and features. In addition, Columbus came out to site and dug down to large rock located in coring. This rock may well have been part of a megalithic monument which would be from ENII; the thick-butted flint axes may relate to later use of this tomb.

7. BREbbd: Engelsborg (aka the Midwife Site)

A Late Ertebølle settlement along Bregninge Å at the head of the Saltbæk Vig was encountered in our survey. The site lay on a small rise at 2.5 m asl and covered an area of roughly 53 × 31 m, oriented in an east–west direction, directly across the stream from Smakkerup Huse. The rise is part of the extensive beach ridge that borders the margins of the Saltbæk Vig. The rich finds from the surface collection at the site included 742 pieces of worked flint and suggested that this could be an important site if organic materials were preserved. Testing in the low areas, to the east and partly toward the bay where the terrain falls sharply adjacent to the settlement zone on the small rise, however, indicated that potential organic materials had been eroded and were no longer present.

Test excavations were conducted in late June and early July, 1995. The owner of the land, a midwife, was unfavorable with regard to our investigations and gave her permission only on the condition that no mechanical power was used. The site continued onto the next property, Engelsborg, to the west, but only three test holes could be excavated there (T6, 15, and 21) as a part of the area was overgrown with trees and another used as a pig stye.

The testing involved 21 1 m² test pits placed in rows at 10 m intervals in the longitudinal direction of the site, or approximately north–south, as well as perpendicular to the direction of the settlement and the coastline, approximately east–west (Fig. 3.14). In some cases, the location of a test pit had to be adjusted due to conditions of the terrain. In every test pit, the northern wall, running east – west, was drawn

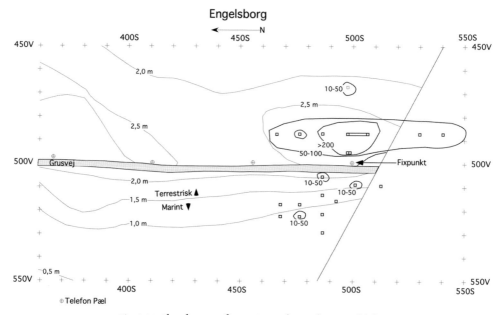

Fig. 3.14. Sketch map of test pits and trench at BREbbd.

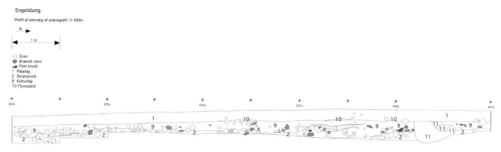

Fig. 3.15. Trench 1, Section profile. West wall. BREbbd. Hollow = stone, grey = burned stone, black = flint. Layer 1 = Plow zone, 2 = beach ridge, 9 = culture layer, 10 = eolian sand.

in order to have a series of sections perpendicular to the direction of the settlement and coastline.

A preserved cultural layer was investigated in more detail by hand-digging a trench (Trench 1) with a total length of 10 m connecting the test pits T7 and T16 (Fig. 3.14). For Trench 1, a section profile of the west wall of this trench appears in Figure 3.15. Two adjacent square meters were excavated in relation to a hearth (T11 and T20). Artifacts were collected by layer from each test pit and each square meter in the trench; no subdivision of the layers was made. Regarding the recording of the artifacts, Table 3.6 includes the total amount of lithic artifacts from the surface collections as well as the excavation.

Table 3.6. Flaked stone artifacts from BREbbd: Engelsborg.

Type	Surface Collection	Test pits All layers	Test trench Plow zone	Test trench Cultural layer	Total
Flake	483	1517	1032	781	3813
Blade	103	67	58	66	294
Microblade	0	5	6	5	16
Burned flint	22	186	141	89	438
Axe sharpening flake	5	3	0	4	12
Flake core	52	20	6	5	83
Blade core	7	2	0	0	9
Microblade core	3	1	0	0	4
Knife on flake	0	1	1	0	2
Retouched flake	7	2	0	0	9
Lateral	2	0	0	0	2
Distal	2	2	0	3	7
Blade knife	4	0	1	0	5
Retouched blade	0	2	0	0	2
Lateral	9	2	1	2	14
Distal	2	4	1	0	7
Denticulated flake	2	0	0	0	2
Notched pieces	0	0	3	1	4
Projectile points	1	20	12	11	44
Flake axe	17	1	0	3	21
Core axe	8	2	0	0	10
Specialized core axe	2	0	0	0	2
Burin on flake	0	1	2	0	3
Microburin	2	0	0	0	2
Round flake scraper	0	1	1	1	3
End blade scraper	7	0	2	1	10
Small borer on flake	2	0	0	0	2
Total	742	1839	1267	972	4820
Weight	17.1 kg	18.3 kg	4.1 kg	4.2 kg	43.7 kg
Sherd	0	0	0	12	12

There was a total of ten body sherds from Engelsborg, all of Ertebølle type, with a wall thicknessws of 1.0–1.3 cm. in addition there were two small pieces of fired clay daub with a woven or regular imprint on one surface. The daub had no temper, grains, or structure that might distinguish it as a fragment of pottery.

The location of the coastline at the time of settlement is uncertain. However, a shoreline of unknown age followed the 1.5 m elevation contour where a boundary was seen between terrestrial and marine/freshwater strata in the test pits west of the field road. Beach ridge formations were present in test pits at the elevation of 1.5 m asl and above, but no gyttja layers were present.

In all the test pits located below 1.5 m asl (T1, 2, 8, 10, 12, 17–19), laminated layers of sand and gyttja (layer 5), typical of the coastal zone, were present in addition to a gyttja layer about 0.5 m thick (layer 6); the bottom of the gyttja layer was reached in T1. This gyttja layer was absent in the test pit with highest location (T2).

A purely marine environment in the form of a compact layer of cardial shells (layer 8) was seen in the test pit T8 closest to the sea. The test pits below the elevation 1.5 m were largely empty of artifacts and without traces of a discard layer. The amount of wood in the gyttja (layer 6) shows that the preservation of organic matter was excellent. The marine deposits must therefore be younger than the settlement site but their precise age is otherwise unknown.

The section with the cultural layer helps describe the deposits at the site. The plow zone was an approximately 20 cm thick layer of brown sandy humus mixed with smaller stones (layer 1). Pockets of eolian sand (layer 10) were preserved at the transition between the plow zone and the cultural layer. The intact culture layer (layer 9) varied in thickness from 8 cm to 40 cm and consisted of gray to black–brown sand. The upper part of the layer was almost stonefree. The bottom of the layer was very irregular with several depressions that may be pits, especially in the southern part of the trench.

Beneath the entire stratigraphic sequence was a beach ridge consisting of yellow to brown sand mixed with large amounts of gravel and rocks (layer 2). Four areas at the site had a distinctive appearance.

Area A

At 505–507 m South was an area with irregular depressions that most likely were humanly made pits. A pit is likewise visible in the section of test pit T16. The culture layer was grayish–black in this area.

Area B

A depression with dark, almost black, dense and hard fill without stratification was found in the area at 501.3–501.8 m S. Immediately towards the south in the same depression was a pile of cooking stones, perhaps related to a fireplace? Very few artifacts were found in this area.

Another fireplace was found in test pits T 11 and 20, 12 m west of the trench (497–499 m S/491–492 m W). The feature was a pit of 50 × 35 cm, up to 13 cm deep and filled with black–gray sand mixed with charcoal, burnt flint, and fire-cracked stones. Only the bottom part of the feature was preserved. The cultural layer was completely plowed up in this area and most of the flint appeared in the plow zone (219 pieces).

Area C

Three successive lenses of a dense and hard, dark brown soil with higher content of organic material or more clay than the remaining cultural layer were found at 499.7–500.8 m S. Beneath these lenses the layer was very gravelly and full of pebbles; the gravel seemed to come from burnt stones. The three lenses were recorded where the cultural layer was thickest and where the greatest number of cooking stones were found. These lenses may represent a sequence of fireplaces.

Area D

A disturbance with a greyish–brown fill of a lighter color than the cultural layer was found in the northern end of the trench at 497.8–498.6 m S (layer 11).

Summary

Engelsborg was a Late Ertebølle coastal settlement belonging to the Stationsvej phase. The preserved part of the settlement included a cultural layer with pits and fireplaces. In one place several successive fireplaces appear to be located above one another. Any discarded organic materials from the site had been removed by erosion at the time when the coastline around 1.5 m in elevation was formed. The coastline contemporary with the settlement must either coincide with 1.5 meters elevation or be situated at a lower elevation. There was no trace of a shell midden.

The remarkable aspect of the Engelsborg site was the discovery of the intact settlement layer, in contrast to almost all other coastal sites where the actual living surface had been eroded away by transgressions and only outcast and redeposited materials were preserved. It was important to note the absence of organic materials on the occupation surface and nearby areas. For this reason we concluded investigations at this site.

8. RAKbdl (aka Birkhøj)

Field survey and a test excavation documented the presence of a late EN–MNA 1 site belonging to the TRB. The excavation consisted of a 9.3 m machine-excavated test trench (1) and a series of 1 m² test pits excavated by hand (T1–8). Some artifacts were present but all were in the plow layer, except a small number which were found in redeposited layers in two test pits (T6–7). No intact features or cultural layers were encountered. The site is part of a continuous spread of material that extends from Illerup Sand to Svenstrup and is exposed on the sandy elevations in the terrain (at 5 m asl). Many of these elevations contain traces of Early Neolithic settlement. An unclassified burial mound sb. 82, called Birkhøj, lay immediately west of the field.

The trench (9.3 m long, 0.9 m wide and 1.8 m deep) was dug with a machine on a terrace down the slope to the north, in hopes of revealing a possible outcast layer with residues of organic material. The profile showed that there was originally a freshwater lake (layer 11), which subsequently became a peat bog (layer 10), over a sand layer (layer 9, presumably eolian sand) followed a later layer of peat mixed with sand (layers 7–8) probably deposited in connection with the late Atlantic transgression, according to Christian Abildtrup in consultation with Bent Åby. The upper layers are plow zone and eolian sand. A local thin layer of charcoal was found in layer 7 in the south end of the ditch, a few features and bones were found under the charcoal layer. A large patch of charcoal was found on the bottom of the trench at approximately 2 m depth.

The extent of the site was investigated by digging eight test pits in two north–south rows along the eastern edge of the field (T1–2) and 35 m further west (T4–8). An east–west row along the southern boundary of the field was formed by T2-T3-T4. The test pits were excavated with a trowel and the soil dry-sieved in a 4 mm screen. A color change in the sediments in T6 meant that this square was expanded by 1 m² to the west (T7). The feature contained a charcoal concentration but appeared redeposited. There was some animal activity in the area. With the exception of T6-7, all finds come from the plow zone; the largest number appeared in T5 and T6-7, as well as T3. The large volume of finds in the T5-T7 squares may reflect an erosion from the higher part of the field to the south, but it is clear that the center of the field has been in this area, while T1–2 were at the edge of the field.

Flint

The diagnostic tools include three fragments of flint axes and a chisel polished on all four sides and dating from EN–MN A, as well as ten polished flint axe flakes dating from the Neolithic. The relationship of a thick-butted flint axe to the site is unknown. A fragment of the butt end was found in a pile of stones picked up by a machine collecting potatoes. The axe may have been picked up in a field other than the remaining artefacts.

A couple of large 'bear-hunting' arrowheads can only be dated to the period between younger Kongemose and the Early Neolithic. A transverse arrowhead with extended corners on the cutting edge was produced from a flint flake rather than a blade and probably dates from the Neolithic. An oblique transverse arrowhead of Vedbæk type dates from Younger Kongemose. An atypical rhombic arrowhead might date from Kongemose as well. A fine-denticulated piece, ten large scrapers made on flint flakes (Fig. 3.16), and the large proportion of flakes to blades among the unretouched flint pieces support the dating of the majority of the site to the Neolithic period. In all 767 pieces of flint were found at the site, mainly flakes.

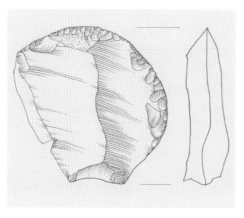

Fig. 3.16. Circular scraper on large flake. 6.3 cm in length (drawing: Kurt Petersen).

The surface collection yielded three fragments of four-sided polished flint axes, a neck fragment of a broken, four-sided polished chisel, and a polished fragment which may be from a thin-butted flint axe. The polished axe fragments in T6 were from a four-sided polished axe, probably thin-butted. Projectile points from the site included a transverse arrow made on an irregular flake with impact bulb near one corner (length 3.3 cm, width 2.2 cm). The shape is most similar to the Stationsvej type, but the arrow could be Neolithic given the raw material. A large transverse arrowhead with almost parallel long sides, made on a flake (length 5.1 cm, max. width 1.5 cm) may be placed in Younger Kongemose but there are extremely large transverse arrowheads in the TRB (Wadskjær 2018). These 'bear arrows' were used from Younger Kongemose through the Early Neolithic. A transverse arrowhead (length 3.1 cm, max. width 1.5 cm), similar to the Vedbæk type but the diagonal index seems smaller, dating perhaps to younger Kongemose was also recovered as was a possible rhombic arrowhead with continuous retouch from the tip of the arrow in an oblique/curved course to the diagonally opposite corner. The arrow is atypical, possibly Kongemose? The classification and number of the flaked stone finds from RAKbdl are tabulated in Table 3.7

Table 3.7. Classification and number of the flaked stone finds from RAKbdl.

	Surface	Trench 1	T1	T2	T3	T4	T5	T6 Plow zone	T6	T7 Plow zone	T7	T8	Sum
Flake	427	0	21	10	81	37	201	84	4	111	27	5	1008
Blade	52	1	2	2	6	1	5	4	1	5	0	1	80
Burned piece	67	0	7	3	27	9	31	10	1	19	11	1	186
Flake core	6	0	0	0	1	0	0	0	0	1	0	0	8
Microblade core	1	0	0	0	0	0	0	0	0	0	0	0	1
Blade core	1	0	0	0	0	0	0	0	0	0	0	0	1
Retouched flake	1	0	0	0	1	0	1	1	0	0	0	0	4
Flake, bifacialtly ret.	0	0	0	0	0	0	0	1	0	0	0	0	1
Flake laterally ret.	3	0	0	0	1	0	2	0	0	0	0	0	6
Flake distally ret.	0	0	0	0	0	0	0	0	0	0	0	0	0
Blade laterally ret.	1	0	0	0	0	0	0	0	0	0	0	0	1
Blade distally ret.	1	0	0	0	0	0	0	0	0	1	0	0	2
Blade knife	7	0	0	0	0	0	0	0	0	0	0	0	7

(Continued)

Table 3.7. Classification and number of the flaked stone finds from RAKbdl. (Continued)

	Surface	Trench 1	T1	T2	T3	T4	T5	T6 Plow zone	T6	T7 Plow zone	T7	T8	Sum
Fine denticulate	1	0	0	0	0	0	0	0	0	0	0	0	1
Proj. Point	5	0	0	0	0	0	0	0	0	0	0	0	5
Polished axe	8	0	0	1	0	0	0	0	0	0	0	0	9
Thin-necked	0	0	0	0	0	0	0	2?	1?	0	0	0	0
Thick-necked	1	0	0	0	0	0	0	0	0	0	0	0	1
Scraper	1	0	0	0	0	0	1	0	0	0	0	0	2
Large skin scraper	4	0	0	0	0	0	0	0	0	0	0	1	5
Large wood scraper	6	0	0	0	0	0	0	0	0	0	0	0	6
Sidescraper	3	0	0	0	0	0	0	0	0	0	0	0	3
Endscraper on blade	9	0	0	0	0	0	0	0	0	0	0	0	9
Double scraper	1	0	0	0	0	0	0	0	0	0	0	0	1
Shouldered scraper	1	0	0	0	0	0	0	0	0	0	0	0	1
Scraper w. Snout	0	0	0	0	1	0	0	1	0	0	0	0	2
Large flake borer	2	0	0	0	0	0	0	0	0	0	0	0	2
Total flint (exc. Surface)		1	30	16	118	47	241	103	7	137	38	8	767= 746
Total weight (g)		53.4	76	33	414	205	520	329.4	100	492.9	76	58	
Trækul tilstede		+							+				
Sherd	0	0	2	0	8	2	51	2	2	5	1	0	73
Weight (g)			7.5		8.6	10	93						

Ceramics

Seventy-two sherds were collected in total, with 69 definitely belonging to the Funnel Beaker culture (Fig. 3.17). Four sherds with vertical striations on the belly date from the Middle TRB (EN2–MN II). Two sherds decorated with designs of filled-out ribbons most likely date from MN I. The remaining sherds are undecorated side sherds and can only be dated to TRB in general. Two fragments of the neck and upper belly belong to small to medium size funnel beakers with a diameter at the neck-belly transition of 14 cm and 18 cm.

T1.   One historic sherd broken in two parts, Very fine grained. Thickness: 0.3 cm.

T3.   Eight sherds, five of which are small with a maximum diameter of less than 1 cm. Seven sherds are undecorated. A decorated sherd shows a ribbon design with a row of nail imprints framed by small angular imprints, dates most likely to MN I.

T4.   Two undecorated side sherds, date TRB.

T5.   In all, 45 undecorated and six decorated side sherds, 93 g, all date from TRB. A decorated side sherd (2.5 × 1.5 cm) shows two ribbon designs filled with a zipper motif impressed with spatula stamp. Date MN I. One belly sherd of a beaker is decorated with deep vertical incised striations. A mini-beaker has a wall thickness of 0.3 cm and is represent by one belly sherd. The vertical lines are deep and fairly dense (7 lines per 3 cm). A third vessel, probably a small funnel neck beaker, measures 14 cm in diameter at neck–belly transition. The vertical lines are placed with same distance as the second vessel (7 lines per 3 cm). A fourth vessel, also a Funnel Neck beaker, has a diameter of 18 cm at the neck–belly transition. Diameter, but no decoration, was preserved. The undecorated side sherds vary in size from a maximum thickness of less than 1 cm (27 sherds), <2 cm (13 sherds), <3 cm (4 sherds) and <4 cm (1 sherd).

T6.   A total of ten sherds, weighing 39 g, including eight undecorated side sherds from TRB and two sherds younger than prehistoric. T6 Plow zone: two undecorated side sherds with a max diameter of less than 1 cm, TRB.

T7.   Plow zone. Four undecorated side sherds, two sherds with a maximum thickness of <1 cm and two sherds measuring 2 × 2 cm, wall thickness: 0.7–0.8 cm. TRB. In the same layer was a black, very fine-grained sherd fired at high temperature, decorated with one line, younger than prehistoric.

T6–7.   'Cultural layer'. Two undecorated side sherds each measuring 2 × 2 cm, TRB. One rim sherd with a thickened rim edge, decorated with a horizontal incised line, diameter 16–18 cm, younger than prehistoric.

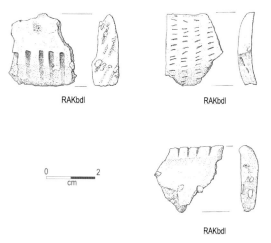

While two arrowheads indicate hunting in the area during the Kongemose period, the actual settlement site dates from the Middle TRB period MN I (3300–3100 BC) or EN 2–MN II (3500–3100 BC) based on the designs of the pottery. The flint tools with four-sided polishing indicate the same

Fig. 3.17. Sherd drawings from RAKbdl (by Kurt Petersen).

time period. The thick-butted flint axe may not be related to the settlement; it dates from the final TRB or early Corded Ware culture (3000–2600 BC).

9. RAKbay

Remains of Mesolithic settlement found by survey, covered an area of *c.* 1480 m² and revealed 269 pieces of flint, including two core axes, two flake axes, and three arrowheads from the Younger Kongemose. The settlement is located at 0.0 m elevation on land that was created by the reclamation project in Saltbæk Vig, i.e., on former seabed. The sediments are very sandy with cardium and some oyster shells. The area is cultivated today. The settlement of RAKbay was found by survey in 1989 and later tested, in 1992. A test excavation of 4 m², as well as seven corings, showed that a single layer existed about 0.6 m below the field surface but no intact cultural layer remained. This layer might be an erosion surface, possibly wind-blown. The few diagnostic artifacts were found during survey; only waste materials were found at the test excavation. Projectile points indicate a dating to Younger Kongemose and older Ertebølle.

A series of four test pits of 1 m² were laid out at 20 m intervals west, east and north of T4. Levels were measured relative to the field surface. The four test pits were dug along a drainage ditch and near the eastern boundary of the field. The pits were excavated with a shovel and the earth was sieved through a 4 mm screen.

The simple stratigraphy comprised a plow zone of approximately 30 cm, consisting of light gray sand with a little gravel and pebbles as well as shell pieces. Under a further 30 cm of sand (eolian or beach sand) lay a rocky layer with some artifacts. The rocky layer may be a wind-blown surface. Under the rocky layer, gray–brown sand followed and possibly a layer of gray sand. Groundwater emerged between 1.2m and 1.8 m below ground level. This layer was probably water deposited and the artifacts may be eroded from the original settlement and spread over a larger area. There was no cultural layer or features in connection with the rocky layer. The lithic artifacts are not rolled but are marine patinated. The number of artifacts was limited and without diagnostic piece but show that T1 and T2 were located on the edge of the flint spread, while T3 and T4 were more at the center with more material.

The field was further investigated with seven boreholes located west, east and north of T4. The profiles were described geologically in cores 1–5, as well as T4. There were no features or intact culture layers. Findings from the plow zone of, among other things, a rhombic arrowhead and a transverse arrowhead indicate a dating to Younger Kongemose and Early Ertebølle, which corresponds to the flint distribution in a low position on the ridge. The flint inventory from RAKbay appears in Table 3.8.

10. RAKbbn

This site is located on the former island of Vrøj at the mouth of the Saltbæk Vig. The site was discovered originally by Columbus who reported large numbers of core axes

Table 3.8. Flint inventory from RAKbay.

	Surface	T1	T2	T3	T4	Sum
Flake	217	6	12	26	49	310
Blade	29	0	0	0	0	29
Burned piece	11	0	0	0	0	11
Core, flake	7	0	0	0	0	7
Core, blade	4	0	0	0	0	4
Core, microblade	1	0	0	0	0	1
Ret. blade	1	0	0	0	0	1
Projectile point	3	0	0	0	0	3
Flake axe	2	0	0	0	0	2
Core axe	3	0	0	0	0	3
Round flake scraper	1	0	0	0	0	1
Total flint	362	6	12	26	49	362

as well as one Maglemosian point and one rhombic point. Site appears to be either Kongemose or perhaps mixed with some Maglemosian, which would be unusual.

The site was tested in 1992 with four test pits of 1 m². Two distinct cultural layers were recorded: an upper layer of beach sand and gravel with artifacts rolled and white patinated and a lower layer of dark brown humus containing artifacts that were fresher and less patinated, as well as intact oyster shells. At a depth of 90 cm we hit moraine sediments which confirmed that there was Pleistocene antiquity to the islands at the mouth of the inlet.

11. RAKbdg (aka Vildsvinepladsen)

This site has a designation in the Danish National Register of Raklev sogn, Ars herred (Holbæk), Vestsjællands amt, Stednummer 03.01.03. A settlement from TRB (late EN) was found on a rise next to a former coastal area. A series of 1 m² test pits (T1–12) was dug on dry land and a test trench (Trench 1) was excavated in the former wetland for the purpose of uncovering organic material and possible discard layers belonging to the site. However, all artifacts were found in the plow layer and no organics or intact culture layers existed. The site is part of the Early Neolithic occupation that is found on almost all the 'higher' areas, i.e., 2.5–5.0 m asl, which extend as small hills from Illerup Sand in the east to Svenstrup in the west. The Mesolithic arrowheads show that these sandy 'ridges' have also been favored hunting areas in past times.

The settlement RAKbdg was found in 1991 and was later tested in 1993. This large settlement, estimated at 3264 m², was located on a slope 5 m above a low marsh area. In the next field was a herd of wild boars with piglets, hence the name given to the place. The profile in Trench 1 showed that there was originally a freshwater lake with a calcareous mud at the bottom. At one point the lake grew and moss (sphagnum) peat formed. A layer of eolian sand was deposited. Thereafter, the area was again wet, likely associated with the Atlantic transgression and consequent groundwater leading to the deposition of a layer of detrital mud. In addition, there is a layer of mud-mixed sand and then horizons of eolian sand.

Test excavations took place in 1993. Twelve test pits were excavated by shovel and soil was sieved through a 4 mm screen. A 23.5 m long trench was excavated by machine. For the sake of the crops, the sample holes were laid along the edge of the marshland. T1 was placed in the SW corner of the field and T2–5 at 10 m intervals to the north along the west side of the field. An east–west row of test pits T6–9 was set out along the southern edge of the field at a distance of 10, 20, 40 and 50 m from the SW corner. A further three test pits T10–12 were placed in an east–west row with 10 m spacing, 47 m from the west side and 30 m from the south edge of the field. Trench 1 was placed in a grassy area between the southern edge of the field and the wild boar area, so that the trench went from the higher terrain down into the low marsh area to expose the stratigraphy and uncover any possible discard zones. The trench was located 50 m east of T1 and 3 m south of the southern boundary of the field.

Geological reconnaissance was conducted by Christian Hans Abildtrup. In order to understand settlement in the area we wanted to know if the wetland was part of former marine waters with access to the cove or a freshwater lake. Abildtrup therefore reviewed the profile in trench 1 and drew two profiles, one more coastal 3 m from the zero point at the beginning of the ditch and one out in the wetland about 21 m from the zero point. The profile indicated that there was originally a freshwater lake which later filled in as peat bog. A subsequent mud layer was associated with the Atlantic transgression. A number of soil samples from the latter profile were analyzed for sulfur content as a test of whether the layers were marine. The interpretation was that the high sulfur content reflected anaerobic conditions at the front of and below an overgrown peat bog.

The find material comprised only a few diagnostic items. Phasing the pottery was difficult. Three pots belonged to the TRB period: an undecorated heat-affected sherd was found in the survey, as well as two sherds in T12, a reddish–brown sherd with a coarse grain and damaged surface, as well as a light brown sherd with coarse, partially broken surface, and decorated with remnants of two half-arcs. It is uncertain with which technique the arcs were stamped: two-string cord or cardium? The sherd from T12 could be Virum style. Another four modern sherds were found in T12.

The flint inventory (Table 3.9) ranges from older Maglemose, in the form of a geometric microlith with fully retouched long side and base (right), to the Neolithic, represented by two finely denticulated pieces and two large round scrapers on flakes. Of the 13 transverse arrowheads, eight are very large, 3–5 cm long, with skewed edges. Several have convex sides, some are twisted, one has cortex preserved. A large transverse arrowhead is on a two-sided flake almost like a mini-flake axe. These oversized transverse arrowheads can also occur during the Neolithic (Vang Petersen 2008).

Table 3.9. Flint inventory from RAKbdg.

Type	Surface Collection	Test Pits	Total
Flake	89	404	493
Blade	5	13	18
Burned	16	79	95
Flake core	2	0	2
Fine denticulate	1	1	2
Burin spall	0	1	1
Ret. flake. distal	1	0	1
Transverse point	8	5	13
Microlith	0	1	1
Hammerstone	0	1	1
Large skin scraper	1	0	1
Large wood scraper	0	1	1
Total flint	123	506	629
Flint weight	1443.2 g		
Pottery	2	6	8

The other five transverse arrowheads are of normal size, 1.5–2.5cm long but all are fragmented; three are missing a small corner of the edge, one is missing a corner of the neck, one is an edge fragment. The conclusion that the Vildsvinepladsen dates from EN II is based on the one sherd in Virum styte and the flint inventory. Due to sand movement and cultivation, no intact layers of culture or features were found; all finds were in the plow zone.

12. RAKbba (aka Illerup Sand)

This site is officially designated in the Danish National Register as Raklev sogn, Ars herred, (Holbæk), Vestsjællandsamt, Stednummer 03.01.03, NM sb. 319. The TRB settlement at RAKbba was found through a 45-minute survey in October 1989 and later in a test excavation in July 1993. Survey documented the presence of a Late TRB EN–MNA 1 site, but no organics or culture layer was detected in the test excavations. All finds were in the plow zone. The sample excavation consisted of a 2 m machine-excavated test trench (Trench 1) and 4 m² test pits excavated by hand (T1–4). This site also forms part of the series of Neolithic sites on the high ground between Illerup Sand and Svenstrup in the eolian sandy elevations of the terrain. The site is located on one of the sandy slopes at c. 5 m asl.

The northeast corner of the field was a lowland covered with redeposited soil. A trench (Trench 1) was dug here parallel to the eastern edge of the field. The ditch was 5 m inside the field and 5 m south of the field's northeast corner. It was 2.0 m long, 1.0 m wide and 1.3 m deep and excavated with a machine to expose any wetland deposits with outcast materials or residues of organic matter. no wetland was detected and there were neither finds nor organics. Stratigraphy from below: moraine clay with gravel, 32 cm sand, 20 cm dark brown sand with organic material (probably redeposited peat), 6 cm eolian sand, 10 cm sand with humus, an older plow zone, 48 cm sandy fill.

The site belongs to the late EN–MNA I to judge from the one ornamented sherd, a small funnel beaker. The flint inventory fits nicely with this dating. Out of 17 fragments of sharpened axes, seven derive from four-sided polished thin-butted flint axes (EN–MNA I), a fragment of a dagger, and a flake knife, pointing most toward late EN. A large transverse 'bear arrow' and a fine tooth, denticulated piece suggest EN. The many large scrapers and a single flake axe could also belong to late EN–MNA I. Several objects are from later contexts. One arrowhead is a prelude to a Late Neolithic type. A number of pots are from the Iron Age.

This is fairly homogeneous material from the Middle TRB. The vast majority of the finds come from surface collection, so the site must be almost destroyed. However, the presence of ceramics could indicate that material is still being plowed up but intact organic material was not found. The site must be seen in the context of the contemporary widespread settlement on Illerup Sand and its surroundings, identified by numerous sites recognized in that area (RAKbaf, bap, baq, bbe, bbt, bdj, bdl and bdm).

13. VISbao (aka Smakkerup Huse)

This is the site we excavated on a large scale and the subject of the next chapter.

Summary

We learned a very important lesson with the testing program, specifically that the period of the transition between the Mesolithic and Neolithic was one of maximum transgression and consequent erosion of latest Mesolithic and earliest Neolithic settlement and outcast layers. Very few places have *in situ* deposits either as a cultural layer in a settlement or as an outcast layer from this critical transition period. There is relatively little primary evidence for this transition along the coast of the Saltbæk Vig. This of course makes our focus on the transition to agriculture in southern Scandinavia more difficult. At the same time, it may help to explain why there is so little *in situ* evidence available for this period.

Eolian sand was observed in many of the test excavations and likely marks a period in the landscape history of Saltbæk Vig associated with the drainage of the area at the end of the 19th century. Because this sand normally buries archaeological materials that are Mesolithic and Neolithic and is directly beneath the plow zone it is unlikely that it was deposited prior to recent times. The exposure of large areas of sand when the attempt to drain the Saltbæk Vig was made would seem to be the most likely time for this deposit to have developed.

It was also the case that large oyster shells were encountered in many of the Mesolithic sites but not in the Neolithic ones. Because many of these Mesolithic sites were redeposited in secondary position by the transgressions, there were no intact middens. Nevertheless, the presence of these shells, including burned examples at Smakkerup Huse, suggest that oyster was a common food source in this area in the Mesolithic and that *køkkenmøddinger* may well have been present at some sites.

There were several candidates for larger excavation including TMMbdv, the Early Neolithic site on top of Lindebjerg, TMMbfv, Saltmade, with the fish fence and trap, or BREbbd, Engelsborg, with the Mesolithic settlement area. In the end we chose to begin larger excavations at a rich Mesolithic site, VISbao, Smakkerup Huse. We had tested this site in 1989 and knew that it had potential. We thought we would be able to excavate other sites in the Saltbæk Vig area later in the project but large excavations can become long-term projects. This one certainly did.

Chapter 4

Smakkerup Huse

Introduction

The choice of Smakkerup Huse as the first (and only) major·excavation of the Saltbæk Vig Project was largely fortuitous. The locality was not identified through survey. In fact, the site probably would not have been recognized in field survey as it is in pasture and therefore covered with grass. Columbus found the place many years ago and he and Bjarne Larsen did some digging at the site in the 1970s when they were young. Columbus also took Lisbeth to do a small excavation at the site in the 1980s. It was surprising to see the better quality of preservation of the 1970s artifacts, compared with the materials we excavated in the mid-'90s. No doubt the lowering of the water table, acid rain, and the general drying of the sediments are responsible for the poorer preservation of more recent materials.

We knew about the site from conversations with Lisbeth and, in fact, did a test excavation there in 1989 while waiting for the harvest and the fields to be ready for survey. We knew that preservation at the site was good and that it offered a chance for finding bone and wood artifacts from the Mesolithic. We did not know we would spend three years (1995–1997) at the site and the rest of the allotted time for the Saltbæk Vig Project.

Carl and Bente Jensen, the property owners, were most kind and hospitable during the many weeks we spent there. My second daughter Erika joined us for the summer season in 1996. I was a bit anxious before she arrived about whether she would take to the hard, but delicate, work in the mud. It would be difficult if she didn't, but it all worked out and she quickly became one of our best crew members.

Part of the site was under a railroad bed from the 18th century, when a train and tracks connected this area to a larger network for transporting sugar beets to the factory. The railroad grade may also have protected some of the site at Smakkerup Huse. We had to remove some of the old railroad bed over the area of our excavations.

Excavations at Smakkerup Huse

Smakkerup Huse is a Middle and Late Ertebølle site. It is important because it provides stratigraphical evidence of the Littorina transgressions in the area, because it offers an example of a shoreline activity area with fishing and a boat landing, because of insights the organic remains provide about the economy and seasonality of the settlement, and because of an unusual painted pebble. The Smakkerup Huse excavations are only briefly summarized in this volume as the results of the investigation have been presented in previous publications (Hede 1999; 2003; Larsen 2000; Price *et al.* 2003; Price and Gebauer 2005).

Smakkerup Huse is located on the inlet at the headwaters of the former Saltbæk Vig on western Sjælland just north of Kalundborg (Fig. 4.1). The prehistoric site was located directly on the coastline at the juncture of the Bregninge stream and the inlet (Fig. 4.2). Today the water level in the inlet is kept artificially low at 1.5 m below modern sea level, making it possible to excavate the site from dry land. This area would have been a small island during the higher sea levels of the Late Atlantic and Subboreal transgressions. The island was about 1 km² in size as defined by the 2.5 m elevation contour. At Smakkerup Huse the Mesolithic deposits on land such as the living area, possible kitchen midden, and burials, etc.,

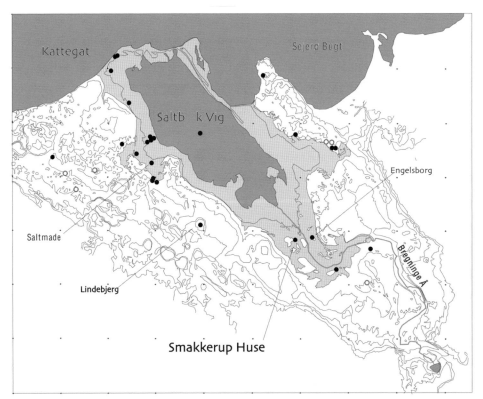

Fig. 4.1. The Saltbæk Vig inlet showing the site of Smakkerup Huse, the neighboring Late Ertebølle site of Engelsborg and the Early Neolithic long barrow at Lindebjerg. Saltmade is an Early Ertebølle site. The light gray around the Saltbæk Vig is the reclaimed land between 0.0 and -1.5 msl.

had been removed by wave erosion during the Subboreal transgression. Only the off-shore activities were preserved including an *in situ* fishing and boat landing area from the Middle Ertebølle, discarded objects, and material washed out from the cultural layers on land.

During the four field seasons in 1989 and 1995–97 (Fig. 4.3), the prehistoric coastline was explored over a stretch of about 40 m. In 1989, a 43 m long trench, 1 m wide, was made from higher to lower elevations on the former coast at Smakkerup Huse. This excavation produced a transect through land, beach, upper foreshore, and marine deposits, documenting the proximity of the site to the prehistoric coastline. This northwest facing coast was heavily exposed to erosion by the sea. However, a sheltered area was found in the lee of the east side of a small point on the shoreline. Perhaps a meander of the Bregninge River carved this curved niche and also created the depression in this area during the meltwater runoff from the last glaciation.

Excavations in 1995–97 exposed this area (Fig. 4.4). An *in situ* fishing and boat landing area from Middle Ertebølle was recovered in this sheltered place. The excavation was done in units of 1 m² following the geological layers subdivided into levels of 10 cm thickness when necessary. All sediments from the excavations were water-sieved in order to recover small

Fig. 4.2. 1852 map of Saltbæk Vig and Bregninge. Red star shows location of Smakkerup Huse.

Fig. 4.3. Excavation and crew at Smakkerup Huse: Kasper Johansen, Gitte Gebauer, and Mike Stafford.

objects from the deposits. Some small 1 m² tests were dug by hand and long trenches were dug by machine. Careful excavations by hand took place in the larger units expanded from the trenches.

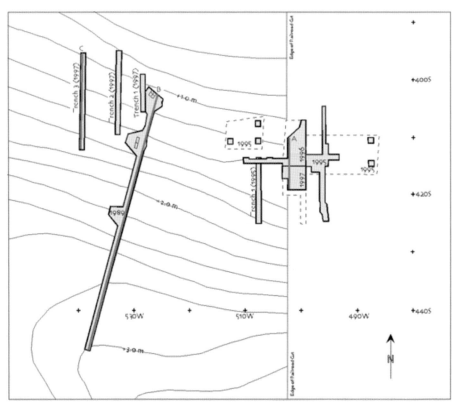

Fig. 4.4. Excavations at Smakkerup Huse. Year of excavation is noted for the various units. The site grid has an arbitrary 0/0 datum. Contour interval is 25 cm. The vertical line near the center of the plan marks the edge of the railroad bed. The section in Fig. 4.6 was made in the trench from 1989.

Geology

The sedimentary sequence at Smakkerup Huse displayed a complicated interaction of transgressions and regressions by the sea, as well as the effects of the isostatic rebound of the land following the last glaciation (Fig. 4.5). The geologists Nanna Noe-Nygård and Signe Ulfeldt Hede studied several sections at the site. The following comments about the stratigraphy are based on their investigations as well as information from the cultural remains (Hede 2003; Price *et al.* 2003; Price and Gebauer 2005). Three episodes of transgression were represented: High/Late Atlantic, and an early and a later high stand during the Subboreal transgression.

Prior to human occupation at Smakkerup Huse the local environment must have included a freshwater swamp and a woodland populated by alder, elm, and oak trees. The original shore was a beach ridge (layer 41 and 39) from the last glaciation, bordering the freshwater peat with a lot of wood (layer 8), probably created by the rising ground water level during the early Atlantic Transgression.

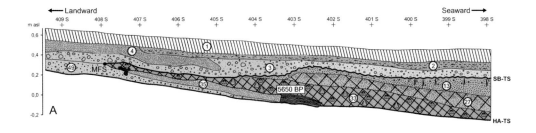

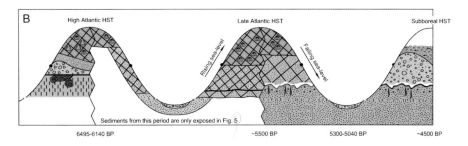

Fig. 4.5. Geological interpretation of the deposits in Trench 2 at Smakkerup Huse. A. Drawing of a portion of the section at Smakkerup Huse. B. Interpretation of deposits in terms of transgressions and regressions.

This peat is dated to from a piece of wood found in the peat in a core. A section drawing of 10 m of the trench appears in Figure 4.6 and a photo of the section in Figure 4.7.

The radiocarbon dates from Smakkerup Huse and their calibrations are shown in Figure 4.8. Continued rising groundwater at the beginning of the High Atlantic Littorina transgression killed off the trees and produced a drowning horizon of grey sand, tree stumps and fallen tree trunks (layer 35). An *in situ* elm tree trunk from the top of this layer was dated to 5060 BC. A fully marine environment was created when the High Atlantic Littorina transgression flooded the Saltbæk Vig area. This transgression created the most marine environment at Smakkerup Huse when marine sediments were deposited in their most landward position. The maximum flooding surface was found at an elevation of about 0.80 m asl and is used as a proxy for the coastline at this time period. The top of this deposit reflected the regression following the High Atlantic Littorina transgression; a lower sea level and a brackish environment was indicated by increasingly sandy marine gyttja and the decreasing size of marine mollusks. Based on a re-evaluation of the Vedbæk investigation two transgressive events, the High and the Late Atlantic transgression, can be merged into a single event beginning around 4800 BC and ending shortly before the beginning of the Subboreal around 4000 BC (Christensen 1995; Hede 2003).

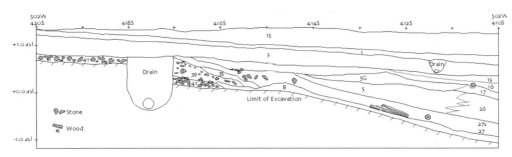

Fig. 4.6. *A 10 m stratigraphic section at Smakkerup Huse. North–south running section at the sheltered area used as fishing zone and boat landing. Layer description: 15. Railroad fill. 1. Plow zone. 3. Sand, gravel, and stones from the later Subboreal Highstand. 13. Sand mixed with gyttja, pebbles and crushed shells. Erosion horizon from the early Subboreal highstand. 16. Sterile brown sandy gytja. Early Subboreal transgression. 5G (gravel) organic rich sand with gravel and pebbles and the associated brackish bay deposit of shell gyttja, layer 17. 5. Organic rich sand, fine grained, and the associated brackish bay deposit of shell gyttja, layer 26. Together layer 5 and 5G form the 'sandbar', 27. Marine shell gyttja mixed with more sand toward the top and towards the coast. Grading into a more marine shell gyttja toward the bottom and seawards, layer 33, not in this section. High Atlantic transgression. 35. Grey sand and fallen tree trunks. Beginning of High Atlantic transgression. 39. Sand mixed with gravel and pebbles. Shoreline erosion. 8. Freshwater peat. 41. Pleistocene beach ridge.*

Fig. 4.7. *Section B, 43 m stratigraphic section at Smakkerup Huse, 1989.*

The first habitation at Smakkerup Huse was related to these marine deposits and is dated by a burned hazel nutshell to 4940 cal BC and by a bone point to 4990 cal BC. Soot on a fragment of a ceramic lamp found at the western end of the site was dated to 4470 cal BC. These dates indicated a Middle Ertebølle, the Stationsvej phase, or slightly earlier period of occupation.

The subsequent deposits involved a sandbar in close proximity to the shoreline deposits. The interface between the sandbar and the brackish bay deposits is an almost solid heap of shells, mainly small *Cardium* and only a few oyster shells. The organic rich sand and the marine shell gyttja coarsened upwards to coarsegrained sand mixed with gravel and pebbles reflecting a high energy environment close to the coast amid continued sea level fall. A dog bone has been dated to 4230 cal BC. The artifactual materials indicate that

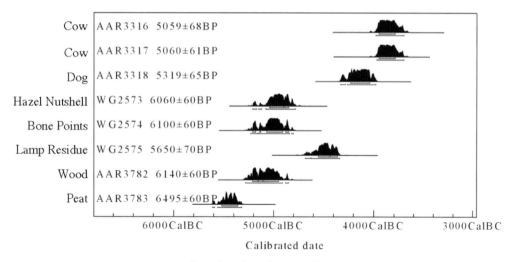

Cow	AAR3316	5059±68BP
Cow	AAR3317	5060±61BP
Dog	AAR3318	5319±65BP
Hazel Nutshell	WG2573	6060±60BP
Bone Points	WG2574	6100±60BP
Lamp Residue	WG2575	5650±70BP
Wood	AAR3782	6140±60BP
Peat	AAR3783	6495±60BP

6000CalBC 5000CalBC 4000CalBC 3000CalBC

Calibrated date

Fig. 4.8. Radiocarbon dates from Smakkerup Huse.

the layer was deposited during the Late Ertebølle, the Ålekistebro phase. Artifacts in this layer were either thrown out from the site or washed out from deposits on land. These layers document a clearly flooded transgressive surface by the high number of cultural remains that were washed out from deposits on land and were now lying horizontally or following the slope of the marine layers. This is the time of maximum transgression in Saltbæk Vig; it occurred during the Late Atlantic/ Early Subboreal and dates somewhere between 4200 and 3600 cal BC. Two bone fragments of domestic cow from this layer have been radiocarbon dated to 3930 cal BC and 3920 cal BC. These two fragments are probably remnants of an Early Neolithic horizon at the site.

The deposit associated with the subsequent rise in sea level was a sterile, brown sandy gyttja layer on top of the transgression surface. This layer reached only as far landwards as the previous brackish bay deposits. The following erosion horizon of sand mixed with gyttja, pebbles, and crushed shells was deposited during the high stand of the early Subboreal transgression at a time when the isostatic uplift outpaced sea level rise. Relative sea level started to fall and a reed swamp formed a growth horizon in the sediments during the time of the lowest sea level in the Subboreal. The artifacts in this layer were similar to those at the top of the sandbar. They were either washed out from cultural layers on land or redeposited from the underlying layers.

A transgressive surface of erosion marked the renewed rise in sea level during the Subboreal period. The transgression removed the habitation area on land and reached an elevation of approximately 2.5 m asl. Landwards, very coarse sediments, a mix of sand, gravel, and rocks, were deposited in a high-energy environment; finer particles were deposited seawards. Except in the sheltered area these transgressive deposits cut into the older, near shore sediments. Two pieces of polished axes were found in this layer supporting a date to the Subboreal and Neolithic. In terms of artifacts this rich layer included a mix from all the occupations at Smakkerup Huse, but organic remains were not preserved. Recent plowing and fill for the railroad track topped the sequence.

Results of excavations

The intact fishing area and boat landing were found in the first marine horizon related to the High Atlantic transgression and regression and the Middle Ertebølle habitation. A scattered pavement of cobble stones extended 3–4 m along the coast and the same distance from the shore. The most landwards distribution of the marine gyttja is used as proxy for the coastline. In addition, four large flat stone slabs and about ten smaller flat stones were placed as stepping-stones to facilitate foot traffic 6–7 m from the shore through the reeds to open water. Similar stone pavements have been found at other Ertebølle sites like Tybrind Vig and Bloksbjerg (Andersen 1985; Westerby 1927 respectively). A wreck of a dugout canoe with a fireplace (several examples are known) was lying at the end of stone-filled area perhaps indicating an area of open water. A total of 48 bone awls were found, mainly within the cobble stone area, some stuck between the stones of the pavement. The bone awls were probably used as spear tips for fishing. No leisters were found. A woven wicker fragment from that area might be part of a fish trap. The wicker was made using heather or willow in the same double plaiting-single twig pattern as a piece found at Tågerup across the Øresund in Sweden (Karsten and Knarrström 2001a, 289). Wooden stakes of hazel were found both in vertical and horizontal positions (17 versus 25 stakes respectively) and might have been used for stationary fish traps as at Halskov (Pedersen 1997, 124), or for tying up smaller fish traps or canoes; the positions of the stakes did not reveal a regular pattern.

Fig. 4.9. Red deer antler and steppingstone at Smakkerup Huse.

Other cultural remains found in this layer include discarded waste and washed-out materials from the settlement on land. A large pair of red deer antler attached to the skullcap was located next to a stepping-stone (Fig. 4.9). Several points of the antler had been broken off or removed by cutting. The antler rack might have been placed here to preserve it for the future or it might have been garbage and tossed out after the best parts had been used. An antler axe with shaft hole near the base of the older Ertebølle type (Andersen 1995b) also

Fig. 4.10. *Fishing and boat landing area showing the shoreline, a cobble stone pavement, flat steppingstones, the canoe wreck and two other canoe fragments, a complete set of antlers, two bark sheets, besides a number of vertical wooden stakes.*

belongs to this horizon together with a pointed antler weapon with a shaft hole, an antler retouchoir, a cut piece of antler and one of bone, a bird bone needle, and a hairpin, 4 bone points and 2 fish hooks. Closest to the coast in a zone about 1.0–1.5 m wide, the sediments were almost completely organic and packed with wood chips — probably from the production of canoes, burned and worked pieces of wood, wooden sticks, twigs and roots, pieces of bark, nutshells and cooking stones. Among the washed-out materials retrieved further from the shore were two sheets of bark, perhaps for use as floor cover, similar to what was found at Lystrup Enge (Andersen 1996). Several pieces of tree fungus appeared; one large fragment had been worked to a felt-like condition. Most cultural remains were recovered within 5 m of the shoreline; beyond this distance only a few wooden stakes and boat fragments were found.

The Late Ertebølle horizon was much richer in cultural remains than the Middle Ertebølle layers but included the same repertoire of finds. Table 4.1 shows the number of finds in the Middle and Late Ertebølle layers. The mixed deposits from the Subboreal (Layer 3) included material eroded from the settlements through Middle and Late Ertebølle as well as the early Subboreal. In general 12–16% of the finds derive from Middle Ertebølle, the bulk of the cultural remains come from Late Ertebølle layers, and 20% of the flint was found in the mixed Subboreal deposits. Organic remains such as fauna, fish bones, nutshells, and wooden objects were not preserved in the mixed Subboreal layer.

The flint found at Smakkerup Huse comprised 26,693 items, including unretouched pieces, cores, and burned pieces. The retouched flint comprises only 588 pieces or 2% of the flint (Table 4.2). Of the retouched flint, the axes make up 9.2%, the points 55.8%, retouched flakes 8.8 %, and retouched blades 17.5%. These four categories make up 91.3% of the total retouched flint from the site, and 89.3–94.3% of the individual layers. Other tool types like different kinds of scrapers (1.3–3.9%), drills (3.0–5.5%), and burins (0–4.5%) account for 6–10% of the retouched flint in the individual layers. The appearance of these tool types is highly variable. The chronological difference in the flint inventory between the Middle and Late Ertebølle layers is reflected in the proportion of core and flake axes: 71% core axes and 29% flake axes in Middle Ertebølle, 22% core axes and 78% flake axes in Late Ertebølle (Table 4.3). The predominance of flake axes is typical of Late Ertebølle. Specialized core axes are present in both horizons, but those from the Middle Ertebølle period derive from the western end of the site.

Change in projectile point types was both limited and very gradual (Table 4.4). The Middle Ertebølle form, the Stationsvej type, was dominant throughout the sequence constituting 50–79% of the points in the Middle and Late Ertebølle layers as well as the mixed deposits from the final Subboreal layer (Vang Petersen 1984). Between 2% and 7% of arrowheads of the Trylleskov type were present throughout the sequence. The latest type, Ålekistebro, was absent in the Middle Ertebølle layers and made up 10% and 27% of the arrowheads in the Late Ertebølle and the final Subboreal layers respectively.

Table 4.1. Percentages of different categories of finds at Smakkerup Huse dating from Middle and Late Ertebølle and the mixed deposits from the Subboreal.

Layer	33/27	55,5G,13	3	Total
Period	Middle EB	Late EB	Mixed/Sub-B.	
Flint	12	68	20	26,693 pieces
Fauna	13	86	1	1762 bones
Fish bones	15	85	0	421.8 g
Nut shells	16	83	1	302.6 g
Pottery	7	93	0	17 sherds
Wooden stakes	49	51	0	86 stakes
Bone awls	86	14	0	54 awls
Antler/bone tools	65	35	0	23 pieces

Fauna includes the bones identified to species. Fish bones and hazelnut shells measured by dry weight in grams. Antler/bone tools include worked pieces other than bone awls.

Table 4.2. Amount of retouched artifacts from the different layers at Smakkerup Huse.

Layer	33/27	%	5	%	5G	%	13	%	3	%	Total	% ret. flint
Period	Middle EB		Late EB		Late EB		Late EB		Mixed			
Axes	14	21.2	11	7.6	6	6.9	6	4.7	15	9.6	52	9.2
Points	14	21.2	88	61.1	50	57.5	74	58.3	99	63.5	328	55.8
Ret. flakes	9	13.6	15	10.4	10	11.5	11	8.7	7	4.5	52	8.8
Ret. blades	22	33.3	17	11.8	16	18.4	24	18.9	24	15.4	103	17.5
Scrapers	2	3	0	0	3	3.4	5	3.9	2	1.3	10	2.4
Drills	2	3	8	5.5	0	0	7	5.5	6	3.8	23	3.9
Burins	3	4.5	4	2.7	2	2.3	0	0	2	1.3	11	1.9
Total	66	2	144	2	87	2	127	2	156	3	588	2

Table 4.3. Distribution of core and flake axes by layer at Smakerrup Huse.

Layer	33/27	%	5	%	5G	%	13	%	3	%	Total	
Period	Middle EB		Late EB		Late EB		Late EB		Mixed			
Core axes	10	71	3	27	2	22	0	0	4	27	19	37
Flake axes	4	29	8	73	9	78	1	100	11	73	33	63
Total	14	100	11	100	11	100	1	100	15	100	52	100

Table 4.4. Types of transverse arrowheads by layer at Smakkerup Huse.

Layer	33/27	%	5	%	5G	%	13	%	3	%	Total	
Period	Middle EB		Late EB		Late EB		Late EB		Mixed			
Trylleskov	1	7	5	6	1	1	0		2	1	9	3
Stationsvej	11	79	52	58	49	55	20	57	51	49	183	56
Ålekistebro	0	0	5	6	10	11	6	17	27	28	48	15
Pref./frag.	2	14	27	30	29	33	9	26	21	22	88	27
Total	14	100	89	100	89	100	35	100	101	100	328	101

Pottery

There is no evidence of polished flint or other flint artifacts typical of Funnel Beaker below the mixed Subboreal layer. The pottery in the Middle and Late Ertebølle layers includes 17 sherds: one from an oval lamp; eight sherds belong to a small cup with a pointed bottom, typical of Ertebølle; a low neck fragment with a splayed rim, also typical Ertebølle; and some side sherds. None of the sherds is particularly thick walled; four are less than 1 cm thick and could be interpreted as Funnel Beaker sherds (Gebauer 1995; Koch 1998). However thin-walled Late Ertebølle pottery has also been found at the Mesolithic site of Ringkloster (Andersen 1998).

Fauna

The bone and shell finds document the subsistence activities of the inhabitants of Smakkerup Huse. The mammal, bird, and toad bones were analyzed and described by Tine Trolle Larsen and Signe Ulfeldt Hede. Charlotte Sedlacek Larsen reported on the fish remains.

Except for the appearance of cattle in the Late Ertebølle layers, the fauna reveal no substantive evidence of changes in the economy through time at Smakkerup (Table 4.5). The three big game animals: red deer and roe deer, and wild boar make up 95% and 93% respectively in the Middle and Late Ertebølle layers, with a minor change in proportions of red deer and roe deer (Fig. 4.11). Fur-bearing animals might be slightly more important in the Middle Ertebølle; more species are represented in the much larger bone assemblage from Late Ertebølle (12 versus 18 species).

Two species of domesticated animals were found, *Canis familiaris* and *Bos domesticus*. Dogs were found in both Middle and Late Ertebølle layers. Cattle were found in the mixed Late Ertebølle–Early Neolithic layers dating from c. 3930 and 3920 BC. The five cow bones come from different parts of the animal and could be from the same individual. Aurochs had long been extinct on Zealand; these bones can only derive from domesticated animals. The cattle were slaughtered at an adult age suggesting that pasture and fodder was available and providing evidence of herding and the beginning of animal husbandry. It does appear that there was Early TRB presence at the site, albeit one that left few remains.

Table 4.5. Species of fauna in Middle and Late Ertebølle contexts at Smakkerup Huse.

	Bones	Species	Primary game		Domestic		Fur bearing				Wild cat	Beaver	Water vole
					Dog	Cow	Fox	Squirrel	Marten	Otter			
	n	n	n	%	n	n	n	n	n	n	n	n	n
Middle Ertebølle	226	12	215	##	1	–	1	1	1	2	–	–	–
Late Ertebølle	1519	18	##	##	38	4	–	–	3	11	10	3	7
Subboreal	17	4	16	–	–	–	–	–	–	–	–	–	1

	Birds					Marine mammals		Miscellaneous	
	Eagle	Swan	Capercaille	Duck	Blackbird	Grey seal	Ring seal	Toad	Hedgehog
	n	n	n	n	n	n	n	n	n
Middle Ertebølle	2	1	–	–	–	1	–	–	1
Late Ertebølle	–	2	3	1	2	2	1	1	5
Subboreal	–	–	–	–	–	–	–	–	–

For the distribution of red deer, roe deer and wild boar, see Fig. 4.11.

Cattle bones have been found at a number other Ertebølle sites such as Bloksbjerg (Westerby 1927), Dyrholm (Mathiassen *et al.* 1942), Norsminde (Andersen 1991), and Ølby Lyng (Brinch Petersen 1970). A contemporary find of cattle at Åkonge has been placed in the earliest Funnel Beaker (Fischer 2002). Another interesting site in this context is the settlement and long barrow at Lindebjerg dated at 3960–3660 or 3790 cal BC (Liversage 1981; Fischer 2002, 366). Lindebjerg is a plateau hill with several Early Neolithic Funnel Beaker sites, megaliths and some cow bones located only 4–5 km, or less than an hour on foot, from Smakkerup Huse. Test excavations at Lindebjerg were described in Chapter 3.

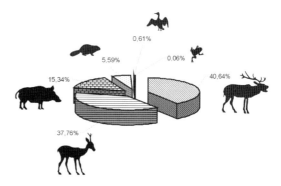

Fig. 4.11. Distribution of the three big game animals and other species at Smakkerup Huse.

Marine foods were important in both periods of the Ertebølle occupation. In the Middle Ertebølle layers documented by the fishing area with fish hooks, fish bones, bone awls, vertical wooden stakes, and the canoe. In the Late Ertebølle fish hooks,

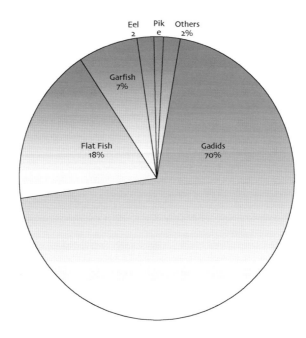

Fig. 4.12. Percentage distribution of fish species.

wooden stakes, boat fragments, many fish bones, and a fish-eating dog with a stable carbon isotope value of –10.2 per mil provide evidence for fishing. At the moment, this dog has the most marine diet in the world for a terrestrial animal. The fish taken were dominated by gadids (70%) and flatfish (18%); other species included garfish (7%), eel (2%), and miscellaneous (3%), in all 12 species (Fig. 4.12). Interestingly only 2% are freshwater fish in spite of the location of the site at a river mouth. The species and the small size of individuals indicate near shore fishing in shallow water during the summer months, perhaps using stationary fish traps (Enghoff 1986). Large individuals of cod and whiting could be caught using line and hook. Hunting of marine mammals and birds appears to have been limited.

Shellfish collection took place in all periods. A number of burned oyster shells are evidence of use for human consumption, probably during the cooler months of the year (Milner 2002). Other mollusks like common periwinkle, cockle, and blue mussel were likely eaten but there is no direct evidence to prove it. A shell midden was not found but could have been eroded.

Flora

Plant materials include both edible food and raw materials that could be used for medicinal or practical purposes (Table 4.6). Roasting or charring show evidence of human use in some cases, while others can only be considered potentially useful.

Table 4.6. *Plant remains from water sieving of soil samples through 2 mm sieve at Smakkerup Huse (identified by Sarah Mason).*

Layer	Co-ordinates	Corylus avellana L.	Quercus robur L./ petraea (Mattuschka) Liebl.	Crataegus L. spp.	Other
5	413S 496W		(abscission scar)		
5	413S 496W		1f pericarp; 2f inner pericarp; 7w + 11f imm./sterile acorn/ cupule; 15± w. buds + several bud scales; (1f wood charcoal)	(8 cf. *monogyna* pyrenes)	4f twiggy wood; 2w + 1f petiole/ peduncle/ receptacle; 1f charred ? parenchyma?
5	414S 494W	1f pericarp			
5	414S 495W	2 whole small nuts			
5	414S 496W		(bud)	(*monogyna* – fruit)	
5	417S 496W		± whole blackened cotyledon		
5+10	414S 496W		1 imm./sterile acorn/ cupule; (1f. ?water–worn wood charcoal)	1 semi-imm. fruit; 1 pyrene	
8	415S 498W		1 cotyledon		
8	415S 498W		1 blackened/flattened cotyledon	(1 blackened pyrene)	
10 local	412S 496W	1f pericarp; 1 nut with weevil hole	1 imm./sterile acorn/ cupule		1 petiole/peduncle
10	413S 496W	5f pericarp	(1 bud)		
12	408S 496W		(1 bud)	1 pyrene	
12	409S 496W		(1 bud)	2 (+1f) pyrenes; (1 imm. fruit)	1f wood charcoal; 1f ? rhizome with node
12	411S 496W			1 blackened pyrene	
12	412S 496W		(1 inner pericarp); 6 imm.sterile acorn/ cupule; (2 buds)	(1 ± mature fruit)	1f wood charcoal; 1f wood; 1f indet. vegetative tissue
12 lower	409S 496W		(1w cotyledon)		

All items are uncharred unless specified - some are blackened but not aparently charred.
Identifications in brackets indicate that identification of taxon is only as cf.; f = fragment, w = whole;
imm. = immature

Fig. 4.13. Jens Nielsen with an example of the two sizes of hazel stakes.

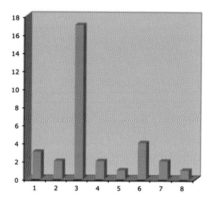

Fig. 4.14. Histogram of hazel stake diameter (cm) at Smakkerup Huse. X axis = stake diameter; Y axis = number of stakes.

The remains listed in Table 4.6 were recovered through water sieving of soil samples through 2 mm nets. Further testimony to the importance of plant resources was provided by the find of a digging stick similar to the one from Lindholm in the Late Ertebølle layers (Dencker 1997, 90).

Active forest management and systematic harvest of hazel for stakes should be considered in this context. Jens Nielsen excavated and described most of these wooden poles (Fig. 4.13). A plot of the diameter of pointed wooden hazel stakes was particularly informative (Fig. 4.14). There were two peaks in this graph at 3 cm and 7 cm corresponding to 7- and 16-year-old harvested branches. It implies that hazel trees were cared for, if not cultivated. Pruning is thought to be important in the case of hazel to produce straight branches for use.

The stakes were made from coppiced hazel. The growth rings indicate that most of the stakes were cut in their 7th year when their diameter was around 3 cm. Based on the interrupted growth in the rings, these stakes were cut either in the spring or autumn. This distinct harvesting pattern shows evidence of active forest management in the Middle Ertebølle, as also seen at Halskov (Christensen 1997, 156). The long straight condition of these hazel poles and the selective years of cutting document the management and maintenance of hazel groves by these Mesolithic foragers. For critique and discussion see Out *et al.* (2020). The sharpened stakes served as posts for fixed fishing equipment and other uses in the waters next to the settlement at Smakkerup Huse.

Approximately five fragments of canoes, dugout from the trunks of lime trees, were found in the deeper deposits at Smakkerup Huse. The largest fragment was found on the bottom of Layer 27. It was 175 cm in length, 36 cm wide, and had the fragmentary remains of a clay-lined fireplace inside the canoe. Several pieces of dugouts were observed as smaller fragments found in section during the excavations. A small woven fragment perhaps of willow branches was probably a piece of a fish trap.

Worked artifacts

The bone and antler artifacts at Smakkerup Huse come from a number of categories. There were 74 examples of bone awls (Fig. 4.15), which served at the tips of fishing spears. There were several sharp bone points. Two bird bone needles were found at the site along with a single bone hairpin. Six fragments of bone fish hooks were recovered in the screening process. Two tooth pendants made from a red deer canine and incisor were found (Fig. 4.16). One amber pendant in the shape of Thor's Hammer was found. The larger tooth was both perforated at the tip of the root and incised around the root with a series of lines perpendicular to the long axis of the tooth.

Antler artifacts included two large pieces, one a complete rack still attached to the skullcap of the animal. Both showed signs of working and cutting. Three antler axes were found, two small with a sharp edge and a shaft hole, and one large, with a sharp edge. Several antler retouchoirs were recovered along with other worked pieces of antler. One spurdog spine had been used as a fine piercing tool (Fig. 4.17). Several carved bone fish hooks were also recovered in the excavations (Fig. 4.18).

Finally, there is the painted pebble (Fig. 4.19): a white quartzite pebble, the size and shape of a medium size potato, painted with a design of curvilinear bands and three dots, two at the wide end and one dot at the other end (Price and Gebauer 2005).

The painted pebble was found at such a seawards position, 10–11 m from the shore, that it is unlikely that a

Fig. 4.15. Bone awls from the site of Smakkerup Huse.

Fig. 4.16. An amber pendant and two tooth beads/ pendants.

Fig. 4.17. Utilized spurdog spine (bottom) compared to modern unused specimen.

current or wave action could have moved the stone from the coastline. It must either have been thrown out from the settlement or dropped from a boat by accident or by choice. Also, the black pigment would only have been preserved if the stone was embedded immediately in the dense marine shell gyttja, which provided a water-logged, anaerobic, and low energy environment. L. Larsson (2000, 36) has suggested that ornamented objects were deposited in the vicinity of, but at the same time outside of the settlement, when the use of the artifact was to be terminated but it was still too powerful to be regarded as ordinary refuse. Sørensen (2019) argues for the shallow water deposition of rare objects based on his discoveries at Syltholmfjord on the Danish island of Lolland. The painted pebble at Smakkerup Huse may have been deposited in a similarly intentional manner. Interestingly the amber pendant was found within 0.4 m of the pebble, but 28 cm higher in elevation in the gyttja.

Discussion

A parallel existence of Ertebølle and Funnel Beaker Culture seems unlikely. The presence of a few domesticates suggests a gradual influx of new elements. Flint technology may be the last domain to change. A similar scenario is reflected in the Mesolithic–Neolithic transition in Schleswig-Holstein (Hartz *et al.* 2002, 336). A find of a specialized core axe in a pit with an Early Neolithic pot in Jutland likewise testifies to the longevity of the Ertebølle flint tradition (Skousen 2008). The early domesticates are pre-dated by the import of several types of Neolithic copper and ground stone axes from Continental Europe (Klassen 2002). It should

Fig. 4.18. Fishhooks carved from bone.

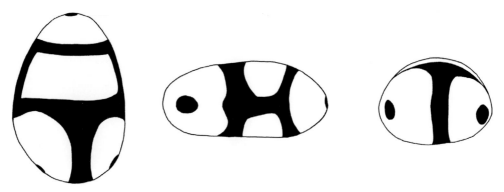

Fig. 4.19. The painted pebble from Smakkerup Huse (approximately half size).

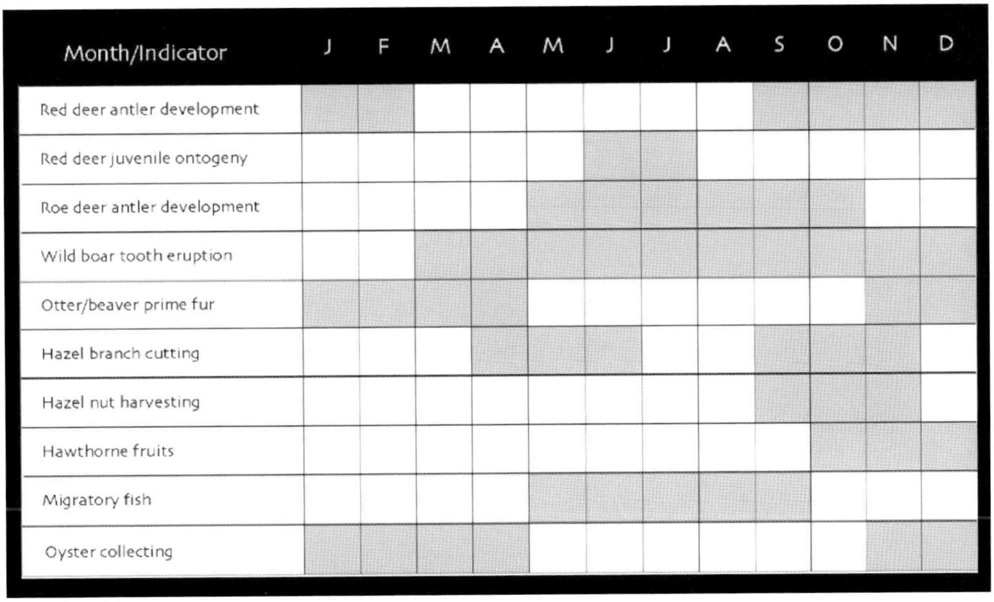

Month/Indicator	J	F	M	A	M	J	J	A	S	O	N	D
Red deer antler development	X	X							X	X	X	X
Red deer juvenile ontogeny							X	X				
Roe deer antler development					X	X	X	X	X	X	X	
Wild boar tooth eruption			X	X	X	X	X	X	X	X	X	X
Otter/beaver prime fur	X	X									X	X
Hazel branch cutting			X	X	X				X	X	X	
Hazel nut harvesting									X	X		
Hawthorne fruits									X	X		
Migratory fish						X	X	X	X			
Oyster collecting	X	X	X								X	X

Fig. 4.20. Seasonality at Smakkerup Huse.

come as no surprise that other elements of Neolithic life could be introduced piece-meal, including the domesticates themselves.

The seasonal indicators from various animals and other resources support an interpretation of a year-round presence at Smakkerup Huse (Fig. 4.20). Unshed red deer antler indicates that animals were killed between September and February. Unshed roe deer antler indicates the period May–November. Red deer calves are born early June and could be hunted in July and August. The birthing time of wild boar in the past is unknown, but spring seems likely, which means piglets could be slaughtered from March to December; the same period as the wild boar tooth eruption took place. Fur-bearing animals would primarily be hunted in the winter. The growth rings on the hazel stakes suggest that some were cut in spring and others in the fall. Hazelnuts and hawthorn were collected in the fall. The eels were present in the summer and early fall; probably most of the fishing took place in summer. Oysters are best in late winter and early spring before they spawn.

The diversity of the subsistence base suggests that this was not a specialized seasonal habitation but, rather, a more permanent residence for a group of people. A continuous year-round habitation cannot be proved or disproved but it seems unlikely the site would be left unattended given the long-term investments in coppiced hazel groves and stationary fish-traps. If sedentism is defined as a place where at least part of the population remains for most of the year, this seems the most likely scenario at Smakkerup Huse. Examples of year-round settlements include other sites like Bjørnsholm (S. H. Andersen 1993b) and Fiskerhuset (Johansson 1999).

Aside from the question of year-round habitation, it would be interesting to know the duration of the settlement(s) at Smakkerup Huse. Together these Middle and Late Ertebølle remains represent a time period of more than a millennium from about 5000 BC to 3900–3800 BC, or about the same length of time as a town like Århus with fortifications dating back to AD 934, has been occupied. A number of Ertebølle sites cover a similar time span, which has spawned a concept of large permanent habitations situated as the main settlement in each fjord system.

At Smakkerup Huse there was no apparent break in the presence of cultural remains throughout the sequence between Middle and Late Ertebølle deposits. The sedimentation record appears to be continuous; except for the transgression surfaces, the sediments grade into one another. The question is whether this apparent continuity represents constant habitation at the site or just constant coastal erosion? If focus of the habitation moved along the coast within the same general area, or was even left for a decade or a generation and then returned to, would such interruptions show up in the archaeological record?

A minor move west along the coast might have taken place in the Middle Ertebølle period where younger elements like specialized core axes and a lamp sherd dated *c.* 4466 BC appeared in the western end of the investigated area. Another Late Ertebølle site, Engelsborg, located within eyesight across the Bregninge River, suggests that the settlement might have moved between the two sides of the river from time to time. At Engelsborg a cultural layer was found without shells but including fireplaces, a number of specialized core axes and a few Ertebølle pot sherds. The outcast layer was gone, no organic material preserved, and no material was available for a radiocarbon date.

Whether the habitation moved along the coast or between the two sides of the river, or two Late Ertebølle sites co-existed across from one another, remains unknown. The data from Smakkerup Huse itself appear to suggest a constant presence at this place at the head of the Saltbæk Vig.

The first settlement at the site must correspond with the Middle Ertebølle boat landing and fishing area. Possibly the Middle Ertebølle habitation was more short-lived and/or included fewer people than the later horizon, or the coastal erosion was more severe since only 12–16% of the different categories of material were found in this horizon. Due to the location of the intact fishing/boating area here, 50% of the wooden stakes and 86% of bone awls were found here (Fig 4.10). Surprisingly other bone and antler tools and worked pieces are also better represented in the Middle Ertebølle layers (65% of the 23 objects). For some reason the composition of the flint inventory was also different, aside from the chronological difference in axe and point types. The Middle Ertebølle flint contained 21.2% axes, 21.2% points, 13.6% retouched flakes, and 33.3% retouched blades, whereas every one of the subsequent Late Ertebølle layers included fewer axes (4.7–7.6%), many more points (57.5–61.1%), about the same amount of retouched flakes (8.7–10.4%) and fewer retouched blades (11.8–18.9%). The reason for these differences is not clear. No substantive differences were found in the economy except more emphasis on red deer than roe deer in Middle Ertebølle.

Likewise, a Late Ertebølle settlement is to be seen in the rich layer at the top of the sandbar. The sandbar itself represents a slow accumulation of a 0.5 m thick layer of eroded material. Though slightly fewer artifacts were present in the lower part of the sandbar; cultural remains, including 31% of all the flint and 82% of the fish bones from the site, were found throughout this very rich layer. The fact that retouched flint tools and the fauna show up in different proportions suggest that the cultural remains in the sandbar are not just washed out from older Middle Ertebølle layers on land but reflect a continuous habitation at the site. Thus, individual settlement periods cannot be distinguished at Smakkerup Huse.

Conclusions

The animal bones document the presence of a variety of terrestrial and marine species in the deposits. The list of mammals, birds, and amphibians includes red deer, roe deer, wild boar, domestic dog, fox, wildcat, marten, otter, gray seal, ring seal, beaver, red squirrel, water vole, bank vole, hedgehog, toad, duck, swan, blackbird, capercaillie, and white-tailed eagle (see Table 4.5). In addition, several bones from domesticated cow were found in the upper levels at Smakkerup, dated to approximately 3800 BC. Also in this mixed layer were two fragments of polished flint axes and a few possible sherds from TRB vessels.

The most abundant terrestrial species were red deer, roe deer, and wild boar. The fur-bearing species, including the dog, had been skinned to remove the pelts. The bone assemblage was heavily fragmented from marrow extraction and tool manufacture. The fish remains recorded a variety of fresh, brackish, and saltwater species, including cod, whiting, herring, plaice, flounder, common dab, garfish, mackerel, bullhead, spurdog, eel, roach, bream, zander, and pike. Most common were cod and flatfish. The individual fish were generally small, suggesting capture in traps or nets. Most of the fish could have been caught at Smakkerup Huse near the shore, rather than in deep water. The majority of these species were likely caught during the warmer months of the year. The faunal remains contained evidence for hunting activities during the summer, fall, and winter.

Shells from many species were present in the deposits but only the oyster showed distinctive evidence of human utilization. Burned shells were observed in some number during the excavations. It does not appear that a shell midden was present at the site but shellfish, especially oyster, were certainly included in the diet. Oysters were likely collected during the colder months of the year. The combined evidence from the plant and animal remains suggests that the inhabitants of Smakkerup Huse lived at the site year-round.

Eight radiocarbon dates from Smakkerup Huse document a sequence of artifacts and deposits from the Middle and Late Ertebølle. The dates come from both artifacts and natural objects. A date of *c.* 5400 BC records the freshwater peat forming in this area prior to the rise of sea level. A date of *c.* 5000 BC on an oak stump in the lower deposits documents the influx of saltwater in this area and the death of large trees at Smakkerup Huse. Other dates on various artifacts help to verify the age of the remains. Radiocarbon dates on the two cow bones place them in the Early Neolithic.

The evidence from Smakkerup Huse suggests that Holocene hunter-gatherers may well have been less mobile than generally assumed. There is reasonable evidence for sedentary occupation of large settlements in the Mesolithic of southern Scandinavia. The excavations at Smakkerup then document the latter part of the Ertebølle period and affirm that there were foragers living 6000–7000 years ago in sedentary communities, successfully exploiting the resources of both the land and the sea. The occupation of the settlement came to an end with the Early Neolithic, based on the tantalizingly few pieces of cow bone, polished axes, and perhaps pottery.

The evidence tells us a great deal about technology and economy, but little about organization or ideology. We are able to answer some of the when, where, and what questions about Mesolithic hunter-gatherers. We know when and where they lived. We know about their raw materials and tools and the remains of the plants and animals they utilized. But there is still a lot we do not know and much for archaeologists to learn.

In the rearview mirror, perhaps we should have spent a few more years in the Saltbæk Vig area, digging more at Lindebjerg and other places. On the other hand, my sense was that our funding at NSF had probably reached its limit for a while and it was time to move on. We next excavated an inland site at Trustrup, which may not have been such a good choice. But that is an accepted risk in excavation. You do not know until you dig.

Chapter 5

Excavations at Trustrup

Introduction

Our next stop involved an attempt to learn something about inland settlement in the Mesolithic and Neolithic. There are many coastal sites in the Mesolithic. One of the important dichotomies (coast–inland) in the debate about the transition from the Mesolithic to the Neolithic involves the utilization of the interior by Neolithic groups as cultivable land became more important (Fig. 5.1). It was frustrating to realize that so many places in the coastal areas had been hit by the transgressions and that archaeological sites from the transition to agriculture had often been destroyed.

A map of the distribution of Ertebølle sites and pointed-butted flint axes as an indication of activity in the Early Neolithic in the northwest Sjælland region (Fig. 5.2) is informative. Ertebølle sites are almost always near water — coastal, riverine, or lacustrine. Pointed-butted axes, which may have been discarded at the place of use, show a much wider distribution, especially inland.

An inland Early Neolithic site should not have suffered damage from transgressions and perhaps would offer a clearer view of what was happening at the transition. The site at Trustrup in the Lille Åmose seemed to be a good candidate for an inland location. The evidence for an Early Neolithic presence in this area is striking and includes a small long dolmen at a low elevation in the Halleby Å valley and a number of animal sacrifices from the Early Neolithic placed in the Lille Åmose and radiocarbon dated to that period (Price and Noe-Nygaard 2009). Both the Lille Åmose and the Store Åmose play a prominent role in Danish Mesolithic and Early Neolithic archaeology with

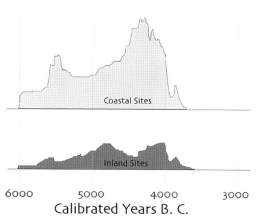

Fig. 5.1. Relative numbers of coastal and inland sites from the Mesolithic (after Persson and Sjögren 1996).

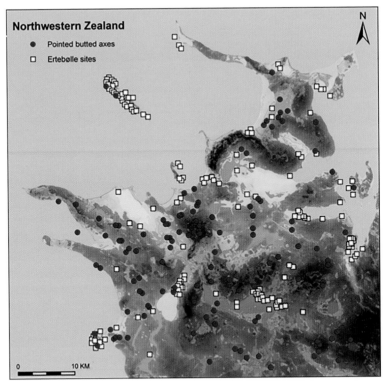

Fig. 5.2. The distribution of Ertebølle sites and pointed-butted axes in the northwest Sjælland (from Schulke 2015).

important sites from both periods in both areas. Both are large bogs that formed in the meltwater lakes of central Sjælland at the end of the Pleistocene (Fig. 5.3).

In retrospect the inland characterization of Trustrup may have been a little hasty. The Little Åmose is a bog and marsh area that lies to the north of Tissø, a lake in the valley of the Halleby stream. The presence of a marine environment in the Little Åmose bog has been debated. It might have happened if the lake of Tissø itself was breached by the sea during the Littorina transgressions. A heavy winter flood in 2005 offered a view of the Ll. Åmose flooded with water (Figs 5.3 and 5.4) and made it seem more likely that this area was indeed marine at the beginning of the Subboreal. Our investigations at Trustrup documented water-deposited sediments at the base of our stratigraphic cuts at the site, but whether these deposits came from fresh, brackish, or saltwater is uncertain.

A second reason for looking into this inland zone was Max Raffn. Max is an amateur archaeologist who lived in the Little Åmose and knew of a number of sites in the area where he had collected archaeological materials. Max is quite a character and very persuasive. He has been raising sturgeon in a garden pond in his front yard for years and dons a scuba mask and snorkel to check on them. In essence Max talked us into digging at Trustrup.

Testing at Gravhøjsmarken

We tested a small site near Trustrup called Gravhøjsmarken, located in Buerup parish, Løve herred, Vestsjællands amt, 03.02.02. Gravhøjsmarken was situated at the northwest corner of a little ice-block lake between the Halleby Å and the Lille Åmose, where coring had documented the presence of substantial Holocene organic deposits in the lake. In late July 2002 five 1 × 1 m test pits were placed in an area where Max Raffn had reported a number of finds from both the Mesolithic and the Early Neolithic. Max has collected c. 30,000 artifacts from the area, dominated by Early Neolithic materials including seven pointed-butted polished flint axes and 18 thin-butted axes, 156 fine denticulated pieces, and 242 flake knives. In addition, Max recovered 116 flakes from polished axes. The collection included 70 flake axes and more than 1500 scrapers, most of which probably belong to the Early Neolithic component of the

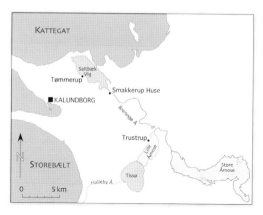

Fig. 5.3. Location of Åmose area in relation to the Saltbæk Vig.

Fig. 5.4. A photo of winter flooding north of Tissø in 2005 provides evidence of the low-lying nature of this area. The Trustrup site is at the right corner of the woods in the upper left (photo: Lisbeth Pedersen).

site. There were both peat and gyttja deposits in the test pits excavated at the site. Two of the five test pits contained a few flaked stone artifacts that had a stone age appearance, but no diagnostic pieces were found. Well-preserved bone remains were encountered in one square. Unfortunately we did not find sufficient material here to justify further excavations. Several other localities around this place appeared to be of interest in a search for Early Neolithic settlement.

Excavations at Trustrup

Excavations were conducted at the site of Trustrup in the Little Åmose over three field seasons in 2001–2003 (Fig. 5.5). The first season involved a few days of testing various places where Max reported finding archaeological remains. Major excavations

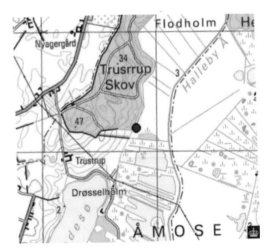

Fig. 5.5. Location of Trustrup excavations in western Sjælland.

Fig 5.6. Excavations at Trustrup, 2002.

were conducted in 2002 and a few days finishing up were spent in 2003. Excavations at Trustrup in 2002 were conducted for 4.5 weeks. Approximately 40 square meters were opened and the archaeological deposits excavated (Fig. 5.6). All sediments from the cultural horizon were water-screened and a variety of stone, ceramic, and bone remains were recovered.

The site is located at, and partly in the southeast corner of, Trustrup Forest. To the east is the now overgrown and drained basin of the Little Åmose. Below the freshwater sediments are meltwater sands. To the west, the terrain rises and the subsoil here consists of meltwater sand or gravel (Fig. 5.5). Elevated near the forest edge, c. 40 m from the excavation, there is an active spring. Between there and the excavation are massive deposits of spring limestone (Danish: *kildekalk*) or travertine that have also been detected in the western part of the excavation.

The geological investigation of the site revealed that it lay in the discharge zone of the spring on the hillside that was depositing substantial amounts of *kildekalk* above the archaeological site. This carbonate deposit was responsible for the preservation of bone at the site. At the same time, however, accumulation of this carbonate in the bone material and subsequent wet–dry processes caused heavy fragmentation of both bone and ceramics. As a consequence, these materials are found only in very small pieces, making identification difficult. A radiocarbon date was obtained on one bone fragment of 3860 cal BC, suggesting that the part of the site indeed dates from the very beginning of the Neolithic. However, distinctively Neolithic materials were found only in the plow zone among the archaeological materials. Because of the fragmentation of material and the absence of other organic remains, excavations were concluded at this locality.

Excavation involved a long trench with a U-shaped extension and a few test pits (Fig. 5.7). Investigations revealed two distinctive horizons under the plow layer, parts of which were subject to systematic excavation. Most of the settlement inventory was flint implements and waste, some ceramics, a few bone points, and numerous small pieces of broken bone. Also included were fish bones, a flake axe, and a small bead made from a pierced circular piece of freshwater mussel shell. A brown peat layer (layer P) containing a substantial amount of archaeological material was found above a well-defined mud layer (layer CL), also with artifacts. The finds from the two layers appear to belong to the same cultural phase, though the stratigraphy suggests that at least two settlement episodes occurred.

The physical excavation of each square meter was similar. The plow layer was excavated by hand and encountered prehistoric remains were collected, bagged, and kept separate. The upper cultural layer, an ancient peat horizon, was carefully excavated with trowel and usually water sieved in a 4 × 4 cm screen. The finds were bagged and kept separate. The lower cultural layer, probably a freshwater mud or gyttja, was also carefully excavated with trowel and water sieved and the finds bagged and kept separate.

No prehistoric features were observed or recorded. However, it should be mentioned that in layer P there were quite a lot of fire-cracked stones. It is uncertain whether these represented a disturbed fireplace or discarded cooking stones. Similarly, there was an accumulation of fire-cracked stones in layer CL. Charcoal and flint have been found in connection with the stones, suggesting that there may have been a disturbed

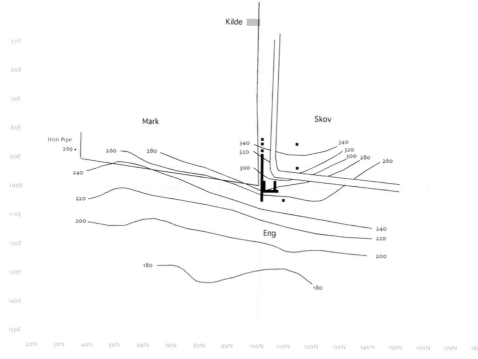

Fig. 5.7. Plan of excavations at Trustrup, 2002. The spring to the west of the site is marked Kilde. The forest at Tustrup is marked Skov. Mark is the field.

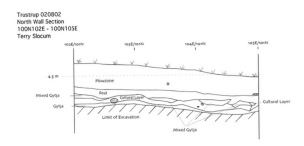

Fig. 5.8. Profile drawing from Trustrup, north wall,
100N102E–100N105E.

fireplace. Disturbances of the site deposits, however, were generally clear and included animal passages and drainage ditches.

The stratigraphy at the site was relatively straightforward (Fig. 5.8). PZ (plow zone) was a homogeneous brown loam. Where the plow zone lay directly on the underlying peat the boundary was sharp but it often diffuse and difficult to distinguish from the plow zone sediment. SA was a sand with a large silt component, yellow to orange due to differential oxidation. This was probably trench spoil from the bottom of the modern adjacent ditch. It occurred as a discrete lamina in the fill of the intrusive pits. P was a very dark brown decomposed peat that retained a fibrous texture. This deposit was probably not detritral mud as we initially thought. It was probably a peat developed primarily from decomposed reeds that invaded the shallow shore as the water level receded or as the lake filled with organic sediment. CL (cultural layer) was a brown loam with snail shells, some pre-cipitate carbonates and a high organic component. We called this the 'cultural layer', 'cultural horizon', 'middle', or 'outcast zone' since it consistently contained the bulk of the artifacts. Most of the artifacts were probably deposited in this sediment but it is possible that some continued to be deposited directly into the overlying peat once it had begun to form. According to Nanna Noe-Nygaard this was an organic mud (gyttja) that formed along the shallow lakeshore. KK (*kildekalk*) was a pale gray clay loam (possibly illuviated clay, i.e., from a B horizon) with a large $CaCO_3$ component increasing with depth upslope. Very hard porous lime may comprise more than 20% of the deposit by volume. This deposit can be distinguished from the basal sediments which are a calcareous mud. It is not known whether this material represents one or more settlement episodes per se, or whether it is exclusively superimposed material from the underlying brown peat. Of course, a combination of both options cannot be ruled out.

In sum, on top of a supposed lake deposit is a cultural layer. This layer appears to consist of organic mud (layer CL) deposited near the shore of the lake basin. The layer is strongly dehydrated, but organic matter in the form of bones is present, albeit in a more or less degraded state. Arrowheads, ceramics, and other datable materials point toward the Ertebølle culture's Stationsvej phase. This is probably an outcast layer along the shore of a dry land area.

The mud (CL) is covered by a layer of a more peaty nature (P). The layer may have emerged as a result of a lower water level than before or as a result of the lake being filled with organic material and thereby giving rise to peat moss. The peat contained a great deal of cultural material, especially towards the bottom of the layer, where the especially heavy objects lay deepest, perhaps as a result of sinking in the layer. It is not known whether the peat surface at one point constituted an actual dwelling area during dry periods or whether it is a matter of discarding artifacts on a damp floor. The former is considered a viable possibility.

Flint artifacts

The flint finds are detailed in Table 5.1. There were approximately 10,925 pieces of worked flint weighing 61 kg. The number of burned pieces of flint totaled 2019 of the total flint, about 18.5%. The number of soft-hammer blades was 565 compared to 155 hard-hammer specimens and the total number of blades 987, compared to 7631 flakes. Flake cores totaled 50 while only eight blade cores were recovered. There were 135 points and 24 preforms for points; 14 flake axes and four specialized core axes. In the each of the categories of retouched flakes and blades, blade knives, and scrapers there were 11 or fewer examples along with eight blade borers. Several of the blade knives had retouched concave edges.

Table 5.1. Flint artifacts at Dragsholm.

	No.
Burned	2019
Flakes	7631
Soft-hammer blade	569
Hard-hammer blade	155
Total blades	987
Flake core	71
Blade core	8
Retouched flake	8
Retouched blade	11
Blade knife	2
Point	135
Point preform	24
Flake axe	14
Core axe	4
Blade scraper	11
Blade borer	8
Total no,	10,925
Weight (g)	61,097.7

Other artifacts

There were also a number of medieval or modern objects in the plow zone, including fragments of glass, bottlecaps, horseshoes, and pieces of iron that suggest residence or at least dumping in this area.

Trustrup pottery

(Anne Birgitte Gebauer)

Most of the pottery is Ertebølle that is often broken between individual U-shaped clay coils revealing indentation from fingers, fingertips, and nails. The maximum thickness of an individual sherd is 13 mm, most sherds are 10–13 mm thick. The maximum size of a visible temper grain is 7 mm, but most are 5–6 mm. The size and shape of the pots cannot be determined. At a fragment of a base, the point is not heavily offset from the rest but joins the vessel wall in a smooth oblique angle. One sherd has chamotte temper (burned clay), an Ertebølle feature.

About five sherds could be Funnel Beaker (Neolithic) because of their denser, fine-grained structure. Some show an 'N' or oblique coil structure. One sherd is curved like the belly of a Funnel Beaker and is only 7 mm thick. Another sherd appears to be a fragment of a flat vessel base. The only decorated sherd came from a straight, slightly funnel shaped rim with an edge smoothed with a finger and decorated with nail impressions. The sherd measures 4.4 × 3.6 × 0.8 cm and has a U-shaped coil structure on one side and an oblique pattern on the other. The temper is crushed granite and a bit of quartz with a maximum grain size is 6 mm. The color is a light grayish–brown.

Faunal remains

Kurt Gron classified the bone material that was highly fragmentary and difficult to identify. The identified species and bone counts show the standard suite of Mesolithic fauna with red deer most common, followed by roe deer and wild boar (Table 5.2). Several species are fur-bearing animals. Bones of horse (*Equus sp.*) are notable and rare in a Mesolithic context and perhaps of more recent origin. Seal bones (*Halichoerus sp.*) are unexpected at an inland site but perhaps not so surprising since marine mammals are known from other inland Mesolithic contexts (e.g., S. H. Andersen 1995a). The seal remains again remind us that Trustrup may not have been so far from the sea. The sheep/goat remains came from the plow zone and are probably historic. Fish included cod (a marine species), pike, and catfish. Duck was identified among the eight bird bones.

Conclusions

Excavations at Trustrup in the Ll Åmose in 2002 were conducted for 4.5 weeks. The more diagnostic artifacts at the site point to a relatively late part of the Ertebølle

Table 5.2. Identified animal bones from Trustrup.

Taxon	Common name	NF	MNI
Cervus elaphus	Red deer	508	9
Capreolus capreolus	Roe deer	444	14
Sus scrofa	Wild boar	199	6
Canis familiaris	Domestic dog	49	2
Castor fiber	Beaver	19	1
Equus caballus	Horse	7	1
Lutra lutra	Otter	6	1
Capra/Ovis spp.	Sheep/goat	3	1
Felis silvestris	Wild cat	2	1
Martes martes	Marten	2	1
Vulpes vulpes	Fox	2	1
Arvicola terrestris	European water vole	8	2
Halichoerus grypus	Gray seal	1	1
Total		1250	41

culture. This applies to a large number of arrowheads of the Stationsvej type and a smaller number of possible Ålekistebro type. The dating is supported by symmetrically flat-shaped flake axes, flake knives with concave distal retouching, and specialized core axes. The ceramic material includes the pointed bottom of an Ertebølle pot. Neolithic material is present in the plow zone, along with a number of historical artifacts.

Trustrup was a fairly rich site in terms of stone tools, ceramics, and bone. but it was situated near a carbonate-rich spring which caused substantial breakage in the bone and ceramic material through repeated wet–dry cycles. We did not learn a lot from Trustrup except that people lived there in the Mesolithic and Neolithic and that marine species were included among the food resources, even though brackish or saltwater may have been several kilometers distant.

Chapter 6

Dragsholm and Bøgebjerg

Introduction

The site of Dragsholm is well known in the literature of prehistoric Europe because of the two graves (Fig. 6.1) that were uncovered in the early 1970s (Brinch Petersen 1973; 1974). One of the graves contained the remains of two women, covered with red ochre and buried with animal tooth pendants, a decorated bone spatula, and a bone point. A published radiocarbon date of 5160±100 BP from this grave suggested a Late Mesolithic age for the two females; stable carbon isotope ratios from their bone collagen indicated a diet dominated by marine foods, also a Mesolithic hallmark. The second grave contained a male individual, interred with a large number of amber beads, several flint blades, projectile points of bone and flint, an antler pick or shaft, a bone wristguard, a battle axe, and a small ceramic beaker belonging to the Funnel Beaker tradition. The Early Neolithic contents of the grave were confirmed by a radiocarbon date of 4840±100 BP and a stable carbon isotope ratio in the bone collagen that indicated a primarily terrestrial diet.

These two graves were originally dated closely to either side of the transition to agriculture in prehistoric Scandinavia. The two graves were separated by 1.5 m in space and around 300 years in time, and very distinct contents. The burials are closely linked as well in discussions of the transition to agriculture in southern Scandinavia and remain a continuing subject of interest. Some even suggested that the graves were contemporary and represented a Neolithic male and two Mesolithic females present at the same time and place. In the intervening years, the original radiocarbon dates have been questioned in light of calibration schemes and marine and freshwater reservoir effects.

In response to these questions, new dates from the graves were obtained (Price *et al.* 2007). Samples of human and animal skeletal tissue from the graves were analyzed for carbon, nitrogen, and strontium isotopes. Our results revealed a greater antiquity for the women's grave and several interesting new aspects of the skeletons, the contents, and the graves. The re-analysis also shed light on some problems and solutions in radiocarbon dating and dietary reconstruction using stable isotopes. Our excavations and geological studies revealed part of the settlement and the sea level history of the place, pertinent to understanding the prehistoric use of the area.

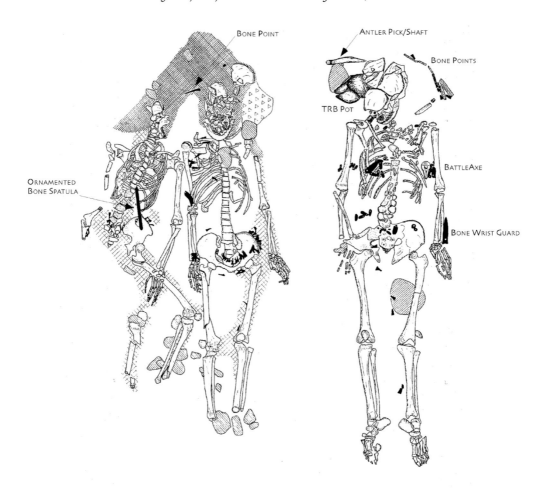

GRAVE I AND II AT DRAGSHOLM

Fig. 6.1. The Mesolithic and Neolithic graves at Dragsholm.

The date and significance of these burials has been debated for a long time. The general consensus is that Mesolithic graves were placed within settlements (Brinch Petersen 1974; Larsson 1997). I thought that this place might have deposits both from the Late Mesolithic and Early Neolithic.

So, at the same time that the redating of the skeletons was being done we began excavations at Dragsholm. I met initially with Arne Andersen of the local Odsherreds Museum, which was responsible for the site, to obtain permission. The excavations were done under the auspices of the Odsherreds Museum (now a part of the regional Museum Vest Sjælland in Holbæk) in conjunction with Arne Andersen. All materials from the excavation are stored with that Museum. I spoke with the original excavator, Erik Brinch Petersen, to let him know of our plans. I also met with the owners of

Dragsholm Slot, Inge Merete and Peter Bøttger, to gain permission for our excavations, which they graciously granted.

This was exciting stuff for me given the importance of the site and the opportunity to uncover Early Neolithic materials *in situ*. The very dense deposits of material at Dragsholm pointed to substantial occupation at a strategic location ideal for obtaining marine resources. We found Mesolithic materials that corresponded in time with the grave of the two females at Dragsholm. The remains included several decorated antler axes, many animal tooth beads and pendants, and lots of bone tools, in addition to copious amounts of flint and some pottery. The new date we obtained for the Early Neolithic male skeleton, however, came from a time when the

Fig. 6.2. Excavations at Dragsholm.

Dragsholm locale was largely under the waters of somewhat higher seas and a corresponding occupation layer was not encountered, perhaps eroded away during the marine transgression. Domestic cattle bones, polished flint axes, and Funnel Beaker pottery in secondary waterlain sediments testified to an Early Neolithic occupation that had been redeposited by the higher waters of the seas. I have come to believe that most occupations from the Early Neolithic period along the coast were destroyed by transgressions at the beginning of the Subboreal. That might also help explain why they are preserved in the higher levels of some shell middens in Jutland.

In conjunction with the trial excavation in 2002 (Fig. 6.2), several test trenches were excavated in the surrounding terrain to gain a better understanding of the fossil fjord area. These excavations were conducted simultaneously with the activities at Dragsholm. This resulted in the discovery of a previously unknown Mesolithic site located approximately 300 m southwest of Dragsholm Castle at the eastern foot of the 12 m high Bøgelund Bakke. This site, called Bøgebjerg (aka Bøgelund Bakke), is approximately 160 m north-north-east of our other excavations at Dragsholm. Bone and wood preservation was better at Bøgebjerg than in the lower area of excavation designated as Dragsholm near the drainage canal. This area of Bøgebjerg with waterlogged deposits appears to have suffered less desiccation from field drainage.

Our final report on the excavations appears here, led by a discussion of the landscape, geology, and sea level changes in the area. A description of the excavations follows, and details of the finds of flint, pottery, bone, and other significant items are provided. There is a brief section on the excavations at Bøgebjerg. Our report concludes with a discussion of the important findings and information that we obtained from this part of the project.

Excavations at Dragsholm

Archaeological investigations were conducted from 2002 through 2004 at the Stone Age site of Dragsholm in northwest Sjælland, Denmark (Figs 6.2 and 6.3). Our international team labored here to expose layers with cultural material from the Late Mesolithic and Early Neolithic periods that were known to exist at the site from the previous excavations of the graves in 1973.

Fieldwork was undertaken to learn more about the age and context of the site and the character of the prehistoric occupations. The testing and excavations that took place at Dragsholm resulted in the recovery of a large quantity of stone, bone, and ceramic artifacts. In addition to the usual range of Stone Age materials, we also found the fragments of three antler axes, a number of fish hooks, tooth pendants, part of a human jaw, a large lugged TRB sherd, and an abundance of fish bone.

A preliminary account of our excavations appeared in a report on the re-analysis of the burials (Price *et al.* 2007). That article documented our findings that the two graves (Fig. 6.1) were 1000 years apart in age, with the two Mesolithic females in one grave dated to *c.* 5983±38 BP (AAR-7417) on the collagen in a red deer bone artifact in the grave and the Neolithic male in the other grave dated to 4903±46 BP (AAR-7416) on table 6.1 on human bone collagen. The two graves were in no way contemporary.

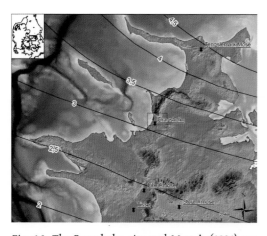

Fig. 6.3. The Dragsholm site and Mertz's (1924) sea level rise estimates with inset of location in southern Scandinavia (prepared by Niels Skytte using data from the Danish Geodata Agency).

Landscape and geology

The archaeological site of Dragsholm (UTM Coordinates: 649868 6183038, the designation in the National Site Archive is Fårevejle sogn, Odsherred herred, Holbæk amt. KUAS journal Stednr. 030403-503) lies on the north side of the Dragsholm Kanal, approximately 1 km east of the coast of Sejerø Bugt and the Storebælt, at the base of a distinctive peninsula known as Ordrup Næs. The site is situated a few kilometers to the south of a high hill landscape called the Vejrhøj Buerne (Weather Hill Arches), part of a major end moraine complex along the northwest coast of Sjælland (Fig. 1.18). The maximum height of Vejrhøj is 121 m asl. These ridges were formed by the Young Baltic ice stream during recessions and successive re-advances through the Storebælt strait from 18,000–16,000 years ago, toward the end of the Pleistocene (Houmark-Nielsen and Kjær 2003).

The area is called Dragsholm (the island by the portage) and that term also is used for the castle that dominates this area (Fig. 6.4). Dragsholm Slot is one of the oldest stone buildings in Denmark. The original Dragsholm Castle was built around AD 1215 by the Bishop of Roskilde. Figure 6.5 shows the location of Dragsholm Slot overlooking the waterway between Sejerø Bay and the Lammefjord in 1771 before it was drained. Along the coast of Sejerø Bay, to the west of the castle, is a raised area of sand dunes. East of the dunes, the Dragsholm Kanal runs today across low ground, following a former sea connection to the waters of the bay. The canal was dug from Drags Mølle (2 m asl) on the shore of the former Lammefjord, draining its waters into Sejerø Bay. Dragsholm Canal was excavated when the Lammefjord was reclaimed from the sea in the 19th century.

Fig. 6.4. *Dragsholm Slot today with Sejerø Bay in the background.*

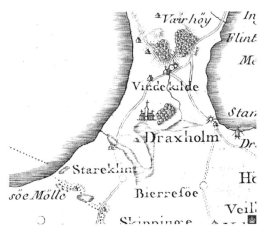

Fig. 6.5. *1771 military map of the Dragsholm area.*

The castle was built here early on because of the strategic nature of the place. The only land passage to Odsherred and the northwest part of the island of Sjælland, between the Sejerø Bugt and the Lammefjord, was across the narrow isthmus of land at Dragsholm. This land bridge was 2–3 km wide and consisted largely of wetlands and marsh. It would have been transgressed by a sea only 2 m higher than present day.

The castle is situated on a distinctive rise in the landscape and overlooks an area to the southwest of small ridges and lowlands on both sides of the canal. One of the higher points in the area north of the canal is Bøgebjerg (aka Bøgelund Bakke) at +12 m asl. Excavations of a Middle Ertebølle site were conducted here as well and are described at the end of this chapter. From the small hill of Bøgebjerg, a low (+5 m asl), narrow ridge runs about 180 m directly south, ending as the low rise where the graves were found in 1973. Another low ridge (+2 m asl) runs perpendicularly to the east approximately 40 m to a second small rise. This

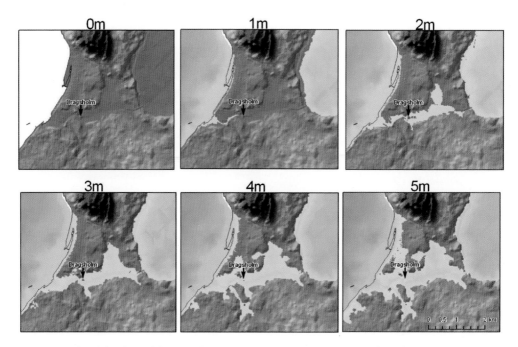

Fig. 6.6. Simulated flooding of the Dragsholm inlet between the Lammefjord (right) and the Storebælt in 1 m increments (drawing: Niels Skytte).

second small rise was the location of the test trench excavated by Per Poulsen of the National Museum in 1974.

Figure 6.6 shows the simulated effects of raising sea level in this area by increments of 1 m. Estimated high water levels during the Atlantic climate episode were 3–4 m (Fig. 6.2) in this part of Denmark (Mertz 1924). At this level the waters of the inlet became a strait between the Storebælt and the former Lammefjord.

The graves at Dragsholm were found on the first low rise near the canal. In this area, the earth from the canal excavation had been dumped to raise the land surface, improve it for cultivation, and to spread out the excavated fill. The top of the small rise had been heavily eroded both by marine transgression and agricultural activity. The place with the Dragsholm burials is situated where the highest beach lines of the Littorina transgressions occur, between 3.5 m and 4.5 m asl.

The small rise with the burials, along with part of the alluvial plain to the south, was once an island beside a strong current in the connection between the Lammefjord and Sejerø Bay. The very coarse-grained sediments in the excavation trenches, the abraded condition of some of the bone material, and the high quantity of fine charcoal pieces in various layers are characteristic of a high energy zone with erosion of the upper foreshore and beach environment.

During the maximum transgressions of the late Atlantic and early Subboreal, *c.* 4000 BC, sea level in this area was +3 m to +4 m higher than today. The elevation of the small rise is only +4.75 m asl, so that it would have been heavily washed by high tide and storm. The field in which the rise sits has been under cultivation since the land was drained and plowing has further reduced the higher areas. In fact, this plowing was responsible for the exposure of the Mesolithic women's grave and the initial recognition of the importance of the site.

The 2002–04 archaeological investigations

Our archaeological project at Dragsholm took place over three field seasons, with 1 week of work in 2002, 8 weeks in 2003, and a final 3 weeks in 2004. The project initially involved a testing phase in order to determine the extent of the archaeological horizons and moved subsequently into larger trench excavations of parts of those deposits. In total, 11 trenches and 12 test pits were excavated to determine the depth and extent of the cultural layers and to search for features and additional graves. The 2002 (50 m²), 2003 (182 m²), and 2004 (16 m²) excavations at Dragsholm opened a total of 248 m², including test pits and trenches, to depths varying between 0.60 and 2.25 m below ground surface. These excavations were concentrated in the southeast quadrant of the area where cultural materials were best preserved (Fig. 6.7). We excavated perhaps 2% of the potential deposits so that a great deal of material remains at the site.

Preservation of organic material was generally good, although it varied by depth. Bone and flint finds were numerous in the upper, Early Neolithic layer (6). Flint artifacts in layer 6 were marine patinated and slightly rolled; ceramics were eroded and usually only larger pieces survived. Bone material in this layer was usually larger, rolled, and somewhat eroded. Fish bone and nutshells were rare in the Early Neolithic layer, probably washed away by the transgressions. There were, in fact, few features and fewer special items recorded because these layers were reworked by water so that the exact location of most finds was not particularly significant.

Flint and bone were also present in the Ertebølle layers (7a–c, 8) lower in the section, but considerably fresher than samples recovered in the Early Neolithic layer (6). Flint artifacts in the lower, Ertebølle layers generally had sharper edges and lacked the distinctive white marine patination of the upper Neolithic layer. Ertebølle pottery was present and a number of sherds were collected. Fish bone and burned hazelnut shells recovered in these lower layers were likewise plentiful and well preserved. Burned hazelnut shell was common in the water-screened material from the Mesolithic layers (7c and 8) and was collected and bagged separately. The discovery of concentrated deposits of fish otoliths in these lower layers was a welcome (but time-consuming) surprise. In addition, in layer 8, there were occasional remnants of wooden stakes.

Excavation in the Mesolithic layers produced 11 fish hooks and fragments and almost 30 bone awls/points. These may all have been lost while fishing in this area

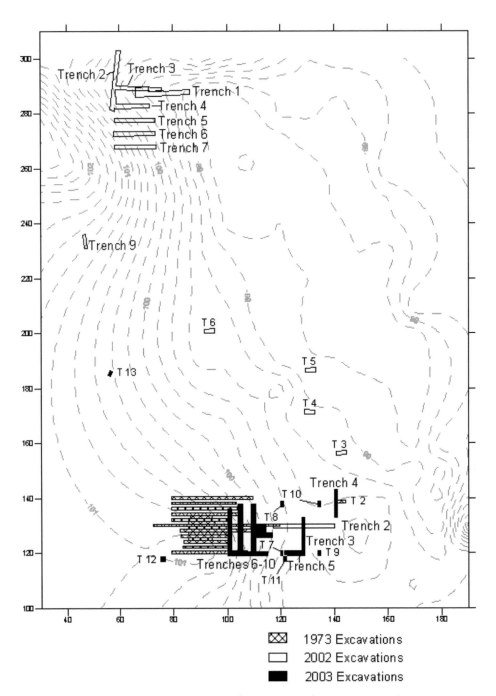

Fig. 6.7. Plan of Dragholm excavations (1973, 2002–2004). Contour interval is 25 cm.

when the water level was higher. In addition to bone hooks and point finds, fragments of three antler axes were recovered in the excavations of Ertebølle layers (see below).

Toward the end of the field season, five long trenches (Trenches 6–10) were dug by machine through the plow zone and the canal fill deposits on the east side of the small rise of the Dragsholm graves to expose the sterile ground surface underneath and to search for features or additional graves. We were hoping to find intact terrestrial deposits but to no avail. Finally, the digging machine was used to excavate another deep test pit (T12) to the north of the Dragsholm rise to see if any deposits remained in this area. Only a handful of artifacts and no features were observed in this entire area.

Archaeological layers

The stratigraphic section from Test 11 at Dragsholm (Fig. 6.8) provides a good overview of the sequence of archaeological layers and depositional context. This was the deepest section that was excavated and it exposed the typical sediments in the southeast quadrant of the former small island at Dragsholm. Two culture horizons were identified in this area of shallow water, including an upper Early Neolithic layer (layer 6) and a lower series of layers of Ertebølle materials (layers 7a–c, 8). These materials likely represent the redeposited remains from substantial occupations from these periods and there is some Mesolithic material deposited *in situ* in layer 8. A sequence stratigraphy of Test 11, compiled by Nanna Noe-Nygaard, is presented in Figure 6.9.

Layer 1: Plow zone, a dark brown sandy, humic layer composed primarily of the sediments removed and dumped on adjacent dry land during the digging of the canal.

Layer 2: The unplowed deposit of canal fill itself, which is a mix of humic and sandy layers also containing archaeological materials and shell. It is clear that the path of the canal cut through archaeological deposits in the area. This layer may also contain pockets of dark decomposed sandy peat (Layer 3) that probably represent the former ground surface following the retreat of the sea here in the middle Holocene. This area was likely a wetland from the time of that retreat until the recent drainage of the region. Layer 3 could not be distinguished in this section. (Layer 4 is drainage pipe ditch fill that was encountered in other parts of the site but was not visible here.)

Layer 5: Beneath the peat (Layer 3), was a fine white sand deposit with some gravel, perhaps eolian in origin This layer may have formed during the period of marine transgression when the *ribbe-dobbe* (sand ridges and intervening lows) landscape to the west was developing along the coastline. Layer 5 was sterile and continuous across the site area except above +4 m asl. One suspects that this eolian activity affected the entire west coast of Sjælland.

Layer 6: A regression horizon with fine white sand, gravel, and large rolled stones. Artifacts, bones, and some shell and charcoal were present. The cultural material in this horizon is largely Early Neolithic, confirmed by several cattle teeth and bones and TRB pottery. Flint artifacts are moderately rolled and marine patinated. The deposit must represent a final episode of erosion and deposition at the site as the sea was retreating from its high stand of the early Subboreal. Two radiocarbon dates from this layer are 4050–3770 cal BC (AAR-8774; 90.5%) and 4260–3990 cal BC (AAR-8778; 85.4%) (Table 6.1).

Layer 7: A rich and complex succession of gray medium-grained sands with two major lenses of cultural material in the middle and lower parts of the layer. The cultural materials in this layer are Mesolithic, belonging largely to the Middle Ertebølle. This layer likely represents a series of transgressive deposits. The upper part of the layer (7a) was often leached with vertical streaks of oxidation and, in some areas, substantial accumulations of iron oxide. This layer contained a moderate number of artifacts. Two radiocarbon dates from layer 7 are 4810–4520 cal BC (AAR-8779; 92.6%) and 5260–4800 cal BC (AAR-8781; 80.5%) (Table 6.1). A second horizon (7b) comprised coarse-grained sand grading into 7a above. Very few artifacts were recovered from layer 7b. Layer 7c was a darker, gray sand layer with substantial cultural material. The dispersal of large quantities of charcoal likely produced the gray color in this layer. Shell lenses were present above 7c in some parts of the stratigraphy. Cultural finds from 7c include ceramics and distinctive Late Mesolithic projectile points. This material is lightly rolled and probably secondarily reworked by the transgressive wave action.

Layer 8: A layer of rust to gray colored sand and pebbles (variable in color across the excavation units) with an abundance of fish bone and hazelnut shell along with artifacts and other bone. This layer was likely largely *in situ*; the flint from it is fresh and unrolled. The cultural material in this layer is outcast material and appears typologically to be Middle Ertebølle. The chronology of the Layer 8 cultural material has been confirmed by three radiocarbon dates on a red deer bone of 5019–5000 cal BC (AAR-8189) and on charcoal of 5320–5040 cal BC (AAR-8781; 95.4%), and 5480–5200 cal BC AAR-8780; 80.5%) (Table 6.1).

Layer 9: A grey–brown clayey sand. This layer was sterile and, together with the lowest two layers, likely represents marine deposition during the early transgression of the fjord.

Layer 10: A bedded, down-sloping, coarse orange–brown sand leached with accumulations of iron toward the bottom of the layer. Layer 10 was also sterile.

Layer 11: A fine to medium-grained orange–brown sand, bedded and sterile. Excavation of Trench 11 ended in this layer at a depth of 2.2 m below ground surface (+0.73 asl).

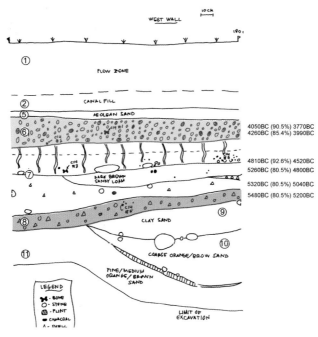

Fig. 6.8. Dragsholm 2003. Test 11 Section. West Wall. 1 m. Radiocarbon dates are given and sample location marked on the section (drawing: Terrence Slocum).

As sea levels rose following the end of the Pleistocene, the Dragsholm area was gradually flooded by a series of transgressions during the Atlantic and early Subboreal periods. A combination of isostatic rebound and eustatic sea level rise resulted in a number of minor transgression and regression cycles called the Littorina transgressions (Iversen 1937; Jessen 1937; Berglund 1971; C. Christensen 1994; 1995; K. Christensen 1997; Maagaard Jakobsen 1981; 1983). The narrow land barrier between Dragsholm and the Lammefjord was breached by the sea already during the High Atlantic Littorina transgression. Odsherred (the northwest corner of Sjælland) was then separated from the rest of the larger island of Sjælland.

In terms of human settlement, these transgressions may have interrupted or ended the Mesolithic occupation at the site, and the Early Neolithic materials are younger than the major transgressions. If we use the date for the Mesolithic grave as the time of that occupation it would be *c.* 4300 BC, while the Neolithic grave dates to 4903±46 BP = 3710–3650 cal BC.

Chronology and radiocarbon dating

The archaeological materials from the site at Dragsholm date from the Late Mesolithic Ertebølle and the Early Neolithic Funnel Beaker (TRB). We obtained a total

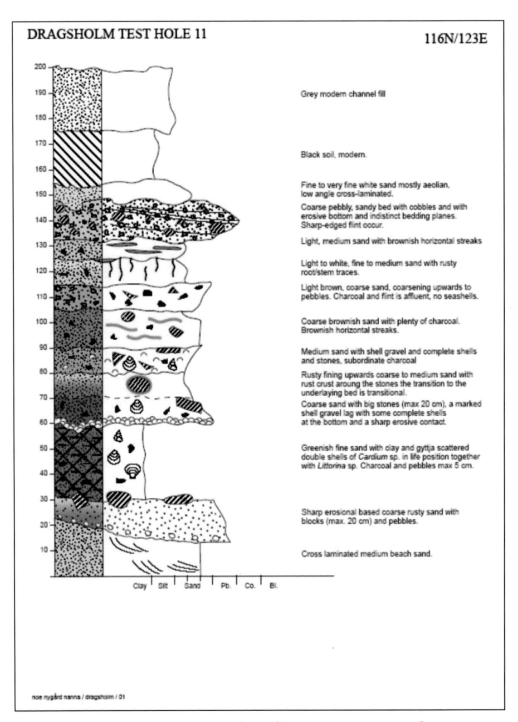

DRAGSHOLM TEST HOLE 11

116N/123E

Grey modern channel fill

Black soil, modern.

Fine to very fine white sand mostly aeolian, low angle cross-laminated.

Coarse pebbly, sandy bed with cobbles and with erosive bottom and indistinct bedding planes. Sharp-edged flint occur.

Light, medium sand with brownish horizontal streaks

Light to white, fine to medium sand with rusty root/stem traces.

Light brown, coarse sand, coarsening upwards to pebbles. Charcoal and flint is affluent, no seashells.

Coarse brownish sand with plenty of charcoal. Brownish horizontal streaks.

Medium sand with shell gravel and complete shells and stones, subordinate charcoal

Rusty fining upwards coarse to medium sand with rust crust aroung the stones the transition to the underlaying bed is transitional.

Coarse sand with big stones (max 20 cm), a marked shell gravel lag with some complete shells at the bottom and a sharp erosive contact.

Greenish fine sand with clay and gyttja scattered double shells of *Cardium* sp. in life position together with *Littorina* sp. Charcoal and pebbles max 5 cm.

Sharp erosional based coarse rusty sand with blocks (max. 20 cm) and pebbles.

Cross laminated medium beach sand.

Clay   Silt   Sand   Pb.   Co.   Bl.

noe nygård nanna / dragsholm / 01

Fig. 6.9. Sequence stratigraphy for T11 (drawing: Nanna Noe-Nygaard).

of 21 radiocarbon dates on various samples from the site (not including duplicate samples from the graves), including the graves and human skeletons, that fit with this chronology, with two exceptions (Table 6.1). These come from more recent cow bones and probably reflect the incorporation of these samples in the sediments that were removed during the digging of the canal or our excavations. Here we focus on dates that were obtained from the excavations in 2002–2004. The majority of these samples come from Test 11 and were used to date the succession of deposits in that profile (Fig. 6.8).

The remaining dates are from various parts of the excavation. There is a date on a heavy bone chisel from the test excavated by Per Poulsen in 1974. The stable carbon isotope ratio of the sample was –21.5‰, which clearly indicates a terrestrial diet. This artifact belongs to the Neolithic and the bone probably comes from a domestic cow. The isolated human mandible fragment found in 2003 was dated to 6310±60 BP (AAR-7425; 4940–4610 cal BC), roughly contemporary with the two Mesolithic females. This individual also had a substantial intake of marine foods. The human remains, in addition to the mandible fragment, included two loose teeth. A red deer bone from

Table 6.1. Radiocarbon dates from Dragsholm.

Lab. ref.	Material	Sample context	Radiocarbon determination BP	Date cal BC (2σ)*	Percentage probability
AAR-8780	Charcoal	1.63 m asl (T1 1#5)	6320±70	5480–5200	80.50
AAR-8782	Charcoal	1.55 m asl (T1 1#8)	6240±55	5320–5040	95.40
AAR-8781	Charcoal	1.7 m asl (T1 1#7)	6090±70	5260–4800	95.40
Beta 308061	Charcoal	Test 11, C14#9, North 8	6130±40	5210–4980	95.40
AAR-7417	Bone, spatula	Meso. Grave	5983±38	4900–4810	95.40
AAR-7425	Bone, human	Mandible	6310±60	4940–4610	95.40
AAR-8725	Bone, human	Mandible	5910±60	4940–4610	95.40
AAR-8779	Bone, ?roe deer	1.93 m asl (T11#3)	5835±65	4810–4520	92.60
AAR-7414	Bone, femur	Meso. grave DR A	5787±43	4710–4550	
AAR-7415	Bone, femur	Meso. grave DR B	5775±49	4710–4550	
Bet 308060	Charcoal	Test 11, C14#6, North 7b	5840±30	4640–4610	95.40
AAR-8778	Charcoal	2.1 m asl (T11#2)	5330±60	4260–3990	85.40
AAR-8774	Bone, *Bos. d.*	TP2, Paulsen, 2.5 m asl	5150±65	4050–3770	90.50
AAR-7418-2	Antler pick	Neo. Grave	5090±65	3940–4800	
AAR-7416	Bone, femur	Neo. Grave DR D	4903±46	3710–3650	
BA-10654	Bone, *Bos. d.*	125N128E (7a-9)	4490±30	3350–3080	95.40
BA-10656	Bone, *Bos. d.*	126N/128E 3-3	3985±30	2580–2460	95.40
BA-10655	Bone, *Bos. d.*	114N123E 6-8	2075±25	180–30	95.40

*dates rounded out to 10 years according to Mook (1986); calibration: Stuiver *et al.* 2022

Layer 7b in Trench 5 was dated to the Mesolithic, Middle Ertebølle: *c.* 4760 cal BC (BA-10660). Several samples of cow bone were dated to confirm a date to the Early Neolithic but, as noted, only one of the three examples fell in that period. The other two were more recent.

Flaked stone

The majority of the archaeological remains at the site, with the exception of fish bone and nutshell, were pieces of flaked stone. A variety of lithic material was recovered in the excavations at Dragsholm; a few examples of ground stone artifacts were also found. These major categories of stone artifacts are described below. A total of 1293.89 kg of flint were collected, approximately 70,911 pieces. Table 6.2 shows the number and percentage of pieces per category of flaked stone artifact by layer. Percentages are calculated on total artifacts minus burned pieces. The distribution of flaked stone artifacts by excavation unit is available in the museum report.

The flint assemblage is generally typical of the Ertebølle period. Flakes and blades are the most abundant artifacts and this pattern is reflected in the numbers of flake and blade cores as well. Burned flint pieces were tabulated and usually constitute 3.8–27.1% of the total flint in a layer. This burning is normally the result of accidental exposure to fire in the settlement area. The proportion of burned pieces in a layer is a function of the amount of burning in an occupation and the sorting of flint by size and shape by water activity during erosion and redeposition.

Artifacts from Layer 6 are usually marine patinated and rolled (Fig. 6.10), while lithic materials from Layers 7 and 8 are in better condition and have undergone less exposure. The artifacts from Layer 8 (Fig. 6.11) are almost pristine with sharp edges and little to no patination. Artifacts assigned to Layer 9 were in the transition between layers 8 and 9 and probably belong chronologically in Layer 8. The absence of polished axe from in Layer 6 is surprising. Lithics from this layer are generally not distinct from those in the Mesolithic layers and a number of core axes were present in Layer 6. This layer is probably a reworked mix of Neolithic and Mesolithic materials eroded from the top of the small rise with the burials and from nearby areas.

In comparison of the contents, it is important to keep in mind that the layers are redeposited. Layer 6 appears to be a higher energy deposition with some sorting, favoring larger and heavier artifacts. Layers 7 and 8 seem to have been deposited in lower energy conditions; there is very little rolling of materials and preservation of nutshell and fish bone tends to confirm the rather gentle deposition of these materials. The variation in proportions among the categories in Layers 7a, 7b, and 7c also likely reflect the sorting caused by water reworking at different levels of energy. The higher percentages of flakes in Layer 7b and 7c, for example, reflects the higher number of small artifacts in these levels, many of which were nondescript flakes. In fact, there are no substantial differences among the artifact categories in the excavated layers.

Table 6.2. Counts and percentages of various categories of flaked stone artifacts from Dragsholm.

Layer	Weight	Burnt	Flakes	Blades	FlCo	BlCo	RF	RB	BlKn	PT	PTPRE
6	261,623	1822	11728	1476	1227	132	62	54	35	130	131
%			46.08	5.80	4.82	0.52	0.24	0.21	0.14	0.51	0.51
7	158,201	701	8913	873	774	144	42	23	22	81	90
%			44.7	4.4	3.9	0.7	0.2	0.1	0.1	0.4	0.5
8	76,134	255	5458	703	410	48	20	24	11	45	49
%			47.3	6.1	3.6	0.4	0.2	0.2	0.1	0.4	0.4
9	unknown	44	490	108	137	15	4	2	3	3	9
%			67.0	14.8	18.7	2.1	0.5	0.3	0.4	0.4	1.2
7a	20,970	203	494	57	143	22	3	2	2	1	13
%			21.7	2.5	6.3	1.0	0.1	0.1	0.1	0.0	0.6
7b	38,109	243	4175	184	137	29	11	4	1	42	22
%			54.2	2.4	1.8	0.4	0.1	0.1	0.0	0.5	0.3
7c	66,877	220	3346	468	252	51	23	12	7	31	14
%			53.2	7.4	4.0	0.8	0.4	0.2	0.1	0.5	0.2

Layer	FlAx	CoAx	BlSc	BlBo	Total	Total burnt	Sum ret.	% ret.
6	56	60	22	17	15130	13,308	567	4.3
%	0.22	0.24	0.09	0.07				
7	8	25	10	3	11008	10,307	304	2.9
%	0.0	0.1	0.1	0.0				
8	2	5	7	1	6783	6528	164	2.5
%	0.0	0.0	0.1	0.0				
9	2	1	1	0	775	731	25	3.4
%	0.3	0.1	0.1	0.0				
7a	3	5	2	0	747	504	False	0.0
%	0.1	0.2	0.1	0.0				
7b	1	6	3	1	4616	4373	91	2.1
%	0.0	0.1	0.0	0.0				
7c	1	10	3	1	4219	3999	102	2.6
%	0.0	0.2	0.0	0.0		39,750	1253	3.23

FlCo = flake core; BlCo = blade core; RF = retouched flake RB = retouched blade; BlKn = blade knife; PT = point; PTPRE = pre-point; FlAx = flake axe; CoAx = core axe; BlSc = blade scraper; BlBo = Blade borer.

Fig. 6.10. Points, knives, and a flake borer from Layer 6. 116N127E Trench 11.

Fig. 6.11. Points and flake tools from Layer 8 at Dragsholm.

The primary difference between the layers is the Neolithic material (cow bones, Funnel Beaker pottery, and a few distinctive lithic pieces) present in Layer 6, mixed with Mesolithic materials.

The proportion of retouched tools in Mesolithic assemblages in southern Scandinavia is low, generally on the order of 5% or less of the total lithic assemblage (Stafford 1999). At Dragsholm total retouched artifacts comprise 3.2% of the total lithic assemblage (not counting burned pieces). This value varies by layer depending on the nature of the deposit. Retouched artifacts are listed in Table 6.2 in the categories of retouched flakes and blades, blade knives, points, point preforms, flake and core axes, blade scrapers, and blade borers. The most common categories of the retouched tools are points, retouched blades, retouched flakes, and axes. Unusual pieces such as hammerstones, burins, flake and core borers, axe-sharpening flakes, and the like were noted and are discussed below.

A wide range of artifacts were recovered, reflecting substantial settlement activity. Flakes dominate the assemblage. These are the unretouched waste products of lithic production and occur in a wide range of sizes and shapes. Unretouched blades are also an important component of the artifact assemblage. Cores for the manufacture of flakes and blades are also common among the recovered flaked stone artifacts. The retouched assemblage is dominated by points (and point preforms) and axes, including both core and flake axes. The core axes are generally small. Several fragments of specialized core axes were noted, in addition to one intact example. Core axes were likely a multi-purpose woodworking tool, while the flake axe was a more general, heavy, edged, multi-purpose tool used on a variety of materials (cf. Juel Jensen 1988, 178; Knutsson 1982, 90; Havstein 2012, 93; Solheim *et al.* 2018). In general, the frequency of flake axes increases while core axes become less common during the Ertebølle period. A similar chronological change among the flint axes at Dragsholm is seen in the shift towards a predominance of flake axes in Layer 7, but there are a large number of core axes in Layer 6, perhaps as a function of water sorting of larger and heavier pieces. In addition to the core and flake axes enumerated in Table 6.2, there are other examples of axe utilization, including axe-sharpening flakes (15); specialized core axes are represented by one complete example and seven sharpening flakes. There are two fragments of unpolished Neolithic axes.

Projectile points (Fig. 6.11) are transverse, typical of the Middle and Late Ertebølle. The leading and trailing edges of the point are the sharp edges of a blade and the sides are retouched. The leading edge is usually broader than the trailing edge and flares out slightly. The most common variants belonged to the Middle Ertebølle following the typological chronology of Vang Petersen (2008). Point preforms are usually fragments of flakes or blades intended for the production of projectile points, usually identified by concave retouch on one side of a rather flat flake or blade segment.

Blade knives have a heavily retouched edge and are usually made on large regular blades. Convex retouch on the distal end of the blade constitutes one variety of these blade knives. Borers are common. In addition to the artifacts listed in Table 6.2, there are a number of other finds among the flaked stone tools including various kinds of borers and chisels: flake borers (10), core borers (14), core picks (6), and flake chisels (2). Scrapers are present but rare. There are several kinds of steep-edged scrapers on blades (2), on flakes (13), and on cores (3). There is one long, serrated blade which resembles a small saw. Burins are not infrequent; there are at least 28 burins or spalls, in addition to seven microburins, and five drills on backed bladelets. There are several hammerstones of flint (3), probably from recycled cores.

Ground stone

There was one greenstone trindøkse (a groundstone axe) recovered in Layer 7b (Fig. 6.12). It is complete and approximately 11 cm in length. A trindøkse typically is a cylinder of hard, heavy stone that is shaped by pecking. The butt end is tapered and nicely rounded; the bit end is typically rounded on one side and flat or concave on the other. The butt end is sometimes facetted as if it has been used as a hammer or had been hammered. Polish is usually most common on the edge of the bit but sometimes also seen at midpoint, perhaps from hafting, and rarely over more of the surface. Such trindøkse are known from the Middle and Late Mesolithic of southern Scandinavia. In Denmark they are more common in the west of the country.

Fig. 6.12. Groundstone trindøx from Dragsholm.

Pottery (Anne Birgitte Gebauer)

Two major groups of ceramics are represented at Dragsholm – the Late Mesolithic Ertebølle and the Early Neolithic Funnel Beaker Culture. The Ertebølle pottery in Scandinavia was introduced from East Asia and Siberia and further west to the eastern Baltic (Jordan and Zvelebil 2009) as a tradition related to hunter-gatherer societies, while Funnel Beaker pottery developed in central Germany from the interaction of Continental Neolithic cultures, especially Michelsberg, with some influence from Late Lengyel groups, Gatersleben and Jordansmühle (Müller 2011a; Sørensen 2014; Jordan *et al.* 2016). Transitional forms between Ertebølle and Funnel Beaker pottery found at some kitchen middens in western Denmark suggest local involvement of Mesolithic hunter-gatherers continued during the first part of the Early Neolithic (Andersen 2008, 71).

Ertebølle vessels are S-shaped with pointed, flat, or bulb-shaped bases. Vessels are generally medium and large in size; small cups and lamps are known from later Ertebølle deposits. Construction involved coiling and smearing clay ropes into a U-shaped cross- section. Temper is often coarse (e.g., fragmented granite or grog) and sometimes supplemented with plant remains. At Dragsholm the maximum size of visible temper grains is 6–8 mm. Wall thickness is substantial and varied from 10 mm to 21 mm, with an average of 16.8 mm. The ware is porous, often cracked along the coils, and crumbles easily. Several coils show finger imprints along the top. At least four different pots are represented.

The typical shape of Ertebølle vessels on Sjælland with a short, flared neck, a smooth transition to a slightly curved belly, and a pointed bottom is reflected in the fragmented ceramics. Rim and neck of the vessels are flared with the rim slightly thinner than the remaining vessel wall. Fragments from the belly area suggest a rather flat curve. One thick sherd appears to be part of a pointed bottom. Diameters, varying from 22–36 cm indicate the use of medium and large size vessels. Small cups and lamps were not present, and their absence suggests the Middle Ertebølle in terms of chronology. No decorations or food crusts have been found on the Ertebølle pot sherds. All the Ertebølle pottery came from Layer 7. Almost all the material came from three squares in Trench 4, along with a few sherds from Trench 3. No Funnel Beaker material occurred in this layer. There are four unusual pieces of fired clay that may represent fragments of sherds held together by mineral concretions, accidentally burned pieces, or some kind of daub or clay plaster.

Funnel Beaker pottery is usually thin-walled (less than 10 mm thick), tempered with smaller grains, and with a different coil structure than the Ertebølle pottery. Funnel Beaker vessels were built with a flat disc of clay used as the base and clay coils were applied to form the vessel walls. Paddle and anvil technique was used to compress the clay coils and to thin the vessel wall. The use of the paddle produced an oblique pattern in the coils, termed N-structure, typical of Funnel Beaker pottery.

At Dragsholm, the Funnel Beaker pottery clearly differs from the Ertebølle ceramics in terms of an N-shaped coil structure and the thickness of the vessel wall at 5–11 mm, with an average of 7.2 mm. The largest visible grains of temper are only 1–5 mm in diameter. Burned and crushed granite is the most common temper; red feldspar particles occur frequently, but shiny particles like quartz and sand also appear. The colors of the sherds involves various shades of brown – from yellow–brown, reddish–brown, grayish–brown, to almost black–brown. In many cases the outside surface has a red or yellow shade of brown, while the inside surface is darker and greyer. The core of the vessel wall is sometimes black, reflecting firing in a reducing atmosphere.

The shape and number of vessels is difficult to estimate due to heavy fragmentation and poor preservation of the ceramics. However, a minimum of 3–4 vessels is represented, including medium to large Funnel Neck beakers and a large lugged jar. The placement of the lugs on the lower part of the belly of the lugged jar suggests a date in late EN I or perhaps early ENII (Becker 1947, 133; Koch 1998, 114). A date in period EN I is likewise indicated by the limited rim decoration of stabs and finger impressions below the rim. No belly decoration is preserved. Food crusts were observed on the inside of a pot below the rim and on the belly, while cereal impressions were preserved in several of the sherds.

The use of temper similar to Ertebølle pottery in two Funnel Beaker-like sherds stands out. One sherd was tempered with grog or chamotte grains measuring 6 mm in diameter. A neck sherd is very coarsely tempered with sand and large, rounded grains of red feldspar up to 11–12 mm in diameter, but the overall thickness of the vessel wall was only 9–10 mm. The grog-tempered sherd could be a thin-walled Ertebølle sherd redeposited from another layer, while the neck sherd is probably just an example of the variation seen in Funnel Beaker pottery.

Fauna

The enormous bone assemblage from Dragsholm was collected by meter square and level during the excavation, bagged, and weighed. Special finds were noted. This material was analyzed by Kurt Gron with the assistance of Nanna Noe-Nygaard and Jane Richter. The majority of the bone material comes from mammals, with a few examples of fowl and fish (Table 6.3). There are 17 species of mammals with one specimen assignable only to genus and four species of birds, one assignable only to genus, and one species of fish. Most of the fish bones were sorted for separate analysis (see below).

The bone material iss highly fragmented and comprises 17,914 pieces. A total of 1969 fragments have been identified (c. 11%). The proportion of undetermined fragments is unusually high and reflects the rather poor preservation of some of the material. The longest dimension of each of the undetermined fragments was measured – 13,307, or more than 83% of the undetermined fragments, are less than 3 cm, and 9618, or more than 60%, are less than 2 cm. The dimension of a fragment does not in itself determine whether a specimen can be identified. However, the vast majority of

Table 6.3. Identified faunal remains from Dragsholm.

Species	Common name	No.	MNI
Erinaceus europaeus	Hedgehog	3	2
adult		2	1
juvenile		1	1
Sciurus vulgaris	Squirrel	4	1
adult		4	1
Castor fiber	Beaver	8	3
adult		7	2
juvenile		1	1
Arvicola terrestris	Water vole	26	5
adult		23	4
juvenile		3	1
Vulpes vulpes	Fox	9	2
adult		7	1
juvenile		2	1
Canis lupus	Wolf	6	2
adult		5	1
juvenile		1	1
Canis familiaris	Dog	47	4
adult		43	3
juvenile		4	1
Martes martes	Marten	139	5
adult		134	3
juvenile		5	2
Meles meles	Badger	1	1
adult		1	1
Lutra lutra	Otter	7	1
adult		7	1
Felis silvestris	Wild cat	7	1
adult		7	1
Phoca sp.	Seal	1	1
adult		1	1
Halichoerus grypus	Gray seal	23	3
adult		21	2
juvenile		2	1
Sus scrofa	Wild boar	296	14
adult		234	7
juvenile		55	3

(Continued)

Table 6.3. (Continued)

Species	Common name	No.	MNI
neonatal		7	4
Capreolus capreolus	Roe deer	810	20
adult		703	13
juvenile		83	2
neonatal		21	4
foetal		3	1
Cervus elaphus	Red deer	558	11
adult		482	6
juvenile		61	2
neonatal		13	3
senile		2	
Bos domesticus	Domestic cow	22	4
adult		21	3
juvenile		1	1
Phocaena phocaena	Porpoise	7	1
adult		7	1
Homo sapiens	Human	2	1
Cygnus cygnus	Whooper swan	1	
Cygnus olor	Mute swan	1	
Anas platyrhynchos	Mallard	1	
Anas sp.	Duck	1	
Aythya fuligula	Tufted duck	3	
Gadus morhua	Cod	3	

the identified Dragsholm material is from larger animals. In that case the size of the fragment does influence the possibility of reliable identification.

The number of identified bones for each species is given in Table 6.3 and a Minimum Number of Individuals (MNI) is provided for some. The mammal bones are subdivided into categories of adult, juvenile, and neonatal. The term 'adult' is used when the epiphyses have fused with the diaphyses and the permanent dentition has erupted and is in wear. The term 'juvenile' is used for bone elements with fully grown epiphyses and when the deciduous tooth row is in wear (Schmid 1972). The term 'neonatal' is used when bones have a porous structure due to incomplete calcification and the tooth row is erupting, and usually not in wear (Schmid 1972). Measurements were made following von den Driesch (1978). Foetal denotes unborn individuals and senile refers to mature individuals in their later years.

With the exception of the domestic cattle, most of the species present are typical of Mesolithic sites in southern Scandinavia (e.g., Noe-Nygaard 1995; Ritchie *et al.* 2013b), particularly wild boar and both roe and red deer. Domestic dog is well represented and probably served as a hunting companion as well as food. Several fur-bearing species are present in the assemblage including wild cat, otter, beaver, squirrel, red fox, wolf, as well as seal, but marten bones were particularly abundant and may reflect a focus on this species for fur. The cattle bones are not abundant (27) and are confined to Layer 6, the Early Neolithic horizon. It is also important to note the role of marine species in the faunal assemblage. In addition to the abundant fish bones, discussed below, at least two species of seals and the harbor porpoise are represented among the fauna. Two species of swan and at least two species of duck comprise the fowl. A few examples of large cod bones were included in the material for faunal analysis but, as noted, a separate study of the fish bone was undertaken (see below). As is always the case, some of these species may be more recent than the archaeological layers but ended up among the fauna as they live in the ground, e.g., hedgehogs and water voles come to mind.

Burned teeth were noted among several of the fur-bearing species and cut-marks and canine-tooth chewing marks were observed on several wild boar specimens and the bones of roe and red deer. There were examples of burning of teeth and intentional fragmentation of the bones among the larger mammals as well.

Most of the fragmentation of the bone assemblage appears to be the result of systematic, functional breakage for the purpose of marrow extraction. Much of this activity is likely from the Mesolithic period, as dairy products probably supplied the fat and protein for Early Neolithic groups in southern Scandinavia (e.g., Isaksson and Hallgren 2012; Gron *et al.* 2015).

Fish

Fish bone was common in the water-screened material from the Mesolithic layers (7a–c, 8) and was collected and bagged separately from the other faunal remains (Fig. 6.13). This material was analyzed by Ken Ritchie. Excavations in the summer of 2002 produced a total of 722 g of fish bone. In 2003, 6806 g were sorted and bagged. Excavations in 2004 recovered approximately 4650 g of fish bone which was water-screened through 4 mm mesh. Experimental sifting of samples through nested geologic screens of 4 mm, 2 mm, and 1 mm mesh indicate that very small fish bone present at the site were missed in the 4 mm screens at ratios of 1:1–4:1. Previous analysis had suggested that 10–30 bones were present in each gram of fish bone collected and produced estimates of 50,000–150,000 individual elements for the excavated part of the site. Species present include the cod family (cod, saithe, haddock), flatfish (flounder, dab, sole, plaice, and/or turbot), mackerel, eel, garfish, and dogfish. The codfish and flatfish make up the majority of the assemblage. An additional item of note was the large number of cod family otoliths (ear bones) recovered from Layer 8. Excavation of Layer 8 in 4 units (m²) resulted in a total of 1648 otoliths representing at least 824 individual fish. Size estimates from comparison with modern otoliths place most of these fish in the 1–3 kg range – an impressive amount of food.

Layer 6, a sandy layer with a high content of rock and archaeological materials, likely contains materials eroded from higher areas during the final major marine transgressions. Ceramic typology and the presence of cattle teeth suggest a Neolithic date for the level, but in any case, very little fish

Fig 6.13. Fish bone from one sample of sediments from one square meter of excavations.

bone was recovered from these deposits. Layers 7a–c are sandy deposits distinguished from each other by the particle size, iron oxidation marks, and color (probably resulting from different inclusions in the sand such as charcoal). As Layers 7c and 8 were deeper than expected and contained huge amounts of fish bone, a checkerboard sample strategy was devised, collecting fish bone only from every other square. These deposits are interpreted as being a consequence of marine reworking, although less extreme than in Layer 6. Materials in these deposits date to the Middle Ertebølle, based on lithic typology and the presence of Mesolithic ceramics. The deepest level to produce significant amounts of fish bone is Layer 8, thought to be partially *in situ* outcast deposits. Typologically, the materials date to the Middle Ertebølle period, a conclusion supported by a radiocarbon date on a red deer bone of 5019–5000 cal BC (AAR-8189).

Some 40,502 specimens from 18 families of fish were identified at Dragsholm. Family and species identifications from levels in Layers 7 and 8 are provided in Table 6.4. Two trends of interest were observed: (1) a decreased emphasis on the cod family through time along with an increase in flat fish (and other species), and (2) a decrease in the size of fish from earlier to later levels. The gar and mackerel are summer visitors to Danish waters.

Focus on Layers 7b, 7c, and 8 shows clear changes through time. Cod and its relatives (cod family) decrease from *c.* 75% to 65% to 53% from layer 8 to 7c to 7b. Flat fish increase from *c.* 21% to 28% to 37%. Other species increase from 3.8% to 7.5% to 9.8%. Based on these numbers, there was a clear shift through time in the species represented in the Dragsholm midden.

A change in the size of fish – decreasing from older to younger levels – is seen both in the vertebra divided by the raw number of grams and the net number of grams reduced by the weight of non-identified material. This interpretation is supported by the results of the geologically screened samples – also showing an increase in smaller fish through time. A third line of evidence for a decrease in fish size through time

Table 6.4. Identified fish bones from Dragsholm.

Level	Torsk-family	% torsk-family	Fladfisk	% fladfisk	Hornfisk	Pighaj	Makrel	Ulk	Ål	Knurhane	Fjæsing	Sild	Laks	Total non-torsk or -fladfisk	% non-torsk or -fladfisk
7A	288	70.9	86	21.2	1	6	0	13	2	3	6	1	0	32	7.9
7B	1029	52.9	727	37.4	71	37	7	30	12	28	1	3	1	190	9.8
7C	2861	64.9	1221	27.7	82	74	77	45	29	11	4	6	1	329	7.5
8	734	74.9	209	21.3	14	5	11	1	1	5	0	0	0	37	3.8
Total	4914	63.4	2243	29.0	168	122	95	89	44	47	11	10	2	588	7.6

comes from measuring the first vertebra of cod family fish. Layer 8 first vertebra have a mean size of 6.94 mm (n = 25, std dev. = 1.51, median = 6.70); Layer 7c: mean = 5.70 mm (n = 126, std dev. = 1.12, median = 5.60); Layer 7b: mean = 5.13 mm (n = 40, std dev. = 1.04, median = 4.95) and; Layer 7a: mean = 5.67 mm (n = 6, std dev. = 1.02, median = 5.75). The mean measurements correspond to fish sizes of 43.3 cm, 36.8 cm, 33.7 cm and 36.6 cm, respectively (regression formula from Enghoff 1991). This decrease in fish size may indicate increasing reliance on fish traps.

Seasonal indicators

Faunal remains from some species can be used to estimate season of site use. The majority of the seasonal indicators point to spring and summer, while winter indicators are few. Another aspect to consider is that the preservation of the bones of newborn animals is poor and may be under-estimated.

Bones of fawns of *Capreolus capreolus* (roe deer) are present in the Dragsholm material. They most probably derive from animals a few weeks of age. As *C. capreolus* gives birth in May (Schimmelmann 1935), these fawns were likely hunted in May or June. Antler development starts after shedding in November–December and antlers are fully grown in March or April (Schimmelmann 1935). In the Dragsholm material there are two fragments of developing first year antlers from a young buck and nine fully grown unshed antlers. The presence of these antlers indicates hunting from March until mid-autumn. Due to the general state of preservation of the bone material, shed antlers are not likely to be identified.

Bones from *Cervus elaphus* (red deer) fawns probably derive from animals a few weeks of age at the time of death. As *C. elaphus* gives birth late in May or in June (Schimmelmann 1935), these fawns were killed in June–July. Shed as well as unshed antlers of *C. elaphus* were identified. Shed antlers, however, might have been collected at any time of the year and are generally disregarded as a seasonal indicator. Antlers of *C. elaphus* are fully grown and attached from September to February.

Very young *Sus scrofa* piglets are present in the bone assemblage. As the time of birth is estimated to be from late April until mid-May (Noe-Nygaard 1988), these piglets from Dragsholm most probably were killed in May.

Only a few bird bones were present in the bone assemblage, of which three originate from juvenile birds, probably from the time before they left the nest. The breeding season of *Aythya fuligula* (tufted duck) is from late April to May–June and of *Cygnus olor* (mute swan) from late April to early June (Løppenthin 1967), so the presence of the juvenile birds reflects summer activity.

The seasonal indicators are summarized in Figure 6.14 and suggest that the site may have been occupied in all four seasons. Warmer temperatures in late spring and summer provide the context for many indicators. Autumn and early winter is also evidenced by the presence of traditional fur-bearing animals, such as *Martes martes* (marten) and *Castor fiber* (beaver), which are usually hunted in the autumn. There are fewer indictors available during the colder months of the year. While continuous habitation cannot be confirmed by these indicators, it is certainly a possibility. The contemporaneous sites of Agernæs (Richter and Noe-Nygaard, 2003), Tybrind Vig (Trolle-Lassen 1985; re-interpreted by Rowley-Conwy 1995), and Ringkloster (Rowley-Conwy 1980; 1995) all seem to have been visited during a certain period of the year. Sites like Smakkerup Huse (Hede 1999; Price and Gebauer 2005; and see Chapter 4), Skateholm (Larsson 1984; Magnell 2006), and Tågerup (Karsten and Knarrström 2001a; 2001b), however, have substantial deposits and more evidence for year-round

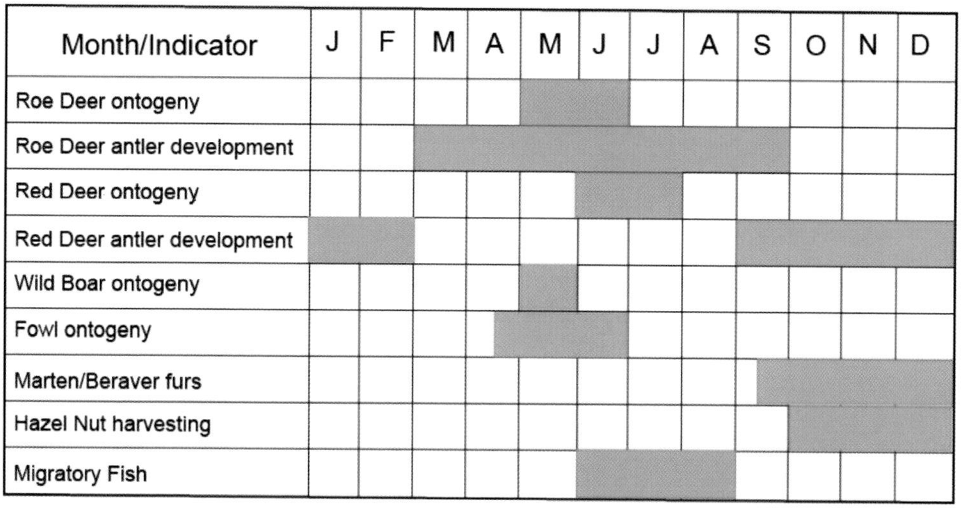

Month/Indicator	J	F	M	A	M	J	J	A	S	O	N	D
Roe Deer ontogeny					▒							
Roe Deer antler development			▒	▒	▒	▒	▒	▒				
Red Deer ontogeny							▒					
Red Deer antler development	▒	▒							▒	▒	▒	▒
Wild Boar ontogeny					▒							
Fowl ontogeny					▒							
Marten/Beaver furs									▒	▒	▒	▒
Hazel Nut harvesting												
Migratory Fish						▒	▒		▒			

Fig. 6.14. Seasonal indicators at Dragsholm.

occupation that can be interpreted as a permanent habitation. Geographically, Drag-sholm and Smakkerup Huse are approximately 25 km apart and both are coastal sites with almost identical mammalian species represented in the bone material. As has been argued elsewhere, we should try to prove that sites were *not* permanent residences, not that they were (Price *et al.* 2018).

Bone and antler tools

A wide range of worked bone and antler objects were found during the excavations, some discussed below. A summary of worked bone objects and their provenience is provided (Table 6.5). In addition, there were a number of non-descript, small pointed pieces of bone and antler recorded as well as several large pieces of worked antler.

Table 6.5. Summary of bone and antler tools recorded at Dragsholm.

North	East	Layer	Comment
112	121	6	1 small round bone
112	121	7	1 trykstok?
114	122	7b char	1 cut antler (long, no base)
114	123	7a/b trans	1 bone prene
114	128	loose	1 bone prene
			1 bone prene
115	121	7b char	1 trykstok
			1 cut antler
			1 cut antler (long shaft)
115	122	7c	1 bone prene (missing)
			1 fishhook (long) broken
115	123	7b	1 fishhook
			1 fishhook
			1 bone prene
115	124	7b	1 bone awl
115	125	8	1 fishhook
			1 bone prene
115	126	7c	1 bone prene
			1 cut antler (blank for axe)
115	128	6	1 bone point
116	127	loose	1 bone dagger
117	128	7c	1 bone borer/awl
118	128	7c	1 bone point
			1 antler pick
119	128	7a/b	1 trykstok

(Continued)

Table 6.5. (Continued)

North	East	Layer	Comment
120	128	7a	1 trykstok
			1 cut antler
121	128	7c	1 perforated seal jaw
122	128	8	1 bone point
122	128	7c	1 worked antler shaft/point
			1 bone point
123	128	7c	1 bone point
			1 bone pin
125	128	8	1 trykstok (antler retouchoir)
126	128	7	1 bone point
			1 bone point
			1 trykstok (antler retouchoir)
			1 trykstok (antler retouchoir)
126	128	7c/8	1 grooved bone
			1 bone point
			1 polished bone
127	128	8	1 fishhook
127	128	7c	1 bone point
128	123	7b	1 bone point
128	140	8 (shell)	1 Perforated antler axe
			1 bone prene
129	140	7c	1 trykstok (antler retouchoir)
130	140	7c	1 bone point
			1 fishhook
			1 bone artifact
131	140	8	1 cut/grooved antler
132	140	7a	1 pointed antler shaft
133	140	7	1 fishhook
			1 fishhook
			1 bone point
			1 polished bone frag
			1 cut red deer antler
133	140	8	1 bone point
133	140	8	1 cut antler
			1 worked antler
			1 worked antler
			1 bone point
			1 bone prene

Fig. 6.15. Sharpened tibia dagger, roe deer bone.

Fig. 6.16. Boar tusk worked into pointed scraping tool.

Fig. 6.17. Bone fishhook.

Several pieces are of particular interest, including two fragments of decorated antler axes, one polished antler axe (butt end with shaft-hole), a sharpened tibia 'dagger' (Fig. 6.15), a boar tusk used perhaps as a fish cleaning tool (Fig. 6.16), a number of fish hooks varying in size and completeness (Fig. 6.17), animal tooth pendants (Fig. 6.18), and three pieces of antler axes.

The worked boar tusk (Fig. 6.16) is pointed at one end, has a sharp edge along its length, and is 'gripable'. Similar examples are known from the Mesolithic elsewhere, e.g., at Friesack in northern Germany (E. David, pers. comm.) and in the Danube Gorges (D. Borić, pers. comm.).

The many fish hooks are fashioned from bone, lacked barbs, and curve from a long stem with a nub on one end to a shorter, pointed end (Fig. 6.17). The animal tooth pendants (Fig. 6.18) are usually canine teeth, often perforated at the end of the root, and taken from several species including dog, red deer, and seal. There is also a perforated seal jaw (Fig. 6.19) among the modified animal remains.

The three examples of antler axes are all fragments, but two of these were found in close proximity, along with the greenstone trindøkse. The association of these objects suggests the contents of a grave. Two of the three pieces have traces of red ochre, also evidence of deposition in a grave. One of the three is a piece of polished antler and one of the two decorated pieces has an area of cross-hatched fine lines on a polished surface on one side of the object (Fig. 6.20). The second decorated antler axe fragment is somewhat larger and includes the shaft hole on one side of the piece. The design on this example is shown in Figure 6.21 and consists of both lines and dots, a combination basically unknown on Danish Ertebølle decorated axes. The meaning of these decorations is unknown but the pattern of dots suggests an animal shape and the band, formed by two lines with intermittent hatching, and wavy 'arms' may be a human or human-like form. Other interpretations are of course possible.

In addition, two small fragments of human remains were encountered in the excavations. These are in addition to the two loose human teeth and the fragment of mandible discussed under radiocarbon dating.

Summary and conclusions

Our archaeological excavations at Dragsholm uncovered large areas around the original burial location, collected new artifactual and human materials, and detailed the stratigraphic context of the site. These excavations opened a series of trenches along the eastern slopes of the small rise of the burial ground and in the adjacent waterlain deposits. The wide trenches on the slope of the rise did not expose any new features or burials. It appears that the graves discovered in 1973 were the only remaining intact burials at the site. At the same time, it seems clear from the discovery of the isolated mandible, tooth pendants, and decorated antler axe fragments in 2003 and two fragments of disarticulated human bone among the faunal material that other graves were destroyed and scattered by wave erosion during the course of several transgressions.

The waterlain deposits at the site indicate at least two, probably three, major episodes of deposition. There is a lower horizon of Early and Middle Ertebølle materials that is largely *in situ* with little evidence of rolling or patination. This lower horizon contains well preserved fish bone and nutshell in great quantities along with other faunal remains. An upper horizon appears to contain Late Ertebølle and Early Neolithic materials according to radiocarbon dates and the contents of the layer. This material is frequently rolled and marine patinated, bone is eroded and not well preserved. Fish bone and smaller artifacts are rare. This upper horizon appears

Fig. 6.18. Animal tooth pendant.

Fig. 6.19. Perforated seal mandible.

Fig. 6.20. Fragment of decorated antler axe with cross-hatching.

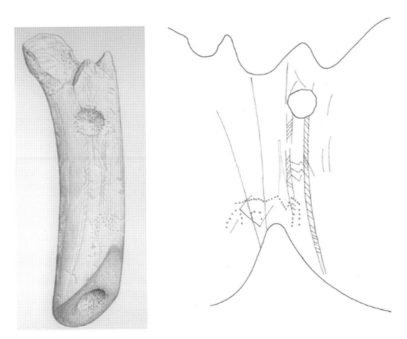

Fig. 6.21. Rollout drawing of fragment of the decorated antler axe with lines and dots. The shaft hole is approximately 2.5 cm in diameter.

to be secondarily redeposited, presumably during a transgression or regression event at the end of the Atlantic climatic episode.

The artifactual materials recovered document occupation in the Late Mesolithic and Early Neolithic. Remains from the Ertebølle date from the Early and Middle parts of this period with little evidence of a Late Ertebølle occupation, when much of this area may have been under water. Distinctive artifacts included decorated antler axes, ceramics, a greenstone trindøkse, and concave truncations on blades. In addition, there are ceramic and stone artifacts belonging to the Funnel Beaker culture (TRB) in conjunction with radiocarbon dates that indicate the presence of Early Neolithic settlement at the site. TRB ceramics were common in the upper cultural layer at the site. Flake axes were found throughout the cultural horizons, but no polished flint axes or fragments were recovered. In total, the artifactual remains, radiocarbon dates, and other information suggest a rather continuous occupation of this propitious coastline of the Kattegat in northwest Sjælland. The fjord created here by rising sea levels during the Atlantic episode would have been a rich area for marine resources. In addition, the opening of this waterway between the Kattegat and the Lammefjord to the east may have created an exceptional situation for the capture of marine resources. The location also has strategic significance as a passage to the north into the peninsula of Odsherred.

The topographic and hydrological history of the area is revealed in the stratigraphy at Dragsholm. The sedimentary succession documents three transgressive cycles. The dates of the three cycles were compared with other northwest Sjælland localities. Together they confirm that the High Atlantic transgression and the late Atlantic/ early Subboreal were the most pronounced and the most inland-reaching transgressions. The timing of the transgressions is well dated and established at four different localities in northwest Sjælland. The height of sea level (*c.* +4 m asl) and the timing of the late Atlantic/early Subboreal transgression make it clear that the Dragsholm locality could not have been occupied at the end of the Atlantic period. At that time, this area would have been largely submerged just at the edge of a high-energy current connecting the Lammefjord and the Kattegat. Early Neolithic materials must have accumulated at the site prior to the last transgression.

Taken together, the evidence from Dragsholm, Fårevejle (Chapter 8), the Saltbæk Vig survey (Chapter 2), and the general absence of earliest Neolithic in much of southern Scandinavia suggests that the first evidence of the introduction of agriculture and a Neolithic way of life may have been largely erased by transgressions at the beginning of the Subboreal climatic episode.

The new investigations at Dragsholm provide an almost complete picture of the archaeological context of the graves and accompanying settlement as well as the Holocene geology of the region. A great deal of new information has derived from these studies including strong evidence that the two graves are approximately 1000 years apart in age and that the two females date from the Mesolithic Ertebølle and that the male is certainly Neolithic. The stray humerus (Individual C) originally found at the burial site comes from the Bronze Age. A third Mesolithic individual, identified from a mandible fragment, was discovered in the new excavations. Stable isotope study of the human remains replicated the earlier collagen carbon results, but investigation of nitrogen and apatite carbon indicates that marine foods, primarily fish, were less important during the Mesolithic than previously believed. New flint, ceramic, bone, and antler artifacts further document Mesolithic and Neolithic occupation at the site.

The Dragsholm area is rich in archaeological sites from the later Mesolithic and it is likely that new settlements and graves will be discovered in the coming years. It is our hope that the results reported here will assist in the understanding of new finds. At the same time, we believe our work has contributed to the resolution of questions regarding the age of the Dragsholm graves and the nature of the transition from the Mesolithic to the Neolithic at this place in western Sjælland.

Excavations at Bøgebjerg

The site of Bøgebjerg belongs to the Middle Ertebølle. The official designation is Bøgelund Bakke, Fårevejle sogn, Ods herred, Holbæk/Vestsjællands amt, Sted nr. 03.04.03. Excavated remains included flint, bone, shell, and wood. The site was excavated in 2003, after testing with one trench (Trench 1) in 2002. A series of six trenches comprising over 140 m² was excavated by machine and hand, with water-screening of some of the deposits (see Fig. 6.2, above).

Radiocarbon dates

Several radiocarbon dates were obtained for the deposits at Bøgebjerg. These included three from the Aarhus radiocarbon laboratory and two from Beijing. An initial determination was made at Aarhus in 2002 to help us date the site. This was AAR-8191, measured on bone (probably from roe deer), dated 4800–4200 cal BC (95.4% probability). Coupled with the absence of pottery at the site, this suggests a Middle Ertebølle age. One (roe deer bone fragment) of the two dates from Beijing returned a Late Neolithic estimate of 2880–2620 cal BC (95.4%) suggesting that not all the bone at the site was contemporaneous.

The remaining dates appear valid and include BA-10660 (4830–4690 cal BC (95.4%)), on red deer bone from Trench 5, Layer 7b; AAR-8775 (5370–4710 cal BC (95.4%)) on charcoal, Trench 2, Culture Layer; and AAR-8776, 5000–4710 cal BC (95.4%)) on red deer antler at 75 cm below surface in Trench 2. All these dates fall in the Early and Middle Ertebølle.

Stratigraphy

The basic geology of the deposits at Bøgebjerg is shown in Figure 6.22.

Layer 1: Topsoil with slump and slide structures.
Layer 2: Dark humified gyttja with peaty substance on top.
Layer 3: Dark fine clay gyttja.
Layer 4: Clean white sand with a few orange iron stripes. A few roots with scattered pieces of charcoal on top.
Layer 5: Medium to fine sand thinning upwards with organic matter decreasing upward, charcoal pieces on bottom.
Layer 6: Coarse sand, upwards increasing to fine pebbles with cobbles and a few roots. The upper part consists of shell gravel mixed with complete shells. Scattered bone fragments and flint artifacts.
Layer 7: Medium sand, coarsening upwards with layers of black organic mud. Scattered rusty roots, possibly tidal dominated.
Layer 8: Clean light green medium sand, with reed stems?

The deposits from Bøgebjerg are somewhat earlier than those at nearby Dragsholm (based on radiocarbon dates, flint typology, and the absence of ceramics), but still within the Ertebølle period. Some of the same processes of transgression/regression with the resultant erosion and redeposition of materials undoubtedly took place here.

Lithics

Flint artifacts from Bøgebjerg were common and
fairly typical for the Middle Ertebølle period
(Table 6.6). A total of almost 129 kg of flint
artifacts were removed from the excavations,
2829 pieces, 56 retouched tools or 1.9% of all
flint artifacts. Points were most common among
the tools. There were several blade knives and
a fragment of a pointed-butted polished axe,
probably intrusive.

Fauna and fish remains

Faunal analysis has not been completed with the
exception of the fish remains.

The majority of the fish bones found at
Bøgebjerg came from Layer 7. The distribution
of fish remains found in these layers is provided
in Table 6.7. A total of 265 g of fish bone was
recovered, all from Trenches 2 and 3. This material has been analyzed (Table 6.8). The Bøgeb-

*Fig. 6.22. Air photo of Dragsholm (lower)
and Bøgebjerg (upper) excavations (Royal
Danish Air Force)*

jerg assemblage was 2592 specimens from ten families. The number of unidentified
vertebrae is fairly high, but this is mostly due to the number of bones that were too
eroded for identification and not because there were a lot of extra species that could
not be identified. Many of the unidentified bones were torsk or flat fish, but these
were not listed if the identification was uncertain.

One preliminary observation of interest is the number of individuals in the cod
family, based on vertebrea. Using 50 as the number of vertebrae in a fish, there are
at least 22 individuals represented by the 1079 vertebra. But looking at the number
of second, third and fourth vertebrae it is clear that there were at least three times
that many fish. This effect is most pronounced in the two units from Layer 3 (see
above). This result suggests that there was some kind of differential deposition of
the heads.

Wooden stakes

A number of worked hazel stakes were found in the excavations. A total of 18
sharpened stakes recorded. Hazel stakes were found in Trench 2 between 73–75E
in three separate levels. The upper zone, Wood 1, is at the top of Layer 7 or the
transition between layer 5 (mud layer over shell layer) and layer 7 (shell layer).
There are other tangled wood and bark pieces. Wood Zone 2 is located under

Table 6.6. Flint artifacts from the excavations at Bøgebjerg.

North	East	Layer	Wt	Whit %	Burn	Flakes	Soft	Hard	Total blades	Flco	Blco	Rf	Rb	Blkn	Pt	Ptpre	Flax	Comments
289	61	1	2551	10	20	468	8	15	26	5				1*	2	2		*transversal, polax pointed butt – bog patination
289	74	*	119	5	1	17	1	1	2									*shell gyttja
289	61	2	1292	10	11	214	1	7	9	4			1*		2	1		*distal, 1flkn
289	59	1	2189	10	39	466	3	21	31	1					5			1ax frag.
289	62	2*	1980	10	12	331	4	9	18			2	1	1				*contact with till
296	58	2	375	15	16	108	0	2	3				1					
293	57	1	1753	20	55	676	9	9	23	1		2	1*		9	2		*w/double ret., 1axfl
289	59	3	1922	25	25	315	11	12	24	2		1	1					1bu
301	59	*	193	0		1											1	*gyttja
289	73	*	400	0		18	1	1	2	1								*træ 3 (?)
303	59	*	215	5	1	15	2	2	6	1								*gyttja

Whit % = white patination; Flco = flake core; Blco = blade core; Rf = retouched flake; Rb = retouched blade; Blkn = blade knife; Ptpre = Pre=point; Flax = flake axe

Table 6.7. Distribution of fish remains by level at Bøgebjerg (Trenches 2 and 3 combined).

	m²	Weight (g)	NISP
Level 1	5	10	97
Level 2	1	<1	1
Level 3	2	60	372
Level 5	3	31	303
Level 7	6	161	1776
Other	4	3	43
Total	21	265	2592

the shell layer at the top of the mud layer under the shell layer, at the same level as the two paving stones. Wood Zone 3 is in the mud under the two paving stones.

Table 6.8. Identification of fish remains from Bøgebjerg.

Vertebra	No.	%
Cod family	1079	49.0
Flatfish	774	35.1
Garfish	77	3.5
Mackrel	20	0.9
Eel	16	0.7
Gurnard	15	0.7
Turbot	13	0.6
Herring	3	0.1
No ID	209	9.5
Cod family		
Basio-occipital	13	
1st vertebra	41	
2nd vertebra	76	
3rd vertebra	75	
4th vertebra	83	
5th vertebra	44	
6th vertebra	28	
Other	719	

Other bones	
Cod family	
Premaxillary	39 (24 left and 15 right)
Maxillary	10 (5 left and 5 right)
Dentary	10 (3 left and 7 right)
Parasphenoid	6
Post-temporal	5 (2 left and 3 right)
Prevomer	5 (2 whole, 2 left and 1 right)
Supracleithrum	4 (2 left and 2 right)
Angular	2 (1 left and 1 right)
Quadrate	1 (right)
Fladfisk	
Os anale	3
Maxillary	2 (left)
Hornfisk	
Dentary fragments	7

Table 6.9. Bone tools from Bøgebjerg.

Object	No.
Bone awls	2
Bird bone awl	1
Bone points	11
Fishhooks	2
Bone prene	14
Antler retouchoirs	2
Bone perçoirs	1
Bone pins	2
Bone chisels	2
Antler axes	2
Worked antler	3

Bone tools

Bone tools uncovered in the excavations are listed in Table 6.9, the range is largely typical of Ertebølle.

Results of excavation

It was found that the terrestrial part of the site, marked by a dark culture layer with flint pieces and fire-cracked rocks, was probably re-arranged due to erosion of the rather sloping terrain, but that a marine discard layer was intact with flint and with good preservation conditions for bones and partially preserved wood in the form of sharpened hazel sticks and massive layers of wood chips. The site was a Middle Ertebølle settlement and thus a bit too early to provide information on the transition to farming.

Chapter 7

Fårevejle Kro

Introduction

Our project intentionally revisited the site of Fårevejle Kro in western Sjælland, known to be a stratified shell midden, originally investigated at the end of the 19th century. The site was about 6.5 km north of Dragsholm and well within our range. Because of our interest in the transition to agriculture during the Atlantic–Subboreal transition and in the geology in this area, this seemed to be a useful place to continue our study. Our plan was to investigate this midden with new questions and excavation techniques as well as radiocarbon dating. Kitchen middens (*køkkenmøddinger*) in other parts of the country were often found with Early Neolithic material in the upper layers of the shell heap and we hoped to find a similar situation here. This site was somewhat higher in elevation than many on the coastline and might have escaped the erosive transgressions we observed elsewhere. I was also very interested in digging a shell midden, one of the classic site types of the Danish Mesolithic. This project was in the Odsherred Museum jurisdiction and again I spoke with Arne Andersen prior to beginning work at the site and arrangements were made with the farmer for excavations on his land.

Excavations at Fårevejle Kro

The shell midden at Fårevejle Kro (aka Vejle Kro) lies in a northwestern corner of the now fossil Lammefjord in western Sjælland, Denmark. The site is situated on the south side of what was in late Atlantic times, *c.* 6000 years ago, a small peninsula on the northwestern shore of the fjord (Fig. 7.1). The peninsula is bounded on the east and southeast by the fairly steep slopes of a hill known as Borrebjerg. These heights decline gradually to the west and the shell midden lies in the first saddle west of Borrebjerg. Today the area of the site is sloping dry land under cultivation. The primary drainage canal for the Lammefjord region runs approximately 100 m to the south on the level ground of the old sea floor.

The site sits at an elevation of 5–7 m asl. During the middle Holocene, sea level was approximately 4 m higher than today in this area and the site would have been almost directly on the coast. Figure 7.2 shows the location of the previous excavations

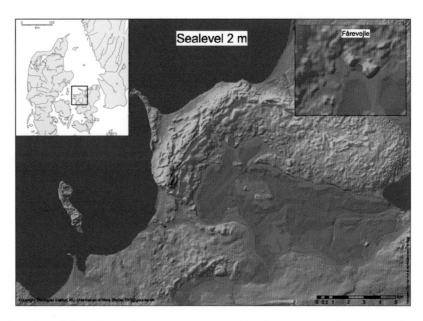

Fig. 7.1. Location of Fårevejle Kro in the western arm of the former Lammefjord; sea level at +4 m asl (Source: Nanna Noe-Nygaard).

Fig. 7.2. Air photo showing GPS survey of the agricultural field and the location of the excavations from both 1896–97 (black) and 2004–5 (red).

at the site in black and the 2004–05 excavations in red, in conjunction with elevation; sea level at the time of occupation was +4.0 m asl.

The official designation of the site in the National Register (Sognebeskrivelse) is Matr. 16c af Høve, Asnæs sogn, Ods herred, Vestsjællands amt., Stednr. A 15991, NM 03.04.01, sb. nr. 137. The coordinates of the site were listed incorrectly in the DKC register and should be 653972/6187975. The coordinates according to the UTM system are 0654041 6188144.

Geology

In the early part of the Holocene this area would have been dry land in the interior of what is today Denmark. As sea levels rose and the Storebælt (the straits between the Danish islands of Sjælland and Funen) flooded, the area was gradually submerged by the Littorina transgressions during the late Atlantic and early Subboreal climatic episodes (Iversen 1937; Jessen 1937; Berglund 1971; Jakobsen 1981; 1983, C. Christensen 1994; 1995; K. Chrisensen 1997; Astrup 2019). As the seas reached higher, the area known as the Lammefjord was created (Fig. 7.3). Maximum sea level in the area was probably +4 m asl according to Mertz (1924). This interpretation corresponds closely with the results of the analysis of cores from Trundholm Mose, 15 km to the north (Kolstrup 1988; Christensen 1995).

A few kilometers southwest of the Fårevejle midden rises the hill of *Vejrhøj* and the *Vejrhøj Buerne*, a major end moraine running along the western coast of Sjælland. This end moraine is fairly steep and prominent and would have protected the whole western area from heavy winds coming from the west and north. These conditions, in addition to the access to the open sea through the inlet at Dragsholm, must have made this area attractive for settlement (Fig. 7.4) – also

Fig. 7.3. An artist's view of the church at Fårevejle from Vejrhøj with the low, forested hill of Borrebjerg near the location of the shell midden at Fårevejle Kro across the small bay of the Lammefjord behind and just left of the church.

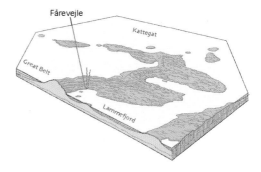

Fig. 7.4. Artist's reconstruction of the landscape of northwest Sjælland in the late Atlantic climatic episode (Schou 1949).

indicated by the presence of other sites in the area dating from the same period as the Fårevejle midden.

Later, during the Subboreal, the water receded, closing off the narrow straits through Dragsholm between the Sejerø Bugt and the Lammefjord. This former waterway between the Sejerø Bugt and the Lammefjord was only 2–3 km wide and largely wetlands and marsh. In order to reclaim the Lammefjord, the Audebo Dam was constructed in the years 1872–74; the first stage of pumping out the diked water began in 1875 and a primary drainage canal was dug from Drags Mølle (2 m asl), linking the former Lammefjord through the Dragsholm inlet, draining the Lammefjord region into the bay of Sejerø. When the site was visited and excavated at the end of the 19th century, the shore of the slowly draining fjord was only 30 m away, and the peninsula crowned by the Borrebjerg was surrounded by marsh (Madsen *et al.* 1900, 112). Today this area is cultivated fields and pasture and the former Lammefjord is famous for the carrots grown there.

Previous investigations

The shell midden at Fårevejle Kro was first discovered by A.P. Madsen in 1894, where he noted a few pieces of shell on the ground surface. Otherwise the place showed little sign of occupation as the slope toward the Lammefjord was quite even and the area was under cultivation. Madsen put in four test pits and concluded that the shell midden was approximately 68 m long and 14 m wide, the shell layer itself about 0.75 m thick. He also found well preserved animal bones and teeth, flint debitage, and a flake axe.

This initial testing led to larger excavations at the site conducted by the National Museum, carried out over nine days in 1896 and 1897 (Madsen *et al.* 1900). Four trenches were excavated perpendicular to the length of the midden. Two of these trenches crossed from one side of the midden to the other. At the north side of trench 2 and trench 4, a cross-trench was excavated perpendicular to the main trench and roughly along the edge of the midden. A total of *c.* 150 m² were excavated, and the estimated size of the midden revised. The shell midden was now suggested to be about 56 m long, 10–11 m wide in the middle, and 0.7–0.9 m thick at a maximum, on average 0.5 m thick. The plow zone covering the shell midden was 15–25 cm deep on average, more along the north and south edges. The plow zone in trench 3 was much thicker, *c.* 60 cm probably due to slopewash, and the shell layer thus thinner in this area.

The shell layer was composed of oyster, *Cardium*, mussel, and *Littorina* shells, in some places identified as distinctive 'meal piles'. In most places, the midden layer was a compact mass of shells without much soil. Surprisingly few artifacts were found in the midden, which was one of the reasons why C. Neergaard indicated in a letter to the National Museum that he did not think the midden was a suitable object of study for 'the Second Kitchen Midden Commission'. Today it is clear that a number of middens from the end of the Mesolithic contain relatively few finds (e.g., Norsminde,

Krabbesholm; Andersen and Johansen 1997). There are also several natural, fossil shell beds known around the former Lammefjord, not far from the site. There are other smaller, cultural shell middens in the area as well. The Fårevejle Kro midden is one of the largest.

Further investigations in 1897 focused on the area behind the midden and revealed a dark, fatty cultural layer, 5–50 cm thick, increasing toward the east, as a continuation of the shell midden. This layer mostly overlay and thus post-dated the shell midden. Both Mesolithic and Neolithic artifacts were found in this area as well as fireplaces. There were few artifacts found in the Mesolithic layers themselves and more from the Neolithic deposits in the dark cultural layer behind the midden. The overall conclusion was that the Fårevejle midden was a stratified shell midden, with layers and a few artifacts from both the Mesolithic and the Neolithic, but not rich enough for further investigations.

The site was collected in 1982–83 by Knud Heinesen, a Danish politician and amateur archaeologist, who donated his collection to the Kalundborg Museum. In 1997, the site was visited as a part of the *køkkenmødding-projekt 1996–97* (Andersen and Johansen 1997). The Fårevejle midden was surveyed, but no tests were put in. The conclusion was that the site should be protected if excavations showed well preserved cultural layers. There are other sites in the Fårevejle area of interest. On the same peninsula as the Fårevejle Kro midden, a couple of hundred meters to the southwest, there are two smaller shell middens. These sites were cored and/or tested as part of our 2004–05 project. In 2010 the site at Fårevejle was purchased by the state and made a protected monument. Several information signs and a small parking area were added along the edge of the field.

2004–05 Fieldwork

Survey, Coring, and Datum

Our initial efforts focused on mapping the field and coring to establish the exact position of the shell midden and to get a preliminary sense of the stratigraphy of the site. The entire field around the site from the road to the drainage canal was surveyed by Lars Jensen from Odense Bys Museer. He mapped the field at a 5 m interval using GPS and set fixed points for the map and excavation. The contour map of the field did not reveal a mound, as was the case in 1894. Fixed points were marked with a nail in the ground and either a ranging rod or a wooden stake. Error was on the order of ±2 cm vertically and less horizontally.

A 2 × 20 m trench (Trench 1) was laid out at 140–142E/100–120N. Given that orientation, our trench was designed to run between the center and eastern excavations from 1896–97 (between længdegrav 1/tværgrav 3 and længdegrav 2/tværgrav 4). This position was confirmed after removing the topsoil of the trench when a relatively recent disturbance appeared at 141E/115N. It was 2 m wide from north to south, the edges straight cut. This must have been part of the third, easternmost trench from

1897, længdegrav 2. With this information we were able to establish the exact position of the 1896–97 excavations in relation to our 2004–05 excavations (Fig. 7.2).

Excavations

The excavations in 2004 were initiated with Trench 1 opened by hand (Fig. 7.5). The topsoil was *c.* 40 cm thick in the upper part of the trench (around 110N) and *c.* 80 cm thick in the lower part (around 106N). This topsoil was removed to the level where crushed shell began to appear. We were able to expose the entire, eroded surface of the midden which appeared as a low mound, sloping upward from the landside to the middle of the midden and downward toward the former shoreline. Later the trench was extended at both ends using a backhoe.

The shell midden itself was excavated by hand using trowels. Excavation proceeded by square meters. The layers were generally excavated in 10 cm 'artificial' levels, but the cultural layers were followed when possible (if they were more than 10 cm thick they were split into two or more levels). All the obvious diagnostic finds, pottery, retouched flint pieces, and large bones were measured in three dimensions and given X numbers. The remaining material, shell and dirt, was water screened through a 4 mm mesh (Fig. 7.6). All small finds – flint flakes and small pieces of bone and the like – were collected and recorded by meter square and level. All features and interesting areas of shell, stone concentrations, and ash dumps on the midden surface were mapped, drawn, photographed and given numbers as features.

On the north (inland) side of the midden, the plow zone was removed to the layer where crushed shell appeared. Behind the midden the plow zone and the subsequent layers were removed down to the moraine sand since finds were rare in these layers (only a very few flakes). To the south, on the fjord side of the midden, we used a backhoe to remove the overburden (from approximately 106N and south). We took off the deposits down to the marine clay where it was seen in the trench. We went approximately 15 m to the south until we hit water running out of the side that collapsed the walls of the trench. Here we stopped. There was no peat or gyttja in this area, which was a disappointment. Any cultural material or an organic layer associated

Fig 7.5. West wall of the northern portion of Trench 1 with shell midden exposed.

with the use of the midden must have been destroyed by storm or wave action or perhaps transgressions and plowing. Trench 1 eventually ran from 90N to 141N, approximately 51 m in length. The shell midden was present in about 11 m of the trench from 105N to 116N.

We continued excavations at the shell midden at Fårevejle. It was clear that the oyster section of the midden – beneath the blacker layer with crushed mussel, *Littorina*, and *Cardium* shells – was composed of more intact shells of oyster, less sediment, and much more bone. There

Fig. 7.6. Screening station for shell midden deposits at Fårevejle Kro.

were clusters of bones in the midden deposits, especially in the oyster layer, that contained a variety of species.

Trench 1 went through the thickest part of the midden, from the north area behind the midden, through the midden, and out into the fossil Lammefjord (leaving a 2 × 2 m² balk in the midden where the shell layers were thickest). The cross-section of the trench provided a good overview of the stratigraphy and formation of the shell midden (Fig. 7.5). It also documented the relationship between the midden and the dark, fatty, cultural layer immediately behind it. To the south, in front of the midden, the trench was carried out into the former fjord but no preserved outcast layers were found. A total of 102 m² was opened in 2004 of which the shell midden makes up approximately 22 m² (approximately 4% of the midden area).

In 2005 we returned to the site to continue the work started in 2004. The 2004 excavations left a number of unanswered questions: Was a pre-midden layer present beneath the shell midden? What was the age of the stone pavements found on the southern border of the shell midden? How do these pavements relate to the latter? Was the shell midden ever transgressed? How much of the shell layers are actually Neolithic? And finally, what is the nature of the dark cultural layer north of the midden? The fieldwork goals of the 2005 excavations were two-fold: to complete the work begun in Trench 1 – excavating the remaining 2 × 2 m balk in the midden and cleaning the bottom of the trench under the midden (to determine if an occupation layer was present), and to put in a new trench to excavate a larger part of the midden and to determine the nature of the dark, fatty, (Neolithic?) cultural layer to the north, partly covering the midden.

The 2 × 2 m balk from 2004 in Trench 1 was re-opened by exposing the north and south walls in order to have control of the section during excavation. The topsoil was removed by hand down to a layer containing shell fragments and then trowels were used for excavating. The midden in this balk was excavated in natural layers, taking all four m² down at the same time. The layers were numbered starting at 1 and collated with the layers on the section drawings. The balk in the midden was *c.* 80 cm thick and covered by 30–40 cm of plow zone.

A location for Trench 2 was selected using the old drawings and descriptions from 1896; the dark, fatty layer was reported to be thickest in the area just east of old 'Tværgrav 3'. Trench 2 (2 × 7 m²) was placed in such a way, that it included the dark, fatty layer to the north behind the shell midden as well as the northern edge of the shell midden (131.5–133.5E/112–119N). The eastern edge of the old 'Tværgrav 3' appeared in this trench along the west section of our Trench 2.

The topsoil was removed by machine down to a layer where crushed shell first appeared. Excavations proceeded as in Trench 1. All features and interesting areas of shell or stone concentrations and ash dumps on the midden surface were mapped. They were drawn on plans (scale 1:10 or 1:20), photographed, and given a feature number (A-numbers). Samples for radiocarbon dating were taken from all major layers by selecting shells (*Cardium edule*) when present and/or charcoal and bone. A total of 14 m² was excavated in 2005 – 4 m² of the midden and the floor of Trench 1 and 10 m² in Trench 2.

Testing

Testing was done at two sites in the vicinity of Fårevejle Kro. Both sites are in the National Registry and were surveyed as part of the *Køkkenmødding projekt 1996-97*. One was estimated to be largely destroyed (03.04.03 sb.527A), the other as fairly promising (03.04.03 sb. 506B). The former site is located in a field used for pasture. Coring in 2005 in this area revealed little shell or cultural material. A few patinated flakes were found at this site, but no diagnostic artifacts. No further work was done.

Site SB#506B was cored and tested. This test pit was 1 × 1 m, excavated after coring showed a layer of shell at a depth of approximately 1 m. This test pit was located in the northeast corner of the back garden of the McEwans' house, approximately 200 m west-south-west of the larger midden at Fårevejle Kro. A section at the test pit shows garden soil and then the dark brown, broken shell horizon we have seen in every excavation of the shell midden at Fårevejle Kro (Fig. 7.7). There was

Fig. 7.7. Photo of test pit at SB#506B.

a thick layer of gray sediment, charcoal, and crushed shell, comparable to the late Early Neolithic/early Middle Neolithic layer at Fårevejle Kro. This grey shell layer sat on top of a thin white layer of oyster shells. The oyster shells covered another layer of grey sediment with crushed shell that sat atop of the white sand subsoil. We encountered a hearth or charcoal layer in the oyster shell layer and a possible post-hole in the floor of the test pit.

Section archive at Fårevejle Kro

At the end of the 2005 season, Per Poulsen of the National Museum made two 'geological' peels or archives from the eastern section of this trench where the shell layer was thickest. He used expanding foam, glue, a fiberglass mat, and wooden frames to create two replicas of the stratigraphy of the midden (Fig. 7.8).

Results of excavations

The site at Fårevejle Kro is a stratified shell midden with both Mesolithic (Late Ertebølle) and Neolithic (late Early Neolithic/early Middle Neolithic Funnel Beaker Culture) layers, based on

Fig 7.8. Per Paulsen and the section peel.

radiocarbon dates, diagnostic pottery, and flint artifacts. As was observed in 1896–97, there were surprisingly few finds from Fårevejle Kro. There was some limited activity at the site prior to the establishment of the midden as evidenced by a few scattered pits. We did not find an extensive, thick, dark brown layer to the north of the midden as reported from the excavations in the late 19th century. There were only remnants of a dark brown layer to the north with very few finds. The extent of this deposit was not determined. We suspect that this layer represents slope wash and perhaps an area of cultivation from the Neolithic. Some of this old deposit may have been incorporated in the modern plow zone. Results from our excavation are discussed below for Trench 1 and 2.

A group of 7–9 individuals (Fig. 7.9) worked for 73 days over two summer seasons in 2004–2005 to expose and record *c.* 114 m² of the site. Our investigations were focused on the shell midden, but we also explored areas to the north and south. In 2004 and 2005 a total of 36 m² of the actual shell midden was excavated; during 9 days in 1896–97 a large group of individuals opened *c.* 89 m². A total of 125 m² of the midden has been excavated to date. The shell midden is estimated to cover 616 m², in which case at least 80% remains. The results of our investigations include both the information about the midden and the finds.

Trench 1

The shell midden at Fårevejle Kro seems to have formed directly on an old beach, which appears as light reddish-brown sand criss-crossed by animal burrows, mostly mole runs. Some pockets and thin bands of large, intact oyster shells are found on top of this layer. The lowest layers of the midden contain mostly whole shells but some crushed shell is also present. None of the layers is exclusively oyster. Small, yet distinct, 'meal piles' were sometimes detected, usually dominated by one species of shellfish. The shells were fairly loosely packed and must have been

Fig. 7.9. Fårevejle field crew 2007. From left: upper row: Carolyn Freiwald, Tia Nielsen, Lone Andersen, Jens Nielsen; front row: Ken Ritchie, Per Paulsen, Terry Slocum, Doug Price, Michael P. Jensen.

covered quite quickly by subsequent deposits. These layers contain numerous artifacts, bone is particularly abundant but also flint flakes, some stone tools, and ceramics are found.

Another interesting detail was a large boulder (*c.* 80 × 50 × 30 cm) found in the middle of the shell layers (140E/112N) – it was in fact the only boulder found embedded in the shells. It was clearly split and turned out to fit perfectly with one of the big boulders embedded in the moraine sand right behind the midden. This indicates that these two areas might have been open at the same time.

All of the oyster shell layers are thought to be Mesolithic (i.e., Late Ertebølle), based on the presence of diagnostic Ertebølle sherds (one from a lamp) and flint tools such as transverse arrowheads, flake axes, and distally retouched blades. Much of the actual shell midden seems to be Mesolithic.

The upper and thinner layers of the midden are composed of crushed shell mixed with sediment, pebbles, and fragments of burned rock. These layers are mainly composed of crushed cockle and mussel shell mixed with some *Littorina*. Oysters are occasionally found in these layers, but they are by no means dominant. One layer, in particular, appears as a fairly thick, grayish–black ash horizon with charcoal and a large number of burned rocks, many of which are part of features. This layer was recognized in both years of the excavations and seems to be present over the full width of the shell midden. The fact that the shells are crushed and the 'ash/charcoal horizon' is extensive may indicate that these surfaces were lying open for a long time. Most of the pottery is found in these layers and appears to be of (Middle) Neolithic date.

Some flint flakes and tools are also present but they are few in number compared to the lower, compact shell layers of Mesolithic date. The shell midden is clearly thicker in the eastern part of the trench, which means that it slopes down toward the west.

There is no sharp division between the Mesolithic and Neolithic layers. The Mesolithic layers contain mostly whole shells, but these are not oysters exclusively as observed in other Danish shell middens; both cockles and mussels are present in these layers, and oysters, albeit smaller and fewer, are present in the topmost crushed shell layers thought to be Neolithic. There is little artifactual evidence that the site was used or material deposited during Early Neolithic I. All of the diagnostic pottery seems to be Middle Neolithic. An overall pattern is seen at Fårevejle where the Mesolithic oyster midden is located slightly more inland than the Subboreal, Neolithic shell deposits, probably a consequence of changing sea level.

Above these layers that make up the actual shell midden, occasional shell pockets were found, but generally the uppermost layer is a humic brown soil containing a lot of gravel and pebbles and a small amount of tiny shell fragments. This layer appears immediately beneath the plow zone. Many burned rocks and rock fragments are also present in this level, some of which are part of features on top of the shell midden. This brown soil layer likely records disturbance of the midden caused by trangression/regression (due to the pebbles and eroded conditions of shells), slopewash from the adjacent hill, and/or cultivation.

Bottom of Trench 1

The floor of Trench 1, from approximately 110–115N, was cleaned and exposed to investigate a possible pre-midden layer observed during the final days of excavation in 2004. The layer is a homogeneous dark brown, silty clay containing some apparently whole (but partially dissolved) oyster shells and a few artefacts. A thin layer of large oyster shells was found at the very top of the subsoil under this clay, oyster shell was found in the clay, and thin bands of oyster shells are found in some places over the clay. The clay deposit does not seem to be congruent with these oyster shell bands.

The clay layer was not evenly distributed and varied in thickness from 5–10 cm – thickest around the boulders in the subsoil. The layer extends from *c.* 110N–115N and was also found in pockets from 120–125N where it remained in depressions in the subsoil. It is found on top of and between the head-sized boulders in the top of the subsoil. Neither the layer nor the boulders are found south of 111N. The layer was cleared to look for pits and features in the surface, but none was found. While excavating, however, a single hearth was observed in a shallow depression in the subsoil.

Since the layer is found beneath the shell midden it should pre-date it. The few artifacts found in the layer are Mesolithic; a few transverse arrowheads were found in top of it. The question, however, is whether this layer is an *in situ* cultural horizon beneath the midden – or not? The layer has a washed-in appearance and occurs primarily in the middle of the trench, thickest around the boulders. It is a homogeneous dark, silty clay containing few artifacts. Layers found beneath other shell middens are often dense with artifacts. It is, however, worth noting that the Fårevejle shell midden contained few artifacts and thus the small number in the clay does not necessarily demonstrate that this is not a cultural deposit. This layer, however, might be naturally deposited silty clay, washed under or leached out of the midden.

Thus, it seems likely that the clay washed under or through the midden, surrounding the thin layer of large oyster shells and the few artifacts observed in the topsoil beneath the midden. This would also explain the fact that the clay is thickest around the small boulders in the subsoil and the few pockets found behind the actual midden area. The only object that may be *in situ* is the hearth (A35) composed of fragments of burned rock in a black charcoal-rich matrix, which was distinct from and covered by the silty brown clay. A sandy subsoil appears beneath the brown silty clay and in some places directly under the shell layers which, as stated above, formed directly on a beach. There seems to have been sporadic human activity on the beach, represented by the thin oyster shell bands and pockets in the top of the subsoil, before the dense accumulation of shell. These activities were probably responsible for the scapulae (X301) found in the subsoil, *c.* 10 cm beneath the dense shell layers. Moreover, large flint flakes, a few tools, and bones were found in the top of the subsoil in various places, behind, under, and in front of the midden, supporting the idea that some human activity took place before the midden accumulated or off midden while it was in use.

Trench 2

Trench 2 intersected the northeast corner of 'tværgrav 3'/'længdegrav 1' from the 1896–97 excavations and 'tværgrav 3' took up almost half of this new trench, leaving about 1 × 6 m for us to excavate right next to the old trench, and 1 × 2 m partly behind it. To the north beneath the plow zone and approximately 50 cm of a grey humic horizon, the dark, fatty layer was encountered. This layer is a dark brown–black silty clay, discolored by bits of charcoal found throughout the layer. It contains some smaller rocks (5–6 cm in diameter), some which appear burned, and small quantities of worked flint. The dark brown layer clearly overlays the shell midden in the 1 × 2 m area just to the north. Right behind the midden it is *c.* 10 cm thick and reaches a maximum of 35 cm over the midden. Where it is thickest, a bottom-most layer right above the shell which is darker and contains more pebbles can be distinguished. In the bottom of this layer behind the midden, a small concentration of flint cores, blades and flakes (X345–X349), and a fragment of a 4-sided polished axe (X370) were found just above the crushed shell horizon. Several Neolithic sherds as well as some flint artifacts were found in the same layer north of the shell midden in Trench 1. This corresponds with observations made in 1896 and 1897 that this layer should be dated to the (early Middle) Neolithic. Whether it represents an *in situ* deposit of a cultural layer is a different question. There are two hypotheses:

1) The layer formed as a result of activities on top of and behind the shell midden
2) The layer was the result of erosion or slopewash from the higher ground immediately north and east of the site, toward Borrebjerg.

The latter option seems the most realistic since it explains the uniform nature and high clay content of the layer. Charcoal, artifacts, and pebbles would thus have been transported from higher ground. A Neolithic site on the top of Borrebjerg was reported earlier and is recorded in the National Registry of sites. Later movement of topsoil from higher ground is also evident at the site since the shell midden and dark cultural layer are covered by 50–100 cm of topsoil and the modern surface, under which the midden is found, is even and smooth. This more recent soil cover over the midden is undoubtedly a result of slopewash and plowing in the last millennium.

Thus, the shell midden does not extend all across Trench 2, but first appears around 118N where it is very thin, *c.* 5–10 cm, and grows thicker toward the south where its maximum thickness was *c.* 60 cm at 112N. The top-most shell layer consisted of crushed shell composed of *Cardium*, mussel, *Hinia* (or *Nassa*) *reticulata*, and *Littorina* shells with some whole *Cardium* mixed with a substantial amount of sediment. In the northern part of the trench this layer was only a few cm thick but it grew thicker to the south. This layer contained flint flakes and tools and few pieces of ceramic and bone.

Under this layer a dark ashy horizon containing a number of burned rocks was found. It was not observed in the northernmost part of the trench, where the crushed shell layer lies immediately on top of whole oyster shells, but is fairly thick in squares 114–115N and encloses two stone-built hearths, one on top of the other (A34 and A36). Under the first stone-built hearth (A34), several blades, a deer tooth, and a complete ground stone Limhamn axe (X537) were found. This layer thins to the south where it is approximately 2 cm thick at 112N. It looks very much like the layer observed in Trench 1 but is less clearly defined.

Under this upper layer, another lens of crushed shell was observed. Around 115N it is thin and sits right on top of the subsoil but in 114N the lens becomes thicker as the old surface sloped more steeply to the water of the fjord.

Beneath this layer in the northern part of Trench 2 (*c.* 116–117N) were several distinct piles of large oyster shells *c.* 10–20 cm thick (Fig. 7.10) and another oyster shell pile was observed in 112N. These piles are composed of loosely packed large oyster shells along with flint and quite a bit of bone and are thought to represent distinct 'meal piles' of the same kind found in the bottom-most shell layers in Trench 1.

Fig. 7.10. Oyster shell piles in bottom layer, Trench 2.

Behind and beneath the bottom-most layers of the shell midden in Trench 2 (some of which are crushed shell and some of which are the oyster piles) the sub-soil/sand is light brown and criss-crossed by many animal burrows. It contains bits of charcoal and some worked flint, especially bigger pieces, exactly as observed in Trench 1, but also a piece of pottery (X595) and a piece of antler (X605) were found. This horizon is thought to represent an old surface or beach where sporadic human activity took place, either before the shell midden was deposited, or right next to it as it was forming.

Summary of stratigraphy

Overall, the stratigraphy generally seems to be the same in the two trenches (albeit Trench 1 contains a thicker part of the midden).

1. Human activity on the old surface/beach before the midden was formed or right next to the midden while it was forming, leaving some scattered whole oyster shells, large flint flakes, and some bone.
2. Deposition of piles of whole shells, mostly oysters but also *Cardium*, fairly quickly covered. A lot of flint and bone artefacts and some potsherds – diagnostic artifacts are Mesolithic.
3. Layers of crushed shell with flint, potsherds, and few bones.
4. Dark charcoal rich horizon with many burned whole and fragmentary rocks, many of which constitute features and hearths.
5. Crushed shell with other sediment, gravel, and many pebbles mixed in. Contains potsherds and a few flakes. Diagnostic artifacts are late Early/early Middle Neolithic. The top of these layers appears disturbed, perhaps due to transgression/regression, slopewash and/or cultivation.
6. The shell midden and the area immediately behind it were covered by a dark, fatty, cultural layer (some of which washes under the shell midden) containing Neolithic artefacts. This layer could be an *in situ* deposit or slopewash containing artefacts coming down from the adjacent hill, Borrebjerg, where a presumed Neolithic settlement was located (according to the DKC record).
7. More slopewash or alluvial deposition. Cooking pit, date unknown but probably younger than Middle Neolithic.
8. Modern slopewash/plow zone.

The bottom layers, composed of whole shells, can be ascribed to Late Mesolithic (ceramic) Ertebølle, while the upper crushed shell layers are Neolithic, Late Early TRB/Early Middle TRB. This observation is based on the distribution of diagnostic artifacts, flint (tools) and ceramics in particular. There is no indication in the stratigraphy or artifact evidence that the site was used or that material was deposited during the Early Neolithic (EN I).

Radiocarbon dating

Radiocarbon samples were collected and sample locations indicated from all drawn sections. Shells (*Cardium edule*) were collected from all the main layers of the midden, as well as charcoal and bones when available in the section. The samples discussed below come from the 140–141E/110N profile excavated in 2005 (Fig. 7.11). This profile was chosen for dating because the layers here appear to be thick and substantial and mostly undisturbed. It was decided to date bone and shell – *Cardium* was chosen as the preferred type of shell. Five *Cardium* shell samples were chosen coming from the following layers: 3, 5, 6, 7B and 8. Two bone samples (a distal metapodial and a fish vertebrae) were chosen for dating, both from layer 7B. We should thus be able to date layers 3–8. The relative chronology/approximate dates are based on diagnostic artifacts in the layers.

Layer 1   appears disturbed, but contains some flint flakes and tools
Layers 2-4 seem to be early Middle Neolithic – the main components are crushed shell and sediment. They contain a relatively substantial amount of ceramics, and very little flint – the latter is most abundant in layer 4 and almost absent in layers 2–3.
Layers 5-9 seem Mesolithic – compact shell layers composed of whole shells. Bone is abundant in these layers, also flint, tools and flakes. Ceramics are also present but not in the quantities seen in the Neolithic layers.

A series of samples for dating was taken (Fig. 7.12). We tried to sample the different main layers throughout the shell midden by selecting shells (*Cardium edule*) and/or charcoal and bone if any could be found. A 10 × 10 cm column sample was also taken from the thickest part of the midden, each layer kept separate, as an archive.

There radiocarbon dates from this site are puzzling (Fig. 7.13). There is no doubt that those from the marine shells complicate the interpretation of the dates, as these determinations are likely to calibrate to be older dates due to the marine reservoir effect. Nevertheless, the majority of the dates fall between 4000 and 3500 BC, the time of the transition to the Neolithic in Denmark. It appears that there was a good bit of mixing and animal burrowing in the midden that may be responsible for some of the discrepant dates that are out of sequence but the radiocarbon determinations tend to confuse our understanding of this site, rather than clarify.

Fig. 7.11. Photo of section 140-141E/110N, South Wall.

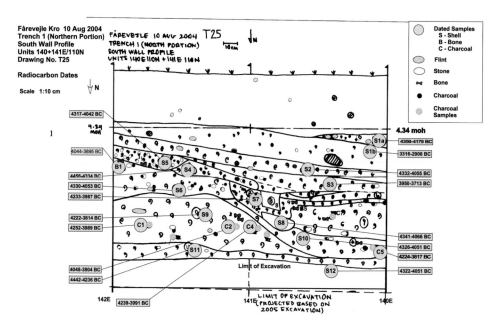

Fig. 7.12. Drawing of section 140-142E/110N, South Wall, with radiocarbon determinations.

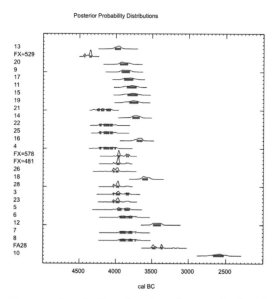

Fig. 7.13. Plot of radiocarbon dates (years cal BC) and probabilities.

Features

A number of features were recognized in the excavations. We found several stone-lined hearths of varying sizes and a number of ash deposits and concentrations of burned, crushed shell, most likely representing fireplaces or dumps. There were a number of post-holes noted in the floor of the excavations and one or two features best described as pavements. These pavements may also have been surfaces for fires as they were usually associated with ash deposits. There were also lenses of yellow clay and ash that were designated as features because of their distinctive attributes. Features recorded during our excavations at Fårevejle Kro are listed in Table 7.1 along with their location and a brief description.

Table 7.1. Features (A=anlæg) recorded at Fårevejle Kro excavations, 2004–2005.

A#	E	N	MOH	Description
1	141	107	3.93	Stone hearth
2	140	107	3.92	Stone hearth = A27
3	141	107–108	3.69	Stone pavement
4	141	114	4.13	Yellow clay lens
5	141	114	4.06	Dark humic lens
6	140	107	3.37	Stone hearth
7	141	114	4.06	Stone hearth
8	141	110	3.84	Ash dump
9	140	105	2.89	Fireplace
10	140	107	3.75	Cardium dump
11	141	113	3.99	yellow clay lens
12	141	112	3.75	hearth
13	141	111	3.51	oyster and charcoal deposit
14	140	114	3.97	Pit with dark humic sediment
15	140	110	4.14	stone hearth
16	140	111	4.49	bottom of A15 or a new hearth
17	141	107	3.7	stone hearth
18	141	106	2.89	concentration of rocks
19	140	110	3.8	burned oyster dump
20	140	110	3.8	ash dump
21	140	111	4.02	ash dump
22	140	111	3.91	ash dump
23	140	110	3.6	ash dump
24	141	116	4.25	bone concentration
25	140	116	4.31	crushed mussel pit
26	141	107	3.23	ash dump/ochre?
27	140–141	108		Stone hearth/pavement = A2
28	140	108		Stone built hearth/pavement
29	141	108		Concentration of (burned) rocks
30	133	119		cooking pit
31	140–141	108–109		Oyster heap
32	133	114		Black charcoal layer (over A33)
33	133	114		Stone built hearth
34				Charcoal layer/hearth
35	140	112–113		Stone built hearth/cooking pit
36	132–133	114		Stone built hearth

MOH = meters over sea level

Artifacts and ecofacts

As noted in 1896–97, the midden contained surprisingly few finds compared to other Danish shell middens. A short description of the various find groups of flint, pottery, animal bone, fish bone, and shell, and worked shell and bone, follows.

Flint

All flint at Fårevejle was collected by meter square and level during the excavation, washed, bagged, and identified by debitage and tool type. The formal tools (axes, points, scrapers, burins, borers, etc.) as well as other possible diagnostic pieces (cores, blades, rejuvenation flakes, retouched pieces, etc.) were usually measured in three coordinates (x, y, z) and given X numbers.

An elaborate blade technology with distinctive projectile points and core axes is the hallmark of the Ertebølle. Stone tools define the chronological phases of the older, middle, and younger Ertebølle (Vang Petersen 1984). Flint points become more regular and symmetric through the period. Core axes were predominant in the early phase, replaced by surface retouched flake axes in the middle phase. Core axes are elaborated with specialized retouched edges in the Late Ertebølle. Blade knives with transverse retouch are common. Burins, scrapers, and borers vary in abundance in the different phases.

A total of 90.7 kg of flint artifacts was excavated at the site. Over two seasons of excavation, we recorded 10,653 stone artifacts. There were 506 burned pieces, 9436 flakes, 542 blades, 80 flake cores, 7 blade cores, 46 retouched flakes, 1 retouched blade, 1 blade knife, 30 points, 4 point preforms, 1 flake axe, 3 core axes, 4 blade scrapers, 2 blade borers, 2 core borers, and 2 core picks. Distal retouch, both straight and concave, was present on a number of flakes and some of these should probably be classified as scrapers. In addition, there were a number of retouched flakes and cores with serrated edges that could be called scrapers. There were at least four burins on various base forms and two axe resharpening flakes (one from a specialized core axe). One of the flake axes was quite large (7 × 9 cm). There were two examples of ground stone artifacts, both Mesolithic, both trindøx, one complete (Fig. 7.14) and the other fragmentary.

Fig. 7.14. Ground stone trindøx from Fårevejle.

The Mesolithic artifacts (small transverse points, flake axes, blade knifes, blade scrapers, and burins) are found in the lower layers of the midden, and Neolithic artifacts (very large transverse points, circular flake scrapers) are found in the upper part. (Flake axes and transverse points are known from ENI, but that period does not appear to be represented by any other evidence in the midden). Flint artifacts were also recovered from the dark cultural layer behind the midden and most of these seem to be of Neolithic age. There is only one example of a polished axe and, unfortunately, this was badly damaged and undiagnostic as to type or probable age. There were very few scrapers or flake axes in the upper levels of the midden. The majority of tools in the upper midden were simple retouched flakes.

Ceramics (Anne Birgitte Gebauer)

Ceramics were encountered throughout the layers and the sherds include both Mesolithic Ertebølle and Funnel Beakers from the late Early Neolithic period EN II (*Virum-gruppen*) and MN A 1b. All ceramics were analysed by Anne Birgitte Gebauer. Ceramics from the 2004–05 excavations are discussed here.

As discussed in previous chapters, pottery appeared after 4700 BC in the Ertebølle period and takes several forms including pointed base cooking vessels, small oval bowls that likely served as oil lamps, and small cups (Andersen 1991; Gebauer 1995). Late Mesolithic Ertebølle pottery is tempered with crushed granite, grog or chamotte, and plant remains. The maximum size of visible temper grains is 6–8 mm. Thickness of the vessel wall varies from 10–21 mm, average = 16.8 mm. The pots are constructed either of round clay coils in U-structure or more compressed coils in H-structure. Several coils showed finger imprints along the top. The ware is porous, often cracked along the coils, and crumbles easily. At least four different pots are represented among the sherds from Fårevejle along with two pointed-bottom pieces in a total of 26 sherds.

The typical shape of Ertebølle vessels, with a short, flared neck, a smooth transition to a slightly curved belly, and a pointed bottom is reflected in the fragmentary ceramics. Rims and necks of the vessels are flared, with the rim slightly thinner than the remaining vessel wall. Fragments from the belly area suggested a rather flat curve. One thick sherd appeared to be part of a pointed bottom. Estimated diameters varying from 22–36 cm from the sherds indicate the use of medium and large vessels. Small cups were not present. No food crusts were observed on the Ertebølle ceramics.

The presence of the Ertebølle pottery indicates a date within Middle to Late Ertebølle, roughly 4700–4000 BC.

Two Ertebølle lamps were found at Fårevejle in the early excavations and were on display in the former museum in Høve for many years. One fragment of a lamp was found in the 2004–05 excavations with the characteristic basin shape and fingernail impressed rim. It seems very likely that this fragment is a piece of one of the lamps found at the end of the 19th century (Fig. 7.15).

Fig. 10. ¹/₂.

en er Tykkelsen betydelig ... eder
e indtrykkede Fordybning ... et har
fuldstændige Kar har ... M langt

Fig. 7.15. Rimsherd of Ertebølle lamp found in 2004 along with published drawing of a lamp from the 1896–97 excavations. Danish 10 and 20 kroner coins shown for scale.

Fig. 7.16. *TRB rimsherd from 2004 excavations at Fårevejle with EN2 decoration.*

Fig. 7.17. *TRB rimsherd from 2005 excavations at Fårevejle with arcade decoration.*

The Funnel Beaker pottery from Fårevejle does not belong to the very earliest Neolithic but rather to late EN I (perhaps even EN II; if not Virum style). The sharply rounded belly, the clearly offset, and fairly high neck exclude a date of early EN I as does the decoration. The zigzag on a neck sherd (Fig. 7.16) points to EN 2, while the rim sherd with arcade decoration (Fig. 7.17) could be early.

Faunal remains

The bone material from Fårevejle was separated by meter square and layer during the excavation, cleaned, bagged, and weighed. Whole bones, teeth, and other possibly diagnostic fragments were measured in three coordinates (x, y, and z) and given X numbers.

The preliminary identification list in Table 7.2 includes all species from all levels in the excavations. Herluf Winge identified the fauna from the 1896–97 excavations (Madsen *et al.* 1900). In general, there is a strong correspondence between the two sets of information. Table 7.2 also lists the few species noted by Winge that did not appear in our excavations including *Bos taurus, Homo sapiens, Castor fiber,* and *Larus argentatus.*

As is usual for Ertebølle settlements, the majority of the bones come from the 'big three' – roe deer, red deer, and wild swine (96% of the NISP). Wild swine is most common, followed by roe deer with red deer a distant third. Fox, wildcat, otter, and marten suggest hunting (or trapping) to obtain furs, while the presence of seal bones shows that aquatic mammals were also pursued. The three sheep or goat bones almost certainly result from the Neolithic occupation of the site. It is interesting that the other domesticate, dog, is only represented by a single specimen (a second phalanx). Butchery evidence in the form of cutmarks (15 specimens) and bones fractured to extract marrow (333 specimens) attest to the exploitation of these animals for food as well as probably for raw materials.

Although only 14 bird bones were identified in the material (Table 7.2), taphonomic losses are suspected to be especially high for these animals and they could well be

Table 7.2. Preliminary species identification and relative abundance at Fårevejle.

Taxon	Common name	NISP	%	MNI	1896–97
Sus scrofa	Wild boar	554	43.2	6	√
Capreolus capreolus	Roe deer	435	34.0	8	√
Cervus elaphus	Red deer	231	18.0	5	√
Vulpes vulpes	Fox	26	2.0	2	√
Felis silvestris	Wild cat	7	<1	1	√
Phoca sp./Halichoerus sp.	Seal unspecified	5	<1	1	
Lutra lutra	Otter	3	<1	1	√
Capra sp./Ovis sp.	Domestic goat/sheep	2	<1	1	
Arvicola terrestris	Water vole	2	<1	1	√
Canis familiaris	Dog	1	<1	1	√
Martes martes	Marten	1	<1	1	√
Apodemus flavicollis	Yellow necked mouse	1	<1	1	
Bos taurus	Domestic cow	–			√
Homo sapiens	Human	–			√
Castor fiber	Beaver	–			√
Anas sp.	Duck unspecified	3	<1	1	√
Alca torda	Razorbill	3	<1	1	
Cygnus sp.	Swan unspecified	3	<1	1	
Uria aalge	Common guillemot	2	<1	1	
Mergus merganser	Common merganser	1	<1	1	
Mergus serrator	Red-breasted merganser	1	<1	1	
Somateria mollissima	Eider duck				√
Larus argentatus	Herring gull				√
Total		1281			

NISP= Number of Identified Specimens, MNI=Minimum Number of Individuals

under-represented compared to their actual importance. This especially true as their value for raw materials (e.g. feathers and bones) may have been higher than their role as food. All the birds are waterfowl, which accords well with a coastal settlement and a subsistence base focused on aquatic resources.

The fish bone assemblage consists of 2943 specimens, of which 2738 are identified to family, genus, or species level (Table 7.3). There are at least 13 different fish present, which fits the pattern of Ertebølle assemblages that tend to have diverse fish taxa even when the number of identified specimens (NISP) is relatively low. The assemblage is dominated by marine species (e.g. gadids) although the flatfish may be mostly represented by flounder that have a brackish or even freshwater tolerance. Eel

Table 7.3. Identified fish bones from Fårevejle

Taxon	Common name	NISP
Gadidae	codfish	1546
Gadus morhua	cod	33
Pollachius sp.	saithe/pollock	1
Pleuronectidae	right-eye flounder	1028
Platichthys flesus	flounder	3
Scophthalmidae	turbot/brill	12
Anguilla anguilla	eel	74
Belone belone	garfish	17
Clupea harengus	herring	8
Cyprinidae	carps and minnows	7
Esox lucius	pike	3
Myoxocephalus scorpius	sculpin	2
Scomber scombrus	mackerel	2
Squalus acanthias	spurdog	1
Salmo sp.	salmon/trout	1
Total		2738

and salmon/trout are diadromous fish that alternate between marine and freshwater environments. The pike and cyprinids are generally freshwater fish but with a certain tolerance for brackish water. Taken as a whole, the assemblage is consistent with a fishery that took place in the immediate environs of the site in the Lammefjord, with possible occasional forays into the nearby Kattegat.

Sampling and recovery methods were consistent throughout the excavation; all excavated materials were wet-sieved with 4 mm mesh. The mesh size of the sieving apparatus is an important consideration when evaluating the recovered fish bone assemblage. The mesh size used at Fårevejle was large enough that it is likely that some bones passed through the screen and were lost, however, testing of the effects of sieve size at two nearby Ertebølle sites on northwest Zealand (Dragsholm and Asnæs Havnemark) demonstrated that the effect was only modest and the results obtained here should be reasonably representative (Ritchie 2010). Another consideration for discussions of the fishery is variability between different contexts of the midden. Although there seems to be a trend towards greater representation of gadids progressing deeper into the midden (Figure 7.18), whether this is due to cultural or taphonomic factors is not clear.

The largest share of the fish comes from the cod family (Gadidae), with cod apparently the most common, supplemented by a small number of saithe and/or pollock. Cod sizes were estimated from measurements of otoliths (Härkönen 1986) and first vertebrae (Enghoff 1994); they are of relatively modest sizes (Figure 7.19) as is common for Ertebølle assemblages (Enghoff 1994).

Flatfish, primarily from the family Pleuronectidae but with a few specimens from Scophthalmidae, are the second most common type of fish remains in the assemblage. As mentioned, flounder remains are definitely present in the assemblage and this species is capable of living in marine, brackish, and freshwater environments. Sizes of the flatfish (Figure 7.20) were estimated from measurements of the first vertebrae and are in line with those from other Ertebølle sites (Enghoff 1994).

Eel are in a distant third place regarding NISP. The sizes of eel based on measurements of cleithra and ceratohyals (Enghoff 1994) range from c. 35cm to 108 cm, with the majority (6 of 9) around 50–65 cm. The rest of the taxa are represented by only a small number of remains each, but the diversity of fish suggests flexibility in the fishery to accommodate short- and long-term fluctuations in the availability of the main prey. The spurdog is only represented by a single dorsal spine that could be a tool (Noe-Nygaard 1971) brought from elsewhere that does not represent part of the site fishery.

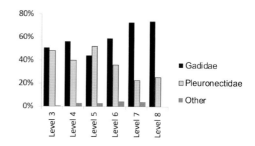

Fig. 7.18. Variability in fish remains (vertebrae only) between levels of the midden.

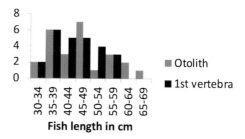

Fig. 7.19. Length of cod reconstructed from measurements of otoliths and 1st vertebrae.

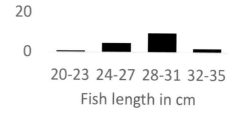

Fig. 7.20. Length of flatfish reconstructed from measurements of 1st vertebrae.

Shell

The following various marine mollusc species were present in the shell midden: oyster (*Ostrea Edulis*), cockle (*Cerastoderma edule/Cardium edule*), mussel (*Mytilus edulis*), edible periwinkle (*Littorina littorea*), peppery furrow shell (*Scrobicularia plana*), netted dogwhelk (*Nassa reticulata*), and a few shells of needle whelk (*Bitium reticulatum*). The first four occur in all the layers in the midden, while the latter three are found more sporadically. Samples of the midden were taken from several sections and shells identified and counted by weight. Table 7.4 is a representative example of one of these

Table 7.4. *Samples of shell midden section for shellfish identification at Fårevejle. Percentages by weight.*

Level	Weight (g)	Volume (l)	% Mussel	% Oyster	% Cardium	% Littorina	% Nassarius	% NoID	% Matrix	% Shell
99	1195	1.2	0.0	0.1	0.0	0.1	0.0	0.3	99.5	0.5
1	2360	1.7	0.6	1.1	0.6	0.3	0.0	5.6	91.9	8.1
2	1785	1.3	2.2	0.0	3.2	0.6	0.4	17.3	76.2	23.8
2A	1020	1	17.5	5.2	3.8	0.0	0.0	24.6	48.8	51.2
4B	3510	3.6	16.9	5.2	13.2	1.0	0.1	22.5	41.1	58.9
10	1370	1.5	25.5	22.4	8.9	0.0	0.0	28.4	14.8	85.2
7A	2230	2.2	15.6	13.6	4.3	0.7	0.6	29.6	35.7	64.3
7	2970	3	11.3	40.4	1.6	0.0	0.1	18.2	28.3	71.7
Total	16,440	15.5								

sampled sections and lists the weight and volume of the sample for each layer along with the percent of the five most common shell species, and the percent of shell and matrix in each sample (99 is the layer number used for the plow zone).

A number of trends are apparent in this table. The amount of non-shell matrix generally increases toward the upper layers in the section and the per cent of shell in each layer decreases by layer. The exception is layer 10 which has a high percentage of shell (mussel shell = 25.5% and oyster shell = 22.4%) which makes up 85.2% of the layer. Oyster shell dominates in Layer 7 and makes up more than 70% of the layer. From layer 7A upward mussels dominate the shellfish by weight.

Seasonality

Based on the occurrence of two migratory fishes, mackerel and garfish, that today appear in Danish waters only during the warmer months of the year, at least some of the fishing must have taken place in the late spring to early fall. However, two cod otoliths were sampled for oxygen isotopes to determine the season of catch for the fish (Ritchie *et al.* 2013a). Results indicated fishing during the late winter/early spring. Although the rest of the faunal remains show mainly summer occupation at Fårevejle, the cod otoliths show winter activity as well. Whether this means the site was inhabited year-round or was subject to periodic visitations in different seasons is an unresolved question (Fig. 7.21).

Worked shell and bone

There was almost no worked shell or bone, only a few pieces. Among the more unexpected finds was a shell bead. It is circular and *c.* 8 mm wide with a whole drilled in the middle and is probably made from oyster (Fig. 7.22). The bead was found while

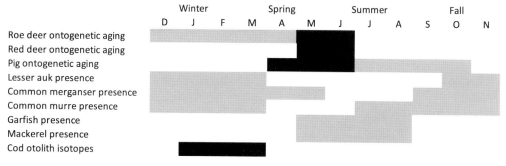

Fig. 7.21. Seasonality information from faunal remains (grey indicates possible occupation in this period, black is definite).

screening material from the bottom-most part of the midden and came out of layers composed of whole oysters. The date is thought to be Mesolithic since the bead is made of oyster shell, and the layer in which it was found is superimposed by layers containing Ertebølle ceramics. This type of shell bead is only known from a few other sites in Denmark (e.g. Trustrup) and probably does not survive easily nor be easily recovered during excavation. One antler *retouchoir* was also recorded in the excavations.

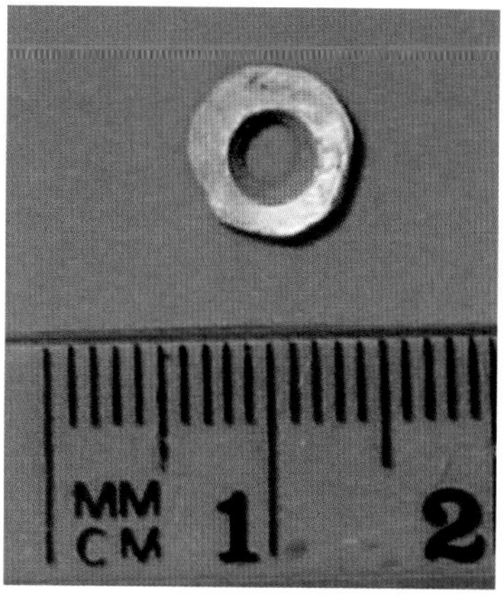

Conclusions

Shell middens are one of the hallmarks of the Danish Mesolithic. The term Ertebølle comes from one of the first recognized humanly-created shell midden

Fig. 7.22. Shell bead found in Mesolithic level at the Fårevejle midden.

sites in the country. For many years these middens have been assumed to be dwelling places (Andersen 2004), but more recent work has brought this assumption into question. Impressions from our work at Fårevejle focus on the rather low quantity of 'settlement' debris – in the form of faunal remains and stone tools – that characterize this site. We suspect that the settlement site associated with this midden was some distance away and that the midden was used occasionally for consuming shellfish and other foods, perhaps for several days at a time given the higher quantity of faunal remains and artifacts in the lower layers. The general absence of burials and artifacts seems to support this perspective.

The midden was also used during the later part of the Funnel Beaker period, perhaps in a different way since the shell species are different and also because the shell and matrix are heavily fragmented, suggesting more or longer human presence at the midden, or perhaps poor preservation given the general absence of heavy oyster shells. Or a combination. Flint in this layer was often marine patinated (white) and rolled indicating that the midden was transgressed at least during storms. The overall pattern of transgressions is clearly visualized in the Fårevejle excavation with regressive succession, where the Atlantic oyster midden is located more inland than the Subboreal, Neolithic midden which is more seaward, with cockles shell deposits. Fish and shellfish obviously continued to be part of the diet in the Early Neolithic and perhaps settlement was closer. The obvious connection is to the Borrebjerg hill-top adjacent to the site. If this was used for settlement or other purposes during the Middle Neolithic it would fit well with the ENII/MNI chronology of the upper part of the midden. The midden area may well have been associated with a nearby settlement.

At the same time, the low density of artifactual material and the rather specialized contents of the midden suggested to me that this was not a residential site during the Mesolithic or even close to one. Clearly, distance to settlement must have been an important factor in the amount and density of cultural contents in shell middens. Jens Nielsen asked why Mesolithic people made big piles of white shells when they just as easily could have spread them out or thrown them back in the water. Jens suggested that perhaps they wanted to mark these places, to create landmarks with large piles of white shells, to make their presence known. Food for thought.

Chapter 8

Asnæs Havnemark

Introduction

In 2005 Jens Nielsen told me about a place along the coast of the peninsula of Asnæs where Late Mesolithic materials were eroding out of a low sea cliff. The site had been found originally by Columbus, the amateur archaeologist Egon Iversen. The owner of the land was Eirik Vinsand and he was most kind in allowing us to work at the site and also provided substantial help in the form of a digging machine and operator. We uncovered the cultural layer at the edge of a sea cliff and excavated a number of square meters. The standard range of stone and bone tools were present along with huge amounts of flint debitage. The quantity of fish bone was also remarkable; much of the matrix in the cultural layer was composed of fish remains. A wide variety of fish species were taken here. We also collected more than 30 bone fish hooks and preforms in the excavations. Seals were also important prey at this location and several different species could be identified among the bones we recovered. Seals still inhabit this end of the peninsula today. One of them kept an eye on us for several days during the excavations.

A large number of birds, including several kinds of eagles and swans, were among the faunal remains. The normal Mesolithic terrestrial species were present but the faunal assemblage was dominated by roe deer. Clearly Asnæs had been a rather special location. At the same time, we have evidence for almost year-round occupation and the use of the location over several hundred years. A report on the excavations at Asnæs Havnemark was published in the *Danish Journal of Archaeology* (Price *et al.* 2018). This chapter contains a summary of that story.

Kalundborg sits at the head of a lovely fjord that extends for more than 10 km between the two peninsulas of Røsnæs to the north and Asnæs to the south (Fig. 8.1). The fjord is one of the deepest in eastern Denmark and has been attractive for human settlement for millennia. There are many prehistoric sites reported in the National Register; more than 100 barrows from the Bronze and Iron Ages, along with substantial remains from the Mesolithic and Neolithic on the peninsula of Asnæs. Asnæs is also well known as a source of very good flint raw material along the beaches and particularly at its west end.

Fig. 8.1. The location of the site of Asnæs Havnemark toward the tip of the peninsula of Asnæs near the town of Kalundborg, Denmark, looking east.

Excavations at Asnæs Havnemark

The site was discovered in 1993, eroding from a small cliff on the north side of the peninsula of Asnæs, by Columbus. A visit in 2005 by Jens Nielsen and I confirmed the location of the site and the threat of continued erosion. The cultural layer contained flint, bone, and pottery diagnostic of the Ertebølle period. A radiocarbon date was obtained on a sample of bone and provided a date of 4340–4040 cal BC (Table 8.2: AA72355). A heavy winter storm in 2006 further eroded the cliff face, exposed more material, and reiterated the danger that the site faced.

The site is named Asnæs Havnemark and its full designation in the Danish national catalog system (*Sognebeskrivelse*) is Årby sogn, Ars herred, Holbæk amt. Stednr. 030110-365 (KUAS j.nr), or Årby 365 for short. The site is located on a small high point along the north coast of the Asnæs peninsula that remains as a slight bulge along the coastline (Fig. 8.1). Excavations took place over five weeks in June and July 2007, intended to determine the extent of the site, expose the cultural layer where it was present, and obtain materials to describe the site and its contents before it was completely destroyed by the sea. The excavations exposed a terrestrial midden deposit and cultural layer that was protected and preserved under a raised beach ridge along the coast, but largely destroyed elsewhere by older erosion and continuing beach ridge formation in this area. The site itself sits on top of beach ridge deposits and moraine clay and was subsequently covered by later beach ridge materials. Significant finds at the site included substantial quantities of fish bone and other faunal remains, an extraordinary number of fish hooks, and medium size pot sherds from typically thick and heavily tempered Ertebølle ceramics. There were also some unexpected finds, discussed below.

Location and setting

The landscape of the peninsula is dominated by the end moraine that is Asnæs (Fig. 1.19, above) and the sea which is gradually changing the shape of the peninsula. The sea erodes and builds along the coast – this process has been ongoing for millennia. The archaeological site of Asnæs Havnemark is in fact in an active area of beach ridge construction. It appears that the Mesolithic settlement was directly on an ancient beach ridge in this area and that there were at least two episodes of occupation. The major focus of our project was the cultural layer that was exposed by wave erosion on the north coast of Asnæs, but we also uncovered a deeper settlement layer at the same place just on top of the moraine surface beneath the beach ridge.

In the early Holocene, the Kalundborg fjord would likely have been dry land, a long stream valley through what became the fjord into the river valley that would become the Storebælt (the Great Belt, the waters connecting the Baltic and Kattegat between the islands of Funen and Sjælland). As sea levels rose during this period, the area flooded and a fjord was created in the narrows between Asnæs and Røsnæs. Maximum sea level in this area was probably +2.0 to +2.5 m asl according to Mertz (1924) and our own observations at the site. The low western end of the Asnæs peninsula may have been inundated, leaving only a few higher, small islands for human occupation. The deep waters of the fjord and the sea of the Storebælt created a rich environment for Mesolithic hunter-gatherers. In all probability, large runs of eels, herring, and other species of fish as well as seals passed along the coast of Asnæs, as is known to have been the case in historical times (Pedersen 1997).

Excavations

We began field work at Asnæs Havnemark in early June of 2007 (Fig. 8.2) by relocating the cultural materials eroding from the small sea cliff and orienting our site grid to that cliff. The site grid is 14° W of North. We laid out a 10 square meter grid across the site and adjacent field to provide complete coverage for our excavations and finds. The site grid was given an arbitrary 100N/100E start. We used the southwest corner of excavation units for designation of meter squares. We placed a fixed point on the top of a deeply buried red wooden stake on the west side of a fence post at UTM coordinates 622680/6171480. The top of the stake was 3.188 m asl. The elevation for the site was obtained by collating the results of two methods: an estimate from the mean tidal height and a surveyed transect from a geodetic fixed point at a residence on the peninsula. From the transect we

Fig. 8.2. Field crew at Asnæs Havnemark: from right, Ken Ritchie, Charlie the Dog, Lone Andersen, Vanessa Smolenski, Terry Slocum, Doug Price, Jens Nielsen, and Kurt Gron.

calculated an elevation of 3.187 which corresponded almost exactly with the sea level measurement which we used as the site fixed point. The UTM coordinates for the site are 622601/6171516, Zone 3.

A contour map was made of the part of the agricultural field in which the site was located (spot heights are plotted on Fig. 8.3). We began a program of hammer coring to map subsurface layers but this was largely unsuccessful because of all the stones in the beach ridge deposits and the difficulty of recognizing the cultural layer away from the coastline. We then turned to 1 m² test pits and excavated six tests south of the coastline in order to determine if the cultural layer continued to the south and what the depth and contents of this layer might be. The two southernmost tests reached moraine subsoil within 30–40 cm indicating that there was little of interest on this surface – no cultural layer and few artifacts. A test pit to the west also contained little cultural material, but a distinct series of beach ridge deposits. It is clear that, to the east, there are more beach deposits. Apparently, beach ridges have been accumulating in this area for millennia. The analysis of the test pit contents suggested that the cultural layer was largely preserved to the north under the raised beach ridge. This was the material eroding along the sea cliff.

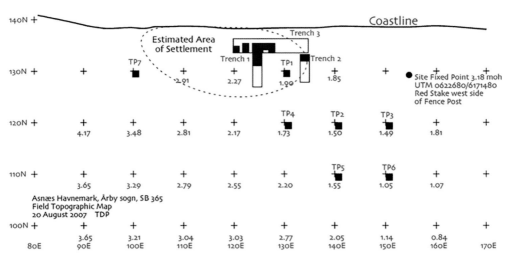

Fig. 8.3. Schematic plan of excavations as Asnæs Havnemark including grid and elevations for the general area of the project.

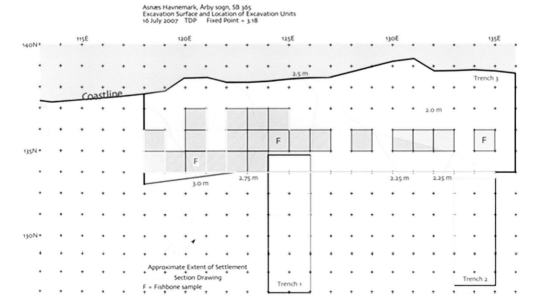

Fig. 8.4. Plan of the excavation trenches at Asnæs Havnemark 2007 with shaded meter squares marking the area of intensive excavation. 2.5 m is the estimated sea height at the beginning of the Subboreal.

After some consideration of the test pit data, we used a backhoe to open a north–south trench (Trench 1) near TP1 (Fig. 8.4). This trench was 2 m wide as excavated by the machine. We then moved approximately 10 m east and excavated a second north–south trench (Trench 2) through the deposits with a similar width. Both trenches were begun to the north, as close as possible to the raised beach ridge that marks the border of the landscape here. Artifacts were collected and sections were drawn to record the finds and context, but we were still searching for the cultural layer which appeared in the north ends of Trenches 1 and 2. A subsequent excavation unit, Trench 3, was dug, running east–west across the Trench 1 and 2 units to uncover these deposits. This excavation by machine removed the raised beach ridge deposits along the coast that had protected the cultural layer from earlier erosion and destruction. The excavated squares are shown in Figure 8.3.

Careful and intensive excavation was undertaken in the cultural layer in Trench 3 and a total of 22 m² were excavated with water sieving of all deposits (Fig. 8.5). This strategy allowed us to obtain a longitudinal sample of the occupation horizon defined by the cultural layer. Sections were drawn in a number of the squares in order to record the stratigraphy and a longitudinal section of Trench 3 was drawn along the south wall of the trench. The estimated extent of the settlement, at least the area of remaining cultural layer, is indicated in Figure 8.4 by the yellow zone. Meticulous

Fig. 8.5. Overview of excavations in Trench 3 looking east.

recovery of fish remains was focused on three squares as indicated in Figure 8.4, with some fish bones recovered from other squares as well.

Stratigraphy

The sediments at the site reflect a mix of terrestrial and marine deposits. The terrestrial moraine is a clay-rich till with gravel, cobbles, and a few boulders. The surface of the moraine contains more sand from mixing with later deposits. The layers on top of the moraine in the area of the site are of marine origin and composed of sand, gravel, and fist size cobbles that were probably thrown up into this area in the process of beach ridge formation along the coast.

This process is visible in the larger stratigraphy of the site. Sediments were generally sandy with varying amounts of gravel and stones associated with the beach ridges. A younger beach ridge had buried the cultural layers that had accumulated on top of the older beach ridge. Beneath the beach ridges at some depth there was a base of ground moraine beneath the older beach ridge. The cultural layer that accumulated atop the older beach ridge was divided into three strata, based on color and content. The bottom of the cultural layer was black with many artifacts. The middle of the cultural layer was brown with shell and artifacts and the upper portion of the cultural layer was gray with shell and artifacts. There was a shell midden present in several squares composed largely of blue mussel shells with some oyster. This midden was no more than 20 cm thick at a maximum. The presence of shell in the deposits was likely responsible for the good preservation of bone at the site.

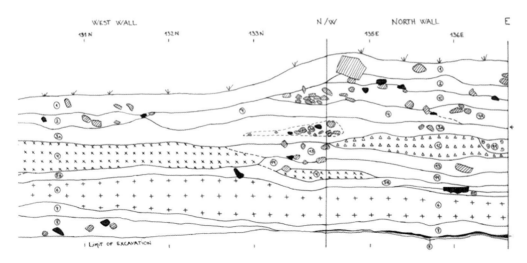

Fig. 8.6. Section drawing of the west wall and the north end of Trench 1. Hatched = rock; black = flint.

Figure 8.6 is a section drawing of the west wall and the north end of Trench 1 that shows the stratigraphy of the site and the location of the beach ridge deposits. Layer descriptions appear in Table 9.1. Figure 9.7 is a photograph of the north wall shown in that section. The thick layers of beach ridge deposits are overlain by an upper cultural layer. The lower cultural layer beneath the beach ridge deposits and on top of the moraine subsurface is seen at the base or the section of the north wall.

Fig. 8.7. Photograph of north wall, Trench 1. Compare with section drawing (Fig. 8.6).

Features

A total of ten features (Danish: *anlæg*) were identified and designated in the excavations at Asnæs Havnemark. These features were photographed, drawn, cross-sectioned, and sampled. They consisted either of a pit or a group of stones distinctive in either abundance or arrangement. Most of the small pits were generally nondescript. No large structures or graves were encountered in our excavations. Of particular interest was a probable Bronze Age cooking pit uncovered at the west end of the excavations, probably part of a linear arrangement of such pits that are a characteristic feature of the Bronze Age. Evidence of at least three such pits were observed in our excavations.

Table 8.1. Layer descriptions for section drawing in Figure 8.6.

Layer	Description
1	Medium brown silty sand - Plowzone
2	Medium gray-brown silty sand with many pebbles and rocks, sandier than plowzone
3A	Light gray sandy horizon with few pebbles
3B	Texture and color the same as 3A but with a pocket of rocks
4	Dark gray silty sand with many rocks and roots (beach ridge)
5A	Very light gray fine sand
5B	Light grayish brown fine sand with many rocks
6	Light grayish brown sandy horizon with many rocks (beach ridge)
7	Medium gray loose sand
8	Gray sandy clay with orange oxidation, a few large cobbles, shell, charcoal and flint
9	Medium gray brown coarse sand with small black inclusions
9A	Same as 9 with more pebbles
10	Medium brown silty sand with some pebbles and a few cobbles
11	Dark gray humic sand with many shell fragments and pebbles (cultural)
12	Light grayish brown sandy horizon with many rocks (beach ridge)
13	Dark brown sand & gravel with pebbles & cobbles, few shell frags, sea snails, black to NE
14	Light grayish brown sand with pebbles and a band of large pebbles across the top
15	Medium to dark gray sand with pebbles, a few flint flakes, and fishbone
16	Black (charcoal) loose sand with mussel shell, fishbone, flint (cultural)

Radiocarbon dating

A total of ten samples of charcoal and bone were sent to the University of Arizona AMS Laboratory for radiocarbon dating (Table 8.2). There is one additional sample from Aarhus collected in 2005 from the eroding section along the sea cliff and two samples of oyster shell AMS-dated in Beijing in 2011. Samples were selected to date different layers and features including several pits. We needed to know when the beach ridges formed and to develop some idea of the length of site occupation. There is also a deeper occupation horizon that appeared in the bottom of Trench 2 that we tried to date (see below).

The radiocarbon dates document the occupation of the site toward the end of the Ertebølle period. Eight measurements range between 5696±63 BP (Table 8.2: AA77189; 4700–4440 cal BC) and 5172±60 years BP (Table 8.2: AA77196; 4080–3890 cal BC). The Beijing (BA) dates are slightly older, possibly the result of a marine reservoir effect from the oyster shell. A plot of the probability curves (Fig. 8.8) indicates the likelihood of at least two episodes of site use (*c.* 4500 cal BC and *c.* 4100 cal BC) and the occupation of this site near or at the time of the transition to agriculture in southern Scandinavia. The last cultural layer likely accumulated over a substantial period of time, perhaps several hundred years at the end of the Atlantic climatic episode.

Table 8.2. Radiocarbon determinations from Asnæs Havnemark (Årby 365).

Lab No	No	Material	Layer	Unit	East	North	$\delta^{13}C$	BP cal	BC 2 sigma range
AA72355	29	bone	Loose find	Tr3	127	134	-22.7	5345±60	4340(99.7%)4040
AA77189	2	tooth	BrSurface	Tr3	122.99	137	-23.9	5696±63	4700(94.5%)4440
AA77190	3	bone	CuLayer	Tr3	124	136.43	-24.7	5197±71	4240(89.3%)3910
AA77191	4	bone	BrSand	Tr3	122.38	137	-22.6	5311±61	4270(95.2%)3990
AA77192	5	charcoal	CuLayer	Tr3	126	132	-23.9	5359±42	4280(54.7%)4140
AA77193	6	antler	BrSurface	Tr3	120	136	-22.9	5298±60	4270(97.7%)3980
AA77195	8	charcoal	Feature A7	Tr3	121	134	-25.7	5668±43	4620(91.3%)4430
AA77196	9	bone	Deep CuLayer	Tr2	124	132	-24.2	5172±60	4080(73.2%)3890
AA77197	10	bone	BrSurface	Tr3	120	135	-24.0	5415±61	4360(86.5%)4140
AA77199	12	food crust	Shell	Tr3	124	135	-25.4	3742±42	2240(90.6%)2030
BA10657A	15	oyster shell	Shell	Tr3	123	136	na	5740±35	4320(99.1%)4090
BA10657B	16	oyster shell	A7-Upper Layer	Tr3	121	134	na	5735±35	4310(100%)4080

Loose: Finds from topsoil or unknown provenience; BrSand: Brown sand over cultural layer (with artifacts); Shell: Shell lens in cultural layer with many artifacts; CuLayer: (Cultural Layer) black with many artifacts; BrSurface: (Gray brown surface) beneath cultural layer. Dates rounded out to 10 years according to Mook (1986).

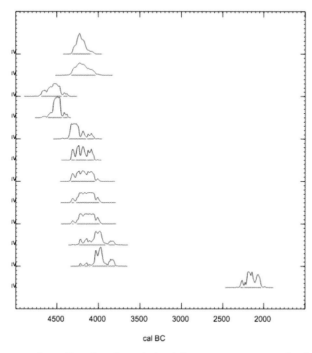

cal BC

Fig. 8.8. Probability curves for radiocarbon dates (cal BC) from Asnæs Havnemark. The transition between the Mesolithic and Neolithic is around 4000 cal BC.

Several comments are necessary at this point. All the dated material has some human association. The dates in general confirm a Late Mesolithic date and fit with the archaeological material we recovered. There appear to be two groups of dates, an older pair around 4500 cal BC (AA77189 and AA77197, Table 8.2) and a series of nine between 4300 and 3910 cal BC that date the primary cultural layer. Several of the dates appear to overlap the transition to the Neolithic around 4000 cal BC. Our attempt to date the lower occupation horizon in Trench 2 was not successful as the bone we sampled provided one of the youngest dates in the series. Perhaps this bone belonged to the upper occupation horizon. The youngest date we obtained, AA77199, which calibrated to 2240–2030 cal BC (3742±42; Table 8.2), was a surprise, but in retrospect makes some sense. This date was on a sample of food crust from an unusual pot that was excavated at the site in the shell deposit in the upper cultural layer. This date is from the Late Neolithic and may be associated with the cooking pit that was uncovered in the northern part of our excavations. If this assumption is correct it would mean that the cultural layer from the Late Mesolithic remained near the surface, not buried by beach ridge deposits, at least through much of the Bronze Age.

Flint

Flint from the site is all shapes, sizes, and several shades – mostly of gray, but there is also some brown (bog patinated). Material from the deeper cultural layer in Trench 2 appears lighter in color than the rest, perhaps due to carbonate accumulation on the flint. Marine patination is minimal in most layers/squares. Very few hammer stones were noted during the excavation. Perhaps the rough preparation of artifacts took place near the sources of flint elsewhere on the peninsula and only finer, finish flaking was done on site at Asnæs Havnemark. There are many small flakes that indicate flintworking at the site. The Asnæs peninsula has lots of high-quality flint, particularly at the west end of the peninsula, so that ready availability is in part responsible for the massive amounts of flint at the site. My impression was that there were more blades at other sites we have excavated, but perhaps the quantity of flint debitage is so much greater here that it masks the importance of blades.

The flint generally is very fresh and sharp. At the same time, some flint materials from the Upper Beach Ridge deposit are wind polished, rolled with worn and fractured edges, and slightly marine patinated. This material gives the appearance of having been in the water briefly and having rolled around with other stone objects. It is probably either from the primary occupation at Asnæs Havnemark that was eroded from former coastline to the north or from the earlier occupation horizon that is buried deeply in Trench 2. Some of the layers in some of the squares show a good bit of burning in the flint (and bone) which appears as lots of broken, burned, gray pieces along with much more color including a reddish tint to many pieces which must have been heated.

There were more than 320 kg of flint artifacts excavated at the site, a total of 45,202 pieces. There are 4992 burned pieces, 31,747 flakes and 2996 blades, of which approximately 1350 were produced using a hard hammer. There are 264 flake cores, 18 blade cores, 49 retouched flakes, 12 blade knives (Fig. 8.9), 284 projectile points (Fig. 8.10) and 33 point preforms, 110 flake axes (Fig. 8.11) but only 2 core axes, neither of which is specialized, and 10 blade scrapers. The core axes, if that is what they are, are poorly made, typical of Late Ertebølle. The flint tools therefore consist primarily of projectile points, flake axes, some distal concave truncated blade knives, a very few scrapers, and a very few possible burins.

Fig. 8.9. A distal concave truncated blade knife from Asnæs Havnemark (Årby 365).

Ceramics (Anne Birgitte Gebauer)

It was our sense that there was a good deal of pottery at Asnæs Havnemark compared to other Mesolithic sites we had excavated. There were *c.* 300 sherds both collected and excavated from the site. The overwhelming part of the pottery from the site appears to belong to the Ertebølle tradition. However, some of the ceramic material is complex and often difficult to classify. Due to fragmentation, little diagnostic information was available on the shape and size of many of the

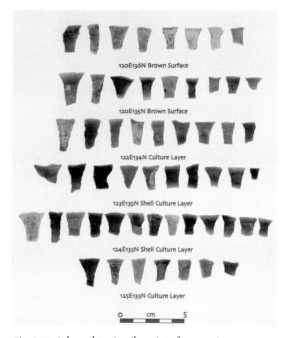

Fig. 8.10. Selected projectile points from various contexts at Asnæs Havnemark (Årby 365).

vessels and distinction between Ertebølle and TRB was often not possible. The description and analysis of the ceramic materials from Asnæs Havnemark was undertaken by Anne Birgitte Gebauer in consultation with Eva Koch, Anders Fischer, and Aikaterini Glykou. The pottery came from two sources. A small group of sherds was collected by Iversen who originally found the site and donated his collection to the museum. The Iversen collection, fewer than 20 sherds, includes only Ertebølle pottery. In addition to the pottery, two very small pieces of fired daub, one with stick impressions and one with some reddish color, were found in the cultural layer.

A much larger group of sherds came from the 2007 excavations, approximately 275 pieces, of which the vast majority appears to belong to the Ertebølle tradition.

Fig. 8.11. Selected flake axes from Asnæs Havnemark (Årby 365).

Fig. 8.12. Round base of Ertebølle vessel.

Most of the pottery consists of body sherds with a thickness of 10–15 mm. Fragments of pointed bottoms were found in three excavation meter squares (Fig. 8.12). An Ertebølle rim sherd with an estimated diameter *c.* 20 cm was found nearby. This rim sherd and one of the base fragments clearly came from larger vessels. Another sherd appears to be part of a small vessel with an estimated diameter of only *c.* 8 cm. Heat spalling typical of Ertebølle pottery is seen on the surface of several body sherds.

Fragments of Ertebølle clay lamps were found in three squares. One fragment has a greyish–brown color on the outside, while the inside is covered with a black crust. Another lamp is represented by three rim sherds that fit together (this group measures 5.2 cm in width, 2.1 cm in height and is 10–11 mm thick) and three body sherds. The rim is turned slightly inwards; finger impressions have been made in the smoothed edge of the rim. The third lamp fragment has a rather uneven surface and a clear bend in the side wall. The rim of this lamp is turned inwards, the edge smoothed and decorated with oblique strokes. The latter two sherds might be from the same object.

Sherds clearly belonging to the Funnel Beaker tradition were found in a number of squares. This TRB classification was confirmed by Eva Koch and Anders Fischer. The sherds seem to represent a total of six or more different vessels of small, medium, or unknown size. They include a rim sherd with possible traces of decoration, a single vessel represented by three concave neck sherds with a total diameter *c.* 24 cm, a sherd showing a clear, sharp angle between neck and belly (Fig. 8.13), a number of body sherds and a flat bottom sherd. Two rim sherds are from a small vessel, possibly a Funnel Neck beaker with rim diameter *c.* 12 cm, and another rim sherd is from a thin-walled vessel with impressions probably made with fingernails in the upper edge of the rim. In addition, there are two sherds with oblique coil construction that are TRB in origin, and several sherds with worn edges that are generally less than 10 mm in thickness and appear to be Funnel Beaker tradition. There is a large convex belly sherd 3.4 × 2.7 cm in size cm in size as well as a concave neck sherd with oblique construction and traces of oblique imprints from rim decoration belonging to the TRB. The general absence of decoration fits well with an Early TRB date for this pottery.

Fig. 8.13. TRB pottery sherd, neck-belly transition.

Some ceramics from the excavations were examined chemically in two different studies. One of these involved strontium isotope ratios and the other employed Instrumental Neutron Activation (INAA or NAA) to characterize some of the pottery.

Strontium isotopes, reported as the ratio ^{87}Sr/^{86}Sr, have been used primarily in human tooth enamel in the study of past mobility. This ratio varies geographically depending on local geology. There are, however, a number of potential applications involving the sourcing or proveniencing of other objects and materials such as pottery, stone, textiles, or fauna. Applications to ceramics are limited, but promising (Makarona *et al.* 2014). The problems that exist involve the measurement of temper vs matrix, the uses and contents of the vessel, and diagenesis. Nevertheless, comparison of strontium isotope ratios in pottery sherds makes possible an objective discussion of the origin of the pot.

^{87}Sr/^{86}Sr was measured on powdered samples of 19 sherds. The descriptive statistics for these measurements included a mean ±1 s.d. of 0.7297±0.0107 with a range between 0.7187 and 0.7656. Figure 8.14 provides a histogram of these values with one presumed TRB sherd and three Ertebølle lamp fragments indicated. The remainder of the sherds are likely from Ertebølle vessels. With the exception of the 0.7656 value for a lamp fragment, the sherds that were analyzed do not appear to be distinct from one another which suggests the same, probably local origin of the clay. The very high value for the lamp fragment may be due to large pieces of granite temper in the sample.

Another way to look for chemical differences in the pottery involves Neutron Activation Analysis (e.g. Bishop and Blackman 2002). NAA uses gamma-rays to measure a wide variety of elements in parts-per-million concentrations. NAA uses the slow 'thermal' neutrons from a nuclear reactor to excite the nucleus of an atom. The neutron strikes the nucleus of an element in the sample, making the atom unstable and radioactive. This nucleus then decays through various processes including

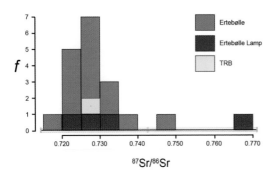

Fig. 8.14. Histogram of 87Sr/86Sr values for 19 sherds from Asnæs Havnemark.

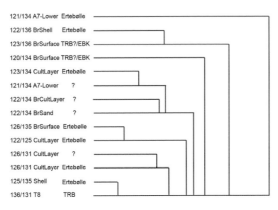

Fig. 8.15. Dendrogram for Neutron Activation Analysis (NAA) results from 14 sherds from Asnæs Havnemark.

the emission of gamma-rays. The number of gamma-ray emissions of a particular energy or wavelength are measured to determine the concentration of the element originally present in the sample. A large range of elements can be measured with high precision.

Elemental concentrations were measured on 14 sherds from Asnæs Havnemark, a set which included lamp fragments and two possible TRB sherds in addition to a range of Ertebølle pottery. The results of this analysis are presented in a dendrogram (Fig. 8.15) which was constructed using Euclidian distance as a measure of similarity and Ward's error for grouping (Hennig *et al.* 2016). Again, as in the strontium isotope analysis, no major differences were detected among the Ertebølle and Funnel Beaker ceramics. If these unusual sherds are indeed TRB, it would appear that they were made from local ingredients similar to the Ertebølle vessels.

Nutshell

Burned hazelnut shell was observed in the excavations and in the water-screened material but was not abundant and could not be systematically collected or counted. Its presence is simply noted here. Such burned nutshell has been reported as very common at some Mesolithic sites such as Smakkerup Huse (Chapter 4; Price and Gebauer 2005) and Duvensee in northern Germany (Bokelmann 2012) and must have been an important food source for Mesolithic groups (Holst 2010).

Shell

There was a substantial deposit of seashells in the upper part of the upper cultural layer composed largely of horse mussels (*Modiolus modiolus*), along with sea snails (*Littorina littorea*), some cockles (*Cardium glaucum*), a few oysters (family Ostreidae), and a small predator snail (*Nassarium pygmaeus*). In places this appeared to have been a midden, *c.* 20 cm in thickness, with a distribution covering several tens of square meters. On the other hand, this may well be a natural deposit of shells accumulated on a beach, especially since the horse mussels are usually found at a depth of 5 m or more, beyond ready human access.

Faunal remains

Preservation at the site of Asnæs Havnemark was very good and the presence of smaller bones as well as larger pieces is a testament to that fact. There was an exceptional amount of faunal material, including enormous quantities of fish bone. It is important to remember that only a small part of the larger settlement that was originally at this location has been preserved and only a small part of that has been excavated, so that the materials found represent only a tiny part of what would have been present. This material is described in some detail below by Ritchie *et al.* (2013b). The non-fish fauna study is part of a larger consideration of Mesolithic fauna at a series of sites in Denmark that was originally the PhD thesis of Kurt Gron (2013) at the University of Wisconsin-Madison and has also appeared in recent publications (Gron 2015).

The bone material from Asnæs Havnemark was separated by meter square and level during the excavation, bagged, and weighed. In addition, any special finds were noted. There were 131 bags of bone material from 104 different levels and units at the site, for a total of 18.02 kg. The faunal material comprises 50,005 identified bones. Of these, 47,760 (95.5%) are fish, 2214 (4.4%), mammals), 29 (0.1%) birds, and two (< 0.1%) amphibians. A total of 799 bones exhibit evidence of burning, including 728 fish bones.

The horizontal and vertical distribution of the faunal remains from the site shows remarkable uniformity. Three layers (culture, shell, and brown) constitute the majority of the vertical provenience information for the samples. The relative abundances of fish from those layers are quite similar, with codfish holding a dominant position of at *c.* 75–87% of all identified specimens. Overall, all classes of faunal remains from the site show uniformity in their relative abundances across contexts and therefore it is reasonable to treat the assemblage as a unit as there is remarkably little change.

Mammals

The identified mammals are listed in Table 8.3. A wide range of species are represented. Numerous long bone fragments are present along with a variety of other bones. For the most part, long bone is fragmented for the extraction of marrow. Several species were identified from only a few bones: red squirrel, otter, mouse, wildcat, and two voles. Fur-bearing animals are present in modest numbers. Otter and wildcat are rare, while fox, beaver, and pine marten are not uncommon. Marine mammals – seal and porpoise – appear frequently among the faunal remains. Since much of the seal material was not confidently identifiable to species, seal specimens were assigned to a general class of 'seal'. This class includes the grey seal (*Halichoerus grypus*) and at least one member of the genus *Phoca*. The Arctic harp seal (*P. groenlandica*) was common in the waters of the North Sea and Baltic during the early Holocene and has been identified at a number of later Mesolithic sites in Denmark (Storå and Ericson 2004).

The identification of mammalian species by skeletal element was tabulated by Gron (2013), along with number of identified specimens (NISP; after Payne 1975) and minimum number of individual (MNI) statistics. The most common species is roe deer, comprising two-thirds (66.5%) of the identified material, deriving from at least 19 individuals. The next most common individual taxon by NISP is wild boar, making up 6.3% of the assemblage and deriving from at a minimum four individuals. However, taken together, seals (Phocidae), regardless of specific identification, comprise 7.4% of the identified material (MNI=5). They are therefore the second most common mammalian prey. The only domesticated species is the dog, represented by at least four individuals and 5.3% of the assemblage.

A few specimens could be assigned ontogenetic age. One very porous roe deer calcaneus, too young to have even developed epiphyses, probably represents a new-born. Additionally, one wild boar specimen died at around 5 months of age based on a recently erupted first mandibular molar, and another specimen died under a year of age on the basis of an unerupted second mandibular molar (Matschke 1967). Additionally, the cervical vertebral fusion of a harbor porpoise specimen indicates an animal of at least 6 years of age (Galatius and Kinze 2003). In all, the sample cannot

Table 8.3. Identified mammal remains from Asnæs Havnemark.

Taxon	Common name	NISP	MNI
Capreolus capreolus	Roe deer	1493	19
Martes martes	Pine marten	65	5
Sus scrofa	Wild boar	141	4
Canis familiaris	Domestic dog	119	4
Erinaceus europaeus	Hedgehog	12	4
Cervus elaphus	Red deer	122	3
Vulpes vulpes	Fox	43	2
Castor fiber	Beaver	21	2
Sciurus vulgaris	Red squirrel	5	2
Lutra lutra	Otter	5	2
Apodemus flavicollis	Yellow-necked mouse	4	2
Phocoena phocoena	Harbor porpoise	14	1
Felis silvestris	Wildcat	2	1
Clethrionomys glareolus	Bank vole	1	1
Arvicola terrestris	Water vole	1	1
Phocidae	Seal	166	5
Total		2214	58

provide a mortality profile for any single species at the site although qualitatively, roe deer are represented by animals of multiple ages and therefore there was probably no clear focus on a particular age class indicative of a more specialized procurement strategy (e.g. Richter and Noe-Nygaard 2003).

The preponderance of roe deer in the material is notable, comprising almost two-thirds of the mammalian faunal remains. Body-part representational data indicate that the deer were not butchered elsewhere or selectively transported (Gron 2015) to the site, an assessment supported by the rather tight distribution of isotopic values (Ritchie *et al.* 2013a) which indicate that these roe deer lived in extremely similar, if not the same, habitats. Despite their high representation in the assemblage however, roe deer were not necessarily the most important species in terms of subsistence. They rarely exceed 25 kg in body weight (Fruziński *et al.* 1982), so multiple roe deer are needed even to approximate one red deer carcass by weight, for example.

There are a large number of seal remains and extensive cutmarks on several elements which indicate their utility to the hunters. The location of the site on this peninsula likely explains this as they generally prefer secluded locations when they haul out (Riedman 1990). The seals may therefore have been clubbed while on land at a haul out location near the site, although hunting with harpoons from boats may have occurred as well.

The location on the Asnæs peninsula may also explain the rather lower numbers of red deer relative to other Ertebølle sites (see Fig. 8.24 below) (Møhl 1971; Skaarup 1973; Noe-Nygaard 1995; Gotfredsen 1998; Enghoff 2011; Price and Gebauer 2005), as limited land area may have restricted the numbers of such a large animal (Geist 1998; Kamler *et al.* 2008). The location would have less affected the abundance of the much smaller roe deer, a species that often lives at higher population densities (Gill *et al.* 1996; Kamler *et al.* 2008).

Birds
Bones from a variety of birds are present, especially long bones from large birds that appear to have been used in the production of fish hooks. Thirteen species of birds were identified among the avian remains, listed in Table 8.4. The presence of each species of bird is determined by the find of single or only a few skeletal elements. The birds can be characterized as divers, waterfowl, or birds of prey. A number of these are large birds including the great auk, swan, and eagle. The presence of the great auk (*Penguinis impennis*) is of interest because this flightless bird, standing approximately 90 cm tall and weighing *c.* 5 kg, became extinct in the mid-19th century. Several examples of third phalanges (talons) from birds of prey are also recorded in the faunal remains. Birds probably would have been hunted with nets or bow-and-arrow; likely taken either as a source of meat (waterfowl) or, in the case of birds of prey, to obtain feathers for fletching or for ornamentation, or to use the bone for other specialized purposes (Clark 1948).

Table 8.4. Identified bird remains from Asnæs Havnemark.

Taxon	Common name	NISP	MNI
Penguinis impennis	Great auk	3	2
Cygnus olor	Mute swan	6	1
Pandion haliaetus	Osprey	4	1
Haliaeetus albicilla	White-tailed eagle	3	1
Aquila chrysaetos	Golden eagle	3	1
Gavia stellata	Red-throated loon	2	1
Podiceps grisegena	Red-necked grebe	2	1
Cygnus cygnus	Whooper swan	1	1
Larus argentatus	Herring gull	1	1
Mergus serrator	Red-breasted merganser	1	1
Podiceps cristatus	Great crested grebe	1	1
Turdus merula	Common blackbird	1	1
Turdus philomelos	Song thrush	1	1
Total		29	14

Isotopic analyses

Bone collagen carbon and nitrogen isotope analyses of the faunal remains were undertaken (Ritchie *et al.* 2013a). The focus of the isotopic studies was on the bones of wild animals and domestic dogs from the site in order to determine the environments from which they were hunted, and as a proxy for human diet (Noe-Nygaard 1988; Clutton-Brock and Noe-Nygaard 1990; Fischer *et al.* 2007; but see Eriksson and Zagorska 2003). Results are listed in Table 8.5.

All wild animals show values that are within normal ranges for southern Scandinavia (Fischer *et al.* 2007). The roe deer show highly consistent values, indicative of an herbivorous diet in a very similar, and probably forested, environment (Gron and Rowley-Conwy 2017). Given the limited width of the Asnæs peninsula, this may indicate a largely forested environment in the Mesolithic if the deer were hunted nearby. The wild boar had higher $\delta^{13}C$ values than the deer, but not higher $\delta^{15}N$. While omnivory cannot be ruled out, this is more likely due to their browsing in more open environments. The grey seal has much higher $\delta^{13}C$ and $\delta^{15}N$ values, as is expected for a marine carnivore. The dogs' values indicate they were eating an almost entirely marine diet, similar to other Mesolithic dogs from Denmark (Fischer *et al.* 2007). It is in this context that the aggregate faunal remains need be understood, in particular the fish.

Fish

A substantial part of the effort of our excavations and analysis involved the fish remains at Asnæs Havnemark, as it was clear that this was a large and important

Table 8.5. Stable isotopes of carbon and nitrogen from Asnæs Havnemark (from Gron 2015).

No.	Taxon	Lab no.	%C	%N	C:N	$\delta^{13}C$ (‰)	$\delta^{15}N$(‰)
AH24-49	Capreolus capreolus	258926	21.78	7.2	3.53	−23.0	4.8
AH40-19	Capreolus capreolus	268260	16.41	5.24	3.66	−22.9	5.5
AH74-15	Capreolus capreolus	268261	18.45	5.82	3.70	−23.1	5.9
AH70-14	Capreolus capreolus	268262	20.07	6.58	3.56	−22.8	5.8
AH73-16	Sus scrofa	268266	17.24	5.74	3.50	−20.9	5.2
AH-84-1	Sus scrofa	284462	35.46	12.70	3.26	−20.9	5.1
AH70-20	Phoca/Halichoerus	268269	18.88	6.37	3.46	-9.56	14.2
AH85-4	Canis familiaris	268272	15.06	4.88	3.60	−11.9	10.1
AH83-10	Canis familiaris	268273	14.30	4.60	3.63	−13.2	11.9

component of the site deposits. Eventually these materials became the focus of a PhD thesis at the University of Wisconsin-Madison (Ritchie 2010) as well as several important publications in Mesolithic studies (e.g. Ritchie *et al.* 2013a; 2013b).

The identified family and/or species of fish in the bone material is listed in Table 8.6. A total of 47,760 specimens were identified from the three trenches from 18 fish families. The fish assemblage from Asnæs Havnemark is remarkable because of its size and diversity. Codfish dominate the assemblage, with eel following at a distant second and other fishes contributing relatively minor amounts. Freshwater fish are rare (only eight cyprinid vertebrae), but diadromous fish include eel, shad, and trout/salmon. These results are very much in accord with the site's location on the Asnæs peninsula with no major bodies of freshwater in the vicinity.

Preservation of the fish bones was generally good and all of the skeletal elements seemed to have been discarded together, though not all elements were recovered and identified in equal proportions. Fish bone was very common in the water-screened material from the site and was collected and separately bagged from the beginning of excavations. These bags have been weighed and the information recorded by meter square and level. Because of the abundance of fish bone in the site deposits, our recovery strategy shifted from water sieving and collecting fish bone from all squares using 4 mm screens to a dedicated sorting process where Ritchie focused on complete recovery from selected squares, using a white table surface for careful sorting and separation of all fish bone from the washed matrix. In addition, 14 small samples (generally 2 liters with one sample of 5 liters) were wet-sieved through nested 4 mm, 2 mm and 1 mm mesh geological sieves to assess the impact of recovery methodology on the final results. All recovered fish material has been analyzed.

Although some identifications are to species level, the predominance of vertebrae (especially from members of the cod family) means that most of the specimens are only identified to the family level. To avoid comparisons between different taxonomic levels, fish families are used to report results. Gadidae are represented by

Table 8.6. Identified fish remains from Asnæs Havnemark.

Family	Species	Common name	NISP
Anguillidae	Anguilla anguilla	eel	3949/598*
Belonidae	Belone belone	garfish	45/-*
Callionymidae	Callionymus lyra	dragonet	1/-*
Clupeidae	Clupea harengus	herring	158/106*
	Alosa sp.	shad	13/-*
Cottidae	Myoxocephalus scorpius	bullrout	601/96*
Cyprinidae	various	carp family	8/2*
Gadidae		codfish	38103/2244*
	Gadus morhua	cod	
	Melanogrammus aeglefinus	haddock	
	Merlangius merlangus	whiting	
	Pollachius pollachius/virens	pollock/saithe	
Gasterosteidae	Gasterosteus aculeatus	3-spined stickleback	-/44*
Gobiidae	Gobius sp.	goby	-/3*
Pleuronectidae		flatfish	897/59*
	Platichthys flesus	flounder	
(possible)	Pleuronectes platessa	plaice	
(possible)	Limanda limanda	dab	
Salmonidae	Salmo trutta/salar	trout/salmon	13/2*
Scombridae	Scomber scombrus	Atlantic mackerel	444/117*
Scophthalmidae		flatfish	1/-*
(possible)	Psetta maxima	turbot	
(possible)	Scophthalmus rhombus	brill	
Squalidae	Squalus acanthias	spurdog	40/1*
Syngnathidae	various	pipefish	-/1*
Trachinidae	Trachinus draco	greater weever	34/9*
Triglidae			136/5*
(possible)	Trigla lucerna	tub gurnard	
(possible)	Eutrigla gurnardus	grey gurnard	
Zoarcidae	Zoarces viviparusviviparous eelpout		18/12*
Total			44461/3299*

Numbers are from the screen-test samples. NISP = Number of Identified Specimens cod, haddock, saithe/pollock, and whiting. Cod are most common at 75.1%, with 5.1% whiting, 1.0% saithe/pollock, 0.4% haddock, and 18.4% unspecified gadid – based on identifications of 898 otoliths. Flat fish are represented by flounder (although plaice and dab may also be present) and turbot/brill. Clupeidae remains consist of both herring and 13 vertebrae of shad *(Alosa alosa* and *A. fallax* are both present in Danish waters)*. The only other Ertebølle sites where shad bones have been recovered are Dragsholm and Henriksholm-Bøgebakken (Ritchie 2010; Enghoff 2011 and see Chapter 6). None of the cyprinid vertebrae could be assigned to species, so it is not possible to say which fish(es) are present from among the several options. Salmonids are also only represented by vertebrae, so it is not possible to state whether these are trout or salmon. Triglids could be either tub or grey gurnard, but only grey gurnard is definitely present. The single specimen that is attributable to dragonet (family Callionymidae) is of note as this fish has only been identified in one other Ertebølle assemblage (Norsminde; Enghoff 1991). Some fishes that are present in the assemblage (i.e. three-spined stickleback and pipefish) were only recovered because of the use of very fine mesh-size sieving.

Another important category of evidence regarding the fish remains at Asnæs Havnemark comes from 898 recovered otoliths. The otoliths were used for estimating fish size based on regression formulas and also isotopically analyzed for information on season of death. For cod, for example, measurements of otolith total length (OL) were used to estimate fish total length (TL) based on the formula (Härkönen 1986, 90):

$$TL = -202.13 + 48.37(OL)$$

Summary data are graphically displayed in Figure 8.16. Estimates range from cod as small as 20 cm (with a weight of *c.* 100 g) up to a maximum of 53 cm (weight *c.* 1.5 kg), with an average of around 33–34 cm (weight *c.* 300 g). Estimates of eel sizes ranged from 42 cm to 86 cm, with an average of approximately 61 cm. The fact that most of the eels are greater than 50 cm in length implies that the majority of the catch were females – perhaps caught during their fall migration (Muus *et al.* 2006). There was not a great deal of variation in the sizes of the flat fish, with an average length of about 25 cm.

The size estimates for the fish are similar to those from other Ertebølle sites in Denmark. Cod usually average around 30–40 cm, slightly larger at Lystrup Enge and Grisby. The largest fish at Asnæs Havnemark estimated from otolith length are not as large as the ones seen at many other sites. There are other elements in the assemblage that indicate larger fish were caught. Eels from the site are similar in size to those seen elsewhere, although the absence of any specimens less than 42 cm is notable. The flat fish from Asnæs Havnemark are also similar in size to those found in other Ertebølle assemblages (Enghoff 1994). The fish bones represent a minimum of hundreds of individuals, demonstrating that fish were a significant part of the diet, even if their precise contribution is difficult to ascertain.

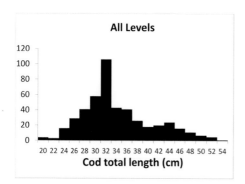

Fig. 8.16. *Total lengths of cod for all levels combined.*

Stable isotope analyses of seven cod otoliths from two Late Mesolithic Ertebølle sites (Asnæs Havnemark and Fårevejle) were conducted to determine the season of catch for the fish (Ritche *et al.* 2013b and see Chapter 7, above). Results indicate fishing during the late winter, spring, and summer. This is a considerably broader fishing season than that estimated solely from the presence of migratory fishes in the assemblages and suggests that fishing played a larger role in the annual subsistence cycle than previously acknowledged.

In regard to the fish, the fact that at least 22 species from 18 different families are present in the assemblage shows that there were many fishes available that the inhabitants could choose to take. While fishes were locally available in higher or lower numbers depending on the species, the many bones of codfish (and to a lesser extent eel) demonstrate that they were the preferred catch. The rocky, exposed shoreline near the site, the predominance of codfish (including large individuals of cod and haddock), and the recovery of numerous fish hooks and preforms suggest that angling (possibly offshore in boats) played a major role in the fishery. This interpretation is supported by the very low incidence (0.1%) of weever, a species often used as a marker of fishing with stationary structures (Enghoff 1994). A further indication of the importance of the cod fishery is the otolith evidence showing that they were caught at different times of the year. That most of the eel are larger than 50 cm and thus presumably females points to eel fishing in the fall when they were migrating from freshwaters into the sea (Muus *et al.* 2006). Some of the smaller fish hooks could have been used in this fishery but it is also possible that nets, traps, or spears were employed during this event. Access to good cod fishing grounds and migrating eels in the fall may have been the reasons behind why the site is located far out on the Asnæs peninsula, a setting that was the location of an important historical fishery for several different species (Drechsel and Petersen 1988).

Human remains

A fragment of a human mandible with four teeth attached was excavated in unit 122E135N and at least five other human teeth were recovered in the excavations. A few small pieces of human bone and tooth were also identified during the sorting and identification of the faunal remains. These materials were forwarded to the Anthropology collections associated with the Forensic Anthropology Section of the Department of Forensic Medicine at the Panum Institute in Copenhagen. The presence of these human remains in the deposits at Asnæs Havnemark strongly suggests that there were Mesolithic burials at the site.

Bone modification

Burning, butchery, and tool production were all ways that bone at Asnæs Havnemark was modified by human activities. Less than 1% of the mammal material is affected by burning, indicating that most cooking occurred after removal of meat from the bones. Other options involve meat being either cooked (stewing, earth ovens) or preserved (drying, smoking) by methods that would not result in burnt bones. Burning is the principal manner in which the fish remains have been modified, although this was a fairly rare occurrence. Despite the fact that a total of 728 fish bones from the 4 mm sieving assemblage exhibit signs of burning (ranging from partial blackening to complete calcination), this is a small percentage (*c.* 1.6%) when considered in the context of over 47,000 identified specimens.

Fig. 8.17. One of the bone fishhooks found at Asnæs Havnemark.

Evidence of butchery (including sawing, cutmarks, scrape marks, etc.) was present on some mammal bones, although any systematic patterns are obscured by the condition of the bone material. Nearly all the appropriate mammal bones were marrow-fractured, and no systematic choice of one species over another is evident. Other than the previously described burning, osteological evidence for how fish were prepared is scant. There were almost no cutmarks observed during the analysis and skeletal element representation provides little additional information about butchery methods.

Bone tools were generally limited to the 43 fish hooks and preforms (Fig. 8.17), along with six roe deer antler retouchoirs, bone points (5), bone awls (4), bone needles (2), and two tooth pendants. One of the tooth pendants was made from the reticular canine or grandeln tooth of a red deer (*Cervus elaphus*; Fig. 8.18; S. Sørensen 2016). The root had been perforated for attachment. Such pendants are often found in graves and again provides another argument for burials at the site.

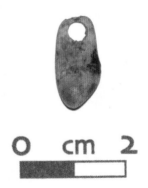

Fig. 8.18. Grandeln tooth from red deer made into tooth pendant.

The bone fish hooks and preforms were a special category of artifacts from this site (Fig. 8.19). There were 25 finished hooks and 18 preforms. These specimens were in various states of preservation, both complete and fragmentary. Several of the preforms exhibit preliminary engraved lines to mark the outline to be cut from the bone.

In general, relatively few bone specimens were worked or prepared for the manufacture of tools. However, one aspect particularly worthy of note is the degree and specificity of working traces found on bones of domestic dog (Fig. 8.20). In total, 119 fragments of bone are attributable to dog. Of this number, nearly every long bone is worked in a very similar fashion, with minor differences probably owing to variations in bone morphology. Regardless of the specific long bone to be worked, the flattest surface was first selected and then incised on either side, to prepare a relatively flat section of cortical bone with parallel edges. Subsequently, the prepared section was incised perpendicular to the edges in order to weaken, and eventually remove, a flat and broadly rectantular piece of bone.

This prepartion resulted in a preform for making fish hooks. While the majority appear to be made from the long bones of dogs, one of these came from a swan ulna (*Cygnus* sp.). Several preforms show the general method of making fish hooks from the flat pieces of bone (Fig. 8.21). Several hooks could apparently be made from piece of bone by hollowing out the curvature of the hook and snapping off the nearly complete object.

Seasonality

The faunal remains provide another means for examining the seasons of site use at Asnæs Havnemark. Multiple lines of evidence including animal behavioral ecology,

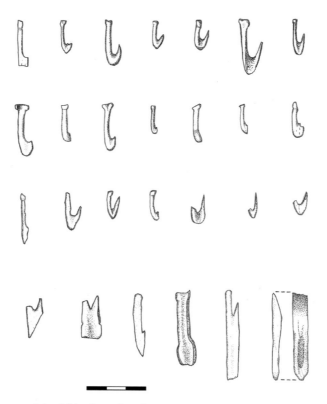

Fig. 8.19. Some of the fishhooks and preforms from Asnæs Havnemark. The scale is 3 cm.

oxygen isotope analysis of cod otoliths, and ontogenetic ageing of select species indicate use of the site in all seasons of the year. As Sørensen (2017, 31) noted, at large coastal settlements from both the Kongemose and the Ertebølle periods all seasons of the year are usually represented in the faunal remains.

The presence or absence of birds at specific times of the year can be a useful tool for establishing the season of occupation at archaeological sites. Seasonal information is restricted to species with migratory patterns. The seasonal information from the birds at Asnæs Havnemark is limited. The golden eagle, mute swan, white-tailed eagle, herring gull, red-breasted merganser, grebes, song thrush, and common blackbird (Table 8.5) are all possible year-round residents in Denmark (Génsbøl 2006). The osprey only leaves in winter and the whooper swan is only absent in summertime. Red-throated loons seasonally migrate through Denmark in the spring and autumn (Génsbøl 2006). As there is only a single specimen for most of these species it probably best not to draw conclusions regarding seasonality from this category of evidence.

Migratory behavior is also present in the fish evidence, especially with regard to gar-

Fig. 8.20. Worked groove parallel to flat surface of a dog tibia.

Fig. 8.21. Perpendicular cutting to facilitate snapping off a section of bone with a prepared flat surface.

fish and mackerel that are present in Danish waters from the late spring to early fall. The presence of bones from both these species in the assemblage, albeit in limited numbers, strongly suggests summer occupation at Asnæs Havnemark. Three diadromous fishes (eel, shad, and salmon/trout) provide some evidence for site use during spring and fall as they are most easily caught during migration, although individuals could also have been taken at other times of the year (Muus *et al.* 2006).

In contrast with the evidence from migratory fish, the predominance of codfish in the assemblage (including large examples of cod and haddock) may be evidence for winter occupation, based on comparison with the Danish fishery of the 19th century (Moustgaard 1987). To test this idea, a pilot study using a newly developed methodology was conducted on four cod otoliths to determine in which season these fish were caught. The method relies on three factors: that fish otoliths grow

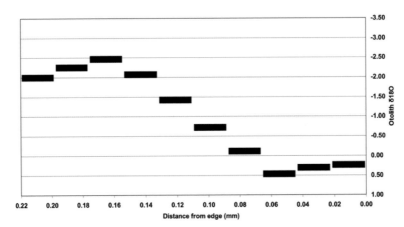

Fig. 8.22. Results from 48 cm long cod. Readings higher (more negative) on the Y axis indicate warmer temperatures and readings farther to the right on the X axis are closer to the time of capture.

incrementally throughout the life of the fish, that they incorporate isotopes of oxygen in ratios that reflect their surroundings, and that the ratio of ^{16}O and ^{18}O in their aquatic environment varies in response to water temperatures (see Hufthammer *et al.* 2010; Ritchie *et al.* 2013b). By comparing the result from the sample taken from the outer edge of the otolith (the area being formed when the fish died) with the annual cycle of water temperature changes revealed by the complete series of samples, it is possible to determine at what time of year the fish was caught. The 48 cm fish, for example, was caught when water temperatures were just beginning to warm from their annual low, corresponding to a seasonality indication of late winter or early spring (Fig. 8.22). Although the sample size is small, these results show that while some cod were caught during the summer, winter and spring were also part of the fishery at Asnæs Havnemark.

Two lines of evidence are available for the estimation of season of occupation using the mammalian remains; the seasonal casting of antlers by deer and the ontogenetic development of, in this case, roe deer and wild boar. Modern roe deer cast their antlers in November and December (Sempéré *et al.* 1992) after which, they grow back in an annual cycle. Several roe deer frontal bones and their attachment points for antlers, the pedicles, are present at Asnæs Havnemark which provide evidence of different stages in this cycle. Uncast antlers still attached to the pedicle, antlers in the process of being cast from the pedicle, and pedicles that have recently cast their antlers, are all present in the assemblage. This indicates that the deer in question died at that stage of their life cycle. The recently cast antlers that have not yet started to regrow and the antlers in the process of being cast are therefore very strong indicators of a late autumn, or early winter time of death.

Figure 8.23 summarizes the cumulative seasonality information from the animal remains. In aggregate, there is evidence for a human presence at Asnæs Havnemark

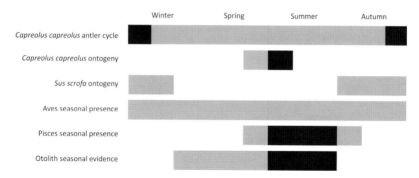

Fig. 8.23. Seasonality at Asnæs Havnemark (black indicates higher confidence, grey less confidence).

for much of the year with the caveat that visits need not have been continuous. It is, nonetheless, apparent that hunting and fishing took place in similar seasons. It would seem that there is good evidence for year-round use of the site and very strong evidence for human presence in the summer.

Interpretation

The site location, faunal assemblage, and tool technology all point to the conclusion that the people who lived at Asnæs Havnemark oriented their lives towards the sea. Isotopic evidence indicates that seafood was the most important part of the diet. The overall impression of animal use at the site is one of both focus and breadth. In this sense, the diet of the inhabitants appears to be similar to the pattern known from many other Ertebølle sites. While the assemblage is strongly dominated by fish of the cod family and roe deer, there is a wide range of other species present. With availability of these primary food sources insured, other animals could be incorporated into the subsistence regime as opportunity arose.

There is variability in Ertebølle faunal use that has not generally been recognized. While the same species are generally present in most assemblages, their relative abundance varies widely among sites. Five other sites from Denmark (Bjørnsholm on the Limfjord in northern Jutland, Vængesø III in east-central Jutland, Tybrind Vig on Funen, Nivågård in northeastern Sjælland, and Smakkerup Huse in northwestern Sjælland) have reasonably large faunal assemblages excavated with methods appropriate for recovering a good sample of fish remains (Bratlund 1993; Price and Gebauer 2005; Andersen 2009; Enghoff 2011; and see Chapter 4, above). The assemblages from these sites help to demonstrate that broad differences in fishing practices existed within the larger framework of available resources.

Examining the different families of fish at these sites makes it apparent that, generally, the same species of fish were caught. Despite this exploitation of common species, the fisheries were actually quite variable when relative abundances are considered. At most sites, a majority of the specimens are from one type of fish, but

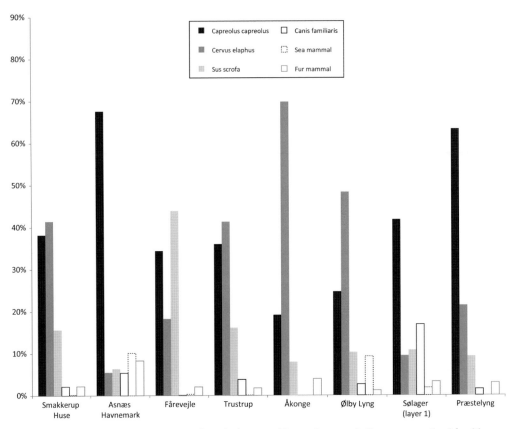

Fig. 8.24. Variation in relative abundance (NISP) of mammal bones from Ertebølle sites on Zealand (Møhl 1971; Skaarup 1973; Noe-Nygaard 1995; Gotfredsen 1998; Hede 2003; Gron 2013; Ritchie et al. 2013b).

that type varies between codfish, flat fish and eel (most often codfish). The fact that mostly the same types of fish are found at Ertebølle sites throughout Denmark, but in widely varying abundances, points to fully competent fishing capabilities tailored to local conditions.

The same pattern is seen with the mammal bone, even if restricted to only Ertebølle sites on Zealand (Fig. 8.24). The same mammals are generally present at these sites. Where dissimilarity occurs it ca n often be attributed to the local availability of species. The relative abundance of species is quite different at individual sites. Variability is observed particularly among the three main terrestrial game animals (red deer, roe deer, and wild boar), as well as sea mammals and fur-bearing species. The faunal material from Asnæs Havnemark highlights this variability and underscores the reality of differences among certain classes of resources.

These comparisons show that within almost all classes of animals exploited by Ertebølle hunters and fishers, there is a great deal of inter-site variability. While the same animals generally occur in all assemblages, the focus of the subsistence at each site represents adaptation to local conditions. In the case of Asnæs Havnemark, the location of the site may, to some degree, explain the preponderance of just a few species in the archaeological material. However, a major caveat is that while this is the case, the breadth of species and range of classes of animals utilized remains quite impressive, indicating an ability to employ multiple hunting and fishing strategies to fully exploit local resources. We take this to strongly indicate that in the face of either seasonal or atypical environmental stresses, Ertebølle hunters at Asnæs Havnemark had the knowledge and skills to readily switch between vastly different classes of resources as needed.

In other words, despite the preponderance of roe deer and codfish remains, the Asnæs Havnemark assemblage is the result of a highly flexible hunter-gatherer subsistence strategy able to adapt to local, seasonal, and longer-term shifts in resource availability. In turn, this means that environmental stresses would have less impact to create major changes in general subsistence patterns. Because of this flexibility, we contend that substantive environmental changes could not have been the major causal force for the introduction of agriculture at the end of the Ertebølle period. The evidence we have presented greatly weakens such arguments.

Conclusions

The Asnæs peninsula has been associated with fishing for generations. There is an historical fishing village on the south coast of the peninsula with well-known fixed weirs (Pedersen 1997). There are former fisherman's houses and processing buildings 2 km east of the site of Asnæs Havnemark. A herd of seals is still often seen off the west end of the peninsula. The area is also a well-known hunting place today and both roe deer and pheasants are taken in large numbers.

The site is unusual for a number of reasons and has substantial potential to provide information on the transition to agriculture in this region. The radiocarbon dates now available place the site at the time of the transition to agriculture in southern Scandinavia, *c.* 4000 cal BC. The deposits are terrestrial, rather than waterlain, and a portion of the settlement area is intact. The cultural layer appears to represent a short-term occupation, lying between two episodes of beach ridge formation. Beach ridge deposition at this elevation must have taken place during a time of higher sea level, likely during the Littorina transgression at the end of the Atlantic climatic episode. This event fits extremely well with the radiocarbon dates for the site and also provides important information on potentially significant environmental changes at the end of the Mesolithic period.

Beyond the normal assemblage of materials that characterize a Late Mesolithic site in this region, there are high numbers of stylistically homogeneous projectile points, distinctive flake axes, bone fish hooks and preforms, seal bones, large bird bones, and an extraordinary amount of fish bone at Asnæs Havnemark. The rich occupation layer, including a fragment of a human jaw, suggests a substantial residential settlement on this coast. While a variety of species are represented, eel and cod are very common. In addition, a large quantity of ceramic material was recovered in the test excavations. This abundance of pottery includes both pointed-bottom vessels and oval lamps from the Late Mesolithic, as well as several examples of Early Neolithic ceramics. The site is of interest for a number of reasons including the coastal location, the unusual ceramics, the nature of the fishery, and the focus on specific game species.

The cod family dominates the fish assemblage, while roe deer account for the vast majority of the mammal remains. Despite the preponderance of these two species of animals, the assemblage presents an impressive variety of other fish, mammals, and birds. Different skills and procurement strategies are required to obtain terrestrial game, fur animals, seals, raptors, waterfowl, and the various species of fish. The wide variety of animals represented in the Asnæs Havnemark assemblage indicates that the people who lived there were proficient in a number of different hunting and fishing techniques. The predominance of roe deer in the mammal material and cod in the fish material indicates a distinct degree of economic specialization. However, it is important to remember that the inhabitants of Asnæs Havnemark were not so much constrained by the availability of animals in the vicinity of the site, as drawn there because of the prey that were present.

There is also evidence of contact with others in the ceramics at the site. Assuming contemporaneity, the unusual pottery, TRB in tradition, suggests some contact with early farmers either in Denmark, southern Sweden, or across the Baltic in northern Germany. The unusual types of pottery, however, appear to be locally made. The abundance of food in the form of marine resources and roe deer found at the site suggests that food stress was not an issue for the local population. Such evidence argues that more food was not a concern when Ertebølle hunter-gatherers were replaced by farmers.

Chapter 9

Conclusions

The conclusions to this book are in fact a distillation of what I have learned over the last 40 years or so that I have been doing archaeology and going to Denmark. Most of this will concern professional issues rather than personal ones, but I cannot help but mention some of the things that I have observed and felt in that period. Several dichotomies distinguish the people of northern Europe from the south: butter not olive oil, meat and potatoes not pasta and tomatoes, protestant not catholic, blonde not brunette, beer not wine. In general, Danes are liberal on most issues, cosmopolitan in taste, demanding in design, frugal, family-focused, socially – rather than individually – oriented, and pay some of the world's highest taxes – a fascinating combination of old-fashioned morality and post-modern perspectives. It it is a country where almost everyone knows the names of famous furniture designers. In Denmark I have experienced warm relationships, lifelong friends, a caring society, a welfare state that takes care of almost everyone, an emphasis on quality and equality, and both a long and a broad perspective on the future. Denmark is often rated as one of the happiest countries in the world but they must take that survey in the summer. Winter weather is rather depressing, dark, and dreary.

It is important to take stock of what was gained from the many years of fieldwork in Denmark. We learned a good bit about the Mesolithic. The easy availability of high-quality flint meant that there was an abundance of sizable lithic material present at most Mesolithic sites. At the same time, the number and diversity of formal tool types is really quite limited. Retouched tools comprise less than 5% of most assemblages. A rather standard set of artifacts was used. Projectile points and axes are common. Scrapers, burins, and borers vary in proportion from site to site, but are usually not found in large numbers. The lithic industry of the Mesolithic in this area verges on the mundane. Other technologies in wood, bone, clay, and stone are also rather simple. Ertebølle pottery, for example, is well known for its rather crude form, heavy temper, and low firing temperature. At the same time, of course, these tools allowed Mesolithic hunter-gatherers to do what they needed to do.

My overall impressions from these decades of encounters with the Mesolithic are many. Distinctive characteristics of the period include a broad diet of plants and animals from both the land and sea. Certain resources – nuts, fish, and shellfish – were particularly visible in the archaeological record. Marine foods were clearly an important component of diet. Sites were often directly at the coast. Plant foods were utilized as well in large quantities, especially rich hazelnuts that must have been abundantly available. Sites were often large and cultural deposits substantial. More seasonal indicators were available that pointed to longer settlement use and residence. The impression is of bigger and longer-term settlements. Although group size is still nearly impossible to estimate, we are almost certainly talking about tens of individuals, not hundreds. It is still not clear if these settlements were really permanent occupations or involved repeated visits, but Binford's 1980 model of logistic collectors with fixed base camps seems appropriate here. Different kinds of sites are recognizable with varying resource extraction emphases – fur trapping sites, fishing sites, sealing sites, shellfish collecting sites, and others – but in general these places share a number of similarities as well in terms of a rather standard assemblage of domestic equipment and foods.

The equipment in the Mesolithic included the bow and arrow, domesticated dogs for hunting, water transport in the form of canoes, a variety of fishing gear such as nets, hook and line, leisters, weirs, traps, and various ground stone tools for woodworking and grinding. Pottery is used in later Mesolithic northern Europe for cooking and probably storage. In addition, southern Scandinavia was the home of Mesolithic art in a variety of forms and media – carved amber figurines, engraved and decorated bone, stone, wood, and antler pieces. Exchange among groups was operating and there were clearly non-local objects present in the form of exotic stone axes and tooth pendants from foreign animal species. Ritual behavior was visible at the very least in wetland deposits (e.g., Sørensen 2020), burials, and a number of cemeteries from this period.

We learned less about the Early Neolithic. I looked for Early Neolithic sites in western Sjælland for more than 20 years. We do have a number of sites with radiocarbon dates from the time of the transition and slight indications of Neolithic involvement – a few domestic cow bones and polished axe fragments at Smakkerup Huse, radiocarbon dates and some unusual pottery at Asnæs Havnemark, radiocarbon dates at Fårevejle shell midden, the Early Neolithic burial, polished axes, and cow bones at Dragsholm. These are hints only. Clear and distinct *in situ* evidence of Early Neolithic occupation or living floors is difficult to come by. Perhaps we had an example at Lindebjerg (TMMbdr), but there was very little coherent information regarding the arrival of the Early Neolithic in the study area. The lesson here is that ENI had a rather light presence in southern Scandinavia and that much of the evidence has been eroded and redeposited. It is also the case that much of the material identifiable as Early Neolithic has been found in and around sandy areas near the coast.

This problem of low visibility for the Early Neolithic has been noted elsewhere. Christian Juel and Anders Kjær (2015) wrote about the earliest Neolithic at Vedbæk Fjord, Denmark, another coastal area 100 km east of the Saltbæk Vig, which they refer to as an overlooked horizon. They report on a settlement layer dated 3950–3640 cal

BC at the site of Maglemosegård. This Early Neolithic layer consisted of small concentrations of finds where only the Funnel Beaker ceramics could be definitely dated to the Neolithic. A jaw from a dog was the only domesticated animal. Usually, it is the presence of pointed-butt axes and Funnel Beaker pottery which leads to the identification of a Neolithic horizon. If these artifact types are rare or absent it is very difficult to distinguish between a Late Mesolithic and an Early Neolithic occupation. This problem of visibility is often relevant where Early Neolithic and Mesolithic material are present at the same site. Juel and Kjær also note the problem with transgressions and coastal erosion in locating and identifying the Early Neolithic.

Other experiences, in addition to my years in Denmark and Danish archaeology, have influenced my views on the origins and spread of agriculture and expanded my perspectives on past human diet, inequality, and social complexity. My graduate training at the University of Michigan was deep and intensive; I think what was most important was that I was taught to take a careful and critical view of what I heard and read. Graduate school also focused on fundamental questions in archaeology. A lot of what I have learned has been trying to keep up with those issues. I also gained greatly from graduate student seminars on the origins of agriculture I held at the University of Wisconsin-Madison.

A visit to Góbekli Tepe in Turkey left a major impression. A map of the agriculturally fertile areas of the world really caused me to think. A paper on changes in CO_2 levels in the earth's history by an atmospheric scientist and a follow-up by a biologist, an evolutionary scientist, and an archaeologist made a lot of sense to me. A conference on the Origins of Agriculture, sponsored by the WennerGren Foundation, provided food for thought and helped me put my work in perspective. My own research involving isotopes and human tooth enamel changed my views 180° on human mobility in the past. Experiencing the information explosion that good preservation brings was very important. Ancient DNA research in Europe has focused on the who question in terms of the arrival of the first farmers and offers some intriguing answers. An essay by Polly Wiessner on the emergence of inequality drew me deeper into the subject. These topics and more are elaborated in the following paragraphs.

Góbekli Tepe

Góbekli Tepe made a big impression (Fig. 9.1). Gitte and I were fortunate to visit this site in eastern Turkey several years ago. Góbekli is an absolutely remarkable place, dating from 10,000 years ago, at the very beginning of the Neolithic, containing the most extraordinary architecture. At that time most of the known settlements in the Near East were rather small and undistinguished. As Ian Hodder supposedly said, 'Góbekli Tepe changed everything'. We had heard about the site, but nothing compares with a visit.

Góbekli lies at almost 800 m in elevation atop a mountain in the Fertile Crescent that part of the ancient Middle East where the plants and animals that were

Fig. 9.1. View of some of the large circular structures at Góbekli Tepe. (Image by Mark Cartwright, reproduced under Wikimedia Creative Commons Attribution-Share Alike).

to become domesticated were present in abundance. The site itself covers a huge area, some 8 hectares. The mound or tell (the *tepe*) has a height of 15 m and is about 300 m in diameter. Beneath the mound, Góbekli contains a series of monumental round to oval buildings, erected in an early phase, together with smaller, rectangular buildings around them some of which are contemporary and some of which are slightly later. The monumental buildings are best known as they were the focus of the archaeological investigations. They are around 20 m in diameter on average and have carved stone pillars up to 5.5 m high (equivalent to a two-storey building), often richly decorated with relief carvings – the world's oldest megaliths (Fig. 9.2). There are an estimated 20 of these large circular structures and 200 of the huge pillars at the site. The pillars are often T-shaped and appear anthropomorphic in design. The rectangular buildings are smaller and some have mostly undecorated pillars up to 2 m high. Especially striking is the number of tools related to food processing – grinding slabs, hand stones, pestles, and mortars. These grinding stones and other evidence confirm the importance of preparing cereal grains at the site. The large circular structures were filled in sometime after 8000 BC, probably intentionally buried under debris, mostly flint, gravel, stone tools, and animal bones. The animal bones were dominated by gazelle and aurochs, the wild ancestor of domestic cattle (Peters and Schmidt 2004).

The director of the site excavations, the late Klaus Schmidt (e.g., 2006; 2011; 2012), often described the site as a pilgrimage place for hunter-gatherers. Others have questioned his interpretation. Banning (2011), for example, suggests that some of the large, circular structures at Góbekli may have been residential – domestic as well as ritual in purpose. Banning argues that Neolithic people 'either made no strong distinction between sacred and profane or found the sacred in their daily routines' (Banning 2011, 620). The large amount of domestic refuse and the abundant grinding stones and sickles that are present in these large structures support his hypothesis.

I personally believe that Góbekli was an Early Neolithic site (known as PrePottery Neolithic in the Near East) with some important civic/ceremonial structures that were essential to the community. It may be that these folks were just on the cusp of domesticating plants and animals, but I cannot believe that they were not Neolithic. As Banning notes (2011, 636) the economy of the PrePottery Neolithic was 'mixed traditional hunting and gathering with newer, more controlled exploitation of resources'. The visit to Góbekli left me struck by how spectacular that early site was and how dramatic the changes associated with the emergence of the Neolithic could be.

Fig. 9.2. A stone pillar with carved fox at Góbekli Tepe (Image by Alex Wang, reproduced under Wikimedia Creative Commons Attribution-Share Alike 4.0 International).

Climate change

Discussions of the importance of climate keep popping up in the literature of the transition to agriculture (e.g., Huntley *et al.* 2002; Krossa *et al.* 2017; Lewis *et al.* 2020), increasingly with the growing concern over global warming today. Climatic events from the past are suggested to impact human behavior and be responsible for changes like the arrival of agriculture in northern Europe. Bonsall *et al.* (2002) for example, made the argument that the spread of agriculture to northern Europe, after a delay of more than 1000 years, was due to climate change. They recorded increases in charcoal frequency in Scottish lake deposits at *c.* 7050, *c.* 4450, *c.* 3950, and *c.* 2300 cal BC that they associated with forest fires during *warmer* phases of relatively dry climate. The 3950 cal BC date corresponded to the introduction of agriculture in the

British Isles (although it is a little late for southern Scandinavia). On the other hand, Heiri *et al.* (2004) focused on centennial-scale *cooling* episodes enhancing the spread of early agriculture in the mid-Holocene at approximately 8700–8500 and 6200–5600 BC. Clearly climate was changing, getting warmer or colder, wetter or drier.

The so-called 8.2 k event, the 6.2 k event, and even the 4.2 k event have been indicted for similar consequences (Tinner and Lotter 2001; Huntley *et al.* 2002; Gehlen and Schon 2005; Weninger *et al.* 2006; Budja 2007; Krossa *et al.* 2017). These events represent episodes of climatic disruption, named for the date of occurrence. For some, these 'events' are signposts for climatic change. Warden *et al.* (2017) report a sudden increase in summer temperature at 6000 cal BP and argue that this temperature rise coincided with the introduction of agriculture and thus made farming possible in northern Europe. If this warming caused hypoxia (a decrease of oxygen) in the inshore waters in northern Europe, it might account for the decline in oysters, but these shellfish were quickly replaced with blue mussels in the diet and middens of the region (Lewis *et al.* 2016).

The various reports linking climate change and the spread of agriculture often seem contradictory and unclear. A whole series of catastrophes from elm disease to oyster blights to warmer, drier episodes with forest fires have been invoked as evidence of the role of climate. Theoretically, climate change forces human societies to take new directions by reducing or altering their food supply. Climate change inexorably means less food, but that is hard to justify in northern Europe given the evidence for rich resources.

It is also the case that the spread of agriculture across Europe took place in a series of stands and starts and that each start would have to be correlated with some climatic event for climate change to be an acceptable explanation. Minor climatic shifts do not appear to have been either a limiting or enabling factor for the spread of agriculture. Climate is always changing. Climate change is often an answer for those who cannot accept that humans made the decisions that resulted in the spread of agriculture.

Major climatic change may be another matter. On to atmospheric chemistry. A 1995 article by Rowan Sage asked the question: 'Was low atmospheric CO_2 during the Pleistocene a limiting factor for the origin of agriculture?' He pointed out that the warming of temperature and the melting of glacial ice at the end of the Pleistocene (Fig. 9.3) would have released huge amounts of carbon dioxide from the oceans into the

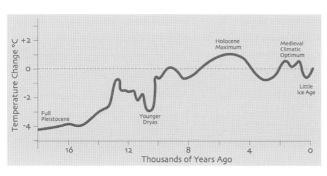

Fig. 9.3. *Average atmospheric temperature over the last 18,000 years (from Sage 1995).*

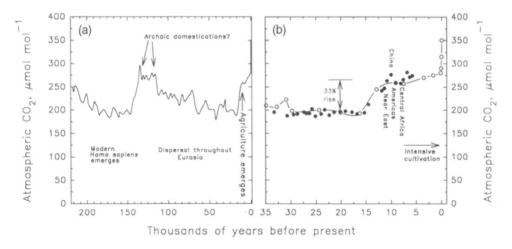

Fig. 9.4. Sage (1995) provided these graphs of changes in CO_2 and plant productivity: (a) depicts atmospheric levels of CO_2 for the last 220,000 years, and (b) shows the change in atmospheric levels of CO_2 for the last 35,000 years with dates for first domesticates for labeled geographic regions.

atmosphere (Fig. 9.4). Carbon storage at the glacial maximum was greatest in the deep oceans (Hodell *et al.* 2003; Hogg 2008) and it is likely that the enormous release of CO_2 with Pleistocene warming derived from that source (Toggweiler 1999). An estimated increase of 33% in atmospheric CO_2 would directly increase photosynthesis and biomass productivity in flora by 25–50%. Plants would grow faster, bigger, and produce more food (Sage 1995).

In essence, Sage recognized a global driver that could explain the relative synchronicity of the origins of agriculture at different spots on the globe at the end of the Pleistocene. In a subsequent article, published in 2001, Richerson and colleagues reiterated Sage's suggestion and pointed out that abrupt climatic changes, dry conditions, and low levels of CO_2 in the Pleistocene would have made agriculture almost impossible, while the Holocene featured more stable climate, moister conditions, and more CO_2, a fertile situation for agriculture. As Richerson *et al.* stated (2001, 404) 'the reduction in climate variability, increase in CO_2 content of the atmosphere, and increases in rainfall rather abruptly changed the earth from a regime where agriculture was impossible everywhere to one where it was possible in many places'.

A map of cropland

An almost accidental encounter with a map (Fig. 9.5) of the areas of pasture and cultivation on earth brought quite an awakening. I noted several things:

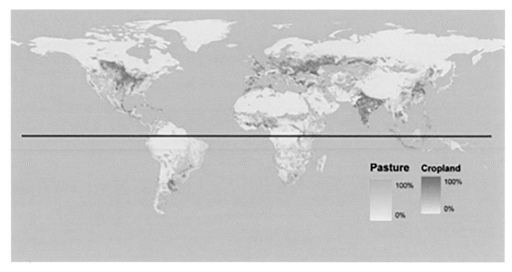

Fig. 9.5. Global map of pasture and cropland today.

1. the actual areas where cultivation is possible (cropland) are quite limited;
2. there was an origin of agriculture almost everywhere there is cultivable land (Near East, Mexico, China, Eastern USA, Subsaharan Africa) early in the Holocene. This also makes it likely that some global cause was at play;
3. agriculture quickly spread into adjacent areas with cropland (Europe, Nile Valley, southwest USA). Clear evidence that agriculture was a very successful new strategy;
4. several other areas probably witnessed their own origins, but we know far too little about them (India, southeast Asia, lowland South America); and
5. the equator runs through northern South America, Central Africa, and Insular SE Asia. Most of the land mass of the earth is in the northern hemisphere. Large parts of the northern hemisphere are too cold for agriculture, beyond the limits of cultivation.

Origins of Agriculture Conference 2009

I helped organize and attended a WennerGren Conference on the origins of agriculture that took place in Mexico in 2009 (Price and Bar-Yosef 2012). Twenty-two of us from all over the world spent a week trying to better understand and explain the origins of agriculture (Fig. 9.6). The people were passionate, the ideas powerful, the information thought provoking. Such small conferences leave an imprint and generate messages and ideas that form and transform our views of the past.

At this meeting I became aware that I was not alone in having trouble finding the earliest Neolithic. One of the most interesting phenomenon noted at the origins of agriculture was not pattern, but variation. In the few places where data on the transition were relatively abundant, there appeared to be a period of chaos, a 'zone of variability', at the origins of agriculture (Weiss *et al.* 2006). This seems to have been a time for the 'auditioning' of many possible new options in human adaptation (Smith 2012). This was the beginning of a new way of life. Visibility is limited; variability is high. It was clear that the first farmers were hard to find, hard to define, hard to identify. I realized that our problems with finding the Early Neolithic in Denmark were not unusual.

Fig. 9.6. Participants in the 2009 WennerGren Conference on the Origins of Agriculture.

Maybe the hardest thing to study is ourselves. It seems to me that the social sciences still do not have good models or theories for incorporating human behavior in explanations. All the data in the world does not necessarily make economists wealthy. That is especially cogent when we are discussing earlier humans in a data-poor discipline. It is hard for me to know what motivated my grandparents, much less people who lived thousands of years ago. Much of the behavior we witness in the past seems strange and often 'unexplainable'. Every change seems new and different and hard to explain. The social sciences and archaeology need some new ideas that better portray the human factor in past behavior.

Isotopes and teeth

For 25 years, in addition to my investigations of the prehistoric transition to farming in northern Europe, I was the director of the Laboratory for Archaeological Chemistry at the University of Wisconsin-Madison. In that capacity I have spent the last 30 years or so working on, among other things, strontium and other isotopes in human teeth as a way to study past human mobility. It still keeps me busy and off the streets in retirement.

The principle is straightforward. Tooth enamel forms during early childhood from the nutrients in our food. Certain isotopes, including those of strontium and lead, are deposited during the formation of enamel and remain there largely unchanged through life and after death. Strontium and lead isotopes vary geographically as a function of the geology we live on. If the isotopes in the tooth enamel of a burial differ from those of the local geology where an individual is buried, then that person is non-local and must have moved during his/her lifetime.

When I first started this work, I thought that early humans were largely sedentary and did not move around very much. After years of study in projects on several continents I now believe that earlier humans were very mobile – that movement was/is a normal part of the human condition.

Seasonality and sedentism

One of the things that I have come to greatly appreciate in archaeology is the importance of preservation at archaeological sites. I do admire the wonders that Paleolithic archaeologists are able to achieve in lieu of well-preserved sites and after millennia of natural processes that have altered the context and conditions under which finds, mostly of stone, are made. *but* in terms of learning more about subsistence, settlement location, settlement duration, dating, and many other things, we need good conditions of preservation. Archaeological fauna make a huge contribution to our knowledge of the past. The question of sedentism is especially important in this context.

The appearance of permanent settlement in human prehistory is one of the more important steps along the path to more complex society (e.g., Harris 1978; Plog 1990; Kelly 1992). Yet the rise of sedentary communities is often thought to be a relatively late phenomenon, appearing with the origins of agriculture, perhaps slightly earlier, perhaps slightly later, depending on the area under consideration and the individual doing the considering. Certainly, the hunter-gatherers who became farmers in Southwest Asia were sedentary before the domestication of plants and animals. But the evidence in general for more sedentary hunters and more mobile early farmers seems convincing, at least in much of Europe. It is now clear that groups of farmers moved quickly into southern Scandinavia where Late Mesolithic groups appear to have been living in sedentary situations. A similar pattern was observed along the Danube between Serbia and Romania where early farmers arrived about 8000 years ago (Fig. 9.7).

Arguments for mobile farmers/sedentary hunters have generally been ignored because of long standing biases we hold concerning hunters and farmers in archaeology and anthropology. Lee and DeVore in the anthropological classic *Man the Hunter* (1968) summarized this view by stating that hunter-gatherers 'lived in small groups and moved around a lot'.

It is time to reconsider. For example, Ruff *et al.* (2015) used measures of relative strength of the upper and lower limb bones from a large sample of Upper Paleolithic to recent European individuals to assess changes in mobility. They documented a gradual decrease in movement with the onset of the Neolithic. Such a gradual change with the introduction of agriculture suggests that sedentism was not a necessary or complete part of the Neolithic package. We need to focus on the corollary that some

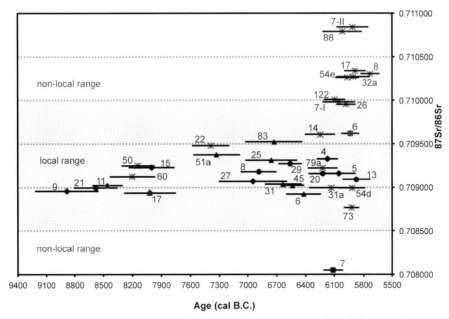

Fig. 9.7. Plot of strontium isotope ratios in human tooth enamel vs age of tooth (Borić and Price 2013).

of the last hunter-gatherers may also have been sedentary and that farmers often moved. Instead of trying to disprove mobility, perhaps we should be trying to disprove sedentary occupation. At the very least we need to remember that subsistence and settlement strategies were never unilateral in prehistory. The nature of residence is situational rather than chronological.

Ancient DNA

Ancient DNA has revolutionized our understanding of parts of the past. Early research in this field focused on modern blood groups, before turning to ancient mitochondrial DNA inherited from female ancestors. Today's aDNA research uses tooth roots or petrous bone from the skull as a source for genetic studies which can identify large parts of the whole genome. The advantage here is that many things about the individual can be identified, including genetic ancestry and kin relationships, disease history, and specific characteristics.

Such studies have had a major impact on our understanding of the relations between the last hunters and first farmers in Europe. These studies provide details as well as more general information. According to recent genomic investigations the first farmers of the southern Levant and Zagros Mountains were strongly genetically differentiated, each descended from local hunter-gatherers. The first farmers in Europe were closely related to the Near Eastern farmers from the Levant and Anatolia who spread westward.

It seems clear today that most of the early farmers in Europe had ancestors originally from the Near East where agriculture began (Haak *et al.* 2005; 2010; Bramanti *et al.* 2009; Hall *et al.* 2012; Skoglund *et al.* 2012; 2015; Hofmanová *et al.* 2016; Lazaridis *et al.* 2016; Omrak *et al.* 2016; Pereira *et al.* 2017). It also appears that almost everywhere the Neolithic went, it was carried by these groups of farmers. Only a few farmers show genetic relationships with the Mesolithic hunter-gatherers who preceded them in Europe. The *who* in the mystery of the Neolithic appears to be the expanding groups of farmers that originally came from the Near East. This is the case in Britain and Scandinavia as well as much of the rest of Europe. In northern Scandinavia, there does seem to have been an eastern group that arrived during the Mesolithic and stayed longer (Malmström *et al.* 2013; Günther *et al.* 2017).

A study by Mittnik *et al.* (2019) provides a glimpse of what is possible with aDNA. This group used a multi-dimensional approach to the burials of members of farming villages dating from the Late Neolithic to the Bronze Age, in a small valley in southern Germany. The research group combined aDNA, isotopic, and archaeological information to show long-term trends in the continuity of wealthy households in the valley, along with the influx of migrants, and the practice of patriarchy. aDNA was able to determine the kinship relations of some of the burials, archaeological information revealed the wealth buried with certain individuals, and strontium isotope analysis was used to examine the mobility of those persons. Women were much more likely to be non-local and probably followed the residence rules of a patrilocal society.

Some answers

Thirty years ago, I thought that I would never know the answers to many of the questions I had about the emergence of farming. Now I think I have a glimpse at some of the answers. It is time to turn to some of the issues that have been at the center of my research: dietary change, complexity, inequality, and the transition to agriculture. These are in fact related.

Changes in diet

Some 40 years ago Henrik Tauber, a Dane, using carbon isotopes in human bone, published a very important study (1981) that demonstrated a major shift in diet from marine to terrestrial foods at the onset of the Neolithic in Denmark (Fig. 9.8). Refinements and additions to his formulation have not changed the general picture (Fischer 2002; Schulting 2018). Similar shifts in diet have been observed in a number of places in northern and western Europe (e.g., Richards and Schulting 2003; 2015). This change in diet has been one of the major puzzles of the transition to agriculture. Why did farmers stop eating seafood and focus on a terrestrial diet? A number of

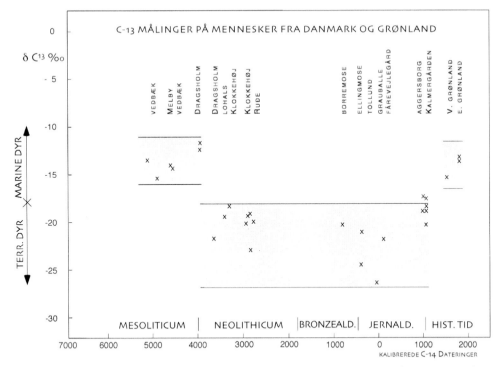

Fig. 9.8. Tauber's graph of δ¹³C vs ¹⁴C age for Mesolithic and Neolithic humans (1981, 333, fig. 2).

explanations have been forthcoming, but few have seemed to provide a viable answer as to why this shift occurred.

Finally, there is now information from molecular and isotopic archaeology that seems to provide a reasonable answer. Salque *et al.* (2013) presented evidence for cheese making in the 6th millennium BC in northern Europe, implying the importance of dairy cattle management. They reported organic residues preserved in pottery vessels that provided direct evidence for early milk use (e.g., Copley *et al.* 2005). Cramp *et al.* (2014a) pointed to evidence for dairy farming at the margins of agriculture in northern Europe and argued dairying probably accompanied an incoming, genetically distinct, population. Gron *et al.* (2015b) have argued specifically for cattle management for dairying in Scandinavia's earliest Neolithic, based on age and sex data from cattle bones. Isaksson and Hallgren (2012) reported milk residues in pottery from the Early Neolithic site of Skogsmossen in central Sweden. And finally, Cramp *et al.* (2014b) argued for the immediate replacement of fishing by dairying by the earliest farmers of the northwest Atlantic coast of Europe. It seems clear today that this diet puzzle has been solved; milk and/or milk products largely substituted for the fish and marine animals that had previously provided fat and protein.

Complexity

Some years ago I rather naively wrote about social complexity in the Mesolithic and suggested that the Danish Late Mesolithic represented an example of complex hunter-gatherers (Price 1981; 1985a). By that I meant those societies were characterized, among other things, by hierarchical organization and differential status. It seemed to me at the time that insufficient consideration had been given to the variability present among prehistoric hunter-gatherer groups and that we were missing some important aspects of human behavior and adaptation with the simplistic concept of small groups of mobile foragers. In 1980 I attended a conference in Amsterdam on *Archaeological Approaches to the Study of Complexity* that forced me to put some of my thoughts and impressions on hunter-gatherer variation on paper. That eventually led to a volume in 1985 called *Prehistoric Hunter-gatherers: The emergence of cultural complexity* that I edited with Jim Brown.

Digging in Denmark, after some years in the sparseness of the Dutch Mesolithic, led to an inflated impression of the Stone Age of southern Scandinavia. I was tremendously impressed with the Mesolithic in Denmark. There was information in features, bones, and other kinds of artifacts that could help interpret more of the essential settlement and subsistence information that interested me. In contrast to the tiny scatters of small flint artifacts in the Netherlands, there was excellent preservation of bones, many large flint artifacts, pottery, features, cultural layers, art, even wooden artifacts. This stuff looked a lot more sophisticated, structured, and complex than what I had seen in Holland. That experience lead to an article in that 1985 book entitled 'Affluent foragers in southern Scandinavia' which suggested that the archaeological evidence there pointed toward more complexity, specifically the possibility of status differentiation and hierarchical organization. However, we know almost nothing about social organization and there is *no* convincing evidence for inequality or hierarchical organization in the archaeological data from southern Scandinavia.

Vines of complexity

I also benefitted greatly from Polly Wiessner's (2002) article 'Vines of Complexity', which I regard as one of the most thought-provoking and inspirational papers in a generation. As she notes in her first sentence (2002, 233) 'The initial stages of the institutionalization of hierarchical social inequalities remain poorly understood'. Wiessner reports on the Enga of highland New Guinea, using oral histories from the last 250 to 400 years. Following the introduction of the sweet potato prior to European contact, significant changes took place among the Enga. The economy was transformed from one based on shifting taro horticulture and hunting and gathering to surplus production based on sweet potato cultivation and intensive pig husbandry (Wiessner 2002). Population grew and there were many new opportunities including the settlement of marginal areas. A sharing of power among hunters, traders, warriors, ritual experts, and managers gave way to hierarchy as a few leaders steered an economy with potential for rapid growth. Competition provided the driver for change. Hierarchy developed over a period of some five to six generations; inequality was inherited by trade managers and war leaders who had achieved control. Institutionalized inequality was a threshold in political evolution where deeply rooted traditions in small-scale societies were altered, setting the stage for more complex polities (Wiessner 2002).

Wiessner describes a situation in which authority and power emerge as hierarchical organization and status differentiation, sponsored by surplus production, developed. Wiessner provides an ethnographic model analogous to the origins of agriculture and the rise of inequality that offers much food for thought.

Conclusions

In terms of the question of complexity in the Stone Age – yes, the Mesolithic archaeology of southern Scandinavia is more complex than the inland areas of central and western Europe (cf., Spikens 2008, 9). Sites are bigger, there is a wider range of plant and animal species in the diet. Because of the unusually good conditions of preservation we are able to see a larger part of the material remains of these groups. There are many more kinds of artifacts made of more materials: stone, bone, clay, wood, fiber, and more. Nevertheless, the vagaries of preservation, coastal location, and the availability of large flint nodules likely exaggerate the differences between these regions. Bailey (2008) for example, suggests that social complexity might not characterize any part of the European Mesolithic.

My overall impression is that the Mesolithic people of southern Scandinavia had a pretty easy life with the availability of rich resources and a technology sufficient for the tasks at hand. I do wonder why interpersonal conflict was rife, at least at certain times, and why indications of traumatic or lethal injuries appear commonly in the mortuary evidence. At the same time, there does not seem to have been a need for more elaborate organizational solutions for the conduct of life. Social inequality was not an aspect of Mesolithic complexity.

In sum and in general, it is my impression that social inequality is rare among hunter-gatherers, especially in prehistory. I have argued elsewhere that status differentiation probably begins in the Neolithic (Price 1995; Price and Bar-Yosef 2010; Nielsen and Sørensen 2018; Price and Gebauer 2019). If we accept that premise, then the range of variation among hunter-gatherer societies in the past is defined not by status, but rather by other aspects of adaptation, group size, duration of residence, technology, and subsistence practices. This range is from less to more complex, using the definition of more parts and more integration. More complexity means bigger groups, longer stays, more elaborate technology, intensified subsistence, broader resource utilization, and the like. Archaeologically, complexity should be visible in larger site size, patterns of exchange, territoriality, more permanent occupation, greater productivity, storage facilities, and a number of other aspects. Social inequality is a potential, but non-essential, quality of complexity among hunter-gatherers. Again, Binford's distinction of logistic and collector hunter-gatherer adaptations is useful.

I spent a lot of time in the field in Denmark, on the lookout for complexity. There are still many mysteries, but I no longer regard the Mesolithic of southern Scandinavia as highly complex. In sum it is my impression that the hunter-gatherers of Mesolithic southern Scandinavia were more complex in terms of subsistence and settlement behaviors compared to some of their neighbors to the north and south. At the same time, social organization and economic activity do not appear to have been greatly elaborated. The technology, though diverse and incorporating a variety of different materials, is rather primary. There do not seem to have been a lot of composite or complex tools as seen in other areas (e.g., Oswalt 1979).

Inequality

A corollary to the larger issue of complexity concerns when inequality and hierarchical organization appeared in prehistory. The subject is discussed and debated. Hayden (2001) would argue that a number of groups in the European Upper Paleolithic were complex. Others suggest that such complexity is a much later phenomenon in the archaeological record. Again, it is important to remember that social inequality is only one aspect of complexity and not necessary for societies to be regarded as more complex. 'Social complexity', *sensu* Bailey (2008), is likely a relatively recent development among a few groups of hunter-gatherers. My own opinion is that social inequality in the form of wealth differences, inherited authority, and status differentiation is largely a consequence of the agricultural revolution (Price 1995; Price and Bar-Yosef 2010; Price and Gebauer 2019). I would be astounded to find evidence of hereditary social inequality in the European Mesolithic.

Current evidence suggests that the search for causality in terms of the adoption of agriculture should focus on the realm of human choice, rather than forcing models requiring changes in climate, environment, or technology. Human groups at the onset of the Neolithic participated in a larger sphere of trade and formalized the higher status of certain individuals in both life and death – through burials and other practices like the display of prestige goods. It seems most reasonable to suggest a scenario in which interaction through exchange networks among farmers, involving both ideas and materials, fostered the spread of agriculture, participation in new forms of social and economic organization, and the rise of hierarchical leadership in society (Price and Bar-Yosef 2011; Price and Gebauer 2019). The reasons that farmers succeeded in Southern Scandinavia can more likely be explained through access to new goods and ideas, rather than new ways of obtaining food.

The Neolithic is associated with the production of surpluses based on domesticated plants and animals and involvement in both local and long-distance exchange networks that intensified economic production and confirmed social differentiation. The evidence for the almost simultaneous origins of agriculture and social inequality from our perspective is very convincing. The introduction of agriculture in northern Europe was accompanied by a number of innovations and changes in economic and social organization. After a period of adaptation – a 'virtual Neolithic' – the beginnings of social inequality likely accompanied the increases in food surplus and a growing population, especially following the introduction of the ard around 3700 BC. The amount of grave goods in some non-megalithic graves and dolmens and the few select graves placed in the earthen long barrows suggest a strong and public focus on particular individuals.

Likewise, the presence of locally made weapons and jewelry in addition to long-distance imported objects displaying wealth and power indicate that certain individuals had achieved new social roles (e.g., Budd *et al.* 2020). A number of these objects, such as oversize flint axes, amber jewelry, copper, and weapons, were prestige artifacts produced not so much to perform practical tasks, but to display wealth, success, and/ or power. The presence of these prestige technologies and the costly metal objects indicates the emergence of new social roles. Interestingly, most prestige objects were deposited individually or as a component of hoards, probably in connection with public ceremonies. Only in a limited number of cases were the weapons and copper objects used as grave goods, presumably celebrating the status of certain individuals, as observed in the grave from Assing (Woll 2003).

Nevertheless, the evidence for social inequality in the Early Neolithic remains tenuous and continues to be debated. Social inequality does not often appear to have been expressed in dramatic displays of individual wealth or power. Social hierarchies may have been weakly developed in terms of individual authority. A group-oriented society is suggested by the collective enterprises such as monument building as well as the hoards and wet area sacrifices. Requirements for labor and leadership are debated with regard to the construction of large causewayed enclosures, but must have been rather small-scale for the burial monuments. Early Funnel Beaker communities seem to have balanced a weakly developed leadership with an ideology oriented towards collective social groups, managed by investing vast amounts of resources in rituals.

Ritual depositions of objects were common during the Funnel Beaker period in Southern Scandinavia. Wetland deposits of single pots are among the earliest deposits in the Neolithic. Later in the Early Neolithic, these offerings included evidence of feasting, the sacrifice of oxen, and in some cases of young people (Koch 1998, 169–71; Bennike 1999). Numerous deposits of polished flint axes, amber necklaces, and pendants

Fig. 9.9. A hoard of amber necklaces, beads, and spacers found in a TRB pot from Sortekær, Denmark (photo: Lennart Larsen, Danish National Museum).

were placed in buried hoards in wet areas (Fig. 9.9) and on dry land. A number of stray finds of weapons, such as battle axes, mace heads and flint halberds, may also have been deliberately deposited (Ebbesen 1998). The offerings, sacrifices, and deposition of highly valued objects represent the removal of an enormous wealth from circulation in society. The collective effort involved in these depositions can be seen as another aspect of the 'public works' employed as part of a corporate strategy to facilitate changes in the social organization of early farmers.

The origins of agriculture

The origins and spread of agriculture constitute one of those big, thorny questions in archaeology that have occupied many people for many decades without obvious solution. The question has been under investigation in Scandinavia for more than 150 years (Fischer 2002). This issue is multi-dimensional, involving climate, environment, people, society, plants, and animals. A huge number of important concepts are potentially involved. These include sedentism, storage, population density, population pressure, resource abundance, niche construction, processing and harvesting technologies, climate and environmental changes, ownership of produce and resource localities, potential domesticates, competition, wealth accumulation, inequality, risk reduction, nutritional requirements, choice, chance, and a receptive social/cultural context, among others.

The origins and spread of agriculture and the Neolithic way of life was a major turning point in the evolution of human society. Farming changed everything. Our ancestors had spent much of prehistory in gatherings or as hunter-gatherers. Our heritage as food collectors, consuming the wild products of the earth, extends back tens of thousands of years. Nevertheless, at the end of the Pleistocene, some human groups began to produce their own food rather than collect it, to domesticate and control wild plants and animals, achieving what is perhaps the most remarkable transition of our entire human past. The norms of hunter-gatherer equality and sharing were revised. Food sharing was transposed into competitive feasting which became a debt-creation mechanism for building alliance.

Agriculture is a way of obtaining food that involves domesticated plants and animals. But the transition to farming is much more than simple herding and cultivation. Bowles (2011) has argued that foraging was more productive than cultivating in the Early Neolithic. One of the things that I have continuously tried to emphasize is that agriculture originates in areas with rich resources, not in regions of deprivation. The origins of agriculture also entail major, long-term changes in the structure and organization of the societies that adopt this new way of life, as well as a totally new relationship with the environment. Whereas hunter-gatherers largely live off the land in an *extensive* fashion, generally exploiting a diversity of resources over a broad area, farmers *intensively* utilize a smaller portion of the landscape and create a milieu that suits their needs. With the transition to agriculture, humans began to truly alter their environment.

Explanations of the origins of agriculture have sometimes been categorized as either push or pull models. Hunter-gatherers are either pushed, forced, to become farmers or they are pulled, drawn by the benefits of a new lifestyle. Population pressure and climate models, for example, push human societies to find new ways to feed growing numbers of members. Social hypotheses usually involve pull, in which members of society are drawn into relationships of inequality in order to benefit from new arrangements that reduce risk or increase wealth.

Basically, this question of the transition to agriculture is a mystery to be solved – who, what, when, where, and why? The *why* of the Neolithic transition remains among the more intriguing questions in human prehistory. There is as yet no single accepted theory for the origins of agriculture – rather, there are a series of ideas and suggestions that do not quite resolve the question. At the same time, of course, the evidence we have is, as usual, limited and scanty.

As we learn more about this transition, it becomes clearer how complex this past was, exhibiting much more variability than we have realized or admitted. This is nowhere clearer than in the origins of agriculture in the ancient Near East. There is more archaeological information from this region about the origins of agriculture than anywhere else in the world – more sites, more excavations, more analyses, more publications, and so forth. Yet new discoveries in the past 30 years have completely altered our understanding of the transition and revealed levels of complexity in the process not even imagined three decades ago.

Three discoveries from the earliest PrePottery Neolithic in the Near East highlight this new perspective, change our understanding of this period in human prehistory, and raise enormous new questions. The finds at Gobekli Tepe in southeastern Turkey have already been discussed. The regional burial ground at Kafar HaHoresh in Israel revealed enormous new variability in the treatment of the dead and indications of emerging social inequality in the PPNB period, *c.* 8500 BC (e.g., Goring-Morris 2005). The economic intensification and competition reflected in the cemetery finds were frequent companions of the Neolithic revolution (Price and Bar-Yosef 2010). Finally, the colonization of the Mediterranean island of Cyprus by Late PPNA and PPNB people carrying domestic plants and domestic and wild animals to the island by boat is an extraordinary story (Guilaine *et al.* 2000; Peltenburg and Wasse 2004; Vigne *et al.* 2011). Agriculture and the Neolithic began expanding very early in the process. In the case of Cyprus, across long distances by sea.

The cultivation of plants and herding of animals did not originate in Europe. Early village society and domestication came to Europe from the ancient Near East. The Neolithic began in Southwest Asia and after some time moved onto the European continent, carried by expanding populations of farmers. In the period just preceding the Neolithic, there was intense utilization of plant food, probably in response to increased levels of carbon dioxide in the atmosphere that came with end of Pleistocene warming. Focus at this time was on the northern Levant (northern Syria and south-eastern Turkey) where changes appeared early and quickly. Particularly noticeable is the range of equipment created for processing plants: sickle blades and grinding stones, along with storage pits and roasting areas for preparing wild wheat. Sites were often located in areas of cultivable land, although such settlements depended on wild cereals. These same locations were occupied during the Neolithic, too, probably because of the quantity and/or quality of arable land. Hunting continued and more immature animals were killed, including gazelles and wild goats, a practice which suggests some human control of these animals.

Between 9000 and 8000 BC, changes in the size, shape, and structure of several cereals indicate that they had been domesticated. The Neolithic, defined by the appearance of domesticated plants, began at that time. Eight species of plants were domesticated during the period between 9000 and 7000 BC, including three cereals – emmer wheat, einkorn wheat, and barley – and four or five pulses – lentils, peas, bitter vetch, and chickpeas. (Pulses are the edible seeds of leguminous plants, such as peas and beans.) Flax also was domesticated during this period and probably used for both oil and fiber; linen is made from the fibers of the flax plant. In this same time period, animals were domesticated, and herding became part of human activity. Goats may have been the first domesticates, apart from dogs, soon joined by sheep, cattle, and pigs.

As the Neolithic developed in the Near East, the first towns appeared. Major changes in human diet and in the organization of society began to take place. The number and the size of prehistoric communities expanded greatly during the Early Neolithic, as populations apparently concentrated in settlements. By 7500 BC, new forms of residential architecture (rectangular houses) appeared. Pottery came into use around 7500 BC to serve as easily produced, waterproof containers for holding liquids, cooking, and storage. Shrines and ritual paraphernalia appear frequently, suggesting the formalization of religious activity. The complete Neolithic package of domesticates, village architecture, and pottery was thus in place shortly before 7000 BC, as the Neolithic began to spread north, south, east, and west.

The spread of agriculture into Europe

There are different questions involved in the research discussed in this book. The transition to agriculture in the past is really two issues, one, the cause(s) of the origins of agriculture which took place in Southwest Asia some 10,000 years ago, and two, the reasons for the spread of farming and the introduction of a Neolithic way of life in southern Scandinavia around 6000 years ago.

Part of the reason for the obscurity of this transition may be the vague or inappropriate questions of archeologists, but certainly a large part reflects the nature of the archaeological evidence itself. This does seem to be a time of chaos, of variation, of auditioning, between the last of the Mesolithic and the fully Neolithic farmers building megaliths after 3600 BC. It is also a time of changing sea levels with transgressions destroying low-lying coastal sites and perhaps removing or redepositing materials associated with the arrival of the first farmers to southern Scandinavia. The combination of erosion and a generally low level of archaeological evidence means that the Early Neolithic is very hard to find and define in some places.

The question of course is how to understand this chaos, this absence of evidence, how to make sense of what is happening at the transition. Explanations of the origins of agriculture (and many other phenomenon) often consider a number of different variables. It is essential to segregate such variables among conditions, causes, and consequences. Conditions for agricultural society would include sufficient population, sedentism, adequate growing conditions, the presence of domesticates and certain knowledge. Consequences of agricultural transitions seem to be population growth, population aggregation, increased trade and craft production, organized religion, and innovation.

Research has focused on settlements and burials, artifacts, and domesticates. Perhaps the answer lies more in a shift in focus from things to behavior, toward social and group activities, and toward the consequences of the new arrangements. A more intensive consideration of the Neolithic following the time of chaos may be informative with regard to the changes that were instituted. Moreover, the introduction of agriculture takes place repeatedly in Europe (and elsewhere) and the fundamentals of the transformation must be quite similar. A change from community to household levels of economic organization, for example, may have accompanied the transition to agriculture, including a shift from communal sharing to familial or individual accumulation. Economic activities such as the production of polished flint axes or battle axes may have become more specialized. Clearly these consequences of the agricultural transition reflect the changes that took place through the black box of the transition itself.

One can think about the arrival of farming in Europe in terms of millennia, 1000 year blocks of time. Plants and animals were domesticated in Southwest Asia after 12,000 years ago, beginning in the 10th millennium BC. The Neolithic village complex of square houses, pottery, and agriculture moved to Europe by the end of the 7th millennium BC. This spread took place both by land, across the Bosporus from Turkey to the Balkan Peninsula, and by sea from Cyprus and Anatolia, through the Aegean, to the Greek mainland.

The 5th millennium witnessed a move out of the Balkans in southeastern Europe along two routes. One along the north coast of the Mediterranean, probably by boat with intermittent stops that left behind villages of farmers and pastoralists. A second movement went inland, crossing Central Europe almost to the shores of the Atlantic. The Mediterranean group is usually described from its pottery as the Cardial Culture; the inland group has an eponymous pottery as well, the Linearbandkeramik (LBK). The final stage of the spread of agriculture, expansion into the British Isles and Northern Europe to the limits of cultivation, took place during the 4th millennium. These movements from Asia to Europe, from southeast Europe to Central Europe and the

Mediterranean, and to the northern limits of agriculture took place quickly as leaps or rushes, preceded by a period of stasis (Rowley-Conwy 2011).

One of the more pronounced trends in the European Neolithic was regionalization, the development of distinctly local traditions. Initial farming cultures expanded over broad regions. Settlements were generally located in open and unprotected spaces, and pottery styles were similar across very large areas. Very quickly, however, population growth and the development of permanent field systems resulted in competition and conflict between groups. By 3000 BC, the continent was occupied by distinctive, well-entrenched farming populations making stone tools and pottery, cultivating, trading, and fighting.

In southeastern Europe developments were dramatic in the Early Neolithic period, and often witnessed the rise of towns. This was a time of cultural fluorescence among a series of cultures in Serbia, Romania, Bulgaria, the Ukraine, and eastern Hungary. There developments were new and remarkable – population numbers increased, large villages and towns appeared as tells and megasites, technological innovations – including the first copper production – flourished, long distance trade expanded, and social inequality was pronounced.

Later Neolithic settlements across Europe were often located in defensible positions and heavily fortified. Pottery traditions became more limited in their distribution. At the same time, trade and exchange expanded in scope. A variety of materials and finished goods were moved long distances across Europe. Obtaining raw materials, manufacturing trade items, and transporting finished goods became an important part of Neolithic economic systems. Flint, for example, was mined in Denmark, Sweden, Holland, Belgium, England, and elsewhere and polished into fine axes for trade.

Once upon a time, when I was in Graduate School in the late 1960s and early 1970s, there was an accepted picture of how farming came to the European continent. The general model involved the expansion of farming groups from the ancient Near East, where farming was invented, across the continent along two major paths, one following the north coast of the Mediterranean and the other moving through Central Europe perhaps following the Danube and other major rivers as expansion reached toward the Atlantic coast of Europe, as previously described. A publication in 1984 seemed to provide confirmation for the existing model of how farming spread by examining the distribution of modern blood groups in light of the few hundred radiocarbon dates that were available for the Early Neolithic at that time. Ammerman and Cavalli-Sforza compiled their theory in *The Neolithic Transition and the Genetics of Populations in Europe*, arguing that the spread of farming increased local population densities, causing the spread of farming by demic expansion into new territory and diffusive gene flow between the Neolithic farmers and Mesolithic hunter-gatherers. Their argument pointed to a regular and systematic trend in the radiocarbon dates that were available at that time for the first farmers in different parts of Europe. The spread of farming into the continent was thought to be almost continuous between approximately 8000 and 5000 years ago.

Over the last 25 years or so, this story has changed a great deal, in part due to new discoveries, more radiocarbon dates, and especially because of ancient DNA studies, the latter of which tell us that the replacement of local hunter-gatherers by incoming Neolithic farmers appears to be the common answer to the *who* question. Migration replaces adoption as the primary response to the *how* question regarding the transition to agriculture. There are now thousands of radiocarbon dates from numerous settlements of early farmers across Europe. The spread of farming across Europe is no longer regarded as constant and continuous but appears more as a series of stands and starts that gradually filled the continent within the limits of cultivation.

The investigation of aDNA using new methods that provide insight into past human genomes offers a radically different set of evidence and perspective on the relationships among the folks involved in the spread of farming and major changes in the prehistory of Europe. It is clear that the spread of the Neolithic was carried out by incoming farming peoples, moving from the ancient Near East initially into the Aegean region and from there throughout southeast Europe, by 6000 BC. Two paths took farmers to the west. One lead along the northern shore of the Mediterranean while the other went through central Europe. These regions were settled by dispersed farming communities, by 5500 BC. There was a long period of stasis, however, before farming spread into northwestern Europe, specifically Scandinavia and the British Isles. It was not until *c.* 4000 BC that domesticates and characteristic Neolithic artifacts began to appear in these areas.

The introduction of agriculture to Scandinavia was remarkably rapid when it finally took place. Within a few hundred years, farming practices had spread from northern Germany to the limits of cultivation in Middle Sweden and to the Oslo Fjord area in Norway. The evidence from aDNA indicates that incoming farmers brought the Neolithic to southern Scandinavia. The Early Neolithic Michelsberg Culture is the best candidate (Müller 2011b; Sørensen 2014; Mischka *et al.* 2015) at present for the source of these migrant farmers (Fig. 1.5). Domesticated plants and especially animals defined these early agricultural groups, along with distinctive Funnel Beaker pottery and the new polished stone axes. These groups began to build monuments in the form of earthen long barrows and eventually the large stone tombs known as megaliths. The first elaborate tombs were for individuals, suggesting status differentiation; later graves were communal and collective. Enclosures and palisades were other distinctive constructions from this period. Conflict in the first half of the Neolithic appears to have been rather rare. A number of individual houses or farmsteads are known from the Early Neolithic, but villages were not a feature of this period. More long-distance exchange is evidenced, particularly in axes, but in other objects as well. The first metal –copper – begins to appear during the Early Neolithic, if not before, probably coming from the Alps or southeastern Europe (Gebauer *et al.* 2020).

A major question concerns the role of indigenous Mesolithic people in the spread of agriculture and whether they were involved in local adoption of agricultural practices or simply pushed aside as farmers moved onto the land. Certainly, local hunter-gatherers in some areas must have participated in this transition, but it does appear that the Neolithic way of life was largely introduced by the arrival of farmers.

The end

Most folks do not realize that archaeology moves at a snail's pace, that knowledge about the past is usually acquired in tiny chunks, that time and money are grossly limited, and research is done in one's spare time. The total annual budget for the US National Science Foundation which provides the major share of funding for the worldwide activities of US archaeologists is *c.* $7.5 million, a tiny fraction of the money spent by many other countries and far below the amount needed to do even basic research.

The truth is that we know very little about the past. In some ways it is amazing that we have learned anything at all. We are trying to reconstruct human behavior and history from a few poorly preserved objects that people lost or discarded. Trash from the past. Fieldwork is one of the joys, but also one of the banes of archaeological investigations. Excavations are hard work and take a long time. They are expensive and the outcome is uncertain. Money and time are hard to come by.

Archaeology can tell us many things if we will support such research, be patient, and listen. Humans have always had to deal with climate change and disease, war and catastrophe; lessons for today are there in the past. Although inequality and hierarchical organization are recent phenomena in human history, archaeology has been dealing with these forms of society for decades and can provide insight into what works and what does not.

The study of variation and increasing complexity is at the heart of archaeological research. The transition to the Neolithic was an extraordinary change in human life. The hunter-gatherers of the European Mesolithic offer a fascinating body of information with which to pursue these questions. Agriculture and social inequality provided the surplus and mechanisms that have resulted in our modern world.

Near the end now, looking back, it was the journey that was important, not the destination. When I was ten years old, I was lucky enough to visit the remains of a massive Roman tomb along a roadside in northern Spain. Standing there, I was completely in awe of the crumbling stone walls of that ancient mausoleum; I wondered who made it, why it was built, how old it was. My parents told me about the Romans and how archaeologists studied such ruins. I decided then and there that I wanted to be an archaeologist. I have been able to fulfil that dream; I still love what I do. Archaeology is a passion and my affair has lasted many years. It is a wonderful career, filled with travel, fieldwork, discovery, ideas, and intellectual challenges, interesting friends and quirky colleagues, demanding and delightful students, and endless ways to learn more about the past. To be able to follow my dream and enjoy what I do is a gift for which I am forever grateful to a large number of family, friends, colleagues, and institutions. I have tried to convey some my experiences and decisions on the way. There is no path, everyone must make their own, of course; this has been mine. It has been a grand journey.

I keep wondering, what's next? Perhaps the final lesson of archaeology is a lingering hope about the future. My strongest sense from what I have learned as an archaeologist remains a basic optimism for our species. In every way, we are artifacts, manufactured over a very long period of time, created by the actions and experiences of our ancestors. We have been on the planet for several million years. In that time, we have evolved from a chimpanzee-like ape to the man on the moon. We have expanded geographically and survived under a wide range of difficult conditions. There is an unusual quality about the human species – the enormous potential in the human intellect, with its remarkable inventiveness for coping with change. A large brain and creativity managed to get us through the very long and arduous periods of the past. For that very reason, the future should be just as exciting.

Bibliography

Allentoft, M., Sikora, M., Sjögren, K. *et al.* 2015. Population genomics of Bronze Age Eurasia. *Nature* 522: 167–172.

Andersen, N. H. 1990. Sarup. Two Neolithic enclosures in south-west Funen. *Journal of Danish Archaeology* 7: 93–114.

Andersen, N. H. 1993. Causewayed camps of the Funnel Beaker Culture. In Hvass and Storgaard (eds) 1993, 100–103.

Andersen, N. H. and Madsen, T. 1978. Skåle og bægre med storvinkelbånd fra Yngre Stenalder. Overgangen mellemtidlig- ogf mellemneolitikum. *Kuml* 1977, 31–160.

Andersen, S. H. 1985. Tybrind Vig. A preliminary report on a submerged Ertebølle settlement on the west coast of Fyn. *Journal of Danish Archaeology* 4, 52–69.

Andersen, S. H. 1991. Norsminde. A 'køkkenmødding' with late Mesolithic and early Neolithic occupation. *Journal of Danish Archaeology* 8, 13–40.

Andersen, S. H. 1993a. Mesolithic coastal settlement. In Hvass and Storgaard (eds) 1993, 65–69.

Andersen, S. H. 1993b. Bjørnsholm. A stratified *køkkenmødding* on the Central Limjfjord, North Jutland. *Journal of Danish Archaeology* 10, 59–96.

Andersen, S. H. 1995. Coastal adaption and marine exploitation in Late Mesolithic Denmark – with special emphasis on the Limfjord region. In A. Fischer (ed.), *Man and Sea in the Mesolithic*, 41–66. Oxford: Oxbow Books.

Andersen, S. H. 1996. Ertebøllebåde fra Lystrup. *Kuml* 1993–1994, 7–38.

Andersen, S. H. 1998. Ringkloster. Ertebølle trappers and wild boar hunters in eastern Jutland. a survey. *Journal of Danish Archaeology* 12: 13–59.

Andersen, S. H. 2004. Danish shell middens reviewed. In A. Saville (ed.), *Mesolithic Scotland and its Neighbours*, 393–422. Edinburgh: Society of Antiquaries of Scotland

Andersen, S. H. 2008. The Mesolithic–Neolithic transition in Western Denmark seen from a kitchen midden perspective: a survey. In H. Fokkens, B. J. Coles, A. L. van Gijn, J. P. Kleijne, H.H. Ponjee, and C. G. Slappendel (eds), *Between Foraging and Farming*, 67–74. *Analecta Praehistorica Leidensia* 40.

Andersen, S. H. 2009. *Ronæs Skov: Marinarkæologiske undersøgelser af en kystboplads fra Ertebølletid*. Højbjerg: Jysk Arkæologisk Selskab.

Andersen, S. H. and Johansen, E. 1992. An Early Neolithic grave at Bjørnsholm, North Jutland. *Journal of Danish Archaeology* 9, 38–59.

Andersen, S. H. and Johansen, E. 1997. Køkkenmøding-projektet – et nyt fredningstiltag. *AUD - Arkæologiske udgravninger i Danmark* 1996, 7–18.

Astrup, P. M. 2019. *Sea-level Changes in Mesolithic Southern Scandinavia: long- and short-term effects on society and the environment*. Aarhus: Aarhus University Press.

Bailey, G. 2008. Mesolithic Europe: overview and new problems. In G. Bailey and P. Spikins (eds), *Mesolithic Europe*, 357–372. Cambridge: Cambridge University Press.

Banning, E. B. 2011. So fair a house: Göbekli Tepe and the identification of temples in the Pre-Pottery Neolithic of the Near East. *Current Anthropology* 52, 619–660.

Becker, C. J. 1939. En stenalderboplads pa Ordrup Nas i Nordvestsjalland. *Aarbøger* 1939, 199-280.

Becker, C. J. 1947. Mosefundne Lerkar fra Yngre stenalder. Studier over Tragt-bægerkulturen i Danmark. *Aarbøger for Nordisk Oldkyndighed og Historie* 1947, 1–318.

Becker, C. J. 1951. Maglemosekultur paa Bornholm. *Aarbøger for Nordisk Oldkyndighed og Historie* 1951, 26–177.

Becker, C. J. 1952. *Nørre Sandegård: arkæologiske undersøgelser på Bornholm 1948-1952*. Copenhagen: Kongelige Danske videnskabernes selskab.

Bennike, P. 1999. The early Neolithic Danish bog finds: a strange group of people! In B. Coles, M. S. Jørgensen and J. Coles (eds), *Bog Bodies, Sacred Sites and Wetland Archaeology*, 27–32. Silkeborg: Wetland Archaeology Research Project.

Berggren, Å., Högberg, A., Olausson, D. and Rudebeck, E. 2016. Early Neolithic flint mining at Södra Sallerup, Scania, Sweden. *Archaeologia Polona* 54, 167–180.

Berglund, B. 1971. Littorina transgressions in Blekinge, South Sweden. A preliminary survey. *Föreningens i Stockholm Förhandlinger* 93, 625–652.

Berglund, B. E. (ed.) 1991. *The Cultural Landscape during 6000 years in Southern Sweden - the Ystad Project*. Oxford: Ecological Bulletin 41.

Bintliff, J. L., Kuna, M, and Venclová, N. (eds) 2000. *The Future of Surface Artefact Survey in Europe*. Sheffield: Sheffield Academic Press.

Bishop, R. L. and Blackman, M. J. 2002. Instrumental neutron activation analysis of archaeological ceramics: scale and interpretation. *Accounts of Chemical Research* 35, 603–610.

Blank, M., Sjögren, K.-G. and Storå, J. 2020. Old bones or early graves? Megalithic burial sequences in southern Sweden based on ^{14}C datings. *Archaeological and Anthropological Sciences* 12 (89) [doi.org/10.1007/s12520-020-01039-9].

Boethius, A. 2018. The use of aquatic resources by Early Mesolithic foragers in Southern Scandinavia. In P. Persson, F. Riede, B. Skar, H. Mjelva Breivik and L. Jonsson (eds), *The Early Settlement of Northern Europe*, 311–334. Sheffield: Equinox Publishing.

Boismier, W. A. 1997. *Modelling the Effects of Tillage Processes on Artefact Distributions in the Ploughzone*. Oxford: British Archaeological Report 259.

Bokelmann, K. 2012. Spade paddling on a Mesolithic lake - remarks on Preboreal and Boreal sites from Duvensee (Northern Germany). In M. J. L. T. Niekus, M. Street and T. Terberger (eds), *A Mind Set on Flint: studies in honour of Dick Stapert*, 369–380. Groningen: Groningen University Library.

Bonsall, C., Macklin, M. G., Anderson, D. E. and Payton, R. W. 2002. Climate change and the adoption of agriculture in north-west Europe. *European Journal of Archaeology* 5, 9–23.

Borić, D. and Price, T. D. 2013. Strontium isotopes document greater human mobility at the start of the Balkan Neolithic. *Proceedings of the National Academy of Science* 110, 3298–3303.

Böse, M., Lüthgens, C., Lee, J. R. and Rose, J. 2012. Quaternary glaciations of northern Europe. *Quaternary Science Reviews* 44: 1–25.

Bowles, S. 2011. Cultivation of cereals by the first farmers was not more productive than foraging. *Proceedings of the National Academy of Science* 108, 4760–4765.

Bradley, R. and Edmonds, M. 2005. *Interpreting the Axe Trade: production and exchange in Neolithic Britain*. Cambridge: Cambridge University Press

Brace, S., Diekmann, Y., Booth, T. J., van Dorp, L., Faltyskova, Z., Rohland, N., Mallick, S., Olalde, I., Ferry, M., Michel, M., Oppenheimer, J. *et al.* 2019. Ancient genomes indicate population replacement in Early Neolithic Britain. *Nature Ecology & Evolution* 3, 765–771 [doi. org/10.1038/s41559-019-0871-9].

Bramanti, B., Thomas, M. G., Haak, W. *et al.* 2009. Genetic discontinuity between local hunter-gatherers and central Europe's first farmers. *Science* 326: 137–140 [doi:10.1126/ science.1176869].

Bratlund, B. 1993. The bone remains of mammals and birds from the Bjørnsholm shellmound. *Journal of Danish Archaeology* 10, 97–104.

Brinch Petersen, E. 1970. Ølby Lyng: En østsjællandsk kystboplads med Ertebøllekultur. *Aarbøger for nordisk Oldkyndighed og Historie* 1970, 5–42.

Brinch Petersen, E. 1973. Dobbeltgraven fra Dragsholm. *Nationalmuseets Arbejdsmark* 1973, 187–188.

Brinch Petersen, E. 1974. Gravene ved Dragsholm. Fra jægere til bønder for 6000 år siden. *Nationalmuseets Arbejdsmark* 1974, 112–120.

Brinch Petersen, E. 1993. The Late Paleolithic and the Mesolithic. In Hvass and Storgaard (eds), *1993*, 46–49.

Budd, C., Bogucki, P., Lillie, M., Grygiel, R., Lorkiewicz, W. and Schulting, R. 2020. All things bright: copper grave goods and diet at the Neolithic site of Osłonki, Poland. *Antiquity* 94, 932–947 [https://doi.org/10.15184/aqy.2020.102].

Budja, M. 2007. The 8200 cal bp 'climate event' and the process of neolithisation in south-eastern Europe. In M. Budja (ed.), *14th Neolithic Studies. Documenta Praehistorica* 34, 191–201.

Christensen, C. 1982. Havniveauændringer 5500–2500 f. Kr. i Vedbækområdet, Nordøstsjælland. *Dansk Geologisk Forening Årskrift for 1981*, 91–107.

Christensen, C. 1993. Land og hav. In Hvass and Storgaard (eds) 1993, 20–23.

Christensen, C. 1994. Lammefjorden, Undersøgelser på 4 lokaliteter i fjorden giver informationer om havniveauændringer og afkræfter formodet forekomst af tektoniske bevægelser af landjorden i atlantisk tid. *Nationalmuseets naturvidenskabelige Undersøgelser* 16, 1–31.

Christensen, C. 1995. The littorina transgressions in Denmark. In A. Fischer (ed.), *Man and Sea in the Mesolithic*, 15–21. Oxford: Oxbow Books.

Christensen, K. 1997. Træ fra fiskegærder – skovbrug i stenalderen. In Pedersen *et al.* (eds) 1997, 147–156.

Clark, G. 1948. The development of fishing in prehistoric Europe. *Antiquaries Journal* 28, 45–85.

Clutton-Brock, J. and Noe-Nygaard, N. 1990. New osteological and C-isotope evidence on Mesolithic dogs: comparisons to hunters and fishers at Star Carr, Seamer Carr and Kongemose. *Journal of Archaeological Science* 17, 643–653.

Copley, M. S., Berstan, R., Mukherjee, A. J., Dudd, S. N., Straker, V., Payne, S. and Evershed, R. P. 2005. Dairying in antiquity III: evidence from absorbed lipid residues dating to the British Neolithic. *Journal of Archaeological Science* 32, 523–546.

Cramp, L. J. E. Evershed, R. P., Lavento, M., Halinen, P., Mannermaa, K., Oinonen, M, Kettunen, J., Perola, M., Onkamo, P and Heyd, V. 2014a. Neolithic dairy farming at the extreme of agriculture in northern Europe. Proceedings of the Royal Society B 281, 20140819 [https://doi.org/10.1098/rspb.2014.0819].

Cramp, L. J. E., Jones, J., Sheridan, A., Smyth, J., Whelton, H., Mulville, J., Sharples, N. and Evershed, R. P. 2014b. Immediate replacement of fishing with dairying by the earliest farmers of the northeast Atlantic archipelagos. *Proceedings of the Royal Society B* 281, 20132372. [http://dx.doi.org/10.1098/rspb.2013.2372]

Dalsgaard, K. 1985. Matrikelkort fra 1844 anvendt til rekonstruktion af det udrænede landskab. *Aarbøger for Nordisk Oldkyndighed og Historie* 1984, 282–302.

Dencker, J. 1997. Stenalderbopladser midt i naturens spisekammer. In Pedersen *et al.* (eds) 1997, 87–92.

Diinhoff, S. 1998. Two hundred years of archaeological survey. *Archaeologica Baltica* 3, 67–86.

Drechsel, C. F. and Petersen, C. G. J. 1988. *Oversigt over vore saltvandsfiskerier i Nordsøen og farvandene indenfor Skagen* 4. Esbjerg: Dansk Fiskerimuseum.

Driesch, A. von den 1976. *A Guide to the Measurement of Animal Bones from Archaeological Sites*. Cambridge MA: Peabody Museum Bulletin 1.

Dunnell, R.C. and Simek, J. F. 1995. Artifact size and plowzone process. *Journal of Field Archaeology* 22, 305–320.

Ebbesen, K. 1975. *Die jüngere Trichterbecherkultur auf den dänischen Inseln*. Copenhagen: Forhistorisk-arkæologisk Institut, Københavns Universite.

Ebbesen, K. 1998. Frühneolitische Streitäxte. *Acta Archaeologica* 69, 77–112.

Ebbesen, K. 2011. *Danmarks Megalitgrave* 1(1). Copenhagen: Attika.

Ebbesen, K. and Mahler, D. 1980. Virum. Et tidligneolitisk bopladsfund. *Aarbøger for Nordisk Oldkyndighed og Historie* 1979, 11–61.

Egfjord, A., Margaryan, A., Fischer, A., Sjögren, K-G., Price, T. D., Johannsen, N. N., Willerslev, E., Iversen, R., Sikora, M., Kristiansen, K., and Allentoft, M. E. 2021. Genomic steppe ancestry in skeletons from the Late Neolithic Single Grave Culture in Denmark. PLoS ONE, January 2021. [https://doi.org/10.1371/journal.pone.0244872]

Enghoff, I. B. 1986. Freshwater fishing from sea-coast settlement – The Ertebølle locus classicus revisited. *Journal of Danish Archaeology* 5, 62–76.

Enghoff, I. B. 1991. Fishing from the Stone Age settlement of Norsminde. *Journal of Danish Archaeology* 8, 41–50.

Enghoff, I. B. 1994. Fishing in Denmark during the Ertebølle periods. *International Journal of Osteoarchaeology* 4(2), 65–96.

Enghoff, I. B. 2011. *Regionality and Biotope Exploitation in Danish Ertebølle and Adjoining Periods*. Copenhagen: Scientia Danica, Series B, Biologica 1.

Eriksson, G. and Zagorska, I. 2003. Do dogs eat like humans? Marine isotope signals in dog teeth from inland Zvejnieki. In L. Larsson, H. Kindgren, H. Knutsson, D. Loeffler and A. Åkerlund (eds), *Mesolithic on the Move*, 160–168. Oxford: Oxbow Books.

Fischer, A. 1982. Trade in Danubian shaft-hole axes and the introduction of Neolithic economy in Denmark. *Journal of Danish Archaeology* 1, 7–12.

Fischer, A. 1989. Hunting with flint-tipped arrows: results and experiences from practical experiments. In C. Bonsall (ed.), *The Mesolithic in Europe*, 29–39. Edinburgh: Edinburgh University Press.

Fischer, A. 1993. Mesolithic inland settlement. In Hvass and Storgaard (eds) 1993, 58–63.

Fischer, A. 1997. Mennesket og havet – bosættelse og fiskeri ved jægerstenalderens kyste. In Pedersen *et al.* (eds) 1997, 63–77.

Fischer, A. 2002. Food for feasting? an evaluation of explanations of the Neolithisation of Denmark and southern Sweden. In Fischer and Kristiansen (eds) 2002, 343–393.

Fischer, A, Rasmussen, P. and Hansen, P. V. 1984. Macro and micro wear traces on lithic projectile points. *Jouirnal of Danish Archaeology* 3, 19–46.

Fischer, A., Olsen, J., Richards, M., Heinemeier, J., Sveinbjörnsdóttir, Á. and Benike, P. 2007. Coast-inland mobility and diet in the Danish Mesolithic and Neolithic: evidence from stable isotope values of humans and dogs. *Journal of Archaeological Science* 34, 2125–2150.

Fruziński, B., Baksalary, J. and Kaluzinski, J. 1982. Weight and body measurements of forest and field roe deer. *Acta theriologica* 27, 479–488.

Furholt, M. 2011. Entstehung der frühen Einzelgräber – Was geshah vor 4800 ahrev im Norden? *Archäologie in Deutschland* 2, 28–29.

Gaffney, V., Fitch, S. and Smith, D. 2009. *Europe's Lost World: the rediscovery of Doggerland*. Birmingham: University of Birmingham Press.

Gaffney, V., Thomson, K. and Finch, S. (eds) 2007. *Mapping Doggerland. The Mesolithic Landscapes of the Southern North Sea*. Oxford: Archaeopress.

Galatius, A. and Kinze, C. C. 2003. Ankylosis patterns in the postcranial skeleton and hyoid bones of the harbor porpoise (*Phocoena phocoena*) in the Baltic and North Sea. *Canadian Journal of Zoology* 81, 1851–1861.

Gebauer, A. B. 1995. Pottery production and the introduction of agriculture in southern Scandinavia. In W. K. Barnett and J. W. Hoopes (eds), *The Emergence of Pottery*, 99–112. Washington DC: Smithsonian Institution Press.

Gebauer, A. B. 1988. The long dolmen at Asnæs Forskov, West Zealand. *Journal of Danish Archaeology* 7, 40–52.

Gebauer, A. B. and Price, T. D. 1990. The end of the Mesolithic in eastern Denmark: a preliminary report on the Saltbæk Vig project. In P. M. Vermeersch and P. van Peer (eds), *Contributions to the Mesolithic in Europe*, 259–280. Leuven: Leuven University Press.

Gebauer, A. B., Sørensen, L. V., Taube, M. and Wielandt, D. K. P. 2020. First metallurgy in Northern Europe: an Early Neolithic crucible and a possible tuyère from Lønt, Denmark. *European Journal of Archaeology* 24(1): 27–47. [doi:10.1017/eaa.2019.73\]

Gehlen, B. and Schön, W. 2005. Klima und Kulturwandel: Mögliche folgen des '6200–Events' in Europa. In D. Gronenborn (ed.), *Klimaveränderung und Kulturwandel in neolithischen Gesellschaft*, 53–74. Mainz: Verlag des Römisch-Germanischen Zentralmuseums.

Geist, V. 1998. *Deer of the world: their evolution, behavior, and ecology.* Mechanicsburg PA: Stackpole Books.

Génsbøl, B. 2006. *Nordens Fugle*. Copenhagen: Gyldendal.

Gill, R. M. A., Johnson, A. L., Francis, A., Kiscocks, K. and Peace, A. J. 1996. Changes in roe deer (*Capreolus capreolus L.*) population density in response to forest habitat succession. *Forest Ecology and Management* 88, 31–41.

Goring-Morris, A. N. 2005. Life, death and the emergence of differential status in the Near Eastern Neolithic: evidence from Kfar HaHoresh, Lower Galilee, Israel. In J. Clarke (ed.), *Archaeological Perspectives on the Transmission and Transformation of Culture in the Eastern Mediterranean*, 89–105. Oxford: Council for British Research in the Levant and Oxbow Books.

Gotfredsen, A. B. 1998. En Rekonstruktion af Palæomiljøet omkring Tre Senmesolitiske Bopladser i Store Åmose, Vestsjælland-Baseret på Pattedyr-og Fugleknogler. *Geologisk Tidsskrift* 2, 92–104.

Gron, K. J. 2013. The Ertebølle Faunal Economy and the Transition to Agriculture in Southern Scandinavia. Unpublished PhD Dissertation, University of Wisconsin-Madison.

Gron, K. J. 2015. Body-part representation, fragmentation, and patterns of Ertebølle deer exploitation in northwest Zealand, Denmark. *International Journal of Osteoarchaeology* 25, 722–732.

Gron, K. J. and Rowley-Conwy, P. 2017. Herbivore diets and the anthropogenic environment of early farming in southern Scandinavia. *The Holocene* 27, 98–109.

Gron K. J., Montgomery, J. and Rowley-Conwy, P. 2015. Cattle Management for dairying in Scandinavia's earliest Neolithic. *PLoS ONE* 10(7): e0131267. [doi:10.1371/journal.pone.0131267]

Gron, K. J., Sørensen, L. and Rowley-Conwy, P. (eds) 2020. *Farmers at the Frontier. A Pan-European Perspective on Neolithisation.* Oxford: Oxbow Books.

Gronenborn, D. 2010. Climate, crises and the »neolithisation« of Central Europe between IRD-events 6 and 4 2010. In D. Gronenborn and J Petrasch (eds), *The Spread of the Neolithic to Central Europe*, 61–80. Mainz: RGZM.

Guilaine J., Briois, F., Vigne, J.-D. and Carrère, I. 2000. Découverte d'un Néolithique Précéramique Ancient Chypriote (fin 9°, début 8° millénaires cal. BC), apparenté au PPNB ancien/moyen du Levant nord. nord. *Comptes rendus de 'Académie des sciences, series 2: Sciences de la terre et des planètes* 300, 75-82.

Günther, T., Malmström, H., Svensson, E. M., Omrak, A., Sánchez-Quinto, F., Kılınç, G. M. *et al.* 2018. Population genomics of Mesolithic Scandinavia: investigating early postglacial migration routes and high-latitude adaptation. *PLoS Biol* 16(1): e2003703 [doi.org/10.1371/journal.pbio.2003703].

Haak, W., Forster, P., Bramanti, B., Matsumura, S., Brandt, G., Tanzer, M., Villems, R., Renfrew, C., Gronenborn, D., Alt, K.W., *et al.* 2005. Ancient DNA from the first European farmers in 7500–year-old Neolithic sites. *Science* 310(5750), 1016-8. [doi: 10.1126/science.1118725. PMID: 16284177].

Haak, W., Balanovsky, O., Sanchez, J. J., Koshel, S., Zaporozhchenko, V., Adler, C. J., Der Sarkissian, C. S. I., Brandt, G., Schwarz, C., Nicklisch, N. *et al.* 2010. Ancient DNA from European Early Neolithic farmers reveals their Near Eastern affinities. *PLoS Biol* 8 [doi:10.1371/ journal. pbio.1000536]

Hall, P., Willerslev, E., Gilbert, M. T., Gotherström, A. and Jakobsson, M. 2012. Origins and genetic legacy of Neolithic farmers and hunter-gatherers in Europe. *Science* 336. 466–469.

Hallgren, F. 2004. The introduction of ceramic technology around the Baltic Sea in the 6th millennium. In H. Knutsson (ed.), *Coast to Coast - Arrival. Results and Reflections. Proceedings of the final coast to coast conference 1-5 October 2002 in Falköbing, Sweden*, 123–142. Uppsala: Wikströms.

Härkönen, T. 1986. *Guide to the Otoliths of the Bony Fishes of the Northeast Atlantic*. Hellerup: Danbiu Aps.

Harris, D. R. 1978. Settling down: an evolutionary model for the transformation of mobile bands into sedentary communities. In *The Evolution of Social Systems*, J. Friedman and M.J. Rowlands (eds): 401–417. London: Duckworth.

Hartz, S. and Lübke, H. 2006. New evidence for a chronostratigraphic division of the Ertebølle Culture and the earliest Funnel Beaker culture on the southern Mecklenburg Bay. In C. J. Kind (ed.), *After the Ice Age: settlements, subsistence and social development in the Mesolithic of Central Europe*, 61–77. Baden-Württemberg Materialhefte zur Archäologie in Baden-Württemberg 78.

Hartz, S., Heinrich, D. an:d Lübke, H. 2002. Coastal farmers – the Neolithisation of northernmost Germany. In Fischer and Kristiansen (eds) 2002, 319–340.

Hartz, S., Lüth, F. and Terberger, T. (eds). 2011. *Early Pottery in the Baltic - Dating, Origin and Social Context*, 465–484. Frankfurt: Bericht der Römish-Germanishen Kommission Band 89.

Hartz, S., Kostyleva, E., Piezonka, H., Terberger, T., Tsydenova, N. and Zhilin, M. 2012. Hunter-Gatherer pottery and charred residue dating: new results on the spreading of first ceramics in the north Eurasian forest zone. In *Proceedings of the 6th International Symposium 'Radiocarbon & Archaeology', Pafos, Cyprus, April 10-15, 2011. Radiocarbon* 54, 1017–1031.

Havstein, J. A. 2012. Skiveøksene fra Ormen Lange Nyhamna. In Morfologi, framstilling og funksjon. Unpublished Masters thesis, University of Trondheim.

Hayden, B. 2001. Richman, poorman, beggarman, chief: the dynamics of social inequality. In G. Feinman, and T. D. Price (eds), *Archaeology at the Millenium: a sourcebook*, 231–272. New York: Kluwer Academic/Plenum Publishers.

Hede, S. U. 1999. En palæoøkologisk rekonstruktion af en sen atlantisk kystboplads: Smakkerup Huse ved Saltbæk Vig, NV-Sjælland baseret på osteologisk materiale. Unpublished candidate scientist thesis. University of Copenhagen.

Hede, S. U. 2003. Prehistoric settlements and Holocene relative sea-level changes in northwest Sjælland, Denmark. *Bulletin of the Geological Society of Denmark* 50, 141–149.

Heiri, O., Tinner, W. and Lotter, A. F. 2004. Evidence for cooler European summers during periods of changing meltwater flux to the North Atlantic. *Proceedings of the National Academy of Sciences* 101: 15285–15288.

Hennig, C., Meila, M., Murtagh, F. and Rocci, R. 2016. *Handbook of Cluster Analysis*. London: Taylor & Francis.

Hertz, J. and Rigsantikvarens Arkæologiske Sekretaria. (eds) 1987. *Danmarks længste udgravning*. Copenhagen: Poul Kristensens.

High, K., Milner, N., Panter, I., Demarchi, B. and Penkman, K. E. H. 2016. Lessons from Star Carr on the vulnerability of organic archaeological remains to environmental change. *Proceedings of the National Academy of Science* 113, 12957–12962.

Hodell, D. A., Venz, K. A., Charles, C. D. and Ninnemann, U. S. 2003. Pleistocene vertical carbon isotope and carbonate gradients in the South Atlantic sector of the Southern Ocean. *Geochemistry, Geophysics, Geosystems* 4(1), 1004 [doi:10.1029/2002GC000367]

Hofmanová, Z., Kreutzer, S., Hellenthal, G., Sell, C., Diekmann, Y., Díez-del-Molino, D., van Dorp, L., López, S., Kousathanas, A., Link, V. *et al.* 2016. Early farmers from across Europe directly descended from Neolithic Aegeans. *Proceedings of the National Academy of Science* 113, 6886–6891

Hogg, A. McC. 2008. Glacial cycles and carbon dioxide: A conceptual mode. *Geophysical Research Letters* 35, L01701 [doi:10.1029/2007GL032071].

Holst, D. 2010. Hazelnut economy of early Holocene hunter-gatherers: a case study from Mesolithic Duvensee, northern Germany. *Journal of Archaeological Science* 37, 2871–2880.

Houmark-Nielsen, M. and Kjær, K. H. 2003. Southwest Scandinavia 40–15 ka BP: palaeogeography and environmental change. *Journal of Quaternary Science* 18, 769–786.

Hufthammer, A. K., Høie, H., Folkvord, A., Geffen, A., Andersson, C. and Ninnemann, U. S. 2010. Seasonality of human site occupation based on stable oxygen isotope ratios of cod otoliths. *Journal of Archaeological Science* 37, 78–83.

Huntley, B., Baillie, M., Grove, J.M., Hammer, C.U., Harrison, S., St Jacomet, P., Jansen, E., Karlén, W., Koç, N., Luterbacher, J., Negendank, R., and Schibler, J. 2002. Holocene palaeoenvironmental changes in North-West Europe: climatic implications and the human dimension. In G. Wefer, W. H. Berger, K.-E. Behre and E. Jansen (eds), *Climate Development and History of the North Atlantic realm*, 259–298. Berlin: Springer

Hvass, S. and Storgaard, B. (eds) 1993. *Da klinger i muld... 25 års arkæologi i Danmark.* Aarhus: Aarhus University Press.

Isaksson, S. and Hallgren, F. 2012. Lipid residue analyses of Early Neolithic funnel-beaker pottery from Skogsmossen, eastern Central Sweden, and the earliest evidence of dairying in Sweden. *Journal of Archaeological Science* 39, 3600–3609.

Iversen, J. 1937. Undersøgelser over Littorinatransgressioner i Danmark. *Meddelelser fra Dansk Geologiske Forening* 9, 223–236.

Iversen, J. 1973. The development of Denmark's nature since the last glacial. *Danmarks Geologiske Undersøgelse V. række*, 7C, 1–126.

Iversen, R. 2013 Beyond the Neolithic transition – the 'de-neolithisation' of south Scandinavia. In M. Larsson and J. Debert (eds), *North-West Europe in Transition. The Early Neolithic in Britain and South Sweden*, 21–29. Oxford: British Archaeological Report S2475.

Jacobsen, J. 1984. A contribution to the evaluation of archaeological field-surveying. *Journal of Danish Archaeology* 3, 187–198.

Jessen, K. 1937. Den geologisk-botaniske Undersøgelse af Hjortespring Mose. In G. Rosenberg (ed.), *Hjortespringfundet*, 27. Copenhagen: Nordisk Fortidsminder 3 (1).

Johansson, A. D. 1995. The Ertebølle Culture in South Zealand, Denmark. In A. Fischer (ed.), *Man and Sea in the Mesolithic*, 87–94. Oxford: Oxbow Books.

Johansson, A. D. 1999. Ertebøllekulturen i Sydsjælland. *Aarbøger for Nordisk Oldkyndighed og Historie* 1997, 7–88.

Jonsson, L. 1988. The vertebrate faunal remains from the late Atlantic settlement Skateholm in Scania, south Sweden. In L. Larsson (ed.), *The Skateholm Project 1*, 56–88. Stockholm: Almqvist & Wiksell International.

Jordan P. and Zvelebil, M. 2009. Ex Oriente Lux: the prehistory of hunter-gatherer ceramic dispersals. In P. Jordan and M. Zvelebil (eds), *Ceramics Before Farming: the dispersal of pottery among prehistoric Eurasian hunter-gatherers*, 33–89. Walnut Creek CA: Left Coast Press

Jordan, Peter, et al. 2016. Modelling the diffusion of pottery technologies across Afro-Eurasia: emerging insights and future research. *Antiquity* 90(351), 590–603. [doi:10.15184/aqy.2016.68]

Juel, C. and Kjær, A. 2015. The earliest Neolithic at Vedbæk Fjord, Denmark. An overlooked horizon. *Acta Archaeologica* 86, 217–225.

Juel Jensen, H. 1988. Functional analysis of prehistoric flint tools by high-power microscopy: a review of west European research. *Journal of World Prehistory* 2, 53–88.

Juel Jensen, H. 1994. *Flint Tools and Plant Working.* Aarhus: Aarhus University Press

Juel Jensen, H. 1996. TRB sickles and early Danish agriculture: a view from the microscope. *Poročilo o raziskovanju paleolitika, neolitika in eneolitika v Sloveniji* 23, 129–153.

Kamler, J. F., Jedrzejewski, W. and Jedrzejewska, B. 2008. Home ranges of red deer in a European old-growth forest. *American Midland Naturalist* 159(1), 75–82.

Karsten, P. and Knarrström,B. (eds) 2001a. *Tågerup Specialstudier.* Lund: Riksantikvarieämbetet.

Karsten, P. and Knarrström, B. 2001b. Tågerup – fifteen hundred years of Mesolithic occupation in western Scania: a preliminary view. *European Journal of Archaeology* 4, 16–174.

Kelly, R. L. 1992. Mobility/sedentism: concepts, archaeological measures, and effects. *Annual Review of Anthropology* 21, 43–66.

Klassen, L. 2002. The Ertebølle Culture and Neolithic continental Europe: traces of contact and interaction. In Fischer and Kristiansen (eds) 2002, 305–317.

Klassen, L. 2004. *Jade und Kupfer.* Moesgård: Jutland Archaeologocal Society.

Klassen, L. 2014. *Along the Road. Aspects of Causewayed Enclosures in South Scandinavia and Beyond.* Aarhus: Aarhus University Press.

Knutsson, H. 1982. Skivyxor. Experimentell analys av en redskapstyp från den den senatlantiska boplatsen vid Soldattorpet. *C-uppsats.* Uppsala: Department of Archaeology, University of Uppsala.

Koch, E. 1998. *Neolithic Bog Pots from Zealand, Møn, Lolland and Falster.* Copenhagen: Nordiske Fortidsminder.

Kristiansen, K. and Larsson, T. 2006. *The Rise of Bronze Age Society: travels, transmissions and transformations.* Cambridge: Cambridge University Press.

Krossa, V. R., Moros, M., Leduc, G., Hinz, M., Blanz, T. and Schneider, R. 2017. Regional climate change and the onset of farming in northern Germany and southern Scandinavia. *The Holocene* 27, 1589–1599. [doi:10.1177/0959683617702223]

Larsson, L. 1984. Skateholmsprojektet. På spåren efter gravsedsförändringar, ceremoniplatser och tama rävar. *Limhamniana* 1984, 49–84.

Larsson, L. 1985. Karlsfalt: A settlement from the early and late Funnel Beaker culture in southern Scania, Sweden. *Acta Archaeologica* 54, 3–71.

Larsson, L. 1987. Some aspects of cultural relationship and ecological conditions during the Late Mesolithic and Early Neolithic. In A. C. Goran Burenhult, A. Hyenstrand and T. Sjovold (eds), *Theoretical Approaches to Artefacts, Settlement and Society. Studies in Honour of Mats P. Malmer,* 165–176. Oxford: British Archaeological Report S366.

Larsson, L. 1988. The use of the landscape during the Mesolithic and Neolithic in southern Sweden. In H. T. Waterbolk (ed.), *Archeology en Landschap. Bijdragen aan het gelijknamige symposium gehouden op 19 en 20 oktober 1987:* 31–48. Groningen: University of Groningen.

Larsson, L. 1990. The Mesolithic of southern Scandinavia. *Journal of World Prehistory* 4, 257–309.

Larsson, L. 1991. Coastal adaptation in the Early and Middle Holocene of southern Scandinavia. *Journal of Korean Ancient History* 8, 93–118.

Larsson, L. 1997. Coastal settlement during the Mesolithic and Neolithic periods in the southernmost part of Sweden. In D. Krol (ed.), *The Built Environment of the Coast Areas During the Stone Age,* 12–22. Gdansk: Gdansk University Press.

Larsson, L. 2000. Expressions of art in the Mesolithic society of Scandinavia. *Acta Academia Artium Vilnensis* 20, 31–61.

Larsson, L., Callmer, J. and Stjernquist, B. (eds) 1992. *The Archaeology of the Cultural Landscape.* Stockholm: Acta Archaeologica Lundensia 19.

Larsson, M., and Olausson, D. 1992. Archaeological field survey – methods and problems. In Larsson *et al.* (eds) 1992, 473–480.

Lazaridis, I. 2018. The evolutionary history of human populations in Europe. *Current Opinions in Genetic Development* 53, 21–27 [doi: 10.1016/j.gde.2018.06.007].

Lazaridis, I., Nadel, D., Rollefson, G., Merrett, D. C., Rohland, N., Mallick, S., Fernandes, D., Novak, M., Gamarra, B., Sirak, K. *et al.* 2016. Genomic insights into the origin of farming in the ancient Near East. *Nature* 536: 419–424. [doi.org/10.1038/nature19310]

Lee, R. B. and DeVore, I. (eds) 1968. *Man the Hunter*. Chicago: Aldine.

Lewis, J. P., Ryves, D. B., Rasmussen, P., Olsen, J., Knudsen, K.-L., Andersen, S.H., Weckström, K., Clarke, A. L., Andrén, E. and Juggins, S. 2016. The shellfish enigma across the Mesolithic–Neolithic transition in southern Scandinavia. *Quaternary Science Reviews* 151, 315–320.

Lewis, J. P., Ryves, D. B., Rasmussen, P., Olsen, J., van der Sluis, L. G., Reimer, P. J., Knudsen, K.-L., McGowan, S., Anderson, N. J. and Juggins, S. 2020. Marine resource abundance drove pre-agricultural population increase in Stone Age Scandinavia. *Nature Communications* 11. [doi.org/10.1038/s41467–020–15621–1]

Liversage, D. 1981. Neolithic Monuments at Lindebjerg, North-West Zealand. *Acta Archaeologica* 51, 85–152.

Lomborg, E. 1975. The flint daggers of denmark. Studies in chronology and cultural relations of the south Scandinavian Late Neolithic. *Nordic Archaeological Review* 8(2), 98–101.

Løppenthin, B. 1967. *Danske ynglefugle i fortid og nutid*. Odense: Odense University Press.

Maagaard Jacobsen, J. E. 1982. Littorinatransgressioner i Trundholm mose, NV-Sjælland, en foreløbig undersøgelse. *Dansk Geologisk Forening Årsskrift* 1981, 109–117.

Maagaard Jacobsen, J. E. 1983. Littorinatransgressioner i Trundholm mose, NV-Sjælland, supplerende undersøgelse. *Dansk Geologisk Forening Årsskrift* 1982, 59–65.

Madsen, A. P., Müller, S., Neergaard, C., Petersen, C. G. J., Rostrup, E., Steenstrup, K. J. V. and Winge, H. 1900. *Affaldsdynger fra Stenalderen i Danmark. Undersøgte for Nationalmuseet*. Kjøbenhavn: National Museum.

Madsen, B. 1984. Flint axe manufacture in the Neolithic: experiments with grinding and polishing of thin-butted flint axes. *Journal of Danish Archaeology* 3, 47–62.

Madsen, T. 1978. Perioder og periode overgange i neolithikum. *Hikuin* 4, 51–60.

Madsen, T. 1991. The social structure of Early Neolithic society in South Scandinavia. In J. Lichardus (ed.), *Die Kupferzeit als historische Epoche* 55, 489–496. Bonn: Saarbrücker Beiträge zur Altertumskunde.

Madsen, T. 1993. Barrows with timber-build structures. In Hvass and Storgaard (eds) 1993, 96–99.

Madsen, T. 2019. *Continuity and Change. The Development of Neolithic Societies in Central East Jutland, Denmark. Vol. I – Catalogue of Finds* [available at https://www. archaeoinfo.dk/].

Madsen, T. and Juel Jensen, H. 1982. Settlement and land use in Early Neolithic Denmark. *Analecta Praehistorica Leidensia* 15, 63–86.

Madsen, T. and Petersen, J. E. 1984. En tidig-neolitisk anlæg ved Mosegården. Regionale og kronologiske forskelle i tidligneolitikum. *Kuml* 1982–83, 61–120.

Magnell, O. 2006. *Tracking wild boar and hunters: osteology of wild boar in Mesolithic south Scandinavia*. Lund: *Acta Archaeologica Lundensia* Series in 8° 51.

Makarona, C., Nys, K. and Claeys, P. 2014. Sr isotope analysis for the provenance study of ancient ceramics: An integrated approach. In R. B. Scott, D. Brækmans, M. Carremans and P. Degryse (eds), *Proceedings of the 39th International Symposium for Archaeometry, Leuven 2012*, 149–156. Louvain: Centre for Archaeological Sciences.

Mallouf, R. J. 1981. *A Case Study of Plow Damage to Chert Artifacts*. Austin TX: Texas Historical Commission, Office of the State Archaeologist Report 33.

Malmström, H., Linderholm, A., Skoglund, P., Stora, J., Sjödin, P., Thomas, M., Gilbert, P., Holmlund, G., Willerslev, E., Jakobsson, M., Lidén, K. and Götherström, A. 2013. Ancient mitochondrial DNA from the northern fringe of the Neolithic farming expansion in Europe sheds light on the dispersion process. *Philosophical Transactions of the Royal Society B* 370: 20130373. [doi.org/10.1098/rstb.2013.0373]

Mathiassen, T. 1948. *Studier over Vestjyllands Oldtidsbebyggelse*. Copenhagen: Gyldendalske Boghandel.

Mathiassen, T. 1959. *Nordvæstsjællands Oldtidsbebyggelse*. Copenhagen: Nationalmuseet

Mathiassen, T., Degerbøl, M. and Troels-Smith, A. 1942. *Dyrholmen. En Stenalderboplads paa Djursland*. Copenhagen: Munksgaard.

Matschke, G. H, 1967. Aging European wild hogs by dentition. *Journal of Wildlife Management* 31(1), 109–113.

Mertz, E. L. 1924. *Oversigt over de sen- og postglaciale Niveauforandringer i Danmark.* Copenhagen: Danmarks Geologiske Undersøgelse 41.

Milner, N. 2002. *Incremental growth of the European Oyster* Ostrea edulis. *Seasonality Information from Danish Kitchenmiddens.* Oxford: British Archaeological Report S1057.

Mischka, D., Roth, G. and Struckmeyer, K. 2015. Michelsberg and Oxie in contact next to the Baltic Sea. In J. Kabaciński, S. Hartz, D. C. M. Raemaekers and T. Terberger (eds), *The Dąbki Site in Pomerania and the Neolithisation of the North European Lowlands (c. 5000-3000 cal BC)*, 465–478. Rahden/Westfahlen: Leidorf.

Mittnik, A., Massy, K., Knipper, C., Wittenborn, F., Friedrich, R., Pfrengle, S., Burri, M., Carlichi-Witjes, N., Deeg, H., [...] and Krause, J. 2019. Kinship-based social inequality in Bronze Age Europe. *Science* 366, 731-734 DOI: 10.1126/science.aax6219.

Møhl, U. 1971. Oversigt over Dyreknoglerne fra Ølby Lyng. En østsjællandsk kystboplads med Ertebøllekultur. *Aarbøger for nordisk Oldkyndighet og Historie* 1970, 43–77.

Mook, W. G. 1986. Business meeting recommendations/resolutions adopted by the twelfth International radiocarbon conference. *Radiocarbon* 28, 799

Mortensen, M. F., Henriksen, P. S. and Bennike, O. 2014. Living on the good soil: relationships between soils, vegetation and human settlement during the late Allerød period in Denmark. *Vegetation History and Archaeobotany* 23, 195–205 [doi:10.1007/s00334-014-0433-7].

Moustgaard, P. H. 1987. *At vove for at vinde: Dansk fiskeri skildret af A.J. Smidth 1859-63.* Grenaa: Dansk Fiskerimuseum.

Müller, J. 2011a. Early pottery in the North – a southern perspective. In Hartz et al.(eds) 2011, 241–276.

Müller, J. 2011b. *Megaliths and Funnel Beakers. Societies in Change 4100-2700 BC. A Published Lecture.* Amsterdam: Stichting Nederlands Museum voor Anthropologie.

Müller, J. and Petersen, R. 2014. Ceramics and society in Northern Europe. In C. Fowler, J. Harding and D. Hofmann (eds), *The Oxford Handbook of Neolithic Europe Online*, 1–22. Oxford: Oxford University Press. [doi: 10.1093/oxfordhb/9780199545841.013.061]

Müller, J., Hinz, M. and Wunderlich, M. (eds) 2019. *Megaliths, Societies, Landscapes. Early Monumentality and Social Differentiation in Neolithic Europe.* Bonn: Habelt.

Müller, J., J Brozio, J.-P., Demnick, D., Dibbern, H., Fritsch, B., Furholt, M., Hage, F., Hinz, M., Lorenz, L., Mischka, D. and Rinne, C. 2010. Periodisierung der Trichterbecher-Gesellschaften. Ein Arbeitsentwurf. *Journal of Neolithic Archaeology* 2010, 1–6.

Müller, S. 1918. Ordning af Danmarks Oldsager, Stenalderen. *Stenalderens Kunst i Danmark* 1918, 54–76.

Muus, B., Jørgen Nielsen, Preben Dahlstrøm, and Bent Nyström. 2006. *Havfisk og fiskeri.* Copenhagen: Gyldendal.

Nielsen, A. B., Heyman, E. and Richnau, G. 2012. Liked, disliked and unseen forest attributes: relation to modes of viewing and cognitive constructs. *Journal of Environmental Management* 113, 456–466 [http://dx.doi.org/10.1016/j.jenvman.2012.10.014].

Nielsen, J. 2013. *Strejtog gennem Stenalderen i Raklev Sogn.* Raklev: Lokalarkiv.

Nielsen, P.-O. 1977. Die Flintbeile der Frühen Trichterbecherkultur in Dänemark. *Acta Archaeologica* 48, 61–138.

Nielsen, P.-O. 1979. De tyknakkede flintøksers kronologi. *Aarbøger* 1977, 5–69.

Nielsen, P.-O. 1985. De første bønder. Nye fund fra den tidligste tragtbægerkultur ved Sigersted. *Aarbøger for Nordisk Oldkyndighed og Historie* 1984, 96–126.

Nielsen, P.-O. 1998. De ældste langhuse. Fra toskibede til treskibede huse i Norden. *Bebyggelseshistorisk tidskrift* 33, 9–30.

Nielsen, P.-O., and Nielsen, F. O. S. 2020. *First Farmers on the Island of Bornholm.* Odense: Syddansk Universitetsforlag

Nielsen, P.-O. and Sørensen, L. 2018. The formation of social rank in the early Neolithic of Northern Europe. *Acta Archaeologica* 89, 15–29. [doi: 10.1111/j.1600–0390.2018.12190.x]

Noble, G., Lamont, P. and Masson-Maclean, E. 2019. Assessing the ploughzone: the impact of cultivation on artefact survival and the cost/benefits of topsoil stripping prior to excavation. *Journal of Archaeological Science Reports* 23, 549–558.

Noe-Nygaard, N. 1971. Spur dog spines from prehistoric and early historic Denmark. *Bulletin of the Geological Society of Denmark* 21(2), 18–33.

Noe-Nygaard, N. 1988. δ^{13}C-Values of dog bones reveal the nature of changes in man's food resources at the Mesolithic–Neolithic transition, Denmark. *Chemical Geology (Isotope Geoscience Section)* 73, 87–96.

Noe-Nygaard, N. 1995. *Ecological, Sedimentary, and Geochemical Evolution of the Late-glacial to Postglacial Åmose Lacustrine Basin, Denmark.* Oslo: Scandinavian University Press.

Noe-Nygaard, N. and Hede, U. M. 2004. Tissø, Lille Åmose og Store Åmoses Dræningssystemer gennem 18.000 år. I Tissø og Åmoserne-kulturhistorie og natur, *Årbog for kulturhistorien i Holbæk Amt. – Historisk samfund for Holbæk Amt/ De kulturhistoriske Museer i Holbæk Amt* 2004, 127–152.

Noe-Nygaard, N., Price, T. D., and Hede. S. U. 2005. Diet of aurochs and early cattle in southern Scandinavia: evidence from ^{15}N and ^{13}C stable isotopes. *Journal of Archaeological Science* 32, 855–871.

Nørrevang, A. and Lundø, J. 1979. *Danmarks Natur. Landskabernes opståen.* Copenhagen: Politikens Forlag.

Odgaard, B. V. and Nielsen, A. B. 2009. Udvikling i arealdækning i Danmark i perioden 0–1850: pollen og landskabshistorie. In B. Odgaard and J. Rydén Rømer (eds), *Danske landbrugslandskaber gennem 2000 år: Fra digevoldninger til støtteordninger*, 41–58. Aarhus: Aarhus University Press.

Olalde, I., Schroeder, H., Sandoval-Velasco, M., Vinner, L., Lobón, I. *et al.* 2015. A common genetic origin for early farmers from Mediterranean Cardial and Central European LBK Cultures. *Molecular Biology and Evolution* 32, 3132–3142. [doi.org/10.1093/molbev/msv181]

Omrak, A., Günther, T., Valdiosera, C., Svensson, E. M., Malmstrom, H., Kiesewetter, H., Aylward, W., Stora, J., Jakobsson, M. and Gotherstrom A. 2016. Genomic evidence establishes Anatolia as the source of the European Neolithic gene pool. *Current Biology* 26: 270–275.

Out, W. A., Baittinger, C., Čufar, K., López-Bultó, O., Hänninen, K. and Vermeeren, C. 2020. Identification of woodland management by analysis of roundwood age and diameter: Neolithic case studies. *Forest Ecology and Management* 467, 118136. [doi.org/10.1016/j.foreco.2020.118136]

Paludan-Muller, C. 1978. High Atlantic food gathering in northwestern Zealand, ecological conditions and spatial representation. In K. Kristiansen and C. Paludan-Muller (eds), *New Directions in Scandinavian Archaeology*, 120–157. Copenhagen: National Museum.

Payne, S. 1975. Partial recovery and sample bias. In A. T. Clason (ed.), *Archaeozoological Studies*, 7–17. Amsterdam: North Holland.

Pedersen, L. 1997. They put fences in the sea. In Pedersen *et al.* (eds)1997, 124–143.

Pedersen, L., Fischer, A. and Aaby, B. (eds) 1997. *Storebælt i 10.000 år.* Storebælt Publikationerne. Copenhagen: Storebælt Fixed Link.

Peltenburg, E. and Wasse, A. (eds) 2004. *Neolithic Revolution - New Perspectives onSsouthwest Asia in the Light of Recent Discoveries on Cyprus.* Oxford: Oxbow Books.

Pereira, J.B., Coata, M. D., Vieira, D., Pala, M., Bamford, L., Harich, N., Cherni, L., Alshamali, F., Rychkov, S., Stefanescu, G. *et al.* 2017. Reconciling evidence from ancient and contemporary genomes: a major source for the European Neolithic within Mediterranean Europe. *Proceedings of the Royal Society B* 284: 20161976. [doi.org/10.1098/rspb.2016.1976]

Persson, P. 1999. *Neolitikums början. Undersökningar kring jordbrukets introduktion i Nordeuropa.* Gothenburg: Institute of Archaeology, University of Gothenburg.

Persson, P. and Sjögren, K.-G. 1996. Radiocarbon and the chronology of Scandinavian megalithic tombs. *Journal of European Archaeology* 3, 59–88.

Peters, J. and Schmidt, K. 2004. Animals in the symbolic world of Prepottery Neolithic Göbekli Tepe, southeastern Turkey: a preliminary assessment. *Anthropozoologica* 39, 179–218.

Plog, S. 1990. Agriculture, sedentism, and environment in the evolution of political systems. In S. Upham (ed.), *The Evolution of Political Systems*, 177–199. Cambridge: Cambridge University Press.

Price, T. D. 1981. Complexity in 'non-complex' societies. In S. van der Leeuw (ed.), *Archaeological Approaches to the Study of Complexity*, 54–97. Amsterdam: Instituut voor Prae- en Protohistorie.

Price, T. D. 1991. The Mesolithic of northern Europe. *Annual Review of Anthropology* 20, 211–233.

Price, T. D. 1995. Agricultural origins and social inequality. In T. D. Price and G. M. Feinman (eds), *Foundations of Social Inequality*, 129–151. New York: Plenum Press.

Price, T. D. and Bar-Yosef, O. 2010. Traces of inequality at the origins of agriculture in the Ancient Near East. In T. D. Price and G. M. Feinman (eds), *Pathways to Power. New Perspectives on the Origins of Social Inequality*, 147–168. New York: Springer.

Price, T. D. and Bar-Yosef, O. 2012. The origins of agriculture: new data, new Ideas. *Current Anthropology* 52(S4), S163–S174. [https://www.journals.uchicago.edu/doi/10.1086/659964]

Price, T. D. and Brinch Petersen, E. 1987. Prehistoric coastal settlement in Mesolithic Denmark. *Scientific American,* March, 112–121.

Price, T. D. and Brown, J. A. (eds) 1985a. *Prehistoric Hunter-Gatherers? The Emergence of Cultural Complexity.* Orlando FL: Academic.

Price, T. D. and Brown, J. A. 1985b. Aspects of hunter-gatherer complexity. In Price and Brown (eds) 1985a, 3–20.

Price, T. D. and Gebauer, A. B. 2005. *Smakkerup Huse, A Late Mesolithic Coastal Site in Northwest Zealand, Denmark.* Aarhus: Aarhus University Press.

Price, T. D. and Gebauer, A. B. 2019. The emergence of social inequality in the context of the Early Neolithic of Northern Europe. In S. Hansen and J. Müller (eds), *Rebellion and Inequality In Archaeology*, 135–153. Bonn: Habelt

Price, T. D. and Noe-Nygaard, N. 2009. Early Domestic cattle in southern Scandinavia. In N. Finlay, S. McCartan, N. Milner and C. Wickham-Jones (eds) *From Bann Flakes to Bushmills*, 198–210. Oxford: Prehistoric Society Research Papers 1, 211–219.

Price, T. D., Gebauer, A. B., Hede, S. U., Larsen, C. S., Mason, S., Nielsen, J., Noe-Nygaard, N. and Perry, D. 2001. Excavations at Smakkerup Huse: Mesolithic settlement in Northwest Zealand, Denmark. *Journal of Field Archaeology* 28, 45–67.

Price, T. D., Gebauer, A. B., Hede, S. U., Larsen, C. S., Mason, S., Nielsen, J., Noe-Nygaard, N. and Perry, D. 2003. Excavations at Smakkerup Huse: Mesolithic settlement in Northwest Zealand, Denmark. *Journal of Field Archaeology* 28, 45–67.

Price, T. D., Bennike, P., Noe-Nygaard, N., Ambrose, S., Richards, M. P., Brinch Petersen, E., Vang Petersen, P. and Heinemeier, J. 2007. The Stone Age graves at Dragsholm: New dates and other data. *Acta Archaeologica* 78, 193–219.

Price, T. D., Ritchie, K., Gron, K., Gebauer, A. B. and Nielsen, N. 2018. Asnæs Havnemark: Late Mesolithic on the coast of western Zealand, DK. *Danish Journal of Archaeology* 7, 255–276.

Rascovan, N., Sjögren, K.-G., Kristiansen, K., Nielsen, R., Willerslev, E., Desnues, C. and Rasmussen, S. 2018. Emergence and Spread of Basal Lineages of Yersinia pestis during the Neolithic Decline. *Cell* 176 (1–2), 295–307. [doi.org/10.1016/j.cell.2018.11.005]

Rasmussen, L. W. 1984. Kainsbakke A47. A settlement structure from Pitted Ware Culture. *Journal of Danish Archaeology* 3, 83–98.

Rasmussen, L. W. 1993. Pitted Ware settlements. In Hvass and Storgaard (eds) 1993, 114–115.

Rasmussen, P. 2005. Mid-to late-Holocene land-use change and lake development at Dallund S0, Denmark: vegetation and land-use history inferred from pollen data. *The Holocene* 15, 1116–1129.

Richards, M. P. and Schulting, R. J. 2003. Sharp shift in diet at onset of Neolithic. *Nature 425*, 366.

Richards, M. P. and Schulting, R. J. 2015. Touch not the fish: the Mesolithic–Neolithic change of diet and its significance. *Antiquity 80*, 444–456

Richerson, P. J., Boyd, R. and Bettinger, R. L. 2001. Was agriculture impossible during the Pleistocene but mandatory during the Holocene? A climate change hypothesis. *American Antiquity* 66, 387–411.

Richter, J. and Noe-Nygaard, N. 2003. A late Mesolithic hunting station at Agernæs, Fyn, Denmark: differentiation and specialization in the late Ertebølle-culture, heralding the introduction of agriculture? *Acta Archaeologica* 74, 1–64.

Riedman, M. 1990. *The Pinnipeds: seals, sea lions, and walruses.* Berkeley CA: University of California Press.

Ritchie, K. 2010. The Ertebølle Fisheries of Denmark, 5400– 4000 BC. Unpublished PhD thesis, University of Wisconsin, Madison.

Ritchie, K., Folkvord, A. and Hufthammer, A. K. 2013a. Oxygen isotope ratios in cod otoliths used to reveal seasonality of fishing at Late Mesolithic sites in Denmark. *Archaeofauna* 22, 95–104.

Ritchie, K. C., Gron, K. J. and Price, T. D. 2013b. Flexibility and diversity in subsistence during the late Mesolithic: faunal evidence from Asnæs Havnemark. *Danish Journal of Archaeology* 2, 1–20. [doi. org/10.1080/21662282.2013.821792]

Rivollat, M., Jeong, C., Schiffels, S. *et al.* 2020. Ancient genome-wide DNA from France highlights the complexity of interactions between Mesolithic hunter-gatherers and Neolithic farmers. *Science* 6(22). [doi: 10.1126/sciadv.aaz5344]

Rosenberg, A. 2006. *Ullerødbyen.* NoMus 3.

Rowley-Conwy, P. A. 1980. Continuity and change in the Prehistoric economies of Denmark – 3700 b.c. to 2300 b.c. Unpublished Ph.D. dissertation, Magdalene College, University of Cambridge.

Rowley-Conwy, P. A. 1995. Meat, furs and skins: mesolithic animal bones from Ringkloster, a seasonal hunting camp in Jutland. *Journal of Danish Archaeology* 12, 87–98.

Rudebeck, E. 1987. Flint mining in Sweden during the Neolithic period: new evidence from the Kvarnby – S. Sallerup Area. In G. de G. Sieveking and M. Newcomer (eds), *The Human Uses of Flint and Chert,* 151–158. Cambridge: Cambridge University Press.

Ruff, C. B., Holt, B., Niskanen, M., Sladek, V., Berner, M., Garofalo, E., Garvin, H. M., Hora, M., Junno, J.-A., Schuplerova, E., Vilkam, R. and Whittey, E. 2015. Gradual decline in mobility with the adoption of food production in Europe. *Proceedings of the National Academy of Science* 112, 7147–52.

Sage, R. F. 1995. Was low atmospheric CO_2 during the Pleistocene a limiting factor for the origin of agriculture? *Global Change Biology* 1, 93–106.

Salque, M., Bogucki, P.I., Pyzel, J., Sobkowiak-Tabaka, I., Grygiel, R., Szmyt, M. and Evershed, R. P. 2013. Earliest evidence for cheese making in the sixth millennium BC in northern Europe. *Nature* 493, 522–525. [doi: 10.1038/nature11698]

Sarauw, G. F. L., Jessen, K. and Winge, H. 1903. *En Stenalders Boplads i Maglemose ved Mullerup Sammenholdt med Beslægtede Fund.* Copenhaven: H.H Thieles Bogtrykkeri.

Schimmelmann, H. C. 1935. Vore Hjortearter. In M. Degerbøl, L. Bahr, B. Benzon, F. W. Bræstrup, M. Christiansen, J. Holten, A. L. V. Manniche and H. C. Schimmelmann (eds), *Danmarks Pattedyr*, 395–417. Copenhagen: Gyldendal.

Schmid, E. 1972. *Atlas of Prehistoric Animal Bones.* Amsterdam: Elsevier.

Schmidt, K. 2006. *Sie bauten die ersten Tempel. Das rätselhafte Heiligtum der Steinzeitjäger. Die archäologische Entdeckung am Göbekli Tepe.* Munich: Beck.

Schmidt, K. 2011. Göbekli Tepe: a Neolithic site in Southwestern Anatolia. In S. R. Steadman and G. McMaho (eds), *The Oxford Handbook of Ancient Anatolia*, 917. Oxford: Oxford University Press.

Schmidt, K. 2012. *Góbekli Tepe. A Stone Age sanctuary in south-eastern Anatolia.* Berlin: exOriente.

Schou, A. 1949. Danish coastal cliffs in glacial deposits. *Geografiska Annaler* 31, 357–364. [doi:10.2307/520378]

Schülke, A. 2008. Der soziale Raum zur Zeit der Trichterbecherkultur Aspekte der Landschaftsraumnutzung am Beispiel der Verbreitung von Siedlungen und Megalithanlagen in Nordwestseeland, Dänemark. *Journal of Neolithic Archaeology* 8, 1–23.

Schülke, A. 2009a. The social use of space during the Early Neolithic in Northwest Zealand. In H. Glørstad and C. Prescott (eds), *Neolithisation As If History Mattered*, 217–255. Lindome: Bricoleur Press.

Schülke, A. 2009b. Tragtbægerkulturens landskabsrum: udtryk og ramme for social kommunikation. Et studie over Nordvestsjælland, In A. Schülke (ed.), *Plads og rum i tragtbægerkulturen. Bidrag fra Arbejdsmødet på Nationalmuseet, 22 September 2005*, 67–87. Copenhagen: Det kongelige Nordiske Oldskriftselskab, Nationalmuseet.

Schülke, A. 2013. Three concepts of burying the dead – different types of megalithic monuments and their ritual and social significance. In M. Furholt, M. Hinz, D. Mischka, G. Noble and D. Olausson (eds), *Landscapes, Histories and Societies in the Northern European Neolithic*, 113–124. Bonn: Habelt.

Schülke, A. 2015. The diversity of settings. Ritual and social aspects of tradition and innovation in megalithic landscapes. In K. Brink, S. Hydén, K. Jennbert, L. Larsson and D. Olausson (eds), *Neolithic Diversities. Perspectives from a Conference in Lund, Sweden*, 465–485. Lund: Acta Archaeologica Lundensia Series in 8° 65.

Schulz Paulsson, B. 2010. Scandinavian models: radiocarbon dates and the origin and spreading of passage graves in Sweden and Denmark. *Radiocarbon* 52, 1002–1017

Sempéré, A.J., Mauget, R. and Bubenik, G. A. 1992. Influence of photoperiod on the seasonal pattern of secretion of lutenizing hormone and testosterone and on the antler cycle in roe deer (*Capreolus capreolus*). *Journal of Reproductive Fertility* 95, 693–700.

Sjögren, K.-G. 2011. C-14 chronology of Scandinavian megalithic tombs. In L. García Sanjuán, C. Scarre and D. W. Wheatley (eds), *Exploring Time and Matter in Prehistoric Monuments: absolute chronology and rare rocks in European megaliths*, 103–120. Menga: Journal of Andalusian Prehistory, Monograph 1.

Skaarup, J. 1973. *Hesselø-Sølager. Jagdstationen der Südskandinavischen Trichterbeckerkultur 1. Arkœologiske Studier.* Copenhagen: Akademisk Forlag.

Skaarup, J. 1975. *Stengade. Ein langeländischer Wohnplatz mit Hausresten aus der frühneolithischen Zeit.* Rudkøping: Meddelelser fra Langelands Museum.

Skaarup, J. 1985. *Yngre Stenalder på øerne syd før Fyn 1985.* Rudkøbing: Meddelser fra Langelands Museum.

Skaarup, J. 1993. Megalithic graves, In Hvass and Storgaard (eds) 1993, 104–109.

Skoglund, P., Malmström, H., Raghavan, M., Storå, J., Hall, P., Willerslev, E., Gilbert, M. T. P., Götherström, A. and Jakobsson, M. 2012. Origins and genetic legacy of Neolithic farmers and hunter-gatherers in Europe. *Science* 336, 466–469.

Skoglund, P., Malmström, H., Omrak, A., Raghavan, M., Valdiosera, C. *et al.* 2015. Genomic diversity and admixture differs for stone-age Scandinavian foragers and farmers. *Sciencexpress* 344, 747–750.

Skousen, H. 2008. *Arkœologi i lange baner. Undersøgelser forud for anlæggelsen af motorvejen nord om Århus.* Højbjerg: Forlaget Moesgård.

Solheim, S., Fossum, G. and Knutsson, H.. 2018. Use-wear analysis of Early Mesolithic flake axes from South-eastern Norway. *Journal of Archaeological Science: Reports* 17, 560–570.

Sørensen, L. 2014. From hunter to farmer In Northern Europe. Migration and adaptation during the Neolithic and Bronze Age. Copenhagen: *Acta Archaeological* 85(2).

Sørensen, L. 2015. Hunters and farmers in the North – the transformation of pottery traditions and distribution patterns of key artefacts during the Mesolithic and Neolithic transition in southern Scandinavia. In J. Kabaciński, S. Hartz, D. C. M. Raemaekers, and T. Terberger (eds), *The Dąbki Site in Pomerania and the Neolithisation of the North European Lowlands (c. 5000–3000 cal BC)*, 385–432. Archaeology and History of the Baltic 8. Rahden/Westfahlen: Marie Leidorf.

Sørensen, L. 2020. Biased data or hard facts? Interpretations of the earliest evidence of agrarian activity in southern Scandinavia from 6000 to 4000 cal BC in a theoretical discourse on random down-the-line exchanges and structured migrations. In Gron *et al.* (eds) 2020, 289–316.

Sørensen, L. and Karg, S. 2012. The expansion of agrarian societies towards the North – new evidence for agriculture during the Mesolithic/ Neolithic transition in Southern Scandinavia. *Journal of Archaeological Science* 51, 98–114.

Sørensen, M., Rankama, T., Kankaanpää, J., Knutsson, K., Knutsson, H., Melvold, S., Valentin Eriksen, B. and Glørstad, H. 2013. The first eastern migrations of people and knowledge into Scandinavia: Evidence from studies of Mesolithic technology. *Norwegian Archaeological Review* 46, 1–38.

Sørensen, S. A. 1996. *Kongemosekulturen i Sydskandinavien*. Færgegården: Egnsmuseet.

Sørensen, S. A. 2016. Tooth pendants, their use and meaning in prehistoric hunter-gatherer societies. In M. Sørensen and K.B. Pedersen (eds), *Problems in Palaeolithic and Mesolithic Research*, 225–234. Copenhagen: Academic Books Copenhagen.

Sørensen, S. A. 2017. *The Kongemose Culture*. Copenhagen: Royal Society of Antiquaries.

Sørensen, M., Lübke, H. and Groß, D. 2018. The Early Mesolithic in Southern Scandinavia and Northern Germany. In N. Milner, C. Conneller, and B. Taylor (eds) *Star Carr Volume 1: A Persistent Place in a Changing World*, 305–329. York: White Rose University Press. doi. org/10.22599/book1.

Sørensen, S. A. 2019. Tabt, kasseret eller ofret? *Gefion* 4, 152–175.

Spikens, P. 2008. Mesolithic Europe: glimpses of another world. In G. Bailey and P. Spikins (eds), *Mesolithic Europe*, 1–17. Cambridge: Cambridge University Press.

Stafford, M. 1999: *From Forager to Farmer in Flint. A Lithic Analysis of the Prehistoric Transition to Agriculture in Southern Scandinavia*. Aarhus: Aarhus University Press.

Steinberg, J. M. 1996. Ploughzone sampling in Denmark: site signatures from disturbed contexts. *Antiquity* 70, 368–390.

Strand Petersen, K. 1985. The Late Quaternary history of Denmark. *Journal of Danish Archaeology* 4, 7–22.

Storå, J. and Ericson, P. G. P. 2004. A prehistoric breeding population of harp seals (*Phoca groenlandica*) in the Baltic Sea. *Marine Mammal Science* 20, 115–133.

Stuiver, M., Reimer, P.J. and Reimer, R.W. 2022. CALIB 8.2 at http://calib.org/calib/.

Tauber, H. 1973. Copenhagen dates X. *Radiocarbon* 15, 86–12.

Tauber, H. 1981. [13]C evidence for dietary habits of prehistoric man in Denmark. *Nature* 292, 332–333.

Terberger, T., Burger, J., Lüth, F., Müller, J. and Piezonka, H. 2018. Step by step – the neolithisation of northern Central Europe in the light of stable isotope analyses. *Journal of Archaeological Science* 99, 66–86.

Thrane, H. 1973. Bebyggelsehistorie – en arkæologisk arbejdsopgave. *Fortid og Nutid* 25, 300–320.

Thrane, H. 1991. Danish plough-marks from the Neolithic and Bronze Age. *Journal of Danish Archaeology* 8, 111–125.

Tinner, W. and Lotter, A. F. 2001. Central European vegetation response to abrupt climate change at 8.2 ka. *Geology* 29, 551–554.

Toggweiler, J. R. 1999. Variation of atmospheric CO_2 by ventilation of the ocean's deepest water. *Paleoceanography* 14, 571–588.

Trolle-Lassen, T. 1985. En zooarkæologisk analyse af Ertebøllepladsen Tybrind Vig, baseret på knogler af pelsdyr og kronhjort. Unpublished Candidat magister thesis. University of Aarhus.

Vang Petersen, P. 1984. Chronological and regional variation in the Late Mesolithic of eastern Denmark. *Journal of Danish Archaeoology* 3, 7–18.

Vang Petersen, P. 2008. *Flint fra Danmarks oldtid*. Vordingborg: Danmarks Borgcenter.

Vankilde, H. 2005. A review of the Early Late Neolithic period in Denmark: practice, identity and connectivity. *www.jungsteinSITE.de*

Vankilde, H. 2019. Bronze Age beginnings – a scalar view from the global outskirts. *Proceedings of the Prehistoric Society* 85, 1–27.

Vemming, H. P. and Madsen, B. 1983. Flint axe manufacture in the Neolithic. An experimental investigation of a flint axe manufacture site at Hastrup Vænget, East Zealand. *Journal of Danish Archaeology* 2, 43–59.

Vigne, J.-D., Carrére, I., Briois, F. and Guilaine, J. 2011. The early process of mammal domestication in the Near East: new evidence from the Pre-Neolithic and Pre-Pottery Neolithic in Cyprus. *Current Anthropology* 52, S255–S272.

Wadskjær, A. V. 2018. Neolithic transverse arrowheads – a great misunderstanding. *Danish Journal of Archaeology* 7, 221–240. [doi.org/10.1080/21662282.2018.1523526]

Warden, L., Moros, M., Neumann, T., Shennan, S., Timpson, A., Manning, K., Sollai, M., Wacker, L., Perner, K., Häusler, K. *et al.* 2017. Climate induced human demographic and cultural change in northern Europe during the mid-Holocene. *Scientific Reports* 7, 15251. [doi..org/10.1038/s41598-017-14353-5]

Weninger, B., Alram-Stem, E., Bauer, E., Clare, I., Danzeglocke, U., Jöris, O., Kubatzki, C., Rollefson, G., Todorova, H. and van Andel, T. 2006. Climate forcing due to the 8200 cal yr BP event observed at Early Neolithic sites in the eastern Mediterranean. *Quaternary Research* 66, 401–420.

Westerby, E. 1927. *Stenaldersboplader ved Klampenborg. Nogle Bidrag til Studiet af den Mesolitiske Periode*. Copenhagen: C. A. Reitzel.

Wiessner, P. 2002. The vines of complexity. egalitarian structures and the institutionalization of inequality among the Enga. *Current Anthropology* 43, 233–269.

Woll, B. 2003. *Das Totenritual der frühen nordischen Trichterbecherkultur*. Saarbrücker Beiträge zur Altertumskunde 76. Bonn: Gebundenes Buch.